Introducing

Microsoft Office

FOR

WINDOWS

KEIKO PITTER
TIMOTHY TRAINOR
JEFFREY STIPES

covers
WORD 6.0, EXCEL 5.0, ACCESS 2.0,
and WINDOWS 3.1

McGRAW-HILL

New York St. Louis San Francisco Auckland Bogotá Caracas
Lisbon London Madrid Mexico Milan Montreal New Delhi
Paris San Juan Singapore Sydney Tokyo Toronto

McGRAW-HILL
San Francisco, California

Introducing Microsoft Office for Windows

Copyright © 1995 by **McGraw-Hill, Inc.** All rights reserved. Printed in the
United States of America. Except as permitted under the United States
Copyright Act of 1976, no part of this publication may be reproduced or
distributed in any form or by any means, or stored in a database or
retrieval system, without the prior written permission of the publisher.

6 7 8 9 0   SEM SEM   9 0 9 8 7 6

ISBN 0-07-052068-2

Sponsoring Editor: Roger Howell

Editorial Assistant: Rhonda Sands

Production Supervisor: Richard DeVitto

Interior Design: Gary Palmatier, Ideas-to-Images

Cover Designer: Christy Butterfield

Printer: Semline, Inc.

Library of Congress Catalog Card Number 94-79517

Introducing
Microsoft Office
FOR
WINDOWS

Brief Contents

For more detailed tables of contents, refer to the individual applications' tables of contents.

Introducing the PC and Windows 3.1

Introducing Microsoft Word 6.0 for Windows

Introducing Microsoft Excel 5.0 for Windows

v

Introducing Microsoft Access 2.0 for Windows

Preface

TO THE INSTRUCTOR

The graphical and intuitive nature of Windows has made it, since May 1990, the most popular program for the PC. Microsoft Office for Windows has established itself as a popular and valuable software choice for the educational market at all levels. This book, which is designed as a tool for both classroom use and self-instruction, introduces the major Microsoft Office applications: Windows 3.1, Word 6.0, Excel 5.0, and Access 2.0. (PowerPoint 4.0, which is seldom covered in the introductory course, is not discussed.) The book is an excellent reference tool for readers who have completed the course.

Among us, we have written over two dozen books for all levels of computer learners. The same clear and succinct writing style and streamlined pedagogy that characterize those other books are apparent here.

In the book, each of the four software applications has its own section. Within each section are three, four, or five lessons. Each lesson begins with a series of Objectives that identify the brief, easily learned topics for that lesson. At the end of each major topic is a Practice Time feature that allows students to reinforce or try out what they have learned. At the end of the lesson, a Summary highlights the key concepts, and Key Terms lists the concepts that the student should now be able to understand; these terms appear in boldface in the lesson. A unique feature of this book is the Command Summary following each lesson, a graphic display of the commands presented in the lesson. Finally, Review Questions and thought-provoking, hands-on Exercises allow students to test their knowledge.

Each software section concludes with its own set of learning aids: in-depth Projects test students' learning of the material in the section; a detailed Command Summary recaps all the commands for the application; a Glossary defines the key terms covered in that section; and an Index catalogues the key topics for the section.

A Teaching Materials set is available for each software application covered. Each set contains teaching tips, transparency masters, solutions to "Practice Time" sets, answers to Review Questions and Exercises, and test questions and answers. An instructor's data disk contains exercise solutions and test questions that can be used with McGraw-Hill's RHTest software program.

vii

TO THE STUDENT

This text is designed to provide you with the skills necessary to use Windows 3.1, Word 6.0 for Windows, Excel 5.0 for Windows, and Access 2.0 for Windows, all very powerful and popular software programs. The book is divided into sections, one section for each software application. Each section starts with an Introduction. Do not skip these introductory passages; they explain how the book works and provide tips for using the book successfully.

You are about to begin your travels on the information highway. The skills you learn in this book will help you in your education and will open the doors to the information society.

Introducing
The PC
AND
WINDOWS 3.1

OPERATING SYSTEM

Introducing

The PC
AND
WINDOWS 3.1

KEIKO PITTER

 Mitchell **McGRAW-HILL**

New York St. Louis San Francisco Auckland Bogotá Caracas
Lisbon London Madrid Mexico Milan Montreal New Delhi
San Juan Singapore Sydney Tokyo Toronto

Mitchell **McGRAW-HILL**
Watsonville, CA 95076

Introducing the PC and Windows 3.1

5 6 7 8 9 0   SEM SEM   9 0 9 8 7 6 5

ISBN 0-07-051584-0

Sponsoring editor: Roger Howell
Editorial assistant: Laurie Boudreau
Technical reviewer: Laurie Boudreau
Director of production: Jane Somers
Production assistant: Leslie Austin
Project manager: Gary Palmatier, Ideas to Images
Interior designer and illustrator: Gary Palmatier
Cover designer: Christy Butterfield
Composition: Ideas to Images
Printer and binder: Semline, Inc.

Library of Congress Card Catalog No. 92-82703

Contents

1 Introducing the PC

1

2 Basic Windows Operations

20

3 File Management in Windows

Introduction

INTRODUCING THE PC AND WINDOWS

In today's age of technology, the ability to effectively use microcomputers is an essential skill for nearly everyone.

Introducing the PC and Windows 3.1 acquaints you with the IBM PC and compatibles while providing essential information for productive and enjoyable computing. This tutorial contains fundamental information on Microsoft Windows. Windows is an intuitive and graphical program that helps you use your computer's features and efficiently perform commands.

Using this Module

To use this module, an IBM PC or compatible computer and Windows 3.1 software is required, along with a blank, formatted floppy diskette.

This module is designed to assist you as you complete each lesson. Lessons begin with goals that are listed under the heading *Objectives*. Key terms are introduced in ***bold italic*** type; text to be typed by the user is shown in **bold**. Also, keep in mind the following:

■ This symbol is used to indicate the user's action.

▶ *This symbol is used to indicate the screen's response.*

Alternative: Presents an alternative keystroke "shortcut."

NOTE: This format is for important user notes and tips.

PRACTICE TIME

These brief drills allow the user to practice features previously discussed.

Finally, a glossary of key terms is found at the end of the book.

LESSON

Introducing the PC

OBJECTIVES

Upon completing the material presented in this lesson, you should understand the following:

☐ **The components of a computer system**

☐ **The identity and function of the various components of a computer**

☐ **The characteristics of your computer system**

COMPONENTS OF A COMPUTER SYSTEM

The purpose of a computer system is to process data to produce useful information. A computer system is composed of the following five parts: (1) people (users), (2) hardware, (3) software, (4) documentation/procedures, and (5) data/information. The most important component is the people. There must be users with problems to solve or applications to implement by using the computer. The right hardware and software must be selected to satisfy the needs of the user. Furthermore, the user must understand the proper procedures for producing the result needed, such as how to acquire and enter data and how to obtain the desired output.

The hardware is the physical and visible component of a microcomputer system. IBM and compatible microcomputers come in many shapes and sizes, with a variety of options. Thus, at first glance, we see the differences. A microcomputer, often referred to as a personal computer or a PC, may be small enough to carry and use on an airline flight, or it may be a large unit located on the floor beside your desk. The smallest system boxes are called **laptop computers**. These include **notebook computers**— computers about the size of an 8½-by-11-inch notebook— like the one shown in Figure 1-1. Larger system boxes are called **tower systems** and are often placed on the floor beside the desk. All computers, regardless of size and purpose, have four components: (1) input devices, (2) system unit, (3) output devices, and (4) storage devices.

Figure 1-1

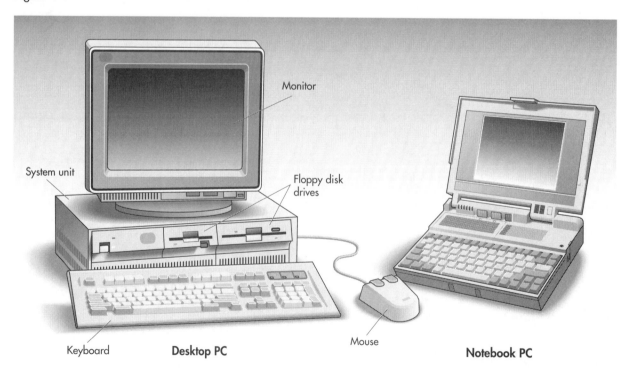

Monitor

System unit

Floppy disk drives

Keyboard   **Desktop PC**

Mouse

Notebook PC

Input devices provide the processor with information for processing. Common input devices include a keyboard, disk drives or a network, a mouse or trackball, and a modem. The **system unit** is the heart and the brain of the computer. It includes the processor unit and the main memory. **Output devices** are used to display, store, and print information. Output devices include a monitor (screen), a printer, disk drives or a network, and a modem. **Storage devices** are used to store information. The information can be written to a storage medium through an output device and can be retrieved using an input device. Common storage devices are floppy disks, hard disks, and cassette tapes.

INPUT DEVICES

All input devices send digital signals to the computer. The signals include the characters sent by the keyboard, movements and clicks sent by the mouse, or graphic images.

Keyboard

The computer **keyboard** resembles that of a typewriter and is used in much the same way. Although there are several keyboard layouts (Figure 1-2), they all provide essentially the same features. In addition to the usual typewriter keys, there are several other keys or groups of keys you should know about.

The keyboard can generate 256 characters. Not all of these characters are visible, and many have special meanings. As is the case on a typewriter, you enter uppercase letters by holding down ⟨⇧Shift⟩ (the key with the broad up arrow) while you press the key or by pressing ⟨Caps Lock⟩ once before pressing the keys. The ⟨Caps Lock⟩ key works similarly to the Shift Lock key on a typewriter. It is a **toggle** key. That means that each time you press the key, a feature is turned on or off. The first time you press ⟨Caps Lock⟩, it shifts the keyboard into uppercase mode. The second time, all letters are returned to lowercase. Some special characters require that you hold down ⟨⇧Shift⟩ even if ⟨Caps Lock⟩ has been pressed. On some keyboards, the ⟨Caps Lock⟩ indicator light indicates whether ⟨Caps Lock⟩, or uppercase, is selected. Both the ⟨⇧Shift⟩ and ⟨Caps Lock⟩ keys are also used, as shown later, to change the function of other keystrokes.

The ⟨←Enter⟩ key is the down-left-arrow key between the main keyboard and the numeric keypad. The function of this key depends on the software package being used. The ⟨←Enter⟩ key may be used to indicate the end of a line (the same as the carriage return on a typewriter) or it may be used to indicate the end of a command (or instruction).

There are 10 or 12 **function keys**, labeled ⟨F1⟩ to ⟨F10⟩ or ⟨F12⟩, across the top or to the left of the main keyboard. These keys provide convenient access to program functions; their use depends on the program being run.

The ⌊Esc⌋ key, usually located in the top left corner of the keyboard, is the escape key. Its use depends on the software; in many programs it is used to cancel an input or operation or to return to a previous menu.

The **numeric keypad** is a group of keys to the right of the main keyboard consisting of numeric keys that have a dual function— either entering numbers or moving the screen position where the entry is made. The screen position where the entry is made is often marked by a **cursor**, which may be a vertical line or a blinking underline character. The function of the numeric keypad can be changed by pressing either ⌊⇧Shift⌋ or ⌊Num Lock⌋. Like ⌊Caps Lock⌋, ⌊Num Lock⌋ is a toggle key. After pressing ⌊Num Lock⌋ once, you generate the characters that appear on the upper half of the

Figure 1-2

keys on the keypad. Press Num Lock again to generate the movement indicated on the bottom half of the key, such as the 4 key to move the cursor to the left. On most keyboards, the Num Lock indicator light indicates whether numeric entry is selected. The numeric keypad also includes a . (period) key; the arithmetic operation keys / (division), * (multiplication), - (subtraction), and + (addition); and an alternate Enter key.

On some keyboards, a second set of cursor movement keys— arrows and keys such as Page Up and Page Down— appears between the main keyboard and the numeric keypad. These keys are not affected by Num Lock. Hence, the presence of these keys lets you leave the numeric keyboard in numeric mode all the time.

The Ins key is the insert key. With many applications, it toggles, or switches, the action of entering data into memory between the insert mode and the typeover mode. When it is in the insert mode, as you edit a line, existing characters move to the right as you insert new characters. In the typeover mode, the characters you type replace the characters already there.

The Del key is the delete key. It has several functions depending on the software. Usually, during data entry, Del deletes the character located at the cursor. This is contrasted with the function of the ←Backspace key, which is located above ←Enter on the main keyboard: ←Backspace deletes the character to the left of the cursor, causing the cursor to backspace. The Del key is often used to indicate items to be deleted. The function of Del is dependent on the program in use.

The Tab↹ key is used in word processing programs like the tab key on a typewriter, moving the cursor to the next tab stop. In programs, Tab↹ is often used to move the cursor from one option to the next on the screen. To move the cursor backward through the options, ⇧Shift is held down while Tab↹ is pressed, written as ⇧Shift+Tab↹.

The Ctrl key is the control key. When issuing a command, Ctrl is held down while another key is pressed. For example, Ctrl+C means that Ctrl is held down while C is pressed. In some programs, the Alt key, which is the alternate key, works the same way as Ctrl. In some programs, Alt can optionally be released before the other key is pressed. The specific control- and alternate-keystroke commands depend on the program.

Each key generates a unique signal to the computer. The function of each key and its recognition by the computer depend on the software being used. Even the method used to correct your typing errors depends on the software being used. You should be getting the idea that, beyond turning it on, learning how to use a computer means learning how to use specific software.

Don't be frustrated or intimidated. If you type in a command for the wrong software, the computer usually just responds with an error message indicating that it doesn't recognize what you typed. These errors do not harm the computer, and most often they do not affect whatever it is you are trying to accomplish. The worst that can happen is that you might have to stop whatever you are doing and start all over again.

Disk Drives/Network

If the information you want to process is stored on a disk, you use a disk drive as an input device. The use of disks and disk drives is explained later.

Sometimes, information you are using resides on a **network**. Interconnected microcomputers form a microcomputer network. One of the computers, called the **file server**, is equipped with large-capacity hard disk drives containing programs and data that can be used by any computer on the network. Reading information from a disk drive on a network is similar to using one on your computer. Ask your instructor about your particular network.

Mouse/Trackball

The **mouse** is a small, handheld device with a roller ball on the bottom. It allows you to send instructions to the computer by moving the mouse around on the desk and pressing one of the buttons on the mouse. When you move the mouse a special cursor, called the **pointer**, moves in the same direction, pointing at the options displayed on the screen. By pressing one of the buttons on the mouse (usually the one on the left), the option pointed to can be executed. Other devices, such as the trackball, work similarly to the mouse. A trackball user moves a ball set in a stationary guide to indicate the pointer movements.

You should become familiar with the following mouse operation terminology:

Point	Position the mouse pointer on top of an object.
Click	Press the active mouse button once.
Double-click	Press the active mouse button twice in rapid succession without moving the mouse.
Drag	After positioning the mouse pointer on a desired object, press and hold down the mouse button while moving the mouse. When the desired new position is reached, release the mouse button.
Drag and drop	Similar to the drag operation, but in Windows 3.1 you can start a program by dragging a picture representing a document (a document icon) and dropping it onto a picture representing a compatible program (a program icon).
Select	Point and click on an object.

Modem

If the information you are using is coming from another computer via a communication line, you may use a **modem**. A modem (modulator-demodulator) is a device that connects one computer to another by a communication line, such as a telephone, through which information can be transmitted.

SYSTEM UNIT

The components of a system unit include the following: the power supply, which may be a battery; a **motherboard**, which holds the microprocessor unit and main memory; and expansion slots.

Microprocessor Unit

The microprocessor unit (MPU), also called the central processor unit or CPU, is the heart and brain of a computer. The **processor** controls all the actions of the computer, including all the mathematical operations on data. The MPU is one of the larger chips on the motherboard. In a PC, this is an Intel 8088, 80286, 80386, 80486, or 80586 chip. The number refers to the design of a specific model of chip. Processor units are characterized by the chip used and the cycle frequency. The newer chips (higher numbers) are compatible with all the design characteristics of the older chips, so they run the programs written for earlier chip versions.

The newer chips are also capable of faster processing speeds. The speed at which a chip processes information is measured as a function of three factors:

Clock speed—the rate at which the MPU processes data. Clock speed is measured in millions of cycles per second, or megahertz (MHz). 80286 chips frequently have processor speeds of 12 to 16 MHz. 80386 chips operate at 16 to 33 MHz, and 80486 chips operate at 33 to 50 MHz.

Word Size—the amount of information the MPU can manipulate at one time. Electronic devices store and process data through a series of switches called **bits**. Different combinations of on (1) or off (0) bits represent data and instructions. Common word sizes are 8, 16, and 32 bits.

Bus Size—the capacity of the input/output path that connects the MPU to external devices such as the monitor or disk drive. The bus size determines how much data is transmitted and received at a time. The bus size for an 8088 chip is 8 bits, 80286 is 16 bits, and 80386 or 80486 is 32 bits. A large bus size increases processing speed because the microprocessor doesn't take as much time to send or receive data.

In general, greater MHz, larger word size, and larger bus size result in a faster computer.

Main Memory

A computer also must store information while data is being processed. That storage place is called **main memory**. The main memory is on the chips on the motherboard. The two types of memory are **random access memory (RAM)** and **read-only memory (ROM)**.

Random Access Memory The RAM stores what you enter into the computer as well as the intermediate results from the computer's calculations. What you enter may be a program or data.

Information in RAM is volatile, meaning its contents are erased when the power to the computer is interrupted or turned off. Thus, it is important when you are using the computer to make sure to save the data on another storage medium from time to time. Otherwise, you can lose all the data you have just entered or processed.

RAM holds anywhere from approximately 128,000 characters, or 128 **kilobytes** (128K), to 640K or more. A character, or a **byte**, is a single letter, digit, or special symbol. The amount of RAM is expandable, which means it can be increased to several **megabytes** (Mb), or million bytes.

For a program to be executed on a computer— that is, for the program instructions to be carried out— the program must first be loaded into RAM. That means the computer must have enough RAM capacity to hold that program. In addition, there must be enough RAM to hold the data being processed. The Microsoft Windows program requires at least 2Mb of RAM.

Read-Only Memory The read-only memory, or ROM, comes already loaded with the information that the computer needs to understand what you enter as you turn the computer on. The information on ROM is not volatile; you can use the information, but you cannot erase or change it. The information that comes on ROM is called **firmware**.

Expansion Slots

The system unit also contains **expansion slots**. Your monitor may be connected to a board in one of these slots. These boards are called interface boards or adaptor cards. They allow a PC to be connected to **peripherals** (devices that perform support functions), such as a monitor or printer. Sometimes an expansion slot contains a memory board that lets you expand the RAM of the computer.

P R A C T I C E   T I M E   1 - 1

Enter the following information on your computer. You may need to consult with your instructor to find out these answers.

My computer is a(n)_____ _____.

My computer has _____ (80286, 80386, or 80486) processor.

My computer _____ (is, is not) attached to a network.

My computer _____ (is, is not) equipped with a mouse or a trackball.

The RAM capacity of my computer is _____.

The speed of my computer is _____ MHz.

OUTPUT DEVICES

Output devices receive information from the computer. The information may be characters and graphics for display sent to monitors and printers, or it may be documents or data sent to a disk drive or modem.

Monitor

The **monitor** has a screen that can display either 80 or 40 columns by 24 or more lines. Most programs use the 80-column by 24-line display. Monitors that produce two tones (green and black, amber and black, or black and white) are called **monochrome**. Three kinds of color monitors that are used include **CGA** (Color Graphics Adaptor), **EGA** (Enhanced Graphics Adaptor), and **VGA** (Video Graphics Array). Also, there are monochrome VGA monitors that show colors in various shades of gray, called a **gray scale**. Technical differences between the types are not discussed here.

The clarity and crispness of display, by which monitors can be compared, is referred to as **resolution**. The resolution of a monitor is defined by the number of **pixels** on a screen. A pixel (picture element) is the smallest discrete image a monitor is able to produce. For example, a monitor can have a resolution of 640 pixels horizontally by 460 pixels vertically (640 × 460). The more pixels displayed, the higher the resolution. Some VGA monitors have resolutions of up to 1024 × 768.

Printers

Four types of printers are in general use today. They are dot matrix, letter-quality, inkjet, and laser printers. Dot matrix printers form characters as a combination of dots and do not produce high-quality output. The number of dots used to form the characters determines how good the resolution of the output is. Some of the better dot matrix printers use 24 dots, or pins. Dot matrix printers can print characters in different styles or sizes and can also print graphics.

Letter-quality printers are like typewriters and produce high-quality output. In most, to change the character style or size, the printing mechanism must be changed, as in an electric typewriter. They cannot produce graphics. They are slower than dot matrix printers and generally cost a little more.

Inkjet printers also use dots to produce characters and graphics. The ink is sprayed toward the paper as a single line of uniform-size drops. Characters and graphics are formed by means of an electric field that deviates the drops up and down as the print head moves horizontally over the paper.

Laser printers produce high-resolution output using laser technology. The result is near publication quality. Laser printers can produce professional-quality graphics. Although they are the most expensive of the four printer types, their popularity for use with microcomputers is increasing.

Printers usually contain several fonts internally. A **font** is a combination of a typeface (what the character looks like) and a size. Typefaces include Courier, Helvetica, Times Roman, and many others. The size is denoted by the height of a capital character on the page, expressed in terms of **points**, or 1/72ths of an inch. Most printers can print proportionally spaced characters, where different letters, such as i and w, are different widths. In contrast, typewriters print all characters the same width. By means of comparison, the Courier typeface in 10-point size prints 12 characters per inch (elite size on the typewriter) and in 12-point size prints 10 characters per inch (pica size).

Some printers can use cartridges to expand the number of fonts available, and almost all dot matrix printers can use **soft fonts**, which are fonts stored on disk until use and then loaded into RAM in the printer for use.

With many applications, when your printer is correctly installed, you can change the font within the software. The options you will have depend on your system, and examples in the lessons in this book may contain font options different from yours.

There is one additional item to note on printers. All printers are either parallel or serial printers. Again, the technical discussion on the difference is not given here. The differences relate to transmission speeds and distances. A parallel printer is connected to a **parallel port** at the back of the computer, and a serial printer is connected to a **serial port** at the back of the computer. A parallel port on a computer is referred to as LPT1 (a second parallel port is called LPT2; the third, LPT3; and so on). A serial port on a computer is referred to as COM1 (then COM2, COM3, and so on). This information is needed because some software is written to work with only parallel printers, whereas other packages let you specify the port where the printer is connected.

Disk Drives

When output is to be used by a computer, data must be in a computer-readable format. The medium most commonly used to store information to be passed on to another computer is a disk, either a floppy disk or a hard disk on your PC or a hard drive on the network. Disks are discussed in more detail later.

Modem

If the output is sent directly to another computer via a communication line, a modem might be used.

P R A C T I C E   T I M E   1 - 2

Enter the following information about your computer. You may need to consult with your instructor to find out these answers.

The monitor attached to my computer is a ___VGA___ (CGA, EGA, VGA) monitor. It is ___color___ (monochrome, color).

The printer attached to my computer is a ___Laser HP___ (give brand name and model).

It is a ___laser___ (dot matrix, letter-quality, inkjet, laser) printer and is connected to ___LPT1___ (LPT1, COM1).

STORAGE MEDIA

A disk is a storage medium. It is used to store information that is needed at a later time. If you recall, a computer has two types of main memory: RAM and ROM. RAM is storage where you can read and write information but it is **volatile**. The moment the computer is turned off or power is interrupted, the information in RAM is lost. ROM is read-only memory, which means you can only read information from it, although it is not volatile. You cannot put on any new information or change information currently on it. Thus, you need a storage medium that is more permanent than RAM and one where you can read and write information, unlike ROM.

When information is written onto a disk, each group of information is stored as a file. If you prepare a letter using a word processor, the letter is stored on a disk as a file with a filename to identify it. A computer program also is stored on a disk as a file, again with a proper filename to identify it. Most application software has commands to let you store and retrieve files from a disk.

A filename is made up of two parts: the name and an optional extension. The name is between one and eight characters in length, and the extension is between one and three characters in length. The extension is often assigned by the application program to distinguish the data file according to its use. Almost any character can be used in a filename and extension, except a blank space and the following set of characters.

. , " / \ [ ] ; : | < > + = * ?

When a complete filename is required, you must give both the filename and extension, separated by a period (.).

Two types of disks are used with a PC: **floppy disks** (Figure 1-3) and **hard disks**. Although they operate in a similar manner, floppy disks are flexible and portable, whereas hard disks are rigid metallic platters. Floppy disks are used with floppy disk drives (referred to simply as disk drives in this book), and hard disks are housed in a hard disk drive unit. Hard disks are explained in a little more detail at the end of this section.

Floppy Disks

The disks used on a PC are either 5¼-inch or 3½-inch floppy disks and either double-density or high-density. All these disks are referred to simply as disks in this manual, although they are also referred to as diskettes. These disks are very similar in function and operation, with some subtle differences (Figure 1-3).

A disk stores data as magnetic spots on a circular piece of Mylar that has a metal-oxide coating. The disk is inside a protective jacket (for 5¼-inch disks) or plastic cartridge (for 3½-inch disks). The larger ones are called floppy disks because the Mylar material is pliant, and in the protective jacket, 5¼-inch disks can "flop" (flex) back and forth. The 3½-inch disks come in rigid plastic cartridges, so the term does not really apply to them. Nevertheless, they also are often referred to as floppy disks and never as hard disks. The cartridge on a 3½-inch disk protects the diskette inside much better than the jacket on a 5¼-inch disk.

The information on a disk is stored along concentric recording positions on the disk known as **tracks** or **cylinders**. Information may be stored on both sides of the disk. A double-density disk has 40 tracks per side on each 5¼-inch disk and 80 tracks per side on each 3½-inch disk. A high-density disk has 80 tracks per side on each 5¼-inch and 160 per side on each 3½-inch disk. The storage capacity on a 5¼-inch disk is approximately 360K for double density and 1.2Mb for high density, and on a 3½-inch disk it is approximately 720K for double density and 1.44Mb for high density.

N O T E :   If you have a high-density disk drive, you use high-density disks. If you have a 360K or 720K disk drive, you use double-density disks. You can use double-density disks in a high-density disk drive, although the capacity of the disk still is limited to 360K or 720K. Consult the DOS manual for more information.

The information is written onto and read from the disk through an opening in the jacket or cartridge. The circular Mylar disk inside spins like a phonograph record, and a **read-write head** accesses information. In the case of 5¼-inch disks the opening is visible and is called the **access window**. A 3½-inch disk has a mechanical shutter that opens automatically to reveal the access window when the disk is inserted in the disk drive and closes automatically when the disk is taken out.

Most 5¼-inch disks have a small notch on the side. This is the **write-protect notch**. If you cover the write-protect notch, the disk is protected from being written over or changed. When you purchase disks, gummed tabs are provided for this purpose.

N O T E :   If you have covered the write-protect notch with a gummed tab, check periodically to make sure the tab is securely in place. Many disk drive problems occur from gummed tabs coming off and getting stuck inside the drive. This is also true of labels you might have attached to the disk.

A 3½-inch disk can be write-protected using the **write-protect tab**. It is write-protected (cannot change information) when the small plastic tab

Figure 1-3

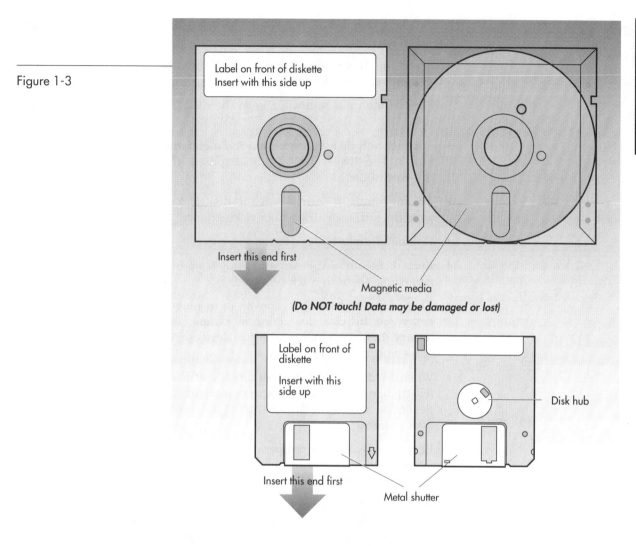

on the back is moved to reveal the hollow opening. When the opening is closed, the disk is not write-protected (and you can read or write information).

When you purchase a disk, it does not contain any information. The disk must be prepared so it is able to store and retrieve data. The process of preparing a disk to accept data is called *formatting* a disk; this is explained in a later lesson.

N O T E :   A high-density disk drive will read information written by a double-density disk drive. However, a double-density disk drive may have problems reading information written by a high-density disk drive.

Care and Handling of Floppy Disks

You must use proper care in handling 5¼-inch disks because they are very fragile. A 3½-inch disk is well protected and quite sturdy. However, care must be taken in handling either type of disk. Here are some suggestions for floppy disk care and handling:

- Insert the disk in the disk drive with the access window (for 5¼-inch) or metal end (for 3½-inch) first, label side up.

- For 5¼-inch disks, always keep the disk in its envelope when not in use.

- For 3½-inch disks, never open the mechanical shutter while a disk is out of the drive. Doing this exposes the surface to dirt, dust, fingerprints, etc.

- Do not touch the surface of the disk through the access window or wipe the surface with rags or tissue paper.

- Do not let disks collect dust.

- Keep disks out of the sun and away from other sources of heat, which can cause them to warp or lose data.

- Keep disks at least 2 feet away from magnetic fields, such as those generated by electrical motors, radios, televisions, tape recorders, library theft detectors, and other devices. A strong magnetic field will erase information on a disk.

- When writing on a disk label already attached to the disk, use only a felt-tip pen. Never use any sort of instrument with a sharp point. Also, never use an eraser. Eraser dust is abrasive and may get on the Mylar disk surface.

- Keep disks at room temperature before use (a disk just brought in from a cold blizzard has shrunk enough in size that its tracks are not where the system expects to find them).

- Never open the drive door or remove a disk while the drive is running—that is, while the red in-use light on the front of the disk drive is on. If you do, you can damage the data on your disk.

- Check to make sure the gummed write-protect tab and external labels are on securely.

Hard Disks

A hard disk unit is a sealed enclosure containing one or more rigid metallic platters (usually an aluminum platter covered with an oxide coating). This enclosure may be installed in the same case as the processing unit (internal hard disk) or in a separate case (external hard disk). A hard disk is sometimes called a ***fixed disk***.

N O T E :   Hard disks are also available on adaptor cards that are inserted in unused expansion slots in the computer. These are called **hard cards**.

Hard and floppy disks use similar principles. Both record data in tracks. The advantage of a hard disk is greater storage capacity and speed. You can install 20-, 30-, or even 600-megabyte hard disks on the computer. The access speed of a hard drive is two to ten times faster than that of a floppy disk.

Care of Hard Disk Drives

A disk drive is a sensitive mechanical device and should be treated as such. Because it has moving parts, it is even more sensitive than the computer. You should not drop it, jar it sharply, or plug it in or unplug it when the computer is on.

The read-write head on a floppy disk drive should be cleaned periodically. A minute amount of dust, dirt, oils, or magnetic oxide particles on the disk-drive head can cause problems. When you transport the disk drive, insert the cardboard packing disk (that accompanied the drive when it was purchased) or a blank floppy disk to protect the drive's internal mechanism.

A hard disk is even more susceptible to physical damage because of its design. You must be very careful not to move the unit without first properly positioning (***parking***) its read-write head. You must also use extreme caution when shutting down the system to avoid turning off power when the hard disk is writing data.

Identifying Disk Drives

A PC comes with one or more installed floppy disk drives. Some have a hard disk drive installed. Each disk drive must be connected to a disk interface board, or disk controller card. The disk controller card, in turn, is inserted into one of the expansion slots in the computer. If there is only one drive, it is known as drive A. If there are two floppy drives, they are drives A and B. A hard drive is usually drive C.

P R A C T I C E   T I M E   1 - 3

Enter the following information on your computer. You may need to consult with your instructor to find out these answers.

There are ___l___ (how many) 3½-inch disk drives on my computer.

There are ___0___ (how many) 5¼-inch disk drives on my computer.

There is a hard disk on my computer.___Y___ (Y/N)

Visually identify which drive is drive A.

STARTING THE COMPUTER

A PC can be started from a floppy disk drive or from a hard drive. In this book, the steps for starting from a hard drive are given because running Windows requires that you have a computer with a hard disk. To start a computer from a hard disk, make sure there is no floppy disk in drive A and then turn on the computer and the monitor.

Depending on how your computer is set up, the computer may offer you a chance to reset its internal calendar. It is most likely that your computer is equipped with a clock, a battery-run device that keeps track of date and time even when the computer is turned off. If that is the case, you do not need to change the time or date unless you specifically want to. The calendar format is month-day-year, with the numbers separated by hyphens. On September 29, 1993, for example, you could enter 9-29-93. The format for time, often entered in 24-hour clock format, is hours:minutes:seconds, with the numbers separated by colons. If you want to enter 2:35 P.M., you enter 14:35.

Eventually either a standard or a customized screen is displayed.

N O T E :   When you start a computer by turning on the switch, you are said to have performed a **cold start**. You can restart the computer when it is already on without turning the power switch off. This is done by simultaneously holding down the Ctrl and Alt keys while you press Del. This is called a **warm start**, because the computer is already on and, thus, warmed up.

DISK OPERATING SYSTEM (DOS)

The ***disk operating system***, or ***DOS***, is a series of computer programs or files that are designed to do the different tasks of controlling, coordinating, and managing all the components of a computer. The computer needs DOS to interpret and execute actions such as loading a program or saving, copying, and deleting files.

Two common operating systems for PCs are PC-DOS and MS-DOS. PC-DOS was written for IBM by Microsoft. Other IBM-compatible computers use MS-DOS (Microsoft DOS). DOS versions are referred to by numbers such as 1.00, 2.10, 2.11, 3.20, 3.30, 4.01, and 5.0. Although higher number DOS versions have more capabilities, and in some instances more DOS commands, they are compatible with earlier versions. To run Microsoft Windows you need DOS version 3.1 or higher.

P R A C T I C E   T I M E   1 - 4

Enter the following information about the disk operating system on your PC. You may need to consult with your instructor.

The version of DOS being used on my computer is ___3.30___.

S U M M A R Y

In this lesson, various components of a computer are presented.

☐ **The function of a computer is to process data and produce a result.**

☐ **The microprocessor unit (MPU) is the brain of the computer.**

☐ **Random access memory (RAM) is where both programs and data are temporarily stored during processing. It is volatile memory.**

☐ **Read-only memory (ROM) contains firmware.**

☐ **Expansion slots are where peripheral devices are connected.**

☐ **The three kinds of color monitors are Color Graphics Adaptor (CGA), Enhanced Graphics Adaptor (EGA), and Video Graphics Array (VGA).**

☐ **Computer output can be passed to another computer via disk or modem.**

☐ **Input components include keyboard, mouse, disk drive, and modem.**

☐ **In general, there are two types of disks: floppy and hard. The two sizes of floppy disks are 3½-inch and 5¼-inch.**

☐ **Information on a disk is accessed through an access window. On a 3½-inch disk, the access window is protected by a mechanical shutter.**

☐ **A disk can be write-protected.**

K E Y   T E R M S

access window
bus size
byte
CGA
click
clock speed
cold start
cursor
cylinders
disk operating
  system (DOS)
double-click
drag
drag and drop
EGA
expansion slots
file server
firmware
fixed disk
floppy disk
font
formatting
function keys

gray scale
hard card
hard disk
input devices
interface
keyboard
kilobyte (K)
laptop computer
main memory
megabyte (Mb)
modem
monitor
monochrome
motherboard
network
notebook computer
numeric keypad
output devices
parallel port
peripherals
pixels
point
point size

pointer
processor
random access
  memory (RAM)
read-only memory
  (ROM)
read-write head
resolution
select
serial port
soft fonts
storage devices
system unit
toggle
tower system
tracks
VGA
volatile
warm start
word size
write-protect notch
write-protect tab

R E V I E W   Q U E S T I O N S

1. What is the purpose of a computer?

2. Identify three factors that affect a microprocessor's processing speed.

3. What does *volatile* mean?

4. Is a blank space a byte? Explain.

5. Name three types of printers and give an advantage and a disadvantage of each.

6. Why is a disk drive both an input and an output component?

7. Why do you need an external storage device?

8. How is information stored on a disk?

9. What does it mean when a disk is write-protected? How is this done?

10. What is the advantage of having a hard disk on a computer?

CONFIGURATION OF YOUR COMPUTER

Transfer the information you entered in PRACTICE TIME throughout this lesson to this page for future reference.

- My computer is a _____ (name and model are usually found on the front of the system box).

- It contains a _____ (80286, 80386, or 80486) microprocessor chip.

- It operates at _____ MHz.

- It contains _____Mb of RAM.

- The A drive is a _____ (5¼-inch, 3½-inch) floppy disk drive that can handle disks of _____ (1.2Mb, 1.44Mb) capacity.

- The B drive is a _____ (5¼-inch, 3½-inch, none) floppy disk drive that can handle disks of _____ (1.2Mb, 1.44Mb) capacity.

- The C drive is a hard drive with a capacity of _____Mb.

- Other drives available are _____.

- The computer _____ (is, is not) attached to a network.

- My computer _____ (is, is not) equipped with a mouse or a trackball.

- The computer has a _____ (color, monochrome) _____ (EGA, CGA, VGA) monitor.

- The printer is a _____ (name and model are usually found on the front of the printer). It is a _____ (dot matrix, letter-quality, inkjet, laser) printer attached to _____ (LPT1, COM1).

- The version of DOS being used is _____.

- If your computer is attached to a network, describe the commands you must give to start the computer and Windows.

Basic Windows Operations

OBJECTIVES

Upon completing the material presented in this lesson, you should understand the following:

- ☐ **The function of the Windows program**
- ☐ **The parts of a window**
- ☐ **Starting Windows**
- ☐ **Minimizing, maximizing, and restoring windows**
- ☐ **Moving program group icons**
- ☐ **Opening and closing a window**
- ☐ **Opening and closing a program**
- ☐ **Moving a window**
- ☐ **Switching among application windows**
- ☐ **Ending a task**
- ☐ **Changing the shape and size of a window**
- ☐ **Arranging icons**
- ☐ **Getting onscreen help**
- ☐ **Exiting Windows**

WHAT IS MICROSOFT WINDOWS?

As mentioned at the end of Lesson 1, the disk operating system (DOS) is a series of programs and files that are needed by the computer to interpret and execute actions you want the computer to do. Microsoft Windows, or simply Windows, is a program that adds to and expands DOS. It gives you an easier way to work with your computer. DOS is a **command line interpreter**, which means you interface with, or give instructions to, your PC by typing key words on the keyboard. Windows, on the other hand, is a **graphical user interface**, or **GUI** (pronounced "gooey"). A user instructs the computer by selecting small pictures, called **icons**. The label below the icon describes the purpose of the icon. You can run programs, enter and move data, and perform all types of tasks simply by using the mouse to point to objects on the screen. You can use Windows without a mouse, too. However, most people feel it is not as convenient.

N O T E : Versions 4.0 and later of DOS let you give commands by making menu choices with a mouse or keyboard. However, these versions do not use a graphical user interface.

Windows owes its name to the fact that it runs each program inside a separate "window." A **window** is a box or frame on the screen. Because Windows uses standard menu options and symbols, once you've learned how to maneuver in one window, you are well on your way to knowing how to maneuver in all the window applications. Windows also has **multitasking** capability. This means you can have numerous windows on the screen at a time, each executing its own program. Just as each program is contained within its own window onscreen, each running program also occupies its own part of RAM. You can easily switch between programs without having to close one and open the next, which allows you to perform several tasks at the same time. This leads to an **integrated environment** that allows you to transfer information from one application to another or to link different applications so any data changes in one application will automatically be reflected in another.

Windows lets you customize the screen to meet your own needs. It also lets you save the screen from one session to the next, which means there is no standard initial screen each time you start the Windows program. This book gives enough information to enable you to begin to use the Windows environment.

IDENTIFYING PARTS OF A WINDOW

Before starting Windows, you should familiarize yourself with terms used to identify parts of a window. The functions of various components are explained later.

A typical window is displayed in Figure 2-1. The entire screen is referred to as a **desktop**. The outer edge of a window is called the **border**.

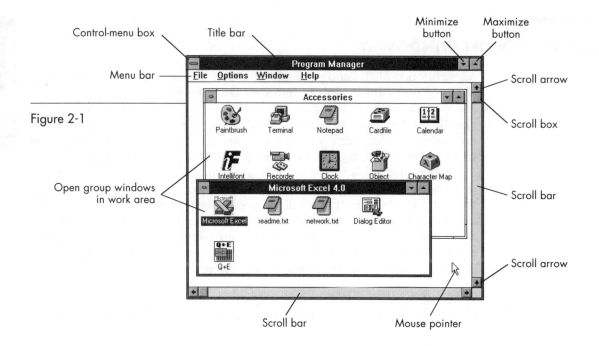

Figure 2-1

The area inside a window is called the **work area**. If you are using a mouse, you will see a single-headed arrow called the **pointer** on the screen. The pointer's movement is controlled by the mouse. The shape of the pointer will change depending on what you are doing. Different shapes are described in this book as they are encountered.

You can make selections using either the mouse or the keyboard. Because making command selections in the Windows environment is done by pointing, the mouse is much easier to use. This book assumes that your computer is equipped with a mouse.

At the top of each window is the **title bar**, which gives the name of the application window that is open. In Figure 2-1, the title is Program Manager. At the left end of the title bar is the **control-menu box**. At the right end of the title bar are two sizing buttons. The **maximize button** is the one with a triangle pointing up, and the **minimize button** has a triangle pointing down. When you click on the maximize button, a **restore button** (this contains two triangles— one pointing up and one pointing down) takes its place. Just underneath the title bar is the **menu bar**, which displays the selections available in this window. In the workspace of the Program Manager window are two open windows. Inside each window are icons with labels— graphical images that symbolize choices or actions.

Figure 2-1 also shows two **scroll bars**: a vertical scroll bar with arrow buttons at both ends at the right edge of the window and a horizontal scroll bar with arrow buttons at both ends at the bottom of the window. These are used to scroll the window vertically and horizontally (respectively) so you can view the parts of the window not currently displayed. Depending on how much of the window is visible, either one or both scroll bars do not appear.

OPERATING SYSTEM

STARTING THE WINDOWS PROGRAM

■ Make sure drive A is empty.

■ Start the computer from the hard drive by turning on the computer and the monitor. If your computer is on a network, follow the procedure for starting from the network.

▶ *The screen will display a DOS prompt, such as C:\> or a menu.*

■ If your screen displays a DOS prompt, type **WIN** and press ⏎Enter. If your screen displays a menu, make the menu selection for Windows.

▶ *A screen similar to the one in Figure 2-2 is displayed. However, because Windows can be set up to have several different appearances when loaded, your screen may not look at all like Figure 2-2.*

Figure 2-2

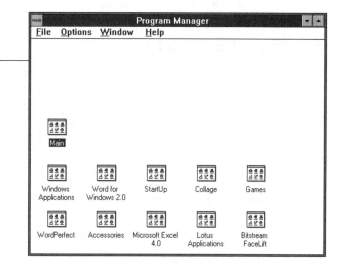

NOTE: If you are not able to start Windows following the instructions above, ask your instructor for procedures to start Windows using your particular setup.

PRACTICE TIME 2-1

Take some time to identify different parts of the window.

The Initial Windows Screen

As mentioned earlier, there is no standard initial screen for Windows. The screen displayed may be the final screen saved from the previous Windows session. If your initial screen does not show the Program Manager window similar to the one in Figure 2-2, find the description below that is closest to your screen and follow the instructions given. Here, only the keyboard instructions are given; the same things could be accomplished using the mouse. Also, these instructions may not mean anything to you right now, but they will make sense to you later.

■ Do one of the following:

- If your screen shows a single icon with the label Program Manager, press [Alt], [Spacebar], then R.

- If the Program Manager window fills the entire screen, press [Alt], [Spacebar], R.

- If the screen is blocked to show several windows with labels in the title bar, press [Ctrl]+[F4] (hold down [Ctrl] and press the [F4] function key). Repeat this until Program Manager is the only window on your desktop.

Selecting a Menu Choice

The menu bar contains the names of several menu options. When you select a menu option, a menu of commands called a ***drop-down*** or ***pull-down menu*** appears beneath the option. You can select a menu option using either the mouse or the keyboard command. In this book most instructions are given for the mouse. When appropriate, however, keyboard alternatives are presented.

The following are general instructions for using the mouse and the keyboard. There are often several ways to enter commands in Windows. Only one way is explained here.

To select a menu option using the mouse:

■ Point and click on a menu option.

▶ *A box with commands, the drop-down menu, appears underneath the option.*

■ To make a selection from the drop-down menu, point and click on a command.

■ To cancel the menu without selecting a command, point and click anywhere on the desktop outside the drop-down menu.

NOTE: You access the control menu by clicking on the control-menu box, the dash or underscore button at the left of the title bar.

Starting the Windows Program **WN25**

OPERATING SYSTEM

To select a menu option using the keyboard:

- Each menu option has one underlined letter. To select a menu option, hold down [Alt] and press the character that is underlined in the menu option. For example, you select the File menu by holding down [Alt] and pressing F ([Alt]+F).

    ▶ *A box with commands, the drop-down menu, appears beneath the option.*

- To select a command in the drop-down menu, press the character that is underlined in the desired command.

- To cancel the menu selection, press [Esc]. If the drop-down menu is displayed, pressing [Esc] once closes the drop-down menu. Pressing [Esc] a second time removes the highlight from the menu bar.

NOTE: The control menu is displayed by pressing [Alt], [Spacebar]. You do not need to hold [Alt] down while you press [Spacebar].

Now try it.

- Point and click on Options.

    ▶ *The Options pull-down menu appears.*

- Click anywhere outside the pull-down menu.

    ▶ *The pull-down menu disappears.*

- Press [Alt]+F. That is, hold down [Alt] and press F.

    ▶ *The File pull-down menu appears.*

- Type **N** to select New.

    ▶ *The New Program Object dialog box is displayed.*

- Click on Cancel or press [Esc].

P R A C T I C E   T I M E   2 - 2

1. Display the Options menu.

2. Select the Auto Arrange command. Auto Arrange is a toggle command, which means that the first time you select it, a checkmark appears in front of it indicating that it has been selected. The second time you select it, the checkmark disappears, indicating that the feature has been turned off. The purpose of the Auto Arrange command is explained later.

3. Make sure the Auto Arrange feature is turned off.

SIZING A WINDOW

Maximizing a Window

When a window is maximized, it fills the entire screen. You maximize a window when that window is the only thing you want to see on the screen, such as when you are doing word processing and want to see as much of the document as possible.

■   Maximize the Program Manager window by clicking on the maximize button, the upward-pointing triangle button at the right edge of the Program Manager title bar.

▶   *The Program Manager window fills the entire screen. The maximize button turns into a restore button.*

Restoring a Maximized Window

A maximized window is restored to its previous size by clicking on the restore button or by selecting Restore from the drop-down menu beneath the control-menu box.

■   Restore the maximized window by clicking on the restore button, the button at the top right corner of the screen with both upward- and downward-pointing triangles.

▶   *The Program Manager window is reduced to its previous size.*

Minimizing a Window

A window is minimized when it is reduced to an icon on the screen. You minimize a window when you want to clear the window but still want the application visible.

■   Minimize the Program Manager window by clicking on the minimize button, the downward-pointing triangle button at the right edge of the Program Manager title bar.

▶   *The Program Manager window is reduced to an icon.*

Restoring a Minimized Window

Again, changing the icon back to its previous size is called restoring.

■   Restore the minimized Program Manager window by double-clicking on the Program Manager icon. Learning to double-click may take a bit of practice.

N O T E :   Maximizing, minimizing, restoring, moving, and sizing windows may be performed by using the keyboard. First press [Alt]+[Spacebar] to view the control menu. If you are working with multiple windows, you then press [→] until the appropriate control menu appears.

P R A C T I C E   T I M E   2 - 3

Try maximizing, minimizing, and restoring using both the mouse and the keyboard. When you are comfortable with these tasks, maximize the Program Manager window.

MOVING PROGRAM GROUP ICONS

The icons that appear on the Program Manager work area are called ***program group icons***. Each icon represents groups of related programs. These icons can be moved around within the Program Manager window to a location that is most convenient for you.

N O T E : If, for some reason, some or all of your icons disappear, select the Arrange Icons option from the Window menu.

■ Move program group icons within the Program Manager window by dragging the icon with the mouse.

OPENING A WINDOW

To run a program in a group, first open the group window. The group window contains icons for each program in the group. Suppose you want to run a program in the Accessories group.

■ Open the Accessories window by double-clicking on the Accessories group icon.

▶ *The Accessories window, similar to the one in Figure 2-3, is displayed. If your Windows program has been customized, your window may look different.*

Figure 2-3

NOTE: From the keyboard, you can open any window by pressing Alt +W to display the Window drop-down menu. You then type the number of the group program option you want, or press an arrow key until the option is highlighted and then press ←Return.

You will now maximize the Accessories window. You might notice that there are two sets of sizing buttons: one set for the Program Manager window and another for the Accessories window. If the Program Manager window is partial screen size (not maximized), then the maximized Accessories window will only fill that partial screen size remaining. Also note the left corner of the title box in each window. Each window has its own control-menu box. The upper control-menu box controls the Program Manager window and the lower box controls the Accessories window. With a mouse, the command can be carried out by clicking on the appropriate box. You will use the keyboard this time, which means you will use → and ← to specify which control-menu box to use.

■ Maximize the Program Manager window, if you haven't already.

■ Press Alt and then Spacebar.

▶ *The drop-down menu for the Program Manager control-menu box appears.*

■ Press →.

▶ *The drop-down menu for the Accessories control-menu box appears.*

■ Press **X** to maximize the Accessories window.

P R A C T I C E   T I M E   2 - 4

Restore the Accessories window.

STARTING A PROGRAM

The icons in the Accessories window represent programs or applications that are available. Starting a program is also called *launching* a program. You will launch one now for practice.

■ Launch the Clock program by double-clicking on the Clock icon.

▶ *The pointer changes into an hourglass to indicate you must wait while Windows launches the application.*

▶ *The Clock program window opens on the screen.*

The clock may be displayed either as an analog or digital clock. You can change the setting.

■ Click on the <u>S</u>ettings option in the menu bar of the Clock window to display the Settings pull-down menu.

▶ *The drop-down menu is displayed.*

N O T E : If you accidentally click on the Program Manager or Accessories group windows, the clock will disappear! Don't panic; the clock is still on your desktop, but it's hidden behind the Program Manager window. To switch back to the Clock window, hold down [Alt] while you press [Esc] once.

P R A C T I C E   T I M E   2 - 5

1. Experiment with various options in the Settings menu such as:

   • Set the clock to digital mode and then back to analog mode.

   • Select No Title. Then double-click on the Clock window to display the title again.

2. Maximize the Clock program window.

3. Restore the Clock program window.

MOVING A WINDOW

When you want to view more than one application at a time, you may need to arrange your desktop. Windows lets you move windows. You will now move the Clock window to another location.

■ Position the mouse pointer on the title bar of the Clock window.

■ Drag the Clock window to a new position on the screen.

▶ *As you drag the window, an outline appears to help you determine the space the window will occupy when set.*

SWITCHING AMONG APPLICATION WINDOWS

The window displaying the application you are currently working with is called the **active window**. It is distinguished from an inactive window by the color or the intensity of the title bar. Also, the active window always appears in the foreground. Inactive windows may be partially or totally hidden behind other windows. The steps to change the active window are different depending on whether the desired inactive window is visible or not.

First you will make the Program Manager window the active window. The Program Manager window is only partially covered by the Clock window.

NOTE: The Accessories window is not an application. It is a list that is displayed by the Program Manager to show all the programs that are saved under the group named Accessories.

■   Click anywhere on the Program Manager window to make it the active window.

▶   *The Clock window disappears. It is in the background, behind the Program Manager window.*

You will now make the Clock window active. Because it is not visible, you need to first display the Task List. An application is also referred to as a **task**, and the Task List displays all applications that are currently running under Windows, whether or not the windows are displayed.

■   Click on the Program Manager control-menu box.

■   Click on the S<u>w</u>itch To command.

Alternative: Press Ctrl + Esc.

▶   *The Task List dialog box is displayed, as shown in Figure 2-4. Both Program Manager and Clock appear on the Task List.*

■   Make Clock active by double-clicking on Clock.

Figure 2-4

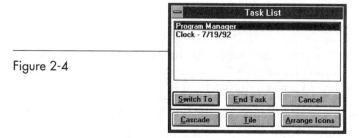

QUITTING A PROGRAM

Many Windows applications have a File menu with an Exit option. You should make a habit of using this option because the Exit command checks to see whether you have saved your work. If not, it will give you the option to do so. As Clock has no File menu, you can close it.

■   Close the Clock program window by double-clicking on the Clock control-menu box.

Alternative: Press Alt + F4 .

▶   *The Clock program is now closed.*

ENDING A TASK

Minimizing a window will also make the window disappear. When you minimize an application window, however, you do not stop the execution of that program. The program is reduced to an icon but continues to run in the background. You can end or switch to the task through the Task List.

■   Launch the Clock program again.

■   Minimize the Clock window.

■   Display the Task List.

If you want to display the clock again, click on the Switch To button. Right now, you want to end the task.

■   Select the Clock program by clicking on Clock.

■   Click on the <u>E</u>nd Task button.

CHANGING THE SHAPE AND SIZE OF A WINDOW

The shape and size of a partial-screen-size window can be changed in a variety of ways, depending on your display needs. There are eight areas on the window border—the four sides and the four corners—that can be relocated.

Right now, you will change the shape and size of the Accessories window. First, move the right border of the Accessories window.

■   Carefully position the pointer on the right border of the Accessories window.

▶   *The pointer changes from a simple arrow to a left- and right-facing double arrow (⇔).*

■   Drag the right window border to a new position before releasing the mouse button.

If you move the right border so some of the icons are hidden, a horizontal scroll bar appears at the bottom of the window. Similarly, if you move the top or bottom border so some of the icons are hidden, a vertical scroll bar appears on the right edge of the window.

N O T E :   At the top or bottom border, the pointer turns into an up-and-down double arrow, and at a corner it turns into a diagonal double arrow.

P R A C T I C E   T I M E   2 - 6

Move the positions of the right border of the Accessories window so a vertical scroll bar appears.

USING SCROLL BARS

The scroll bar is used to view those portions of the window that are not currently visible. To scroll the window you can either click on the scroll arrows at either end of the scroll bar or drag the scroll box, which is the box that appears on the scroll bar someplace between the two scroll arrows.

P R A C T I C E   T I M E   2 - 7

1. Drag the scroll box to scroll the window.

2. Scroll the window by clicking on the scroll arrow.

3. Drag icons around within the window to change their positions.

ARRANGING PROGRAM ICONS

There is a command to rearrange the icons in the window to take advantage of any window shape.

- ■   Select the Window menu.

- ■   Click on the Arrange Icons command.

N O T E :   Icons may or may not be rearranged, depending on how you already moved them around.

If you do not want to bother rearranging the icons manually each time you resize a window, you can select the Auto Arrange command (so a checkmark appears in front of it) in the Options menu.

P R A C T I C E   T I M E   2 - 8

1. Turn on <u>A</u>uto Arrange.

2. Resize the window. Notice how the icons are rearranged.

GETTING ONSCREEN HELP

Windows provides a flexible onscreen help system. Help is accessed from the Help menu option, which is the always the last option on a menu bar.

■   Click on the <u>H</u>elp menu option in the Program Manager window and then select <u>C</u>ontents.

Alternative: Press [F1].

▶   *The Contents screen appears, as shown in Figure 2-5.*

Figure 2-5

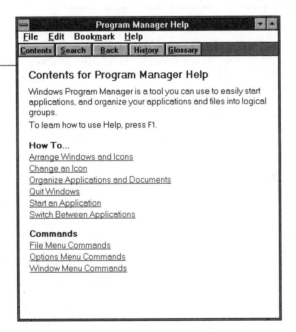

The Help window consists of a title bar, a menu bar, and a work area, like other windows. Below the menu bar is a bar with several command buttons or icons, including Search. The work area contains a read-only document describing a topic. Most help screens contain underlined references to related topics. To view a related topic, select the topic by clicking on it or by using [Tab⇆] to highlight the topic and then pressing [←Enter].

Suppose you need information on how to switch between tasks. You can use the Contents button to view a screen of Help contents or the Search button to access the Search dialog box.

■   Click on the Search command button.

▶   *The Search dialog box appears, as shown in Figure 2-6.*

Figure 2-6

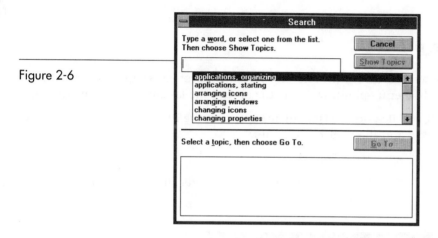

At the top, the dialog box indicates you are to type a word or select one from the list. To select an item from the list, you can scroll until the topic you want is visible and then double-click on it.

■   Type **Switch**.

▶   *The list box highlights the topic Switching Between Applications.*

■   Press ⏎Enter.

▶   *The lower list box displays topics related to the selected topic in the upper box. Here, only one topic is related, which is Switching Between Applications.*

■   Click on the Go To button in the Search dialog box.

▶   *The Switching Between Applications help screen appears.*

The screen describes several ways to switch between applications. It describes how to access the command from the control menu and how to use the alternative, Ctrl+Esc, to open the Task List for switching between applications. On help screens, words or phrases with dotted underlines have definitions that are displayed by clicking on the word or phrase.

To exit Help, you can double-click on the control-menu box or press Alt+F4.

P R A C T I C E   T I M E   2 - 9

1. Spend a few minutes to become familiar with Help. Use the Contents and Search buttons and select related topics. You don't need to memorize the material, but become aware that it is available for you whenever you are using Windows, including during the lessons in this book.

2. When you have finished viewing the topics, exit Help.

ENDING LESSON 2

Always end your Windows session from the Program Manager. This will guarantee you an opportunity to save any work you neglected to store on disk earlier.

■ Double-click on the control-menu box at the left of the Program Manager title bar.

Alternative: Press [Alt]+[F4].

▶ *The Exit Windows dialog box appears. This lets you cancel the command if you did not intend to quit Windows.*

■ Click on the OK command button.

▶ *You exit Windows.*

S U M M A R Y

In this lesson, the basic operations of Microsoft Windows 3.1 are presented.

☐ **Windows is a graphical interface between the user and computer. Most commands are given by selecting icons, as opposed to typing a command, as in DOS.**

☐ **Windows applications use standard commands. Also, Windows has multitasking ability, which lets the user run several programs simultaneously, creating an integrated environment for data transfer between applications.**

☐ **Each application runs within its own window. Each window has standard features, including a border, title bar, and menu bar.**

☐ **Each window can be maximized to fill the screen, minimized to an icon, or shaped and moved on the screen.**

☐ **Users can easily switch between programs.**

☐ **Windows has an extensive onscreen help feature, accessible from the Program Manager Help menu.**

☐ **The user should always properly exit Microsoft Windows before turning off the computer.**

KEY TERMS

active window	icon	pull-down menu
border	integrated environment	restore button
command line	launching	scroll bars
interpreter	maximize button	task
control-menu box	menu bar	title bar
desktop	minimize button	window
drop-down menu	multitasking	work area
graphical user	pointer	
interface (GUI)	program group icons	

COMMAND SUMMARY

Options	**File**
Auto Arrange	Exit

Windows	**Help**
Arrange Icons	Contents

REVIEW QUESTIONS

1. What is Microsoft Windows?

2. How does a GUI differ from a command line interpreter?

3. How do you make menu selections using the mouse; using the keyboard?

4. What happens when you restore a window?

5. How are icons used in Microsoft Windows?

6. What is a program group icon?

7. How do you launch a program?

8. What does the Task List do?

9. How do you switch between tasks?

10. How do you exit from Windows?

EXERCISES

1. Various parts of a Windows screen are listed below.
   a. Describe each part.
   b. Identify each part using the letters in Figure 2-7.

   _____ Title bar   _____ Mouse pointer
   _____ Border   _____ Control-menu box
   _____ Restore button   _____ Scroll bar
   _____ Icon   _____ Minimize button
   _____ Maximize button   _____ Menu bar

Figure 2-7

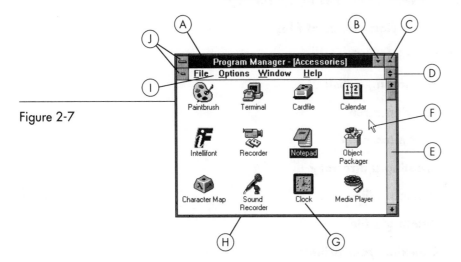

2. Use Windows to perform the following tasks:
   a. Arrange the screen so the Excel, Accessories, and Main group windows are displayed.
   b. Run the Clock program and minimize its window.
   c. Adjust the Program Manager window so the minimized Clock icon is visible.
   d. Move and size the windows so the minimized Clock icon and all the program icons in the three group windows are visible (no scroll bars appear).

3 File Management in Windows

OBJECTIVES

Upon completing the material presented in this lesson, you should understand the following:

- ☐ **The Windows File Manager**
- ☐ **Disk directory hierarchy**
- ☐ **Expanding and collapsing directories**
- ☐ **Viewing filenames in a directory**
- ☐ **Displaying details of files**
- ☐ **Examining file contents**
- ☐ **Formatting a disk**
- ☐ **Copying a file**
- ☐ **Renaming a file**
- ☐ **Creating a directory**
- ☐ **Moving a file**
- ☐ **Deleting a file**
- ☐ **Checking your printer setup**

OPERATING SYSTEM

STARTING OFF

Start the Windows program, following the instructions given in Lesson 2. Make sure the Program Manager is the only window displayed on the screen.

■   Maximize the Program Manager window.

■   Double-click on the Main group icon.

▶   *The Main window, similar to the one in Figure 3-1, is displayed.*

■   Maximize the Main window.

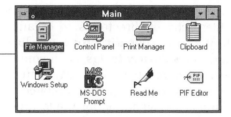

Figure 3-1

The Main group contains the File Manager, Control Panel, Print Manager, Clipboard, MS-DOS Prompt, and Windows Setup. These are applications used to manage the Windows environment and your system resources.

File Manager	Helps you organize the files stored on disk. With it, you can easily find, move, copy, delete, rename, and print disk files.
Control Panel	Lets you customize the way Windows is configured by altering the startup or default settings. You can change such things as the color scheme, the spacing between the icons on your desktop, and even the printer and monitor you are using.
Print Manager	Lets you continue working even while you are printing a file. When you tell a Windows application to print, it sends the file to Print Manager instead of the printer. Print Manager handles the printing task, thus freeing your application for other uses. From Print Manager you can also control the order in which files are printed or halt printing of any file.
Clipboard	A temporary storage area for transferring information within or between applications.

Windows Setup	Assists you in adding new applications and changing hardware configurations.
MS-DOS Prompt	Takes you to the DOS (disk operating system) prompt. Typing **exit** returns you to the Windows environment.

In this lesson, you will work with the File Manager to learn how to perform various tasks involved in managing disk files.

FILES, DIRECTORIES, AND SUBDIRECTORIES

As you may recall from Lesson 1, programs and data are stored on disks as files. As the number of files on a disk increases, you need to keep the disk well organized. This is especially true of large-capacity hard disks. DOS lets you create a hierarchy of directories to organize files on the disk. The original directory, or the **root directory**, can have a number of divisions, called **directories** or **subdirectories**, each containing files that relate to a common subject or application. This way, you can create a directory for each subject or application and place all related files in that directory.

A **pathname** is a designation for the location of files or directories on your disk. The pathname for the root directory is the drive name followed by a colon (:) and backslash (\). For example, the pathname for the root directory for drive C is C:\. The pathname for the directory called EXCEL within the root directory is C:\EXCEL; the pathname for the subdirectory called DATA within the EXCEL directory is C:\EXCEL\DATA; and the pathname for a file called BUDGET.XLS in the DATA subdirectory is C:\EXCEL\DATA\BUDGET.XLS. The diagram below illustrates the directory structure, called the **directory tree**.

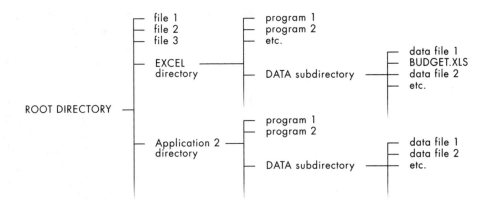

OPERATING SYSTEM

THE FILE MANAGER

The File Manager can be used to view the directory tree and files stored on a disk. The program can also be used to view the contents of some types of files; to copy, move, rename, and delete files; to create and remove directories; and to format disks.

■ Launch the File Manager by double-clicking on the File Manager icon. The File Manager icon looks like a two-drawer file cabinet.

▶ *The File Manager window opens, similar to the one displayed in Figure 3-2.*

NOTE: If your screen looks drastically different (just one window in the work area), click on the <u>V</u>iew menu option and then select the T<u>r</u>ee and Directory option.

Figure 3-2

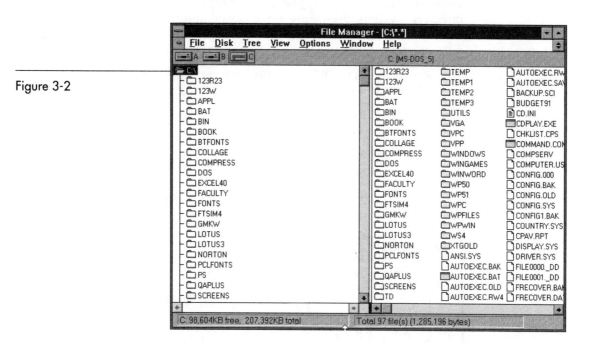

The File Manager application window contains a menu bar with seven menu options, and there are two windows in the workspace. The window on the left displays the directory tree of the selected drive, and the one on the right displays contents, or the directory, of the selected directory (the directory selected in the directory tree window).

Under the title bar of the File Manager window, icons representing the disk drives on your system are displayed. One of the drives is selected (a box appears around it), and the workspace displays the directory tree for the selected drive. The directory tree graphically shows directories, or the branches, in the root directory of the selected drive. Each directory is represented by an icon depicting a file folder.

The file folder icon for the root directory is at the top of the tree. In Figure 3-2 the root directory, c:\, is selected and the icon is an open folder. Hence, the directory window on the right displays the files and subdirectories in the root directory.

- Scroll the left window until the Windows directory is displayed.

- Select the Windows directory by clicking on it.

   ▶ *The icon for the Windows directory turns into an open folder.*

Notice that the directory (right-hand) window changes to show the contents of the Windows directory.

Expanding and Collapsing Directories

The Windows directory may contain one or more subdirectories. To display subdirectories, you **expand the directory**, and to remove the display of subdirectories, you **collapse the directory**. You expand or collapse a directory by double-clicking on it. Depending on whether the Windows directory is currently expanded or collapsed, you may have to reverse the following instructions.

- Expand the Windows directory by double-clicking on the Windows directory icon.

   ▶ *Subdirectories in the Windows directory are displayed, as shown in Figure 3-3.*

- Collapse the Windows directory by double-clicking on the Windows directory icon.

   ▶ *The subdirectories are no longer displayed.*

Figure 3-3

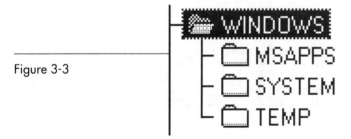

N O T E :   If you want to use the keyboard to expand or collapse directories, choose the appropriate command from the Tree menu option.

P R A C T I C E   T I M E   3 - 1

Try expanding and collapsing other directories. When you are comfortable with these tasks, select the Windows directory again.

Viewing Filenames in a Directory

As mentioned previously, the directory (right-hand) window displays the contents of the selected directory. The title bar shows the pathname for the directory as c:\windows*.*. The *.* indicates that all files and subdirectories in the selected directory are displayed. The following list identifies the types of icons.

Directory icons   These represent directories.

Program file icons   These represent executable (launchable) applications. Their filenames end with one of these extensions: .EXE, .COM, or .BAT.

Document file icons These represent files that are associated with specific applications by their filename extensions, such as .DBF for a database file or .EXL for a worksheet created by an electronic spreadsheet.

Data file icons   These icons are used for all other data files.

Displaying Details of Files

File Manager can also list the files and directories in a different format, with detailed information on the file size and the date and time last modified. First, you will change the display so only the directory window is displayed.

■ Click on the View menu and then select Directory Only.

▶ *The directory tree window disappears.*

■ Show a detailed listing of the files by selecting the All File Details option from the View menu.

▶ *The active window displays each file on a single line, as shown in Figure 3-4.*

Figure 3-4

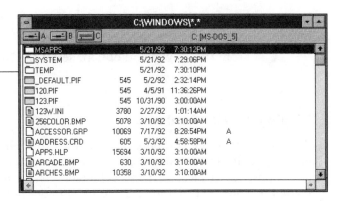

Icons and filenames are displayed in the first and second columns. The third column of the display indicates the file size in bytes. The fourth and fifth columns display the date and the time the file was last modified. The last column displays the ***attributes*** for each file. The attributes contain information DOS uses to determine the kind of operations you can perform on the file. The following describes the various attributes.

R   Read Only. Prevents a file from being changed.

A   Archive. A file that has been modified.

H   Hidden. Prevents a file from appearing in a DOS directory listing, though it is still visible in the directory window.

S   System. Identifies the file as a DOS system file.

Arranging Display of Filenames

You might notice that right now, all filenames are listed in alphabetical order. You can also have files displayed in other orders, such as date or file size.

■   From the Under{View} menu option, select the Sort by Under{Date} command.

▶   *The files are listed in creation-date order.*

P R A C T I C E   T I M E   3 - 2

Try sorting in other orders. When you have tried several options, sort by name again.

Displaying Filenames Only

You can return to the previous display of filenames only, without the file details.

■   From the Under{View} menu option, select the Under{Name} command.

Displaying File Contents

You can display the contents of some files through the File Manager. You can display files with extension .TXT and files with extension .BMP.

Contents of files with the extension .TXT can be viewed and edited using the Notepad program. All you need to do, however, is double-click on the filename. Windows will automatically start the Notepad program.

Right now, you will view the contents of the file SETUP.TXT, but you will not change the file.

■ Use the bottom scroll bar to bring SETUP.TXT into view.

■ Double-click on the icon and filename of SETUP.TXT.

▶ *The Windows Notepad opens, displaying the contents of SETUP.TXT.*

■ Close the Notepad window containing SETUP.TXT by selecting Exit from the File menu or by double-clicking on the control-menu box at the top left.

Alternative: Press ⌷Alt⌷+⌷F4⌷.

NOTE: If, for some reason, you changed the file, a cautionary dialog box will appear and ask whether you want to save the changes. Select the No button.

Files with extension .BMP are graphic files for the Paintbrush application. Again, you will view a file and close it immediately. As before, all you need to do is double-click on the filename. Windows will automatically start the Paintbrush program.

■ Double-click on the icon for ZIGZAG.BMP.

▶ *The Windows Paintbrush program is launched, displaying the image contained in the file ZIGZAG.BMP.*

■ Close the Paintbrush window containing ZIGZAG.BMP by selecting Exit from the File menu.

Alternative: Press ⌷Alt⌷+⌷F4⌷.

NOTE: Both the Notepad and Paintbrush programs are in the Accessories group and can be launched from the Accessories group window.

P R A C T I C E   T I M E   3 - 3

Change the view to display the directory tree only.

Hint: Select the Tree Only command in the View menu.

FORMATTING A FLOPPY DISK

When you buy blank disks, there is nothing on them. A disk must be formatted before you can store information on it. This applies to a hard disk as well. To format a disk means to prepare it to store information.

You will now format a floppy disk. You need a 5¼-inch or 3½-inch disk that either is unformatted or contains information you no longer need. When you format a disk with information already on it, the current content of the disk is erased.

N O T E : As a precaution, the File Manager will not format the active disk, the disk with its directory tree displayed.

■ Place the disk to be formatted in a floppy disk drive.

In the following steps, it is assumed that the disk is in drive A. If you are using drive B, substitute B wherever drive A is mentioned.

■ Click on the <u>D</u>isk option and then select the <u>F</u>ormat Disk option in the pull-down menu.

▶ *The Format Disk dialog box appears as shown in Figure 3-5.*

Figure 3-5

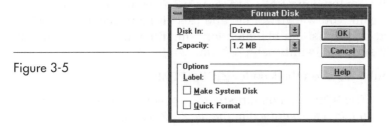

■ If the drive of the disk to be formatted is not correct, specify the right drive by clicking on the button to the right of the displayed drive name. A drop-down list box containing the floppy disk drives on your computer is displayed. Click on the correct drive letter.

The Capacity option refers to the type of disk. If you recall from Lesson 1, there are different types of floppy disks: high density and double density as well as 5¼-inch and 3½-inch. You need to find out what type of disk you are using.

■ If the capacity of the disk is incorrect, display the drop-down list box by clicking on the arrow button to the right. Then specify the right capacity.

The box on the bottom left contains three options.

• You can label the disk with a name of up to 11 characters by clicking in the Label option text box and entering the label. This label is for identification purposes only.

• The Make System Disk check box gives you an option to add the DOS system file, COMMAND.COM, to the disk. Because the DOS 5.0 system file uses about 48K of disk space, you generally will not select that option.

- If your disk already contains data that is no longer needed, you can select the Quick Format check box. This option deletes the files from the disk without reformatting it.

To select a check box, you click on it so that an × appears in the box; to deselect it, you click on the box again so the × is removed.

■ After you specify all options, complete the command by clicking on the OK button or by pressing ⏎Enter.

▶ *A cautionary Format Diskette dialog box (with an exclamation-point icon) appears informing you that formatting erases all data on the diskette.*

■ Confirm that you want to format by clicking on the Yes button.

▶ *A dialog box appears displaying the formatting progress.*

▶ *After formatting, a Format Complete dialog box appears, asking whether you want to format another disk.*

P R A C T I C E   T I M E   3 - 4

1. Format any additional floppy disks you may want to use during the session.

2. When you are finished with formatting, select the No option in the Format Complete dialog box.

3. Minimize the File Manager application.

USING THE NOTEPAD

The Notepad program, which you used briefly earlier, is used for writing and printing short notes. It is a very limited word processing program. Here, you will use it to write a short note that will be saved and used to practice file manipulations and to test your printer setup.

■ Select the Accessories group.

■ Select the Notepad by double-clicking on the Notepad icon.

▶ *The Notepad window appears, as shown in Figure 3-6.*

■ Type the following text:

My name is <*type your name here*>.

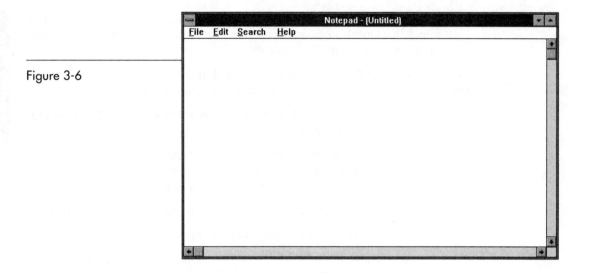

Figure 3-6

You want to save the text in a file on your newly formatted data disk.

■ Click on the File option in the Notepad menu bar and then select the Save As command.

▶ *The Save As dialog box appears as shown in Figure 3-7.*

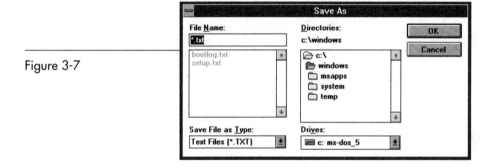

Figure 3-7

The Save As dialog box is used to specify the drive, directory, and filename you want to use to save your text. You want to use your newly formatted data disk. You will save your file in the root directory, using the filename NAME.TXT.

■ If the drive specified in the Drives text box is not correct, display the drop-down list box by clicking on the arrow button to the right. You can then specify the correct drive.

■ Drag to select the content of the File Name text box.

▶ *The directory display changes to a:\ or b:\.*

■ Type the filename **NAME.**

■ Complete the command by clicking on OK or by pressing ⌷←Enter⌷.

▶ *The file is stored on your data disk. The Notepad program automatically assigned the extension .TXT to the filename. You are returned to the Notepad.*

■ Exit the Notepad program.

P R A C T I C E   T I M E   3 - 5

Restore the File Manager from the icon.

CREATING A DIRECTORY

You can create directories and subdirectories using the File Manager program. Suppose you want a directory named JUST4ME on your floppy disk.

■ From the Disk menu option, select the Select Drive command.

■ Specify the drive containing your floppy disk and complete the command by either clicking the OK button or pressing ⌷←Return⌷.

■ From the View menu option, select the Tree and Directory command.

▶ *The file NAME.TXT appears in the directory window.*

■ From the File menu, select the Create Directory command.

▶ *The Create Directory dialog box appears (Figure 3-8). This box lets you specify the new directory name.*

■ Type **JUST4ME** and complete the command.

▶ *The JUST4ME directory appears in the directory tree window.*

Figure 3-8

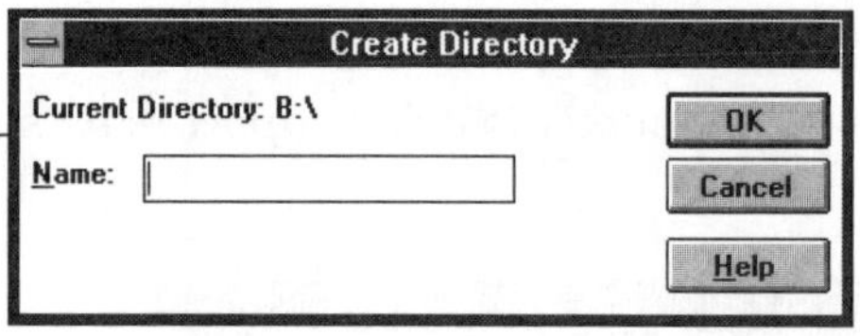

FILE TASKS

Moving a File to Another Directory

Suppose you would like to move NAME.TXT into the directory you just created. When you move a file, the original version is deleted; when you copy a file, the original file is left unchanged.

■ Select the file NAME.TXT.

■ From the File menu, select the Move option.

Alternative: Press F7 .

▶ *The Move dialog box appears as shown in Figure 3-9.*

Figure 3-9

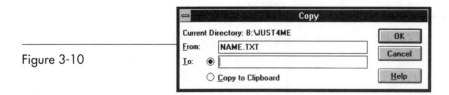

You need to specify the new location for the file.

■ Type **JUST4ME** and then complete the command.

▶ *NAME.TXT is no longer displayed in the directory window.*

■ Select JUST4ME in the directory tree window.

▶ *The JUST4ME directory is displayed. The file NAME.TXT appears.*

Copying a File

You will next copy NAME.TXT to another file, MYNAME.TXT.

■ Select NAME.TXT in the directory window.

■ From the File menu, select the Copy command.

Alternative: Press F8 .

▶ *The Copy dialog box appears as shown in Figure 3-10.*

Figure 3-10

OPERATING SYSTEM

Now you need to specify where to copy NAME.TXT.

■ Type **MYNAME.TXT** and then complete the command.

▶ *Both NAME.TXT and MYNAME.TXT appear in the directory window.*

N O T E :   If you specify only the drive and/or directory in the To box, the file is copied to the specified drive and directory with the same name as the original. If you specify a filename as well, the file is copied to the new location using the new specified filename.

Renaming a File

Sometimes you want to change a filename. Suppose you want to change MYNAME.TXT to ME.TXT.

■ Select MYNAME.TXT.

■ From the File menu, select the Rename command.

▶ *The Rename dialog box appears as shown in Figure 3-11.*

Figure 3-11

```
┌─────────────────────────────────────────────────┐
│ ▬                   Rename                        │
├─────────────────────────────────────────────────┤
│ Current Directory: B:\JUST4ME      ┌──────────┐  │
│ From:    │MYNAME.TXT          │     │    OK    │  │
│ To:      │                    │     ├──────────┤  │
│                                     │  Cancel  │  │
│                                     ├──────────┤  │
│                                     │   Help   │  │
│                                     └──────────┘  │
└─────────────────────────────────────────────────┘
```

You are to specify the new name of the file.

■ Type the name **ME.TXT** in the To box and then complete the command.

▶ *The new filename replaces the old one.*

Deleting a File

You will now delete NAME.TXT from your floppy disk. When you delete a file from a floppy disk, it is gone permanently. You must make absolutely certain that you do, indeed, want to delete the file before proceeding.

■ Select NAME.TXT.

■ From the File menu, select the Delete command.

Alternative: Press ⌐Del⌐.

▶ *The Delete dialog box appears. The file NAME.TXT is displayed.*

If you realize that you wanted to delete a different file, you type that filename. Right now, the information is correct.

■ Complete the command.

▶ *A cautionary dialog box appears to make certain that you do want to delete the file.*

■ Confirm the deletion by clicking on the Yes button.

▶ *The file is deleted.*

NOTE: You can delete a directory using the same command. However, if the directory is not empty but contains files and/or subdirectories, the File Manager will ask you to confirm deletion of the whole subtree structure.

P R A C T I C E   T I M E   3 - 6

Display the contents of the file ME.TXT.

CHECKING YOUR PRINTER SETUP

Before ending this lesson, you will make sure the printer on your system works properly with Windows. If it does not, you need to check with your instructor.

■ From the File menu in the Notepad window, select the Print Setup command.

▶ *The Print Setup dialog box, similar to Figure 3-12, appears.*

■ Make sure your printer name appears under Default Printer.

Figure 3-12

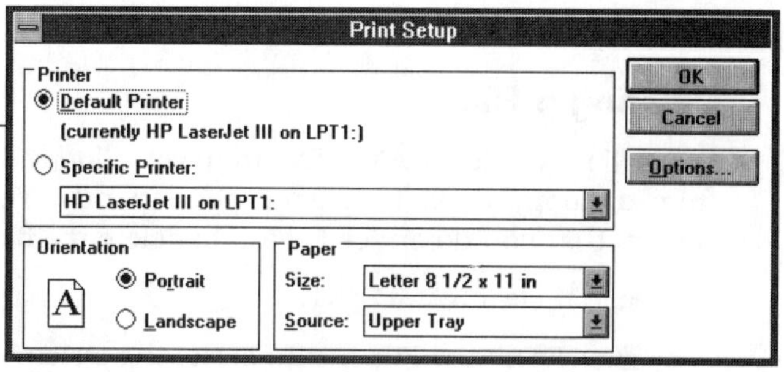

NOTE: If the correct printer does not appear under Default Printer, display the Specific Printer drop-down list box and select the appropriate printer. If your printer is not listed in the Specific Printer list, consult your instructor.

OPERATING SYSTEM

■ Click on the OK button or press ⏎Enter.

Now you can print the text.

■ Make sure your printer is turned on and ready to print.

■ From the File menu, select the Print command.

▶ *The note you just wrote is printed. If it is not printed, consult your instructor.*

■ Exit Notepad.

ENDING LESSON 3

This is the end of Lesson 3.

■ If you have multiple windows open, press Alt+F4 until all windows are closed.

■ Exit Windows and turn off your computer as described in Lesson 2.

■ Remove your data disk from the drive and carefully store the disk.

S U M M A R Y

In this lesson, file management operations in Microsoft Windows are presented.

☐ **The Main group includes the File Manager, Print Manager, and Control Panel programs for managing the Windows environment.**

☐ **Files are stored on disks and arranged in directories.**

☐ **The complete pathname of a file consists of the drive name, all directories and subdirectories leading to the file, and the filename.**

☐ **The File Manager program can be used to do the following:**

• View the directory tree of the selected drive
• View the contents of a selected directory
• Display the specific details (size, date and time last modified, and attributes) of each file on a disk
• Display the contents of a text file or graphics file
• Format floppy disks
• Copy, move, rename, and delete files

KEY TERMS

attributes	directory tree	root directory
collapse directory	expand directory	subdirectory
directory	pathname	

COMMAND SUMMARY

File Manager

```
View
  Tree and Directory
  Directory Only
  Name
  All File Details
  Sort by Date
```

```
File
  Move
  Copy
  Delete
  Rename
  Create a Directory
```

```
Disk
  Format Disk
```

Notepad

```
File
  Save As
  Print
  Print Setup
  Exit
```

REVIEW QUESTIONS

1. How are files organized on a disk?

2. What is a directory?

3. What is meant by collapsing and expanding a directory?

4. What is a directory tree?

5. What pathname would you use to identify the file TEST1.TXT within the TEST directory in the root directory of the disk in drive A?

6. How do you display the contents of a disk directory?

7. What can the Notepad program do? How do you activate this program?

8. How do you create a directory using the File Manager?

9. Why must a disk be formatted?

10. What is the difference between moving and copying a file?

E X E R C I S E S

1. Using a new disk or one without any information you wish to keep, do the following:

    a. Format the disk. Try to give the disk the volume label BUDGET92.

    b. Create two directories on the disk: EQUIPMENT and OPERATING.

    c. In EQUIPMENT, create three subdirectories: OFFICE, INVENTORY, and MAINTENANCE.

    d. Use the File Manager utility to view the file structure on your disk.

2. Launch the Notepad utility.

    a. Write a note to yourself stating what you hope to learn from this course.

    b. Save the note as GOALS on your data disk.

    c. Copy the file to BACKUP on the same disk.

    d. Print the file.

Glossary

access window   An opening on the jacket of a diskette through which information is read from and written onto the disk.

active window   Describes the window to which the next command will apply. If a window is active, its title bar changes color to differentiate it from other windows.

align   To line up.

application window   A window that contains a running application. The name of the application appears at the top of the window.

attributes   *See* file attribute.

bit   Binary digit, the smallest amount of information a computer can hold.

border   Outer edge of a window.

bus size   The capacity of the input/output path that connects the processor to external devices.

byte   A character.

cascade   A way of arranging open windows on the desktop so that they overlap one another, with the title bar of each window remaining visible.

central processing unit (CPU)   *See* processor.

character   A letter, digit, punctuation mark, blank space, or other written symbol used in printing or displaying information.

check box   A small square box that appears in a dialog box and that can be selected or cleared. When the check box is selected, an X appears in the window.

chip   Electronic entity containing one or more semiconductors on a wafer of silicon, within which an integrated circuit is formed.

click   To press and release a mouse button quickly.

clipboard   A temporary storage location used to transfer data between documents and between applications.

clock speed   The speed, in megahertz, used to control how fast the operations within a computer are performed.

close   To remove a document window or application window from the desktop.

cold start   Starting up by turning the computer on and letting the disk start up automatically. The computer is off initially, thus the term cold.

collapse directory   To "hide" additional directory levels below a selected directory.

Color Graphics Adaptor (CGA)   A type of monitor that displays color.

COM port   *See* serial port.

command line interpreter   Software is known to use the command line interpreter when the user gives instructions to the microcomputer by typing keywords on the keyboard.

configuration   The arrangement of hardware and software in a computer system.

control-menu box   The icon that opens the control menu for the window. It is always at the left of the title bar.

current directory   The directory that is currently highlighted in the Directory Tree or whose directory window is the active window.

cursor   A symbol or flashing underscore that shows the position on the screen where an entry is made.

cylinders   Entity composed of all like-numbered tracks from all record surfaces of a disk.

data   Facts and numbers.

default   A value action or setting that is automatically used when no alternate instructions are given. For example, a default drive is where the program looks for data files unless explicitly instructed otherwise.

desktop   The screen background for Windows on which windows, icons, and dialog boxes appear.

dialog box   A rectangular box that either requests or provides information. Many dialog boxes present options to choose among before Windows can carry out a command. Some dialog boxes present warnings or explain why a command can't be completed.

directory   A file or a part of a disk that contains the names and locations of other files on the disk.

directory tree   A graphic display in File Manager of the directory structure of a disk.

disk (diskette, floppy disk, floppies)   A circular object with concentric tracks that is used as a machine-readable medium.

disk drive   Hardware that spins a disk. It reads and writes data onto a disk.

disk operating system (DOS)   A program containing instructions on managing the flow of data between the disk drive and the computer.

document window   A window within an application window. A document window contains a document you create or modify by using an application. There can be more than one document window in an application window.

double-click   To rapidly press and release a mouse button twice without moving the mouse. Double-clicking usually carries out an action, such as opening an icon.

drag   To move an item on the screen by holding down the mouse button while moving the mouse.

drop-down list box   A single-line dialog box that opens to display a list of choices.

drop-down menu   The sub-option menu that appears when an option in the menu bar is highlighted.

Enhanced Graphics Adaptor (EGA)   A type of display device that offers better resolution than CGA.

expand directory   To show currently hidden levels in the Directory Tree.

expansion slots   Slots in the motherboard where you connect the interface boards for the peripherals.

file   A collection of data records with related content; information stored as a named unit on a peripheral storage medium such as a disk.

file attribute   A characteristic of a file— for example, the read-only attribute— that can be changed using File Manager.

filename   The name of a file.

file server   A computer on a network equipped with a large-capacity hard disk drive containing programs and data that can be used by any computer on the network.

firmware   Information that comes on ROM.

fixed disk   *See* hard disk.

floppy disk   *See* disk.

font   A graphic design applied to all numerals, symbols, and characters in the alphabet. A font usually comes in different sizes and provides different styles, such as bold, italic, and underlining for emphasizing text.

format a disk   To prepare a blank disk to receive information.

function keys   Keys ($\boxed{F1}$ to $\boxed{F10}$ or $\boxed{F12}$) that allow special functions to be entered with a single keystroke.

WN58   Glossary
WN58   Glossary

graphical user interface (GUI)   Software is said to use a graphical user interface when a user instructs the computer by selecting small pictures, called icons.

gray scale   The ability to show colors as various shades of gray.

group   A collection of programs in Program Manager. Grouping your programs makes them easier to find when you want to start them.

group icon   The graphic that represents a Program Manager group that is minimized. Double-clicking the group icon opens the group window.

group window   A window that displays the items in a group within Program Manager.

hard disk   Storage medium consisting of a rigid metal platter coated with a metallic-oxide substance upon which data are recorded as patterns of magnetic spots.

hard card   Hard disk that is in the form of an expansion card.

icon   A graphical representation of various elements in Windows, such as disk drives, applications, and documents.

inactive window   Any open window that you are not currently working in.

input   Information transferred into a computer from some external source, such as the keyboard or a disk drive.

input devices   Equipment used to enter programs and data into a computer.

insertion point   The place where text will be inserted when you type.

interface board   A device by which peripheral equipment communicates with the computer.

kilobyte (K)   Approximately 1000 (1024) bytes.

keyboard   System hardware used to input characters, commands, and functions to the computer. The keyboard consists of 83 keys and is organized into three sections: the function keys, the typewriter keyboard, and the numeric keypad.

launching   Starting the execution of an application program. This is usually done by double-clicking on the application icon.

list box   Within a dialog box, a box listing available choices— for example, the list of all available files in a directory. If all the choices won't fit, the list box has a vertical scroll bar.

main memory   A portion of the computer that stores data and instructions. Programs must be brought into main memory before they can be run, and data must reside in main memory before it can be processed.

maximize button   The small box containing an up arrow at the right of the title bar. It can be clicked to enlarge a window to its maximum size.

megabyte (Mb)   Approximately one million bytes (1024×1024 to be exact).

menu   A list of items, most of which are Windows commands. Menu names appear in the menu bar near the top of the window.

menu bar   The horizontal bar containing the menu choices.

microprocessor unit (MPU)   *See* processor.

minimize button   The small box containing a down arrow at the right of the title bar. It can be clicked to shrink a window to an icon.

modem   Acronym for MOdulator-DEModulator; a device that allows computers to use telephone lines for communication.

monitor   A TV-like display device that gives users of microcomputers video feedback about their actions and the computer's actions.

monochrome monitor   A monitor that displays text and graphics in only one color.

motherboard   Main system board; a large board on the bottom of the computer that electronically connects all the individual pieces of a computer.

mouse   A cursor control device that resembles a small box on wheels. As the box is rolled on a flat surface, the movement of the wheel signals the computer to move the cursor on the display screen in direct proportion to the movement of the mouse.

multitasking   The ability to run more than one program at one time without interrupting the execution of another program.

network   A group of computers connected by cables and using special software that allows them to share equipment (such as printers) and exchange information.

numeric keypad   Section of the keyboard containing numeric entry and editing keys.

open   To display the contents of a file in a window or to enlarge an icon to a window.

operating system   The set of computer programs that manages the activities that go on among the keyboard, the video display, and other components.

output   Information transferred from a computer to some external destination such as the display screen, a disk drive, or a printer.

ouput devices   Equipment used to print or display programs and their result.

parallel port   A connection on a computer, usually LPT1, where you plug in the cable for a parallel printer.

pathname   The direction to a directory or file within your system. For example, C:\DIR1\FILEA is the pathname for the FILEA file in the DIR1 subdirectory on drive C.

peripherals   Any device attached to the computer.

pixels   The smallest graphic units on the screen.

point   To move the pointer on the screen until it rests on the item you want to select or choose.

pointer   The arrow-shaped cursor on the screen that indicates the position of the mouse.

port   A connection on a computer where you plug in the cable that carries data to another device.

processor   The heart and brain of the computer; the processor controls all the actions of the computer, including all the mathematical operations on data.

program group   *See* group.

random access memory (RAM)   Storage location where you can both read and write information; volatile memory.

read only memory (ROM)   A storage location from which the user can read information, but to which the user cannot write.

read-write head   Part of a disk drive used to read and write information on a disk.

resolution   The clarity of a monitor.

restore button   The small box containing a down arrow and an up arrow at the right of the title bar. The restore button appears after you have enlarged a window to its full size. It can be clicked with a mouse to return the window to its previous size.

root directory   The highest directory of a disk. The root directory is created when you format the disk. From the root directory, you can create other directories.

serial port   A connection on a computer, usually COM1, where you plug in the cable for a serial printer or other serial communications device, such as a modem.

soft fonts   A font that is downloaded to your printer's memory from a disk provided by the font manufacturer.

storage devices   Devices used to store data.

subdirectory   A directory contained within another directory. All directories are subdirectories of the root directory.

system unit   The hardware component of a microcomputer composed of a processor and main memory.

task   An open application.

text box   A box within a dialog box where you type information needed to carry out the chosen command.

title bar   The horizontal bar located at the top of a window and containing the title of the window.

toggle   A command that alternately turns a feature on and off.

tracks   Recording positions on a disk.

Video Graphics Array (VGA) A type of display device that allows better resolution than EGA.

volatile In referring to memory, the type of memory whose contents are lost when the power is turned off.

warm start Restarting without turning the computer off.

window A rectangular area on your screen in which you view an application or document.

word size The amount of data the processor can manipulate at one time.

work area The area of a window that displays the information contained in the application or document you are working with.

write-protect notch A notch that protects the information on a disk. If it is covered, information cannot be written onto the disk.

write-protect tab A write-protect device on a 3½" disk. The disk is write-protected when the tab is moved to reveal the hollow opening.

Index

OPERATING SYSTEM

Introducing
Microsoft Word 6.0
FOR
WINDOWS

KEIKO PITTER

McGRAW-HILL

New York St. Louis San Francisco Auckland Bogotá Caracas
Lisbon London Madrid Mexico Milan Montreal New Delhi
Paris San Juan Singapore Sydney Tokyo Toronto

McGRAW-HILL
San Francisco, CA 94133

Introducing Microsoft Word 6.0 for Windows

5 6 7 8 9 0   SEM SEM   9 0 9 8 7 6 5

ISBN 0-07-051767-3

Sponsoring editor: Roger Howell

Editorial assistant: Rhonda Sands

Technical reviewer: Sarah Baker

Production supervisor: Leslie Austin

Project manager: Maria Takacs, Graphics West

Copyeditor: Ryan Stuart

Interior designer: Gary Palmatier

Cover designer: Christy Butterfield

Compositor: Graphics West

Printer and binder: Semline, Inc.

Library of Congress Card Catalog No. 94-77137

Contents

WORD PROCESSING

3 Advanced Editing and Multiple Files   57

4 Graphics, Columns, Templates, and Tables   84

WORD PROCESSING

Introduction

A word processing program is a computer program that helps you create, change, and print text. Word processing simplifies the mechanics of preparing documents and helps you to focus on the process of writing.

Introducing Microsoft Word 6.0 for Windows acquaints you with the essential information necessary to create simple to sophisticated documents. Working within the graphical environment of Windows, Word commands and features are presented to increase user knowledge and expertise. This manual is designed to get the user comfortable with the essentials of Microsoft Word 6.0 for Windows and feel confident in exploring the program's capabilities. Not all features of Word 6.0 are covered, and when there is more than one way to accomplish a task, just one method is discussed. The user needs to explore others on his or her own.

Using this Module

Each lesson in this book begins with goals that are listed under the heading *OBJECTIVES*. Key terms are introduced in ***bold italic*** type; text to be typed by the user is shown in **bold**. Also, keep in mind the following:

■   This symbol is used to indicate the user's action.

▶   *This symbol is used to indicate the software's response.*

Alternative: **Presents mouse or keystroke alternatives to keyboard commands.**

NOTE: This format is for important user notes and tips.

P R A C T I C E   T I M E

These brief drills allow the user to practice features previously discussed.

Finally, a series of projects, a command summary, and a glossary of key terms are found at the end of the book.

BEFORE YOU START

To use this book, you need at least an 80286 or higher with at least 4 MG of memory (RAM). If you are installing the program, you need at least 6 MB of space available on your hard disk (the complete installation requires 24 MB of disk space). The computer should also have a floppy disk drive (1.2 MB or greater capacity), a mouse or other pointing device, Windows 3.1 or later, and Microsoft Word for Windows 6.0. The user needs to have a blank, formatted floppy disk. If your configuration deviates from this, consult your instructor. This book assumes that you are familiar with both the basic operation of a computer system and of Microsoft Windows, and with how to use a mouse.

To study this book, you should go through Lessons 1, 2, and the first half of 3. These lessons acquaint you with the basics of word processing. The optional second half of Lesson 3 introduces the merge feature, and Lesson 4 introduces the use of templates, graphics, columns, and tables.

Creating Documents

OBJECTIVES

Upon completion of the material presented in this lesson, you should understand the following aspects of Microsoft Word:

- ☐ **Starting Microsoft Word**
- ☐ **Comprehending word processing terminology**
- ☐ **Giving Microsoft Word commands**
- ☐ **Entering text**
- ☐ **Saving a file to a disk**
- ☐ **Moving through the document**
- ☐ **Selecting text**
- ☐ **Deleting selected text**
- ☐ **Replacing selected text**
- ☐ **Moving and Copying selected text**
- ☐ **Inserting text in an existing document**
- ☐ **Checking the spelling**
- ☐ **Using the Thesaurus**
- ☐ **Previewing and printing the document**

STARTING OFF

Before starting Microsoft Word, you must start the Microsoft Windows program.

■ Start the Windows program. Make sure that the Program Manager is the only window displayed onscreen.

▶ *The installation procedure for Microsoft Word created a program group icon for Word for Windows in the Program Manager window. See Figure 1-1.*

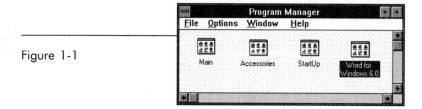

Figure 1-1

NOTE: It is possible that Microsoft Word was installed in the Microsoft Office group window. If so, substitute the appropriate group name in the instruction.

■ Maximize the Program Manager window.

■ Open the Microsoft Word window by double-clicking on the Word for Windows group icon.

▶ *The Word for Windows window, similar to the one in Figure 1-2, is displayed.*

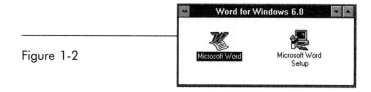

Figure 1-2

The Microsoft Word program group window contains the Word program icon. To start Microsoft Word, double-click on it.

■ Launch the Microsoft Word program by double-clicking on the Microsoft Word program icon.

▶ *If your program is so set up, the Tip of the Day is
displayed. Close the dialog box by clicking on OK or
pressing* Enter*. The Microsoft Word application window
is displayed as shown in Figure 1-3.*

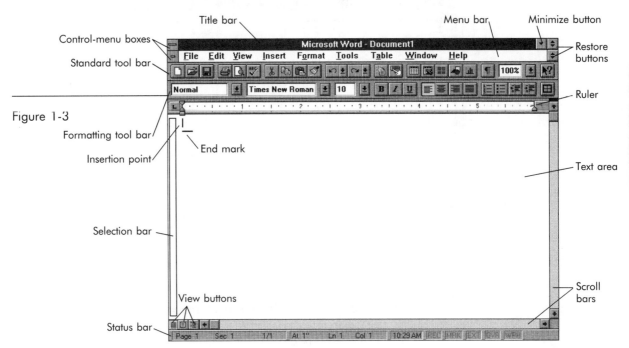

Figure 1-3

The Microsoft Word application window has all the basic components
of a Windows window—a title bar, a menu bar, a control-menu box, minimize, maximize, and restore buttons, and scroll bars. There are additional
elements, such as the **toolbars** and **ruler** below the menu bar, and the
status bar at the bottom. These will be explained later.

You might notice that there are two restore buttons and two control-
menu boxes. This is because, onscreen right now are two windows displayed: the Microsoft Word application window and a new document
window. The new document window is contained within the workspace, or
the area between the menu bar and the status bar, of the Microsoft Word
application window, and the new document window is already maximized.

■ Restore the document window by clicking on the lower restore
button.

▶ *The document window is restored, as shown in Figure 1-4.*

Now you can see the document window more distinctly. The workspace
can contain up to nine documents if your computer has enough available
memory. You might notice that the title bar of the Microsoft Word application window displays Microsoft Word, and that of the document window
contains the name Document1.

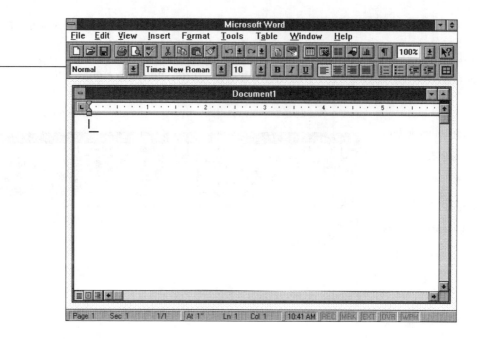

Figure 1-4

■   Maximize the document window.

▶   *Notice that the title bar is changed to Microsoft Word -
Document1 and that the new document window filled out
the workspace.*

The **menu bar**, located below the title bar, contains nine menu options. Microsoft Word commands are accessed either by clicking on the
desired menu option or by pressing the [Alt] key and the key of the underlined letter in the menu option you want. When you select a menu option, a
menu containing the commands, called **drop-down menu**, appears below
the option.

■   Select the Edit option on the menu bar by clicking on it or by
holding down the [Alt] key and pressing [E].

▶   *A drop-down menu appears, as shown in Figure 1-5.*

You can make a selection from the drop-down menu by clicking on a
command or pressing the key of the underlined letter in the command.
Commands that are dimmed are not available to you at this point. (They
require that you've performed some other action.)

Commands followed by an ellipsis (...) will display a **dialog box** in
which you are required to enter additional information such as the name to
call a document. Dialog boxes will be explained as you encounter them in
the lesson.

You will notice that some commands are **toggles**, which means the
command turns a feature on or off each time you enter it. When a toggle
feature is on, a check mark appears before the command option in the
menu, and the check mark disappears when the feature is turned off. In

Edit

Can't Undo	Ctrl+Z
Repeat Typing	**Ctrl+Y**
Cut	Ctrl+X
Copy	Ctrl+C
Paste	Ctrl+V
Paste Special...	
Clear	**Delete**
Select All	**Ctrl+A**
Find...	**Ctrl+F**
Replace...	**Ctrl+H**
Go To...	**Ctrl+G**
AutoText...	
Bookmark...	
Links...	
Object	

Figure 1-5

WORD PROCESSING

other cases, you need to make a selection from a number of options. The selected option will have a bullet (•) displayed before it.

Many commands offer you alternative keystrokes. These appear next to the corresponding command in the drop-down menu. That is, rather than making a selection from the menu bar and from the drop-down menu, commands can be entered by clicking on a tool button or pressing a key in combination with Ctrl, Shift, and Alt keys. When you see Shift+F12, for example, you are to hold down the key marked Shift and press the F12 function key; when you see Ctrl+X, you hold down the key marked Ctrl and press X. These available tool buttons and alternative keys will be given.

To close a menu without choosing a command, click outside the menu or press the Esc key.

■   Close the drop-down menu.

Below the menu bar are two Tool bars: the standard toolbar and the formatting toolbar. They contain buttons that give you quick access to frequently-used commands.

■   Move the mouse pointer on top of the first tool button and let it sit for a moment.

▶   *A description of the button pops up, as shown in Figure 1-6.*

The ruler displays and allows you to change the margins, tabs, and indentation setting.

NOTE: The toolbars and ruler can be hidden from display.

The area below the ruler is the ***text area***. This is the area in which you can enter new text or graphics, review what you have already entered, or change what is there. Of course, as you have not entered anything yet, it is blank. The blinking vertical bar is the ***insertion point***, and the underscore is the ***end mark***. The insertion point shows the position in the workspace where entries are made, and the end mark identifies the end of your document.

Along the left side of the text area is an unmarked area called the ***selection bar***. It helps you select text with the mouse. When the mouse

Figure 1-6

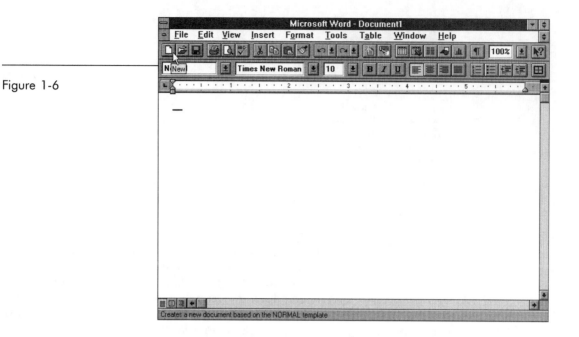

pointer is in the text area, it turns into an I-beam. However, when it is in the selection bar, it turns into a right pointing arrow ⇗.

To the left of the horizontal scroll bar at the bottom are three buttons: Normal View, Page Layout View, and Outline View. These are used to change the way the document is displayed.

At the bottom of the screen is the status bar. It displays the following information about the page that contains the insertion point: the page number; the section number; the total number of pages from the beginning of the document followed by the total number of pages in the entire document; the position of the insertion point measured from the top edge of the page; the line number; and the column number calculated by counting the number of characters between the insertion point and the left margin. It also shows the status of several key on your computer, such as [Caps Lock] and [Num Lock], and of various Word features.

ENTERING TEXT

To enter text, use your keyboard similar to the way you would use a typewriter. As you enter a character, it appears at the insertion point, and the insertion point moves to the right one position. Unlike the keyboard on a typewriter, however, this keyboard does not require entry of a carriage return as you fill a line onscreen. Just keep on typing, because when the cursor gets beyond the right margin, it will reappear at the left margin setting, one line down. When you come to the end of a paragraph, the [Enter] key must be pressed. The [Enter] key breaks the line and moves the insertion point to the left margin, one line down. You have to press the (Enter) key once at the end of a paragraph. Press (Enter) twice if you want to insert a blank line between paragraphs in the text.

If your text fills up the screen, the text will **scroll** up—that is, a new line will appear at the bottom of the screen, and the uppermost line will disappear from view.

CORRECTING ERRORS

If you make a mistake when you are typing text, you may delete unwanted characters by pressing the (Bksp) key. (Bksp) deletes the key to the left of the insertion point. You can then retype the text.

UPPERCASE LETTERS

To enter uppercase letters, hold (Shift) down while you press the character. If you want to type several characters in uppercase, as when you enter a title, press (Caps Lock). To get back into lowercase, press (Caps Lock) again. When you enter certain characters, you have to hold (Shift) down regardless of whether (Caps Lock) has been pressed.

P R A C T I C E   T I M E   1 - 1

Enter the following text:

> **Records of transactions, contracts, and inventories form the basis that allows business to be conducted in an orderly manner. Scribes have been used through the ages to produce copies of business contracts. Inventions that have lowered the cost or increased the speed for an individual to write a document have resulted in increased business productivity. These inventions include paper, pens, and typewriter. The personal computer did not become a success until it became useful for business. Today, word processing is the most common business use of personal computers.**

As you typed in this paragraph, you might have noticed the phe-nomenon called **wordwrap**. As the text gets to the right margin, a word that is too long to fit on the line is moved down to the next line. Words are not split between lines. This feature is included to make reading and text creation easier.

SAVING YOUR WORK

The text that you have just entered is stored in the main memory of the computer. If you turn off the computer or if there is a power failure, you will lose that text. That is why it is important that you save the file on a disk, not only when you quit Microsoft Word, but frequently during your Microsoft Word session. Once a file is on a disk, it is permanently stored. Should there be a power failure, you can retrieve the most recent version of the file from the disk and continue with your work.

N O T E :   This manual assumes that your data disk is in drive A. If you are using a drive other than A, substitute the appropriate drive in the instructions.

■   Make sure a formatted disk is in drive A.

When you save a file, you have two choices: you can use the Save command or the Save As command. If you use the Save command, the file is saved using the filename that appears in the title bar. If there already is a file by that name on the disk, the new file will replace the existing file. If you use the Save As command, you must type a new name for your file.

The first time you save a document, you are forced to use the Save As command no matter which save option you selected. This is to be sure that you give a meaningful name to the document rather than the default name assigned by Microsoft Word.

As mentioned earlier, when you start a new file, Microsoft Word auto-matically gives it a default name, such as Document1. When you save the file for the first time, you use the Save As command and give it a valid and more meaningful name. A valid name for the document, known as the filename, is one to eight characters in number, followed by an optional extension. The extension is a period (.) and one to three additional char-acters. If you do not supply an extension, Microsoft Word automatically assigns the extension .DOC. You can use any character except spaces and the following characters: * ? , ; [ ] + = \ / : | < >. You cannot use a period except to separate the filename from the extension. Right now, use the name MYFILE to save it to the disk in drive A.

■   Select the File menu in the menu bar by clicking on it or by pressing Alt + F, then select Save As by clicking on it or by pressing **A**.

Alternative: Click on the Save tool button 🖫.

▶ *The Save As dialog box is displayed as shown in*
Figure 1-7.

Figure 1-7

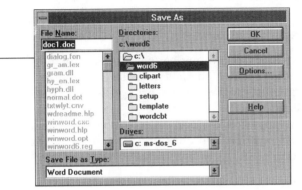

NOTE: Using the Save tool button has the same effect as using the Save command. The file is saved using the current filename.

The insertion point is blinking in the File Name text box. Type the file-name, but do not press Enter.

■ Type **MYFILE**, but do not press Enter.

You need to specify the location of the data disk.

■ Click on the down arrow key at the right end of the Drives list box.

▶ *All available drives are displayed.*

■ Click on a: for drive A.

▶ *The Directories list box displays all directories currently on drive A. If you need to specify the directory, do so by clicking on the directory name.*

■ Complete the command by either clicking on the OK button or pressing Enter.

▶ *The file is saved to the disk in drive A.*

MOVING WITHIN THE DOCUMENT

Suppose, as you read what you typed earlier, you find a mistake or you decide to change the text. If the change you want to make is near the beginning of the text, and if you use the Bksp key to erase all unwanted characters starting at the insertion point, you will have to retype almost the whole text. This is no improvement over using a typewriter. A word processor has a better way. To make corrections like this, you need to learn how to move within the document. That is, you need to learn how to move the insertion point. Text is entered, deleted, or edited at the insertion point.

Using the Mouse

The insertion point may be moved by positioning the I-beam in the desired place and clicking the left mouse button once. If the desired text position has scrolled off the screen, bring it back to the display by clicking on the scroll arrows at either end of the vertical scroll bar at the window's right. When you scroll the text display, however, the insertion point stays in its original position and does not move. Hence, you need to specify the new insertion point.

■ Use the mouse to move the insertion point.

Using the Keyboard

To move the insertion point, use the four arrow keys located on the numeric keypad to the right of the main keyboard (or the arrow keys located between the main keyboard and the numeric keyboard on extended keyboards). The insertion point will move in the direction of the arrow, one position at a time.

NOTE: If you are using the numeric keypad, make sure that Num Lock is turned off.

■ Press ↑.

▶ *The insertion point moves up one line.*

■ Press →.

▶ *The insertion point moves to the right one position.*

If you have a long text, you cannot see all of it onscreen at any one time. As you press ↑ or ↓ repeatedly, the insertion point will keep moving up or down, forcing the screen to scroll. If you keep pressing ↑, the text will scroll down (that is, new lines will appear at the top); if you keep pressing ↓, the text will scroll up (new lines will appear at the bottom).

NOTE: You will quickly learn that the movement of text onscreen is in the direction opposite to the label on the key. The ↑ key lets you view text that was above the screen, and ↓ brings into view text that was below the screen.

It is also possible to move the insertion point a little faster. All you have to do is hold the key down, and the key will keep repeating. If you hold down ↓, the insertion point will zoom down the page. You can return it to the top of the page by using ↑. You will notice, however, that you cannot move the insertion point past the beginning or the end of the text.

You can move the insertion point to the left or right, one word at a time, by holding down the Ctrl key and pressing ← and →, respectively.

WORD PROCESSING

NOTE: On some computers, when giving a combination command with arrow keys, [Num Lock] must be turned off regardless of which set of arrow keys is used. On other computers, the combination only works with the arrow keys on the numeric keypad.

You can move the insertion point to the beginning of the document by pressing [Ctrl]+[Home]. That is, hold [Ctrl] down while you press [Home]. You can move it to the end of the document by pressing [Ctrl]+[End]. Table 1-1 lists various keystrokes for moving the insertion point. (The text you see onscreen right now is not long enough for you to try all of these keys. Just remember them for the future.)

Table 1-1

Key	Action
[→]	Moves one character to the right
[←]	Moves one character to the left
[↑]	Moves one line up
[↓]	Moves one line down
[Ctrl]+[Home]	Moves to the beginning of a document
[Ctrl]+[End]	Moves to the end of a document
[Ctrl]+[→]	Moves one word to the right
[Ctrl]+[←]	Moves one word to the left
[Home]	Moves to the beginning of a line
[End]	Moves to the end of a line
[Ctrl]+[↑]	Moves up one paragraph
[Pg Dn]	Moves down one window
[Pg Up]	Moves up one window

P R A C T I C E   T I M E   1 - 2

1. Move the insertion point to the end, and then to the beginning, of the document.

2. Place the insertion point somewhere in the middle of the document.

3. Try using both keyboard and mouse to move the insertion point.

DELETING TEXT

As you recall, if you make a mistake in typing text, you can correct it immediately by pressing the [Bksp] to remove the unwanted characters, then typing the correct text.

You may delete unwanted characters *anywhere* in the text by adding one step. First, position the insertion point next to the character you wish to delete. Second, press the [Bksp] key to erase the character to the left and the [Del] key to erase the character to the right of the insertion point. Finally, type the correct text.

You can delete text from the keyboard in other ways, too. You can remove the word before the insertion point by entering [Ctrl]+[Bksp], that is, holding down the [Ctrl] key and pressing [Bksp]. You can remove the word after the insertion point by entering [Ctrl]+[Del], that is, holding down the [Ctrl] key and pressing the [Del] key. You can also delete a selected section of text.

SELECTING TEXT

You will now select the sentence beginning "Scribes have ...."

■ Position the insertion point to the left of the capital S of "Scribes have...," then drag the mouse to highlight the entire sentence. To do this, hold down the left mouse button, move the mouse until the sentence is highlighted, then release the button.

Alternative: Position the insertion point anywhere in the sentence, then press [Ctrl]+click (hold down the [Ctrl] key and click the left mouse button).

▶ *The sentence is selected, as shown in Figure 1-8.*

Figure 1-8

> Records of transactions, contracts, and inventories form the basis that allows business to be conducted in an orderly manner. Scribes have been used through the ages to produce copies of business contracts. Inventions that have lowered the cost or increased the speed for an individual to write a document have resulted in increased business productivity. These inventions include paper, pens, and typewriter. The personal computer did not become a success until it became useful for business. Today, word processing is the most common business use of personal computers.

N O T E : If you selected the wrong text, click elsewhere onscreen or press an arrow key to deselect.

Another way to select text is by using the selection bar, which is an unmarked area along the left side of the text area. Once in the selection bar, the pointer shape changes to a right-pointing arrow. Using the selection bar and mouse, you can select a line, paragraph, or entire document with one or two mouse clicks.

Table 1-2 shows ways of selecting text using the selection bar and mouse, as well as keyboard.

Table 1-2

Using Mouse	Select	Using Keyboard	Select
Double-click	Word	Shift + →	One character to the right
Ctrl + click anywhere in sentence	Sentence	Shift + ←	One character to the left
		Shift + ↑	One line up
		Shift + ↓	One line down
Place pointer in the selection bar, point to line, and click	Line	Shift + End	To the end of a line
		Shift + Home	To the start of a line
		Shift + Pg Up	One screen up
		Shift + Pg Dn	One screen down
Place pointer in the selection bar, point to paragraph, and double-click	Paragraph	Shift + Ctrl + →	To the end of a word
		Shift + Ctrl + ←	To the start of a word
		Shift + Ctrl + ↑	To the start of a paragraph
		Shift + Ctrl + ↓	To the end of a paragraph
Ctrl + click anywhere in the selection bar	Document	Shift + Ctrl + Home	To the start of a document
		Shift + Ctrl + End	To the end of a document
		Ctrl + A	An entire document

DELETING SELECTED TEXT

Once text is selected, it can be deleted.

■   Press either Bksp or Del to delete the selected text. Do not move the insertion point.

RESTORING DELETED TEXT

If you realize you didn't mean to remove the text after you've deleted it, you can restore it immediately by using the Undo command.

■   Click on Edit, then on Undo Typing.

Alternative: Press Ctrl + Z or click on the Undo Tool button .

▶   *The text is restored.*

P R A C T I C E   T I M E   1 - 3

Delete the second sentence again.

REPLACING TEXT

You can easily replace a word or phrase with different text.

- Select the text "personal computer" in the next-to-last sentence.

- Type **microcomputer**.

    ▶ *The highlighted text is deleted and replaced by what you typed.*

P R A C T I C E   T I M E   1 - 4

Change "microcomputer" back to "personal computer."

MOVING TEXT

You can also move the selected text from one location to another. This is done using the Cut and Paste commands. The Cut command removes the selected text from a document and places the selection on the Windows *clipboard*, which is temporary storage for information you want to transfer. You can then paste the information where you specify.

Right now, you will move the last sentence.

- Select the last sentence, "Today, word processing is the most common business use of personal computers," as shown in Figure 1-9.

Figure 1-9

Records of transactions, contracts, and inventories form the basis that allows business to be conducted in an orderly manner. Inventions that have lowered the cost or increased the speed for an individual to write a document have resulted in increased business productivity. These inventions include paper, pens, and typewriter. The personal computer did not become a success until it became useful for business. Today, word processing is the most common business use of personal computers.

■ From the Edit menu, select Cut.

Alternative: Press ⌃Ctrl+X or click the Cut tool button ✂.

▶ *The selected text disappears; it has been placed on the clipboard.*

■ Move the insertion point to the space just before the fourth sentence—that is, after the word "typewriter."

■ From the Edit menu, select Paste.

Alternative: Enter ⌃Ctrl+V or click the Paste tool button 📋.

▶ *The text is placed at the insertion point position as shown in Figure 1-10. You may have to insert or delete spaces to make sentence display correctly.*

Figure 1-10

> Records of transactions, contracts, and inventories form the basis that allows business to be conducted in an orderly manner. Inventions that have lowered the cost or increased the speed for an individual to write a document have resulted in increased business productivity. These inventions include paper, pens, and typewriter. Today, word processing is the most common business use of personal computers. The personal computer did not become a success until it became useful for business.

NOTE: To easily access the Copy and Paste commands, you can place the mouse pointer over the highlighted text and press the *right* mouse button. A Shortcut menu appears, as shown in Figure 1-11. The Shortcut menu contains commands related to the item you're working with.

Figure 1-11

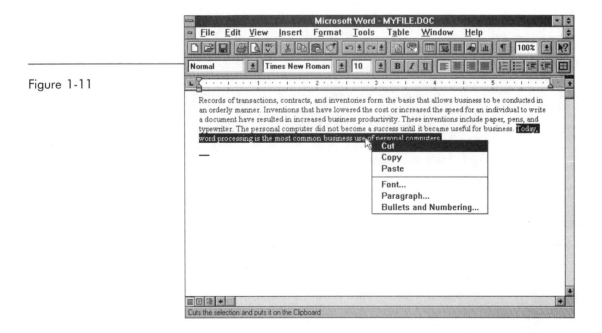

DRAG AND DROP

You will now move the sentence you just moved back to its original position, but using a different method. With **drag and drop**, you can select the text and drag it to where you want it.

- Select the same sentence.

- Position the mouse pointer anywhere on the highlighted text and press the *left* mouse button.

  ▶ *The mouse pointer changes to indicate that you can drag the text, as shown in Figure 1-12.*

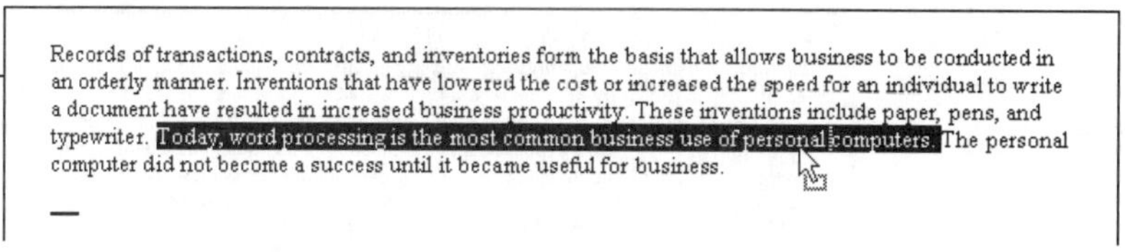

Figure 1-12

> Records of transactions, contracts, and inventories form the basis that allows business to be conducted in an orderly manner. Inventions that have lowered the cost or increased the speed for an individual to write a document have resulted in increased business productivity. These inventions include paper, pens, and typewriter. Today, word processing is the most common business use of personal computers. The personal computer did not become a success until it became useful for business.

- Drag the mouse pointer, that is, hold down the left mouse button and move the insertion point to the desired position, which in this case is after the last sentence.

- Release the mouse button.

  ▶ *The sentence is moved.*

COPYING TEXT

It is also possible to copy selected text. Copying text is different from moving text, in that selected text is not deleted from the original position. To do this, select Copy from the Edit menu, instead of Cut. You can also use the Copy button 🖻. If you want to use the drag and drop feature, hold down Ctrl while you drag the mouse.

INSERTING TEXT

If you need to insert a word in the middle of a sentence, or a sentence in the middle of a paragraph, position the insertion point where you want to begin inserting the text, then look at the status bar. If you see the letters OVR, press the Ⓘₙₛ key. When you press Ⓘₙₛ, the letters OVR disappear. Then you can start typing whatever you want to insert at the insertion point position.

When OVR is not on, any text to the right of the insertion point is pushed across the line to make room for your insertion. When OVR is on, however, the character you type replaces the character the insertion point is on. Ⓘₙₛ is a toggle command. The feature is turned on and off each time you press the Ⓘₙₛ key.

■ Place the insertion point just before the word "Inventions" in the second sentence.

■ Insert the following text just as it appears, *with* the spelling errors:

The earliest writing, cuneiform inscriptoins on on clay tablets, often kept business recrds.

CHECKING SPELLING

Microsoft Word can check your document for misspelled words, two occurrences of a word in a row, and certain types of capitalization errors. The feature helps you proof the document onscreen by comparing each word in the document with a list of correctly spelled words, known as a **dictionary**. When you issue the Spelling command, the program scans the document, flags those words that are not in the dictionary, and for each of these words, suggests words from the dictionary that you might have meant to type.

NOTE: If a word is not in the MS Word dictionary, such as a proper name or a term that is special to a particular industry, Word will flag it as misspelled. You have the option of adding it to a custom dictionary. Once added, the next occurrence of the same word is not flagged.

The program checks the entire document, starting at the insertion point. If you start at the middle, when Word gets to the end of the document, it will ask you if you want to continue checking at the beginning of the document. If you do not want to check all of your document, select that part of document you want to check, then give the Spelling command.

You entered some words with spelling errors in the current document. You will now correct them.

■ Position the insertion point at the beginning of the document.

■ From the Tools menu, select Spelling.

Alternative: Press the F7 function key or click the Spelling tool button 🔲.

▶ *The Spelling dialog box is displayed as shown in Figure 1-13.*

Figure 1-13

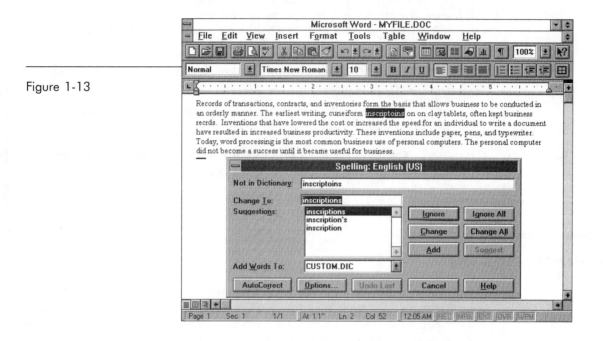

The word "inscriptoins" is highlighted in the document and appears in the Not in Dictionary text box. In the Suggestions list box, the word "inscriptions" is listed and highlighted. As the highlighted word, it also appears in the Changes To text box. Since the highlighted word is correctly spelled, tell Word to replace it in the document.

■ Select the Change button by clicking on it or by pressing [Alt]+[C].

▶ *The correctly-spelled word is inserted. Now the word "on" is highlighted in the document.*

N O T E : If you were to click on Change All instead, all instances of the same word subsequently found in your document are corrected.

Word now tells you that the word "on" is a repeated word. That is, it appears twice in a row. You want to delete the second occurrence.

■ Select the Delete button by clicking on it or pressing [Alt]+[D].

▶ *The second "on" is deleted. Now the word "recrds" is highlighted.*

P R A C T I C E   T I M E   1 - 5

Replace the word "recrds" with the correctly-spelled word. When Word is finished checking spelling, a dialog box appears to notify you. Respond accordingly.

If a word is flagged but is spelled correctly or if a suggested spelling is not given, that word is not currently contained in the dictionary. You can do one of four things: (1) you can add it to a Custom Dictionary by selecting the Add button, (2) you can tell Word to ignore the occurrence of this word this one time by clicking the Ignore button; (3) you can tell Word to ignore the occurrence of this word for the rest of the document by clicking the Ignore All button; or (4) you can edit the word manually. To edit the word manually, place the insertion point in the Change To text box by using the mouse, edit the word, then click the Change option.

After you finish entering text, you should always run it through the spelling checker. It does not catch all your mistakes. For example, if you used "their" for "there," because the word is correctly spelled, the mistake is not caught, but it is still a good aid in creating an accurate document.

THESAURUS

One more available feature should be mentioned: the Thesaurus. Many times, when you are writing a document, you need help finding a word to express your meaning more clearly. The Thesaurus displays synonyms and other words that point to the same idea.

Assume that in the onscreen text, you decide that the word "contracts" in the first sentence is not quite what you wanted to say.

- Place the insertion point anywhere on the word "contracts".
- From the Tools menu, select Thesaurus.

    Alternative: **Press** Shift+F7.

    ▶ *The Thesaurus dialog box is displayed, as shown in Figure 1-14.*

In the dialog box, Word is now saying that the word "contracts" does not appear in the Thesaurus. However, it lists the singular form "contract" as a related word. You can look up a related word in the Thesaurus.

- Select the Look Up button.

    ▶ *Both list boxes display various options for "contract."*

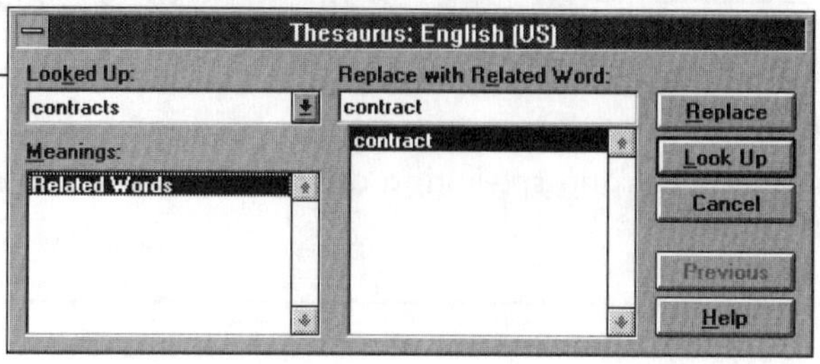

Figure 1-14

The Meanings list box displays different meanings of the word. These include the use of the word as a noun or verb. The list also includes an antonym, or a word with the opposite meaning, and other related words. The Synonyms list box displays words with the selected meaning. The highlighted word in the Synonyms list box also appears in the Replace With text box.

As you select different meanings in the Meanings list box, the content of the Synonyms list box changes to display words with the selected meaning. If you see the word you are looking for in the Synonyms list, select it and click the Replace button. For example, if the word you want to use is "agreement," select it by clicking on it, then click the Replace button. The word "contracts" in the text will be replaced by "agreement." If you did not find the word you are looking for in this list, you can continue the search by doing a Look Up on any of the words listed.

■   Make sure that "agreement" is selected in the Replace with Synonym list box and select the Replace button.

▶   *The word is replaced.*

Because Microsoft Word inserted the singular word "agreement," you will have to enter an "s" at the end to make it plural, in keeping with the rest of the sentence.

■   Insert **s** after "agreement" to make it plural.

SAVING A FILE THE SECOND TIME

Now that you've made several changes to your file, you should save it again. This time, you will save using the same filename.

■   Make sure that the data disk is in drive A.

■   From the File menu, select Save.

Alternative: Press Ctrl+S or click the Save tool button.

▶   *The current document replaces the one on the data disk.*

PREVIEWING TEXT

Before printing the text on a sheet of paper, you can view it onscreen. This is called previewing text.

■ From the File menu, select Print Preview.

Alternative: Click on the Print Preview button 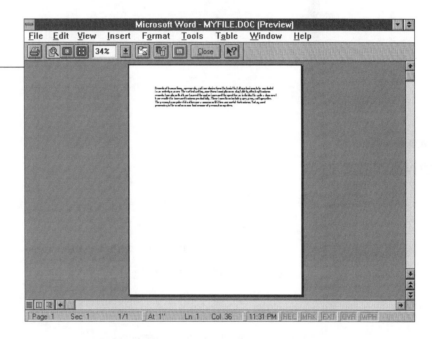.

▶ *A screen similar to Figure 1-15 is displayed. Notice that the mouse pointer turns into a magnifying glass when it's at the top of the document*

Figure 1-15

The screen displays the way your page will look when it is printed. However, the type is too small to read. You can enlarge the display.

■ With the mouse pointer anywhere on the text in the document, click the left mouse button.

▶ *The display is enlarged as shown in Figure 1-16.*

■ Click on the document again.

▶ *The display returns to normal view.*

If you are satisfied with what you see, you can proceed to print. However, if you are not satisfied, you can go back to editing the document without having wasted a sheet of paper.

■ Select the Close button to return to the normal view.

WORD PROCESSING

Figure 1-16

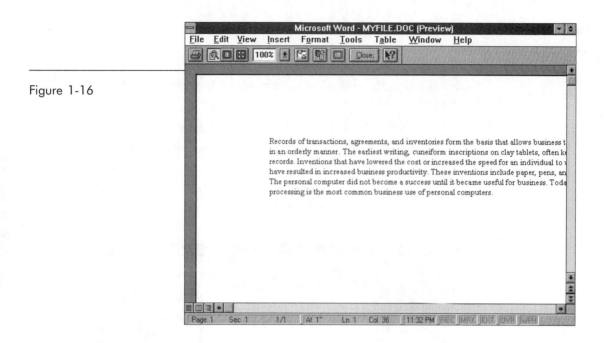

PRINTING TEXT

Now you will print the text.

■   Make sure that your printer is turned on and is ready to use.

■   From the File menu, select Print.

   Alternative: **Press** Ctrl + P .

   ▶   *The Print dialog box is displayed, as shown in Figure 1-17.*

Figure 1-17

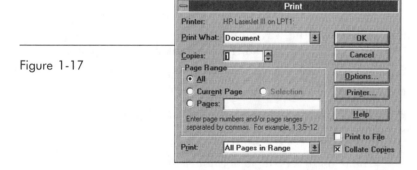

■   Make sure that the printer you are using appears next to "Printer:." If it does not, ask your instructor for help.

For now, do not change option settings.

■ Complete the command by clicking on OK or pressing Enter.

▶ *The text of MYFILE starts to print.*

NOTE: The Print tool button 🖩 gives you a convenient way to print. However, when you print using this button, the Print dialog box is not displayed.

ENDING LESSON 1

You should never quit Microsoft Word by just turning off your computer. *Always* exit to Windows and properly quit Windows before shutting down your system. When you properly exit Microsoft Word and Windows, the program will caution you if any documents have been changed since they were last saved.

■ From the File menu, select Exit.

Alternative: Press Alt + F4.

▶ *If any open documents were changed since they were last saved, a cautionary dialog box appears, giving you a chance to save the document again. Select Yes or No accordingly. You return to Windows.*

■ Quit the Windows session.

■ Remove your data disk from the disk drive.

■ Turn off your computer and monitor.

SUMMARY

☐ **Text is entered at the position of the insertion point. The insertion point can be positioned by using the mouse.**

☐ **Uppercase letters are entered using either the Shift key or the Caps Lock key. To enter special characters that appear on the upper half of a key, the Shift key must be held down, even if the Caps Lock key has been pressed.**

☐ **Words are not split between two lines, but are placed complete on one line through a feature called *wordwrap*. Press Enter only at the end of a paragraph or to insert a blank line.**

☐ **The insertion point can be moved using the keyboard or the mouse.**

WORD PROCESSING

☐ **Pressing [Ins] toggles OVR on and off. In OVR mode, the character you type replaces the one the insertion point is on. When OVR is off, the character the insertion point is on and all characters to the right move over when text is entered.**

☐ **Text can be selected by pointing to the first character with the mouse, dragging the mouse until the text is highlighted, and releasing the mouse button. Text can also be selected using the selection bar and mouse, as well as with the keyboard.**

☐ **Selected text can be deleted, moved, or copied.**

☐ **A valid filename is one to eight characters in length, followed by an optional extension.**

☐ **When you save a file for the first time, you can enter information in the Summary Information dialog box. The information entered is used to later identify and retrieve the file.**

KEY TERMS

clipboard	insertion point	text area
dialog box	menu bar	toggle
dictionary	ruler	toolbar
drag-and-drop	selection bar	wordwrap
drop-down menu	scroll	
end mark	status bar	

COMMAND SUMMARY

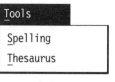

R E V I E W   Q U E S T I O N S

1. Why should you not press [Enter] at the end of lines while entering text? When should it be pressed?

2. What keys move the insertion point without affecting the text?

3. How can you correct typing errors?

4. How do you select a word?

5. What is the purpose of the selection bar?

6. What is the purpose of tool buttons?

7. What is the maximum number of characters that can be used in a filename?

8. Describe two ways to move selected text.

9. Why do you have to save files?

10. Can the Spelling feature find all your errors? Explain.

E X E R C I S E S

1. Enter the text below. Your document need not look exactly as it appears here.
   a. Check the spelling.
   b. Save the file as WD1EX1.
   c. Print the document.

   MEMORANDUM

   DATE: September 10, 1994

   FROM: Lonnie Waters, Social Chairperson

   SUBJECT: Fall Picnic

   Don't forget to attend this year's fall picnic, to be held at the Forest Glade Regional Park on Saturday, September 24, 1994, from 11:00 a.m. to 6:00 p.m.

   There will be lots of events for the entire family. We'll hold a fishing derby, and there will be races and games for all ages.

   You can't beat the price: the food is free to employees and their families. Sign up by the cafeteria.

   And don't forget to bring your umbrellas and rain coats, in case it rains like it did at last year's picnic.

2. Enter the text below. Your document need not look exactly as it appears here.
   a. Check the spelling.
   b. Save the file as **WD1EX2**.
   c. Print the document.

current date

Mrs. Mildred Adams, Librarian
American Historical Society
1776 Freedom Road
Philadelphia, PA

Dear Mrs. Adams:

I am writing a term paper on quotations of American presidents, focusing on their views of how government should be run. It is easy to find famous quotations for some presidents. Washington, Lincoln, both Roosevelts and Kennedy are well-represented in my research notes.

Could you help me find other noteworthy, if obscure, quotes of the presidents? I've tried Bartlett's "Quotations" and several history textbooks in the school library.

Thank you for your time and patience.

Sincerely,

Donna Lee Light

3. Enter the text below. Your document need not look exactly as it appears here.
   a. Check the spelling.
   b. Save the file as **WD1EX3**.
   c. Print the document.

Product Initiative Report:
Water Saddle

Al Jenkins, Product Development

Our department is pleased to announce its latest product invention for advanced testing and market analysis. For years, Cowpokes, Inc. has led the industry in developing innovative products for cattle ranches and rodeos. Recently, our department took a look at dude ranches, and found that

the demand is growing despite a very low return rate. One of the most frequently mentioned complaints of guests was saddle sores.

Therefore, we initiated design and preliminary testing of a revolutionary new water saddle. Like a water bed, its shape conforms to that of the rider, eliminating those bruising pressure points and reducing the tendency to slide about, causing chafing.

The water bag is double sealed in flexible but durable vinyl which simulates the look of cowhide. Preliminary testing indicates more comfort to the rider, but a need to reduce wave oscillations. We have some ideas, but this is a subject for advanced testing.

2 Formatting Documents

OBJECTIVES

Upon completion of the material presented in this lesson, you should understand the following aspects of Microsoft Word:

- ☐ **Using onscreen help**
- ☐ **Opening an existing document**
- ☐ **Recognizing the default format for printing**
- ☐ **Specifying various format options through menu commands and through the tool bars and ruler**
- ☐ **Setting margins**
- ☐ **Setting paper orientation**
- ☐ **Setting tabs and non-printing characters**
- ☐ **Setting paragraph indentation**
- ☐ **Setting line indentation**
- ☐ **Setting a hanging indent**
- ☐ **Formatting bullets**
- ☐ **Setting text alignment**
- ☐ **Centering text**
- ☐ **Setting line spacing**
- ☐ **Setting page breaks**
- ☐ **Formatting page numbering**
- ☐ **Changing font and appearance**

STARTING OFF

Turn on your computer, start Windows, and launch the Microsoft Word for Windows program as you did in the previous lesson. Insert your data disk in a disk drive. If necessary, maximize the Microsoft Word application window.

USING ONSCREEN HELP

If you have difficulty understanding or remembering a command or terminology, you can use the extensive onscreen Help system included in Microsoft Word. The onscreen Help feature of Microsoft Word is similar to Help on all Windows applications.

Let's assume right now that you do not remember how to open an existing document.

■ From the Help menu, select Contents.

Alternative: Press the F1 function key.

▶ *The Word Help Contents screen appears as shown in Figure 2-1.*

Figure 2-1

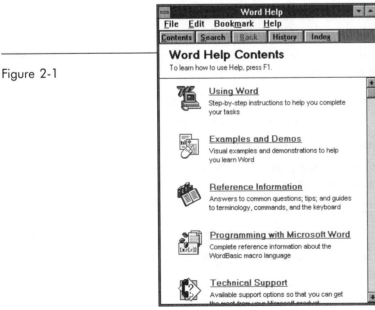

The underlined topics can be selected by clicking on them with the mouse or by pressing Tab or Shift+Tab to highlight the topic, then pressing Enter.

■   Select Using Word.

▶   *A Using Word list of various features appears.*

The list of topics can be scrolled to reveal additional topics. Again, the underlined topics can be selected to reveal further information.

■   Scroll the screen to display File Management options.

■   Select "Opening, Saving, and Protecting Documents."

▶   *A further listing of related topics appears.*

■   Select "Opening an existing document."

▶   *Step-by-step instructions for opening an existing document appear.*

If you want a paper copy of this information, you can select the Print button.

■   Close the How To window by clicking on the Close button or pressing Alt+F4 .

Alternative: **Double-click on the control-menu box at the top left edge.**

■   Close the Word Help window by selecting the File menu, then Exit, or by pressing Alt+F4 .

Alternative: **Double-click on the control-menu box at the top left corner of the Help window.**

You can also do the reverse. That is, given a command, you can get an explanation of that command.

■   From the File menu, select the Open command.

▶   *The Open dialog box is displayed.*

■   Press the F1 function key.

▶   *Information about the Open command in the File menu is displayed.*

■   Close the Help window.

■   Exit the Open dialog box by clicking on Cancel or pressing Esc.

You can also get help on different regions of the screen, such as a tool button.

■   Press Shift+F1 .

▶   *The mouse pointer turns into a question mark ▸?.*

WORD PROCESSING

- Point to the Open tool button 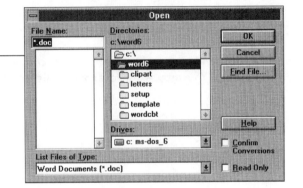 and click the left mouse button.

  ▶ *Again, the Help window describing the Open Document command is displayed.*

- Close the Help window.

OPENING AN EXISTING DOCUMENT

Now let's open a document file. The file to open is myfile.doc, which you saved at the end of the last lesson.

- From the File menu, select the Open command.

  Alternative: Press Ctrl+O or click on the Open tool button.

  ▶ *A dialog box appears, as shown in Figure 2-2.*

Figure 2-2

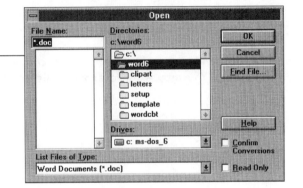

Open
File Name:	**Directories:**	**OK**
*.doc	c:\word6	**Cancel**
	🗁 c:\	**Find File...**
	📂 word6	
	📁 clipart	
	📁 letters	
	📁 setup	
	📁 template	**Help**
	📁 wordcbt	
	Drives:	
	💾 c: ms-dos_6	☐ Confirm Conversions
List Files of Type:		
Word Documents [*.doc]		☐ Read Only

The Open dialog box looks similar to the Save As box you saw in the last lesson. It lets you specify the drive, directory, and filename of the document you want retrieved from disk. You will first specify the drive.

NOTE: If your data disk is not in drive A, substitute the appropriate drive name.

- Click on the down arrow key at the right end of the Drives list box.

  ▶ *All available drives are displayed.*

- Click on a: for drive A.

  ▶ *The Directories list box displays all directories currently on drive A. If you need to specify the directory, do so by clicking on the directory name.*

The File Name list box on the left displays all the files on the data disk.

■   Click on myfile.doc, then complete the command by clicking on the OK button or pressing (Enter).

▶   *The text from the previous lesson is displayed onscreen.*

FORMATTING A DOCUMENT

You may have noticed when you printed the text at the end of the last lesson that it was printed just about the way it was displayed onscreen. Because the screen display and print formats you used were preset by Microsoft Word (you were using the default settings), the document may not have been printed in the format you had in mind.

The layout and formatting of a document is affected through the page setup, paragraph format, and character appearances. Page setup includes such items as the size of the paper and the margins used—items that affect the entire document. Paragraph formats include line spacing, indentations used, and text alignment. You can also change a character's appearance using bold, underline, italics, and different fonts and character sizes.

NOTE: It is possible to divide up a document into sections and define format each section separately. You may want to explore this on your own.

PAGE SETUP

You can change the page setup through the Page Setup command in the File menu.

■   Position the insertion point anywhere in the paragraph.

■   From the File menu, select Page Setup.

▶   *The Page Setup dialog box is displayed, as shown in Figure 2-3.*

The Page Setup dialog box is composed of four different sheets: Margins, Paper Size, Paper Source, and Layout. To display a sheet, either click on the corresponding sheet tab or hold down the (Alt) key and press the underlined character of the sheet name.

Margins

Next, you will look at Margins and Paper Size.

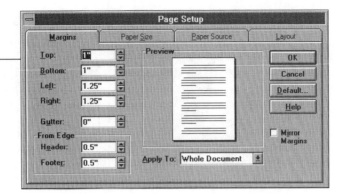

Figure 2-3

■ Select the <u>M</u>argins sheet, if not already displayed, by clicking on the sheet tab or pressing [Alt]+[M].

As you can see, the default setting for top and bottom margins is 1″ and for right and left margins is 1.25″. You will now change the left margin to 2″.

■ Press the [Tab] key until the Le<u>f</u>t margin setting is highlighted or use the mouse to highlight the left margin setting.

■ Type **2**, then press [Tab].

▶ *The Preview display on the dialog box changes to reflect the new setting.*

If you were to complete the command by clicking on OK or pressing [Enter], you would return to the document with changes in effect. Right now, however, let's look at Page Size.

Paper Size

By default, the paper size selected is a standard 8½″ by 11″ and the document has the ***portrait*** orientation, as shown in the Preview display. Portrait is so named because most portraits of people are contained in frames that are taller than they are wide. A sheet printed sideways on the page is printed in ***landscape*** orientation, named because many landscapes are painted on canvases that are wider than they are high. Select paper orientation by using the radio buttons in the Orientation selection box. When a box contains radio buttons, only one button may be selected at any time, like the station selector on many automobile radios. A button is selected by clicking on it with the mouse or holding down the [Alt] key and pressing the underlined character in the selection name.

■ Select Paper <u>S</u>ize.

▶ *The display changes to the one shown in Figure 2-4.*

■ Select Lands<u>c</u>ape by clicking on the radio button in front of it or by pressing [Alt]+[C].

Figure 2-4

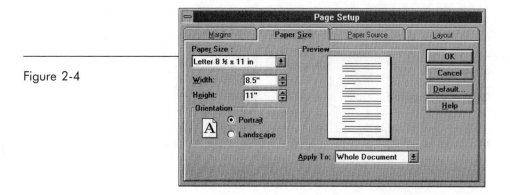

> ▶ *The Preview page display reflects the new orientation. Notice also that the Width is changed to 11".*

■ Go back to the <u>M</u>argins sheet in the dialog box.

> ▶ *The Preview page displayed here also reflects the change in orientation.*

■ Complete the command.

> ▶ *The document displayed onscreen also reflects the change in orientation. You can see that the line length is much longer.*

PRACTICE TIME 2 - 1

Change the page orientation back to Portrait.

THE RULER

At the top of the document window you see the ruler, as shown in Figure 2-5. The ruler displays the margins and custom tab settings for the paragraph that contains the insertion point.

First-line indent marker

Right indent marker

Figure 2-5

Left indent marker

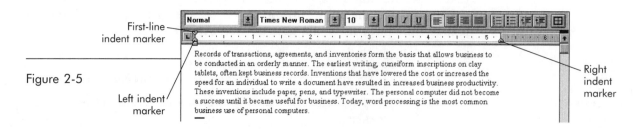

N O T E :   If the ruler is not displayed, choose Ruler from the <u>V</u>iew menu.

The numbers that are displayed along the ruler are relative to the left margin that was set using the Page Setup command. That is, 0″ is the left margin position—which, in this case, is 2″ from the left edge of the paper. In Page Setup, the paper size selected was 8½″ wide, the left margin was set to 2″, and the right margin set to 1¼″. This leaves a line length of 5¼″. This is indicated on the ruler with lighter color between 0″ and 5¼″ position.

As shown in Figure 2-5, the ruler also contains the ***first-line indent marker, left indent marker,*** and the ***right indent marker.*** These will be explained a little later.

P R A C T I C E   T I M E   2 - 2

1. From the Page Setup command, change the orientation to Landscape (this makes the paper 11″ wide). Complete the command.

2. Look at the ruler line as well as the line width of the document by using the horizontal scroll bar.

3. When satisfied, go back to the Page Setup command and change the orientation back to Portrait.

PARAGRAPH FORMATTING

If you need to change the format of just one paragraph for emphasis, position the insertion point somewhere in the paragraph and open the Format menu's Paragraph command. If you want to change the format of more than one consecutive paragraph, select them before giving the command.

Once you set the format for a particular paragraph, any paragraph that is entered below that paragraph will have the same format. That means, when you are entering a new document, if you set a format for the first paragraph, all subsequent paragraphs will have the same format. In an existing document, if you select a paragraph and change the format, other existing paragraphs will *not* be affected. If you were to insert a paragraph, that paragraph would have the format of the one that immediately precedes it in the document.

For most of these commands, there are tool buttons, ruler, and combination keystrokes that will accomplish the same task. Some require that tabs be set at appropriate positions.

TABS AND NON-PRINTING CHARACTERS

Tab settings determine the position of the insertion point each time ⌊Tab⌋ is pressed. When you press ⌊Tab⌋, a ***non-printing*** character is inserted in the document. Hence, if you want to remove the effect of pressing ⌊Tab⌋, you must delete the non-printing character. To make this task easier, however, you can display the non-printing character.

■ From the <u>T</u>ools menu, select <u>O</u>ptions.

▶ *The Options box appears as shown in Figure 2-6.*

Figure 2-6

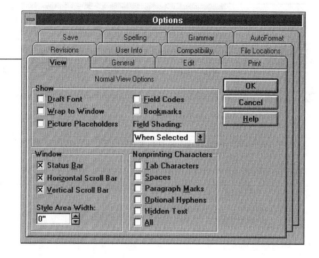

In this dialog box, you select sheets by either clicking on the sheet tab or pressing the ⌊→⌋ and ⌊←⌋ keys.

■ Make sure that the View sheet is displayed.

■ In the non-printing Characters box, select All so that an X appears, then complete the command.

Alternative: Click on the Show/Hide button ⌷.

▶ *The document now displays ¶ where you pressed* ⌊Enter⌋. *Also, dots appear where* ⌊Spacebar⌋ *was pressed.*

■ Position the insertion point at the end of the document, then press ⌊Enter⌋ to position the insertion point at the beginning of a new line.

■ Press ⌊Tab⌋.

▶ *The non-printing character* ⌐ *appears, and the insertion point moves to the 0.5"position.*

■ Press ⌊Tab⌋ several more times.

Each time you press Tab, notice the position of the insertion point. By default, tab stops are set to every half inch, starting at the left margin.

■ Press Bksp to delete tabs. Each time, notice again the position of the insertion point.

To hide the non-printing character, follow the exact same steps you used to display. That is, choose Options from the Tools menu, then click on All (so that X disappears) *or* click on the Show/Hide button.

P R A C T I C E   T I M E   2 - 3

1. Erase all tabs, but leave the insertion point at the beginning of a new line.

2. Hide the non-printing character.

SETTING TABS

You can insert or delete custom tabs. To add custom tab stops, select the paragraph(s) you want affected by the new tab stops, then set the tab stops. You can set the tab by using the ruler or by choosing the Tabs command from the Format menu. If you do not select specific text, tab stops are set for the paragraph that contains the insertion point. When you set a custom tab stop, Word clears all default tab stops to the left of the custom tab stop.

N O T E :   Word stores tab settings in the paragraph mark at the end of each paragraph. If you delete a paragraph mark, not only does the text become part of the following paragraph, but you delete the tab settings for that text.

■ From the Format menu, select Tabs.

▶ *The Tabs dialog box, as shown in Figure 2-7, is displayed.*

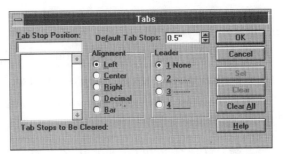

Figure 2-7

To set a tab, type the location in the Tab Stop Position text box, then select the S̲et button. To clear a tab, select the tab setting in the T̲ab Stop Position list box, then select the Cl̲ear button. To clear all tab settings, click the Clear A̲ll button.

The Alignment selection box lets you indicate the kind of tab setting. The default is left. The effects of tab types will be discussed in the next lesson. The Leader selection box is not discussed here.

Set custom tab stops at columns 1″ and 2″. Remember, tab settings are indicated relative to the left margin.

- ■ With the insertion bar in the Tab Stop Positions text box, type **1**, then select S̲et by clicking on it or pressing Alt+S.

  ▶ *1″ appears in the Tab Stop Position list box.*

- ■ Now change the entry in the Tab Stop Position text box to **2**, then select Set.

  ▶ *2″ appears on the Tab Stop Position list box.*

- ■ Complete the command.

  ▶ *The ruler displays custom left tab stops at 1″ and 2″ positions, and all default tab stops to the left have been cleared.*

- ■ Press Tab.

  ▶ *The insertion point is now at the 1″ position.*

- ■ Press Tab again.

  ▶ *The insertion point moves to the 2″ position.*

If you press Tab again, the insertion point will move to the next tab stop at the 2.5″ position, then to 3″, and so on. You will now delete the tab stop at 2″. This should restore the default tabs at the 1.5″ and 2″ positions.

- ■ From the Fo̲rmat menu, select T̲abs to display the Tabs dialog box.

- ■ Select 2″ in the Tab Stop Positions list box.

- ■ Select Cl̲ear, then complete the command.

  ▶ *The custom tab stop at 2″ is cleared.*

You can also insert, remove, and move tab stops using the ruler. To set a tab, click on the ruler where you want a custom tab to be.

- ■ Click the ruler at the 2″ position.

  ▶ *A custom left tab stop is inserted.*

To get rid of any unwanted tab, drag the tab marker off the ruler.

- ■ Drag the custom tab stop at 2″ off the ruler.

  ▶ *The custom tab stop at 2″ is cleared.*

P R A C T I C E   T I M E   2 - 4

1. Set tab stops at various positions by using both the Format menu and the ruler.

2. Try pressing (Tab). Display non-printing characters and look at the effect.

3. When satisfied, hide non-printing character then clear all custom tab stops (Clear All) so that default settings remain in effect.

PARAGRAPH INDENTATION

Let's say now that you want to indent an entire paragraph for emphasis. To do this, you change the values of the left and right indent for that paragraph.

- ■ Place the insertion point at the end of the text.

- ■ Insert at least one blank line by pressing (Enter).

- ■ Type the following:

  The concept behind word processing is a fascinating one. The typewriter has become archaic, stricken by a single technological blow. The concepts of training and productivity have changed, too. The more productive worker is the one who can insert text changes, make corrections, move blocks of text, and otherwise process text rewrites efficiently.

  ▶ *Notice that the new paragraph used the same format as the existing paragraph.*

- ■ Save the document as the file **myfile2** on your data disk.

You want the new paragraph to be indented.

- ■ Position the insertion point anywhere in the second paragraph.

- ■ From the Format menu, select Paragraph.

  ▶ *The Paragraph dialog box is displayed, as shown in Figure 2-8.*

The Paragraph dialog box is composed of two different sheets: Indents and Spacing and Text Flow. To display a sheet, either click on the corresponding sheet tab or hold down the (Alt) key and press the underline character of the sheet name.

- ■ Select Indents and Spacing, if not already displayed.

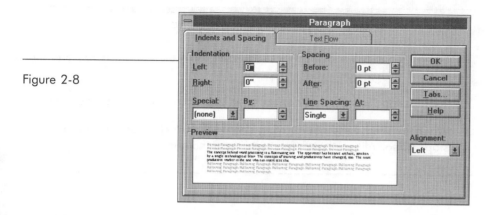

Figure 2-8

In the Preview display box at the bottom, the darker paragraph in the middle shows the format of the selected paragraph as compared to the rest of the document. At the left is the Indentation selection box.

■   In the Indentation selection box, change the Left indent to 0.75″ and press Tab.

▶   *The Preview displays the effect of the new setting on the selected paragraph.*

■   Complete the command by clicking on OK or pressing Enter.

▶   *The document display is similar to Figure 2-9.*

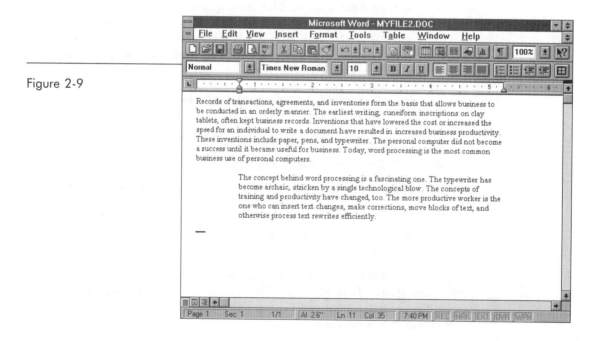

Figure 2-9

Notice the ruler line on Figure 2-9. The left indent marker and the first-line indent marker were both moved to the 0.75″.

■   Position the insertion point on the first paragraph and look at the ruler line; note the position of the first-line and left indent markers.

You can indent the paragraph to the first tab stop position using a tool button.

■   With the insertion point in the first paragraph, click on the Increase Indent button 🖳.

▶   *The first paragraph is indented to the first tab stop.*

■   Click on the Increase Indent button again.

▶   *The paragraph is now indented to the second tab stop.*

Each time you click on the Increase Indent button, the paragraph indents to the next tab stop.

■   Click on the Decrease Indent button 🖳.

▶   *The indentation returns to the previous tab stop.*

P R A C T I C E   T I M E   2 - 5

Bring the first paragraph back to the left margin.

The paragraph can also be indented by dragging both the left indent marker and the first-line indent marker to the desired position. This is done by dragging the little square located just below the left indent marker.

P R A C T I C E   T I M E   2 - 6

Try setting various paragraph indentations through the Format command, tool buttons, and the ruler. When satisfied, make sure that the first paragraph is at the left margin and the second paragraph is indented 0.75″.

LINE INDENTATION

Suppose you want to indent the first line of a paragraph by ½″. One way you can do this, as you just learned, is to make sure that there is a tab stop at 1/2″ and then press (Tab) at the beginning of each paragraph. There is another way. You can set the first-line indent to 0.5″. Once the first-line indent marker is positioned, Word will indent the first line of each paragraph automatically.

- Position the insertion point anywhere in the second paragraph.

- From the Format menu, select Paragraph.

- Select Indents and Spacing, if not already displayed.

- In the Indentation selection box, click on the down arrow by the Special text box.

    ▶   *Additional options are displayed.*

- Select First Line.

    ▶   *The By text box displays 0.5″ and the Preview display shows the change.*

You can increase or decrease the width of the indentation by typing the desired amount in the By text box. Right now, you will leave it at 0.5″.

- Complete the command.

    ▶   *The first line of the second paragraph is indented 0.5″. Also, notice the position of the first-line indent marker on the ruler.*

You can set the first-line indent by dragging the first-line indent marker.

- Drag the first-line indent marker to 0.75″, the same position as the left indent marker.

HANGING INDENT

What will happen if you drag the first-line indent marker to a position to the *left* of the left indent marker? You get a **hanging indent**. In a hanging indent format, a paragraph is indented except for the first line. This format is used quite often in bibliography, such as the following:

Pitter, Keiko. *Using IBM Microcomputers*. 4th ed. Watsonville, CA: Mitchell-McGraw Hill, 1992.

You will try this just to see the effect.

- Make sure to position the insertion point in the second paragraph.

- Drag the first-line indent marker to the 0.25″ position on the ruler.

    ▶   *The first line starts at 0.25″, and the rest of the paragraph aligns at 0.75″.*

1. Drag the left-indent marker and the first-line indent marker to various positions and look at various effects.

2. When you are satisfied, add at least one blank line at the end of the document.

3. With the insertion point at the beginning of the new line, set both the left indent marker and the first-line indent marker to the 0" position. Move the right indent marker to the 3" position.

4. Enter the following text. Make sure to press (Enter) *after* each sentence.

   When a computer is instructed to do a job, it handles the task in a very special way.
   It accepts the information.
   It stores the information until the information is ready to be used.
   It processes the information.
   Then it gives out the processed information.

5. Save the file as file **FILE1.DOC**.

BULLETS

In a bulleted list, a small circle (the **bullet**) appears in front of each item on the list. In Word, the Bulleted format combines bullet with the hanging indent. For each item on the list, a bullet appears at the first-line indent marker position, and the rest of the text appears at left indent marker position.

■ Select the last four sentences entered.

■ Click on the Bullets button 🔳.

▶ *The display is now bulleted, as shown in Figure 2-10.*

To clear the bullet, with the bulleted list selected, click the Bullets button again.

WORD PROCESSING

Figure 2-10

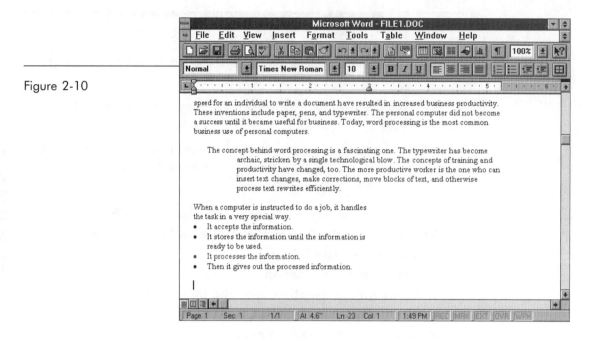

TEXT ALIGNMENT

Right now, the text is displayed aligned at the *left* margin but not at the *right* margin. You can change the alignment so that the text is aligned right, center, or justified. When the text is justified, enough blank spaces are inserted in each line so that both the left and right margins are even.

■ Position the insertion point in the first paragraph.

■ From the Format menu, select Paragraph.

▶ *The Paragraph dialog box is displayed.*

■ Make sure that the Indents and Spacing sheet is displayed.

The Alignment list box appears at the bottom right.

■ Click on the down arrow at the right end of the Alignment text box.

▶ *All four options are displayed.*

■ Select Justified and complete the command by clicking on OK or pressing [Enter].

▶ *The text reflects the change in alignment.*

This could have also been done using the buttons on the toolbar or pressing a combination keystroke. On the toolbar are four buttons for alignment, as shown in Figure 2-11. Right now, the right-most button for Justified is pressed.

Figure 2-11

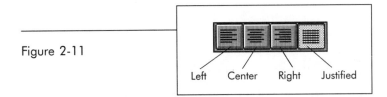

Left   Center   Right   Justified

Using the combination keystroke, left alignment can be entered as Ctrl+L, right alignment as Ctrl+R, center as Ctrl+E, and justified as Ctrl+J.

■ Click on the left-most button or press Ctrl+L for left alignment.

▶ *Text is now left-aligned.*

P R A C T I C E   T I M E   2 - 8

1. Select other tool buttons or press combination keystrokes for alignment and look at the result onscreen.

2. When you are satisfied, set the first paragraph to left-alignment.

CENTERING TEXT

There are times when you need to center text, such as when entering a title. Let's try it.

■ Position the insertion point at the beginning of the document.

■ Press Enter a couple of times to insert blank lines, and then place the insertion point on the first line.

■ Click on the Center button or press Ctrl+E.

▶ *The insertion point jumps to the middle of the line.*

■ Type **LESSON TITLE**.

▶ *The title is centered between the margins.*

N O T E : To center text that has already been entered, select the text, then enter the Center command.

WORD PROCESSING

LINE SPACING

The default setting for the line spacing is single.

■   Position the insertion point anywhere in the first paragraph.

■   From the Format menu, select Paragraph. Make sure that the Indents and Spacing sheet is displayed.

You can see the default, Single, displayed in the Line spacing text box.

■   Click on the arrow to the right of the Line Spacing text box.

▶   *All available options are displayed.*

■   Select Double.

▶   *The Preview display below shows how the document will be spaced.*

■   Complete the command by clicking on OK or pressing [Enter].

▶   *The screen reflects the change in line spacing.*

P R A C T I C E   T I M E   2 - 9

1. Try selecting other options for spacing, each time looking at the Preview box.

2. When satisfied, change the spacing back to Single.

PAGE BREAKS

When you have a long, multiple-page document, Microsoft Word shows you where the printer will advance to a new page. These are known as **soft page breaks** and are shown as a horizontal line in the text onscreen.

As you look over the document, however, you may find that a soft page break occurred at some inappropriate place. For example, you do not want a page break to occur in the middle of a table, or you may want an item to be on a page all by itself. In such cases, you need to manually enter a page break, known as a **hard page break**. A hard page break is inserted by positioning the insertion point where you want the page break to occur and inserting the command for page break.

■   Place the insertion point at the end of the first paragraph.

■   From Insert menu, select Break, then complete the command.

Alternative: Press Ctrl + Enter.

▶   *A line is inserted after the first paragraph, as shown in Figure 2-12.*

Figure 2-12

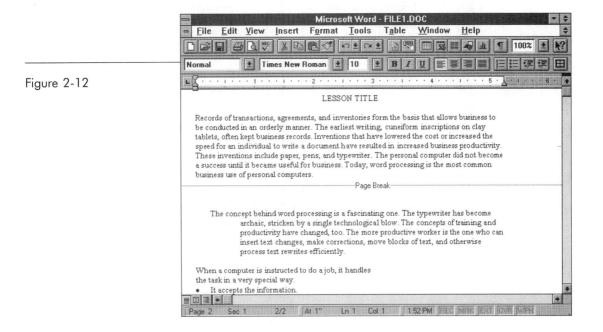

▪   From the File menu, select Preview.

▶   *A page of the document is displayed.*

▪   Click on the Multiple Page button 🖽 at the top.

▶   *This further selection is displayed.*

▪   Drag to highlight 1 x 2, as shown in Figure 2-13.

Figure 2-13

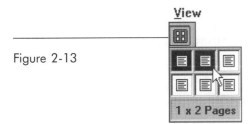

▶   *Two pages are displayed, as shown in Figure 2-14.*

You can see that the first paragraph is on one page and the rest is on the other.

Figure 2-14

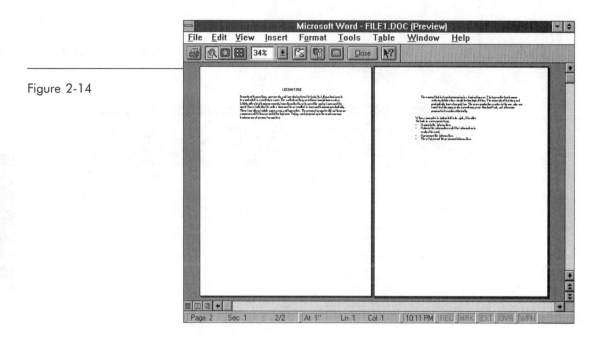

NOTE: From this preview screen, you can print the document by clicking on the Print button.

- Exit the Preview screen by selecting <u>C</u>lose.

Should you decide that you do not want the hard page break after all, position the insertion point just after the break and press Bksp.

PAGE NUMBERING

- When you are creating a multiple page document, you may want to print the page number on each page.

- Position the insertion point anywhere in the first page of the text.

- From the <u>I</u>nsert menu, select Page N<u>u</u>mbers.

  ▶ *The Page Numbers dialog box is displayed, as shown in Figure 2-15.*

You can insert a page number at the top or the bottom of the paper. The bottom is the default selection. Also, the number can appear at the left, center, or right. Right is the default selection. You will use all the default settings.

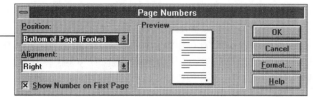

Figure 2-15

NOTE: Through the Format option, you can specify the type of numbers to such as Arab numerals (1,2,3), lowercase Roman numerals (i,ii,iii), or uppercase Roman numerals (I, II, III). You can also specify the starting number for paging.

■ Complete the command.

P R A C T I C E   T I M E   2 - 1 0

1. Preview or print the text to look at the page numbering. You may have to enlarge the display to see the page numbers.

2. Delete the hard page break.

CHANGING FONT

The appearance of characters on your screen and printout is determined by three things, which collectively are called the ***font***: the typeface, the type size, and the appearance.

The *typeface* is the design applied to the characters and given a name, such as Courier, Helvetica, or Times Roman. The typeface is often referred to as the font.

The *type size* of the character will depend on type of font. If the font you chose is ***proportionally spaced*** (different widths for different letters), the size is given in points, measured 72 to an inch. Typical fonts are 10- or 12-point fonts, with 10 being the smaller size. If the font you chose is **monospaced** (each letter requires the same amount of horizontal space), the size is indicated in characters per inch, or cpi. Again, the typical font sizes are 10 cpi or 12 cpi, with 12 cpi being the smaller size.

The *appearance* includes regular, bold, italic, and underline. These can be used in any combination.

You can select an appropriate font for display and printing the document. The style can be varied to emphasize certain information. The font and size will affect the amount of text that can fit on one page of a document.

WORD PROCESSING

To change a text font, select the text you want to change, or position the insertion point where you want to begin typing characters with the new font. If you want to change the default font selection, the insertion point can be anywhere. When you change the default setting, the entire document will use the font specified.

■ Select a section of the text.

■ From the Format menu, choose Font.

▶ *The Font dialog box is displayed, as shown in Figure 2-16.*

Figure 2-16

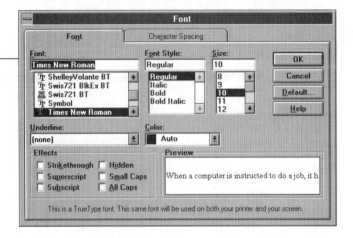

■ Make sure that the Font sheet is displayed.

■ Make a selection in the Font list box.

▶ *The Preview display shows the font selected.*

NOTE: If you want to change the default font selection, select the Use As Default button.

■ When you have the desired font selected, complete the command.

▶ *The selected text changes to the font specified.*

You can also change the font by using the toolbar.

■ Click on the arrow next to the second box from the left on the Formatting toolbar.

▶ *The font options are displayed.*

■ Click on the font name you want.

Depending on the font chosen, you will have different point sizes from which to choose. Size selection is very similar to font selection; you can specify it by using the Character command from the Format menu or choosing the size (to the right of the Fonts) on the Formatting toolbar. Try this on your own.

Try various fonts and sizes, and study the effects.

CHANGING APPEARANCE

You can change the appearance of characters either as you type the text or after it has been typed. As mentioned earlier, appearance includes bold, underline, and italic.

To change appearance while entering text, position the insertion point where you plan to enter text, give the command to change the appearance, type the text, then give the command again to return to normal.

To change the appearance of text already typed, select the desired text, then give the command to change the appearance.

Again, the command can be given through the Font command in the Format menu or through the tool buttons. In the toolbar are three buttons, as shown in Figure 2-17, for Bold, Italic, and Underline.

Figure 2-17

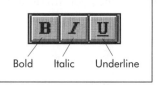

Bold   Italic   Underline

- Position the insertion point at the end of the document.

- Press [Enter] a couple of times to insert a blank line.

- Click the Italic tool button or press [Ctrl]+[I].

- Type the following:

    This text is being entered in italics.

    ▶ *The text appears in italics onscreen.*

- Click the Italic tool button again to return to normal characters.

Now, let's say that you want the title to appear in bold characters. Since it has already been typed, you'll have to select the text of the title, then give the Bold command.

■   Drag the mouse to select the text of the title.

■   Click the Bold tool button or press Ctrl+B.

▶   *The title is now in bold characters.*

■   Click elsewhere to deselect the text.

P R A C T I C E   T I M E   2 - 1 2

Try the underline feature on your own. The combination keystroke for underline is Ctrl+U.

NOTE: Once you decide on a format for selected text, the format can be copied to another section of the document by using the Format Painter tool button. All you need to do is to place the insertion point on the selected text, click on the tool button, then drag on the text where you want the same format applied. You can try this on your own.

ENDING LESSON 2

This is the end of Lesson 2. Exit Microsoft Word as explained in Lesson 1. There is no need to save changes you made to your files.

S U M M A R Y

☐   **Word online Help provides assistance and information on all available features.**

☐   **The default values set by Microsoft Word dictate how a document appears onscreen and on printouts. These values can be changed by using either the menu commands or the toolbars and the ruler.**

☐   **When you press Tab, a non-printing character is inserted in the document. You can treat them like any other character. That is, if you want to delete the effect of a tab, you delete the non-printing character representing the tab.**

☐   **First-line indentation is when the first line of paragraph is indented. To do this, set the tab at the appropriate position and press Tab or set the first-line indent marker to the desired position.**

☐ **In a hanging indent, a paragraph is indented except for the first line.**

☐ **To change the font or appearance of text, you either: (1) give the command, type the text, and enter the command again; or (2) select the text, then give the command to change it.**

KEY TERMS

bullet	landscape	proportionally spaced
first-line indent marker	left indent marker	characters
font	monospaced characters	right indent marker
hanging indent	non-printing character	soft page break
hard page break	portrait	

COMMAND SUMMARY

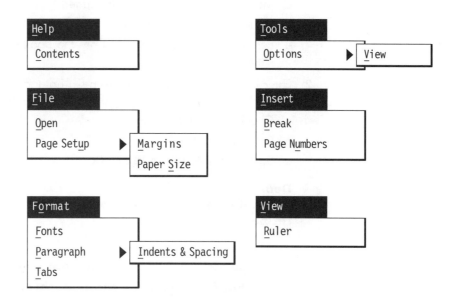

REVIEW QUESTIONS

1. What is the difference between a soft return and a hard return? a soft page break and a hard page break?

2. If you do not specify the left or right margin settings, what values are used?

3. What does "text alignment" mean? What are the options?

4. What does "hanging indent" mean? What commands do you give to use a hanging indent?

WORD PROCESSING

5. How do you indent an entire paragraph?

6. How do you underline characters? Make them bold?

7. What can you do from the ruler?

8. How do you set tabs using the Tabs command? Using the ruler?

9. How do you display two pages at a time during print preview?

10. List the keystrokes needed to make page numbers appear at the top right corner of each page.

EXERCISES

1. Retrieve the letter saved in the previous lesson as WD1EX2.
   a. Make the following changes, get a printout, and save it as **WD2EX1**.
   b. Center the date on the first line.
   c. Make sure that the text is left aligned.
   d. Change the left margin to 4.5" just before "Sincerely."
   e. Remove the quotation marks from the book title, "Quotations." Underline it instead.

2. Enter the following text. (Your text need not look exactly as it appears here. However, you should set new tabs before entering the recipe.)
   a. Check the spelling.
   b. Get a printout.
   c. Save it on the disk as **WD2EX2**.

Dear Jill:
I've just come across the most wonderful spaghetti sauce recipe.

1 pound	**Italian hot sausage**
1 can (4 ounces)	**sliced mushrooms, drained**
3/4 cup	**shredded carrots**
1	**medium onion, grated**
1/2 cup	**chopped parsley**
1 pound	**ground beef**
1 can (28 ounces)	**Italian style tomatoes**
2 cans (6 ounces)	**tomato paste**
1 cup	**dry red wine**
1	**bay leaf**
2 teaspoons	**salt**
1 teaspoon	**basil leaves**

1/4 teaspoon	pepper
1 pound	spaghetti

In a large pan, cook sausage in 1/4 cup water for 10 minutes, tightly covered, stirring occasionally. Remove sausage. In that pan, saute mushrooms, carrot, onion, celery and parsley in sausage drippings until crisp and tender. Remove. Add beef. Cook, stirring frequently, until lightly browned. Remove any excess fat. Return sausage and vegetables to pan. Add tomatoes, tomato paste, wine, bay leaf, salt, basil and pepper. Cover and simmer 30 minutes. Uncover and simmer 2 hours, stirring occasionally. Remove bay leaf. In the meanwhile, cook spaghetti according to directions on package. Serve with grated Parmesan cheese.

Sounds great, doesn't it? It tastes <u>delicious</u>.

Your friend,

Jackie

3. Enter the following text. Your text need not look exactly as it appears here.
   a. Check the spelling.
   b. Get a printout.
   c. Save it on the disk as **WD2EX3**.

IDEA PROCESSING

The phrases "word processing" and "data processing" are becoming more and more prevalent in common language. In the mid-1970s, who owned a word processor? What these phrases actually refer to is idea processing. With the recent growth in computer technology available to consumers, idea processing has rapidly evolved.

In many ways, idea processing has opened previously inaccessible avenues for businesses and individuals:

- Point-of-entry data terminals in a store can immediately register sales and provide data for efficient inventory and management decision.

- Financial models can show a board of directors the cold figures which, in past times, were only available <u>after</u> the decision-making had taken place.

- **Form letters no longer need to be individually typed, using so much secretarial time.**

- **Since businesses and individuals can obtain immediate access to a variety of data sets over phone lines, the possibilities for idea processing seem limited by the mind only.**

And the mind is indeed the crucial element in idea processing. For, without an accurate financial model, the best available data are worthless; without proper thought, inventory and management decisions can be detrimental to the company's well-being; without a specific and detailed method for <u>how</u> data are to be processed, access to timely data is worthless.

3 Advanced Editing and Multiple Files

OBJECTIVES

Upon completion of the material presented in this lesson, you should understand the following aspects of Microsoft Word:

- ☐ **Opening multiple documents**

- ☐ **Switching between document windows**

- ☐ **Copying selected text from one word processing file to another**

- ☐ **Inserting header and footer**

- ☐ **Entering text flush right and decimal aligned**

- ☐ **Including current date**

- ☐ **Finding a particular word or combination of words in a text**

- ☐ **Replacing a particular word or combination of words in a text with a specified word or combination of words**

- ☐ **Using merge**

STARTING OFF

Turn on your computer, start Windows, and launch the Word program as you did in previous lessons. Insert your data disk in the disk drive. If necessary, maximize the Word application window.

OPENING MULTIPLE FILES

As was mentioned in Lesson 1, you can open up to nine documents at the same time in Word if your computer has enough memory. You will now open two files from your data disk: MYFILE and FILE1.

P R A C T I C E   T I M E   3 - 1

1. Open the file MYFILE.DOC on your data disk.

2. Open the file FILE1.DOC on your data disk.

You can see only the content of FILE1.DOC onscreen right now.

Switching Between Windows

You can switch between or among document windows through the Window menu.

■   Select <u>W</u>indow in the menu bar.

▶   *The pull-down menu appears, as shown in Figure 3-1.*

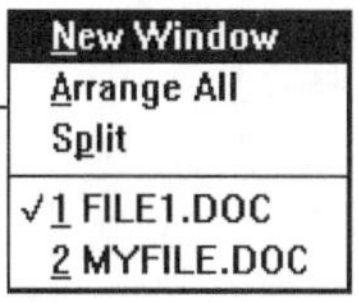

Figure 3-1

```
New Window
Arrange All
Split
√1 FILE1.DOC
 2 MYFILE.DOC
```

The two documents appear as command options. You can select which document to make ***active***. The active window contains the document with which you can work. In the Window menu, the active document has a check mark in front of it.

■   Select 2, the number that appears in front of MYFILE.

▶   *The document MYFILE is made active.*

P R A C T I C E   T I M E   3 - 2

Make the document FILE1 active.

Arranging Windows

You can also switch active documents by displaying both documents at the same time.

■ From the Window menu, select Arrange All.

▶ *The two open windows reduce in size so that they can both be viewed in the workspace, as shown in Figure 3-2.*

Figure 3-2

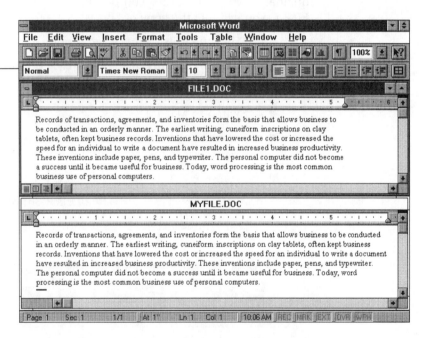

The active window is the one in which the insertion point appears and that has a darker title bar. To make a document window active, click anywhere in the window. You can also maximize the window so that it is the only document window in the display.

■ Click anywhere in the other document window.

▶ *The MYFILE document is now the active window.*

P R A C T I C E   T I M E   3 - 3

Maximize the FILE1 document window.

MOVING SELECTED TEXT BETWEEN DOCUMENTS

Sometimes you need to take a passage of text from one document and insert it into another. In Word, moving selected text between two documents is no different than moving it within a document. You cut or copy selected text onto Windows' clipboard, then paste it.

You will select the second paragraph of FILE1 so that it can be included in MYFILE.

■   Select the second paragraph of FILE1.

The selected text can be cut or copied. When you cut, the text is no longer at the original location. When the selected text is copied, however, the original stays intact. Since you do not want to remove this paragraph from FILE1, you will use the copy option.

■   From the Edit menu, select Copy.

Alternative: Press Ctrl+C or click on the Copy button ⊡.

▶   *The selected text is copied onto the clipboard.*

■   Switch to MYFILE.

■   Position the insertion point at the end of the document. Press Enter twice to insert a blank line.

■   From the Edit menu, select Paste.

Alternative: Press Ctrl+V or click on the Paste button ⊡.

▶   *The selected text is inserted as shown in Figure 3-3.*

Figure 3-3

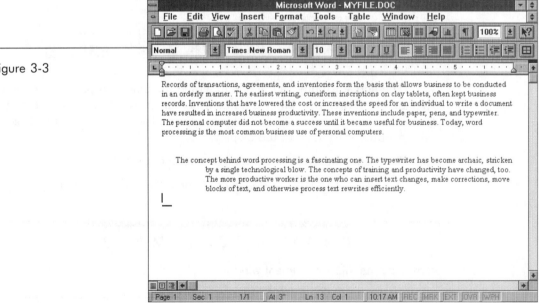

NOTE: If both documents are on display (Arrange All), you can even use the drag and drop feature to copy or move the text between files.

OPENING A NEW DOCUMENT

You will now open a new document.

■ From the File menu, select New.

Alternative: **Press** (Shift)+(N).

▶ *The New dialog box appears as shown in Figure 3-4.*

Figure 3-4

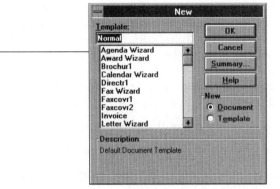

Every Word document is based on a document ***template***, which is a special document used as a pattern to create other documents of the same type. For example, you can create a document template for letters that makes it easy to produce letters of the same format. When you use a template, you no longer have to start from scratch each time you create a document. Tasks such as setting the margins, choosing a font, and creating headers and footers have already been done. Microsoft Word comes with several predefined templates for the most common types of documents. By default, new documents are based on a template called NORMAL.DOT. You can explore other templates on your own.

■ Use the default template selection and complete the command.

▶ *A document window appears.*

P R A C T I C E   T I M E   3 - 4

1. Copy the first paragraph from MYFILE to the new document just created.

2. Arrange all documents.

3. Maximize the FILE1 document.

HEADERS AND FOOTERS

Headers and ***footers*** are lines of text that appear at the top and bottom of every page. They are handy options for displaying information identifying a document. You need to enter these commands only once; the headers or footers will be repeated as specified, starting with the page on which the command was given.

The manner in which headers and footers are specified is similar. Here, only the footer is discussed. You can try the header on your own.

■   Place the insertion point at the beginning of the page.

■   From the <u>V</u>iew menu, select <u>H</u>eader and Footer.

▶   *The display switches to* **page layout view** *and displays the Header and Footer toolbar as shown in Figure 3-5.*

Figure 3-5

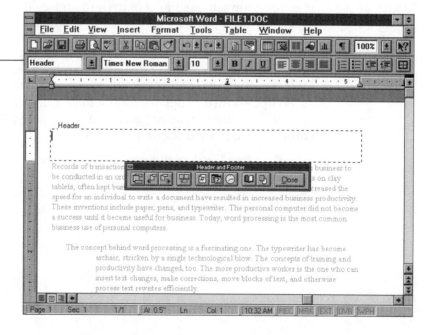

Up to now, your document was being displayed in the normal view. Word was displaying what your text would look like. In page layout view, however, you can see exactly what the document will look like when printed—similar to the Print Preview screen. Whereas in the Print Preview screen, entire pages are displayed at reduced size, the page layout view is similar in size to the normal view. You can switch between normal view and page layout view in the View menu or by clicking on the Normal View and Page Layout View buttons ▣▣ next to the horizontal scroll bar.

Notice the dotted box labeled Header. All you need to do is to type the text to appear as the header.

■   Type the following, but do not press Enter at the end.

Lesson on Advanced Editing - Page

The idea is to display the current page number at this point.

■   Click on the Page Number tool button ▣ in the Header and Footer toolbar.

▶   *Number 1 appears in the header. This is the current page number.*

■   Select Close in the Header and Footer toolbar.

P R A C T I C E   T I M E   3 - 5

1. Insert a hard page break after the first paragraph so that this becomes a multiple-page document.

2. Preview the document to see both pages. The header on the second page indicates Page 2.

CLOSING DOCUMENTS

Closing the document removes the active document from memory without exiting Word. Right now, you want to close all three documents. Each document must be closed individually.

■   From the File menu, select Close.

▶   *A dialog box appears asking you if you want to save the file or cancel the command.*

■ Select <u>N</u>o.

▶ *The document is closed (cleared) without being saved, and another open document becomes active.*

P R A C T I C E   T I M E   3 - 6

1. Close the other two documents without saving changes.

2. Open a new document using the Normal template.

ENTERING TEXT RIGHT ALIGNED

Most of the time, you enter text starting at the left margin. That is, other than line indentation, you want your lines at the left margin. If you also want the text to be even at right margin, you turn the alignment to justified. There are times, however, when you want the text to be entered aligned with the right margin, without regard to the left margin. An example might be when you are entering the date at the beginning of a letter.

■ From the F<u>o</u>rmat menu, select <u>P</u>aragraph. Then set the Alignment to Right and complete the command.

Alternative: **Press Ctrl+R or click on the right alignment tool button.**

▶ *The insertion point moves to the right margin.*

■ Type **current date** and press Enter.

▶ *The text is entered right aligned—even with the right margin.*

P R A C T I C E   T I M E   3 - 7

Set the alignment to left.

WORD PROCESSING

INCLUDING THE CURRENT DATE

Your computer keeps track of time when it is on. If you do not have a battery-operated clock (which stays on when the computer is turned off), you have the option to enter the current date and time when you start up the computer. Nevertheless, there is an internal clock that keeps time and date information. You can have Word insert the current date (as kept by the internal clock) into the document.

■ From the Insert menu, select Date and Time.

▶ *The Date and Time dialog box appears as shown in Figure 3-6.*

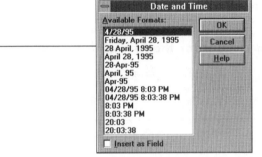

Figure 3-6

The Available Formats box lists all the different ways in which date and time can be displayed.

■ Click on the format you want, say, the fourth one down, and complete the command.

▶ *The current date is inserted at the insertion point in the format you selected.*

N O T E : Note the option to Insert as Field at the bottom of the Date and Time dialog box. When this option is selected, Word inserts the date or time as a field code, which it updates at printing. Also, if the date and time are inserted as a field code, you can update as you work by positioning the insertion point in the date or time and clicking the right mouse button, then choosing the option Update Field in the menu that is displayed.

PRACTICE TIME 3-8

1. Close the current document window without saving.

2. Start a new document and enter the partial letter shown following. The first address and the date are to be entered flush right.

1728 Forest Road
Takoma Park, Maryland
current date

Mr. Gary Bradshaw
Computer Parts Shop
1234 Byte Street
Golden, Colorado 81234

Dear Mr. Bradshaw:

Please accept my order for the following items:

3. Save the text on your data disk as LETTER1.

TAB ALIGNMENT

In the letter you started in Practice Time 3-8, the next step is to specify the items you want to order, the quantity, and the price, as shown below:

50	boxes of diskettes @14.75	$737.50
5	printer ribbons @11.95	59.75
1	diskette container @9.95	9.95

The first column is typed right aligned (at a specific position, +1″ in this case), the second column is typed left aligned (at another specific position, +1.5″ in this case), and the third column needs to be aligned at the decimal point (at position +5″ in this case). You can set the tabs so that this type of data entry is simple.

■ Make sure that the insertion point is at the bottom of the letter. (There should be at least one blank line after the end of the text.)

■ From the Format menu, select Tabs.

▶ *The Tabs dialog box is displayed.*

You will set tabs at +1″, +1.5″, and +5″. However, at +1″, you want to specify right alignment; at +1.5″, left alignment; and at +5″, decimal alignment.

■   Click on <u>R</u>ight in the Alignment box, type **1** in the Tab Stop Position text box, then click on <u>S</u>et.

■   Click on <u>L</u>eft in the Alignment box, type **1.5** in the Tab Stop Position text box, then click on <u>S</u>et.

■   Click on <u>D</u>ecimal in the Alignment box, type **5** in the Tab Stop Position box, then click on <u>S</u>et.

■   Complete the command.

▶   *The ruler appears as shown in Figure 3-7.*

Figure 3-7

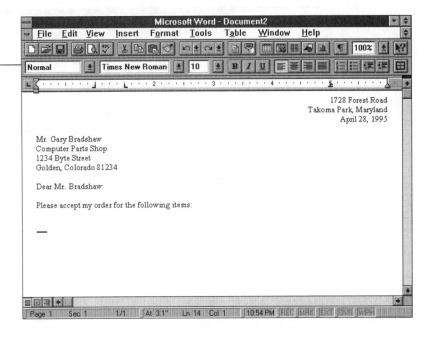

To specify various types of tabs on the ruler, click on the tab style box located at the left end of the ruler. Each time you click, the icon for tab style changes. To set a left tab, make sure that the icon for the left tab is displayed, then click on the ruler at the desired position. To set a right tab, first you make sure that the icon for the right tab is displayed before clicking on the ruler, and so on.

Now you are ready to enter the text.

■   Press Tab.

▶   *The insertion point jumps to the first tab setting.*

■   Type **50**.

▶   *The entry is made flush right at position +1″.*

- Press Tab.

  ▶ *The insertion point jumps to position +1.5".*

- Type **boxes of diskettes @14.75**.

  ▶ *The entry is made left justified at position +1.5".*

- Press Tab.

  ▶ *The insertion point jumps to position +5".*

- Type **$737.50**.

  ▶ *The entry is made with the decimal point at position +5".*

- Press Enter.

P R A C T I C E   T I M E   3 - 9

1. Type in the next two items.

2. Insert a blank line after the third item.

3. Reset the tabs so that they appear every 0.5". (Hint: select Clear All in the Tabs dialog box or drag custom tabs off the ruler line.)

4. Enter the rest of the letter.

   My check for $807.20 is enclosed.

   Sincerely,

   your name
   Enclosure

5. Save the text again, using the same filename.

6. Close the file **letter1**.

FINDING TEXT

There are times when you need to move the insertion point to a specific word that you know is somewhere in the document. Microsoft Word has a command to help you do just that. You can search from the insertion point forward or backwards in a document.

- Open the file MYFILE from your data disk.

Pretend that this is a long document on record management, and you need to find the word "cuneiform" because you have additional information you want to insert.

■ From the Edit menu, select Find.

Alternative: **Press** Ctrl+F.

▶ *The Find dialog box appears as shown in Figure 3-8.*

Figure 3-8

In the Find What box, you need to enter the text you want to find. You can type up to 255 characters in the Find What box. Text scrolls horizontally in the box as you type.

The Search list box shows that you are to search the entire document (All). If you were to press the down arrow at the end of the Search list box, you will see the other two search options.

■ Click the down arrow at the right end of the Search list box.

▶ *You see the options Down and Up.*

Down search means the search is made down the document from the current position of the insertion point, and up search means the search is made from the current insertion point position toward the beginning of the document.

■ Leave the selection at All.

If you do not select Match Whole Word Only, Word will find text that is part of another word. For example, you might be searching for the last name "Thorn," and Word will locate "Thornapple" as well.

If you do not select Match Case, the search is not case sensitive. That is, the text is matched with both upper- and lowercase occurrences within the document. If you select Match Case, however, the search is case sensitive. Microsoft Word looks for an exact match.

Other options are not discussed here.

■ In the Find What box, type **cuneiform**, then select Find Next.

▶ *The first occurrence of the word "cuneiform" is highlighted.*

■ Click on Cancel to close the Find dialog box.

P R A C T I C E   T I M E   3 - 1 0

Find all occurrences of the word "productivity" in MYFILE. (When you initiate
the search, the word "cuneiform" still appears in the Find What box. Just type
"productivity." It will replace the previous entry.)

REPLACING WORDS

In the course of editing a document, sometimes you are looking for a particular word that needs to be replaced. For example, you had written a rather
lengthy report on a client only to find out that there has been a change in
the client's company name. Rather than searching through the entire document visually, looking for any occurrence of the company name and
replacing the name, you'd like Word to find and replace them for you.

P R A C T I C E   T I M E   3 - 1 1

1. Open a new document. Enter the following text, date the letter and add
    an appropriate closing, then save as the file LETTER2.

    Mr. John Smith
    Personnel Office, Republic Engineering
    3570 Fruitland Avenue
    Maywood, OR 97119

    Dear Mr. Smith:

    **This is a letter of application for the draftsperson position
    advertised by Republic Engineering. As you will notice in
    the enclosed resume, my background is just what Republic
    Engineering is looking for.**

    **Please notice also that I have twice been selected as employee
    of the month in my current job. Republic Engineering is surely
    interested in my loyal attitude toward my employer.**

    **I look forward to hearing from you concerning an interview
    date and time. In the meanwhile, could you provide me with
    some information concerning the medical and retirement
    benefits available to Republic Engineering employees?**

    Thank you.

You just found out that Mr. John Smith is no longer with Republic Engineering. The letter has to be sent to Mr. John Matthews.

■ From the Edit menu, select Replace.

   Alternative: Press Ctrl+H.

   ► *The Replace dialog box, as shown in Figure 3-9, is displayed.*

Figure 3-9

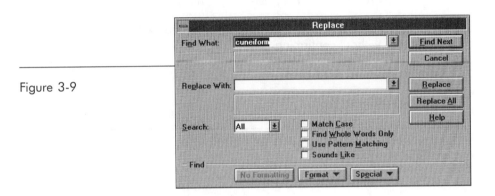

First, you need to specify the character string you want to find.

■ With the insertion point in the Find What text box, type **Smith** (do not press Enter).

Next, you need to specify with what to replace "Smith."

■ Position the insertion point in the Replace With text box.

■ Type **Matthews**.

■ Make sure that the Search text box is set to All.

As you did with the Find command earlier, you must indicate whether to match whole words only or not, and whether you want to do a case-sensitive search. You will leave these unselected.

You have the options of selecting the Find Next button or Replace All button. If you select the Replace All button, you can have all occurrences of "Smith" replaced with "Matthews" without being asked at each occurrence. With the Find Next button, Word will pause after finding the next occurrence.

■ Select the Find Next button to start the search.

   ► *The first occurrence of "Smith" is highlighted.*

■ Select the Replace button.

   ► *"Smith" is replaced with "Matthews," and the next occurrence of "Smith" is found.*

■   Keep on confirming the replacement until all occurrences of "Smith" have been replaced by "Matthews." You will know this is done when no more text is selected.

■   Close the Replace dialog box.

P R A C T I C E   T I M E   3 - 1 2

1. Replace all occurrences of "Republic Engineering" with "Conway Architects" without confirming.

2. Save the letter as **A:LETTER3**.

3. Close all documents.

MERGE

Replace is a good command to use if you are just substituting one phrase with another (or several phrases with several other phrases) one time only. However, if you need to do this many times, such as when sending the same letter to different persons, you should be using the ***Merge*** command instead.

The letter or the document itself, called the ***main document***, needs to be modified to contain the codes where names and addresses should be inserted. Names and addresses, or whatever other information should be merged into the main document, are entered in a separate file, referred to as the ***data source***. The command will then "merge" two files to create as many merged documents as there are sets of information in the data source, with the proper information inserted at indicated positions.

These two files can be created in whatever order you want. What does matter is that the order in which information is supplied in the data source match up with the codes in the main document. Right now, you will create the data source first, then create the main document.

The following letter is the one you want to send out.

WORD PROCESSING

---

current date

Sam Sherman
3983 West Blvd.
Los Angeles, CA 90016

Dear **Sam:**

If you need $2000 worth of equipment right away, it's a
serious matter. And borrowing money to make the
purchase is not always easy. But because you, **Sam**, have
a good credit rating with us, you are now preapproved for
a $2000 credit limit.

If you are interested, give us a call and one of our sales
people will visit you in your fair city of **Los Angeles** right
away. Also, if you need more than the $2000 credit limit,
Sam, please let us know. We'll go out of our way to help
you any way we can.

Sincerely,

In the letter, all text in bold is personalizing information. The idea is to
create as many copies of this letter as you have names and addresses in the
data source, all personalized. That means, within the letter, you need to
specify where to insert first name, where to insert address, city, and so
forth.

You will next use the Mail Merge command.

■ From the File menu, select New.

▶ *The New dialog box appears.*

■ Click on OK or press Enter.

■ From the Tools menu, select Mail Merge.

▶ *The Mail Merge Helper dialog box appears as shown in
Figure 3-10.*

■ Select Create.

▶ *A menu appears with various types of main documents you
might want to create.*

■ Select Form Letters.

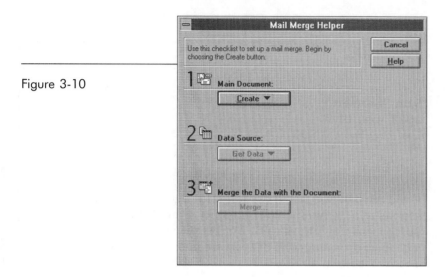

Figure 3-10

> ▶ *A dialog box appears, giving you the option to create the form letter in the document window you've already opened (active window) or in a new document window.*

■ Select <u>A</u>ctive Window.

> ▶ *You return to the Mail Merge Helper window.*

Data Source

The next step is to create a data source.

■ Select <u>G</u>et Data.

> ▶ *You have options to create a data source or open an existing one.*

> ▶ *Select <u>C</u>reate Data Source.*

> ▶ *The Create Data Source dialog box is displayed, as shown in Figure 3-11.*

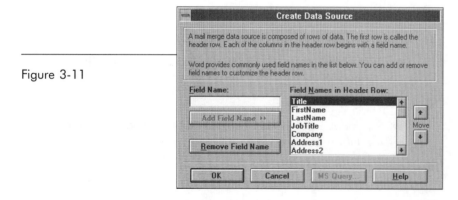

Figure 3-11

The data you enter is organized into data records in a table. The ***field*** names appear in the first row of cells, the header record, and act as column headings for the address information. All information related to a person appears in a row and is referred to as a ***record***. Each record contains fields: a field that contains first name, a field that contains last name, a field that contains street address, and so on. All records in a data file must contain the same fields, listed in the same order.

The first step in creating a new data source is to decide which information you want to vary in each version of the merged document. For the current exercise, you need fields for the following: first name, last name, company, street address, city, state, and zip code.

The next step is to specify the field names to be used. In the Create Data Source dialog box, Word provides commonly used field names in the Field Names in Header Row list box. All you need to do is to add to or remove from the list. If you want to add new field names, a field name can be up to 32 characters. You can use letters, numbers, and underscored characters, but not spaces.

Scroll through the list. The list contains all the field names you need; you just have to remove some.

■ Select Title in the Field Names in Header Row list box, then select Remove Field Name.

■ Similarly, remove other fields so that the only ones left are: FirstName, LastName, Company, Address1, City, State, and PostalCode.

■ When finished, complete the command.

   ▶ *The Save Data Source dialog box appears so that you can save the data file.*

■ Save it as **Customer** on your data disk.

   ▶ *A dialog box appears, giving you the option to enter new records in the data source.*

■ Select Edit Data Source.

   ▶ *The Data Form dialog box appears, as shown in Figure 3-12, ready to accept information.*

Figure 3-12

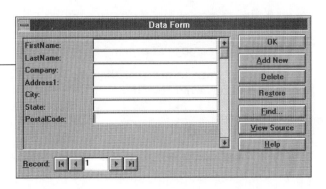

The first record contains information on Kay Gray of Buttons & Banners. The address is P.O. Box 2110, Incline Village, NV 89450.

- Type the first field of the first record. That is, type **Kay** and press Tab.

- Type the second field, **Gray**, and press Tab.

- Enter the other five fields. Make sure to press Tab after each.

Company:	**Buttons & Banners**
Address1:	**P.O. Box 2110**
City:	**Incline Village**
State:	**NV**
PostalCode:	**89450**

- After you've entered the last field, select Add New.

  ▶ *A blank form appears.*

P R A C T I C E   T I M E   3 - 1 3

Enter the information on four other customers. If a field does not contain information (such as no company name given), just press Tab.

George Biehl
Language Technologies
2451 Vegas Valley Drive
Las Vegas NV 89121

Dorothy Durkee
Casino Computers
1255 W. Second Street
Reno NV 89502

Ronald Foss
Heritage Product
P.O. Box 320
Minden NV 89423

Ressa Muller

3000 S. State St.
Ukiah CA 95482

- When you've finished entering the data, complete the command.

  ▶ *The document window for the main document appears, as shown in Figure 3-13. It includes buttons you need to merge field codes.*

You may want to position the mouse pointer over various merge buttons and find out what they do.

Main Document

The first thing you need to type is the name (first and last names) of the person to whom you are writing, followed by the company name one line

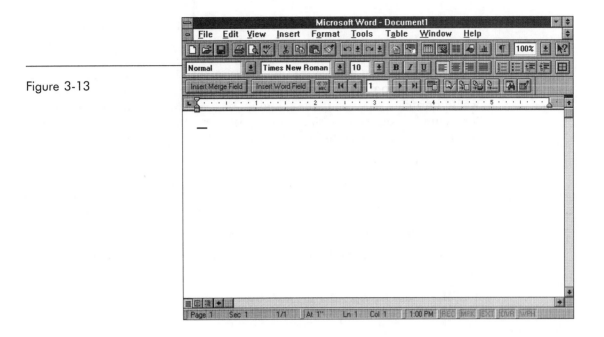

Figure 3-13

down, street address, then the city/state/zip on the next line down. This information has to come from the data file.

■   Insert today's date and press [Enter] three times.

■   Select Insert Merge Field.

▶   *A drop-down menu appears, listing all available fields, as shown in Figure 3-14.*

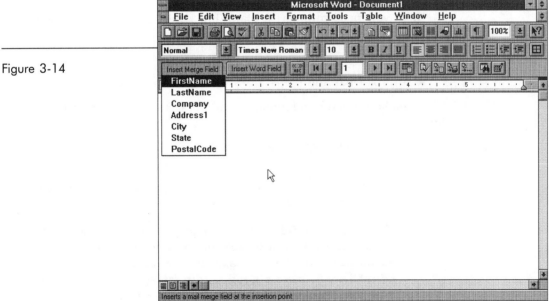

Figure 3-14

■   Select the FirstName field in the Print Merge Fields list box.

▶   *The code <<FirstName>> is inserted in the document.*

When entering field codes into a document, these codes are treated as if they were actual words or blocks of text. Any spacing or punctuation you would normally place in the text should be inserted around the code. Here, for example, you want a blank space between the first name and the last name. Hence, you need to place a space between the two codes.

■   Press [Spacebar].

■   Select Insert Merge Field and select LastName.

▶   *The line now reads <<FirstName>> <<LastName>>.*

■   Press [Enter] to move the insertion point to the next line down.

The second line prints the company name, which constitutes the third field.

■   Select Insert Merge Field, then Company.

■   Press [Enter] to go to the next line.

■   Similarly, enter Address1 on the next line down; and City, State, and PostalCode on the one after. Remember to insert a comma after the City field.

▶   *The screen should look as follows:*

<<FirstName>> <<LastName>>

<<Company>>

<<Address1>>

<<City>>, <<State>> <<PostalCode>>

Next, you need to insert a blank line, then the salutation should be entered.

■   Press [Enter] twice.

■   Type **Dear** and press [Spacebar], but do not press [Enter].

To make the letter personal, you will insert the customer's first name here.

■   Enter the merge code for FirstName, followed by a colon. Press [Enter].

■   Enter the following text. Insert the proper merge code wherever you see <FirstName> or <City>.

If you need $2,000 worth of equipment right away, it's a serious matter. And borrowing money to make the purchase is not always easy. But because you, <FirstName>, have a good credit rating with us, you are now preapproved for a $2,000 credit limit.

If you are interested, give us a call and one of our sales people will visit you in your fair city of <City> right away. Also, if you need more than the $2,000 credit limit, <FirstName>, please let us know. We'll go out of our way to help you any way we can.

Sincerely,

■ Save the file as **MAINDOC** on your data disk.

You can now begin the merging procedure. This is where the information from the data file is merged into the main document. Microsoft Word will create five letters as there are five records in the data file.

■ From the Tools menu, select Mail Merge.

Alternative: Click on the Mail Merge button 📊.

■ Select Merge.

▶ *The Merge dialog box is displayed as shown in Figure 3-15.*

Figure 3-15

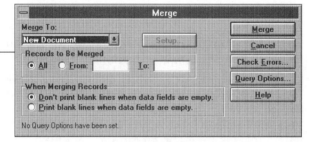

■ Select Merge To by clicking on the down arrow at the right or pressing **R.**

You have two options in merging: (1) You can merge the main document and data source, and print each resulting merged document; or (2) You can merge the main document and data source, and store the resulting documents in a new file.

The second is the default, which you will use.

If you recall, the fifth record, the one on Ressa Mueller, did not contain the Company name. To eliminate the blank line caused by an empty field, make sure that Don't print blank lines when data fields are empty is selected.

N O T E : You could have used either the Merge to Document button or the Merge to Printer button on the Merge toolbar. The task would have been completed using all the default settings.

■ Select Merge.

▶ *Each form letter appears as a document, as shown in Figure 3-16.*

Figure 3-16

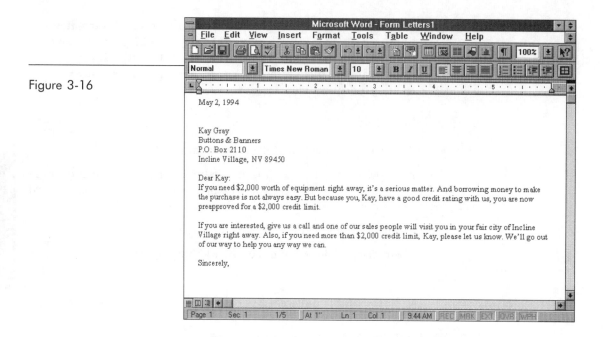

Scroll through the form letters. Notice the fifth letter to Ressa Muller. The blank line (for company name) is eliminated.

You can print these five letters or save the letters as a file. As you can imagine, the information you can merge in a letter is not just limited to mailing information. You can include account balance, due dates, or any other information that needs to be personalized. To include this information, make sure it appears in the data file.

ENDING LESSON 3

This is the end of Lesson 3. Exit Microsoft Word as explained in Lesson 1. There is no need to save changes you made to your file.

S U M M A R Y

☐ **By using the Arrange All command from the Window menu, all document windows are reduced in size and displayed in windows.**

☐ **Copying selected text from one file to another is done with the same procedure as is copying selected text within a file.**

☐ **Headers and footers are lines of text that appear at the top and bottom of every page.**

☐ **The current date, as kept by the computer, can be inserted in a document.**

☐ **Text can be entered flush right, left justified, or decimal aligned at each tab set.**

☐ **In Find or Replace, the text can be scanned in either direction starting from the insertion point.**

☐ **Merge requires two files. The first, the main document, contains the form document, along with all codes necessary to tell Microsoft Word what information is to be merged. The second file, a data source, contains records of data that are to be merged into the primary file.**

KEY TERMS

active window   header   record
data source   main document   template
field   merge
footer   page layout view

COMMAND SUMMARY

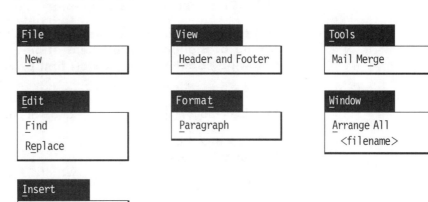

File	View	Tools
New	Header and Footer	Mail Merge

Edit	Format	Window
Find	Paragraph	Arrange All
Replace		<filename>

Insert
Date and Time

REVIEW QUESTIONS

1. What is the purpose of arranging windows?

2. What is the difference between the Cut and Copy commands?

3. What does "right align" mean? How do you enter text aligned right?

4. What does "decimal align" mean? How do you enter numbers with decimal alignment?

5. What is the difference between a normal view and a page layout view?

6. How do you enter the current date in the document?

7. In a find or replace, how do you make search case sensitive?

8. In a find or replace, what happens if you select "Match Whole Word Only"?

9. In Merge, how do you automatically eliminate blank lines for a field that is empty?

10. What are the two files needed in Merge? Explain the purpose of each file.

EXERCISES

1. Enter the following memo. (This exercise also requires you to copy information from the file WP2EX2.)

   MEMORANDUM

   DATE: *current date*

   TO: **All Employees**

   FROM: **Barbara Pettway**

   SUBJECT: **Recipe Contest Winner**

   Jackie Copeland, of the Finance Office, was selected the winner of the food contest held at our annual fall picnic. The following spaghetti recipe won first prize of $25.

   a. Copy the recipe from file WD2EX2 here.
   b. Add the following to ingredients at an appropriate location.

   1/2 cup diced celery
   Parmesan cheese

   c. Check the spelling.
   d. Save the file on the disk as file **WP3EX1**.
   e. Print the letter.

2. Enter the following memo. (This exercise also requires you to copy information from the file WP1EX3 to paste into this document.)

   MEMORANDUM

   DATE: *current date*

   TO: **Market Analysis Department**

   FROM: **Charles Jackson, President**

   SUBJECT: **Water Saddle**

Al Jenkins of Research has come up with a water saddle which shows some promise.

a. Copy the block of text from WP1EX3, beginning with "Recently, our department ..." and ending with " ... causing chafing." Indent both paragraphs 0.5".

b. Add the following:

Please look into the dude ranch market and provide an estimate for product orders over each of the next five years.

c. Check the spelling.

d. Save the file on the disk as **WP3EX2**.

e. Print the memo.

3. Create the following report.

a. Check the spelling.

b. Save as **WP3EX3**.

c. Print the report.

CHILD-WATCH SERVICES COMPANY
TRIAL BALANCE
current date

Cash (111)	$1,780	
Accounts Receivable (112)	1,600	
Equipment (141)	990	
Buses (143)	7,400	
Notes Payable (211)		$7,000
Accounts Payable (212)		1,470
Janet Escamilla, Capital (311)		3,300
	$11,770	$11,770

4 Graphics, Columns, Templates, and Tables

OBJECTIVES

Upon completion of the material presented in this lesson, you should understand the following aspects of Microsoft Word:

☐ **Inserting a border**

☐ **Creating newspaper-style columns**

☐ **Inserting a graphic picture**

☐ **Using a template**

☐ **Creating a table**

STARTING OFF

Turn on your computer, start Windows, and launch the Microsoft Word program as you did in previous lessons. Insert your data disk in disk drive. If necessary, maximize the Word application window.

You will learn the use of columns and graphic pictures by creating a newspaper-style document. Newspaper-style documents have multiple columns on a single page. Text flows from column to column. That is, as you enter text, it fills the first column, then the next column on the same page. When the last column on the page is full, text starts to fill the first column on the next page. When you add or delete text in any of the columns, the remaining text adjusts to keep the columns full. In addition, a newspaper-style document usually has a heading at the top of the first page, and some graphic pictures included in the story.

You will create a newsletter for Sierra Loma Homeowners Association as shown in Figure 4-1.

Figure 4-1

SIERRA LOMA LOG
Newsletter for Sierra Loma Homeowners Association

October, 1995

HOSE BIBS
Many residents have not disconnected their hoses from the outside hose bib since we have had such warm weather. The hose will act as a vacuum and trap the water inside the faucet extension behind the wall. When the water freezes and expands, the pipe may crack under the pressure of the ice. Then when the hose is used, the water runs under your house or into the wall causing substantial damage. Please disconnect your hoses. Should you have a problem, the Association will not be responsible for either the repair to the hose bib or the resulting damage to your home.

HEAT IN UNOCCUPIED UNITS
 If your unit is left vacant, it is important to leave enough heat so as to prevent your water pipes from freezing. Any subsequent damage resulting from frozen pipes will be the homeowner's responsibility, and not subject to insurance claims.

WINDOW WASHING
The Association has had several inquiries as to homeowners wanting their windows washed. The Association does not provide this service. If you check the Yellow Pages, there are several licensed and insured companies available.

MAINTENANCE AND LANDSCAPE
There will be a "skeleton" maintenance crew from November 1, 1995, through March, 1996. Should, if, or when we

have snow, they will be shoveling it from the walks. For your safety, please do not use salt of any kind on the sidewalks. The snow melts when the salt is applied, and refreezes to a slick, icy, and dangerous condition. If you have an area needing "special attention," contact Fred Leisler, maintenance supervisor, at 747-7600.

ASSOCIATION DUES
The monthly homeowners dues per unit will be raised to $96.00, effective January 1, 1996, in order to keep up with escalating insurance, utility fees, and maintenance costs.

Remember, the dues must be paid on or before the first of each month. There is a $10.00 late fee after the 20th. If you have questions regarding your account or your payment history, feel free to call Cindy Anderson, bookkeeper for Sierra Loma Association.

BOARD MEETING DATES
The Board of Directors' meetings are held on the third Wednesday of each month at the Clubhouse, starting at 7:00 p.m. All owners are welcome to attend.

There are four basic steps to creating this document: (1) creating the heading (or title); (2) entering text; (3) specifying the column format; and (4) adding graphics.

Any graphics figures can be inserted either as you enter text or after all text has been entered. You will be saving your document using different filenames at various stages of creation. This way, should you make a mistake with your document, you can start from the previous step.

Depending on the font and character size you use, your document may not look the same as shown in this manual. The example in this manual uses various sizes of Times New Roman.

CREATING THE HEADING (TITLE)

You will first insert the text for title. As you noticed, the title for the newsletter is in characters larger than normal. The character size can be changed by using different sizes as discussed in Lesson 2. You will use 24-point characters.

■ Click on the arrow next to the size indicator on the Formatting toolbar or from the Format menu, then select Font to change the point size to 24.

■ Type **SIERRA LOMA LOG** centered on the line.

P R A C T I C E   T I M E   4 - 1

1. Enter the second line of the title, **Newsletter for Sierra Loma Homeowners Association**. The text is to be centered and entered using 12 point type.

2. Insert a blank line (press Enter twice).

3. Enter the date **October, 1995** right-justified in 10 point type.

4. Press Enter. (Make sure that there is one blank line between the date and the end mark.)

5. Make the entire heading bold.

6. Save the document as **WD4A** on your data disk.

Your document should look like the one shown in Figure 4-2.

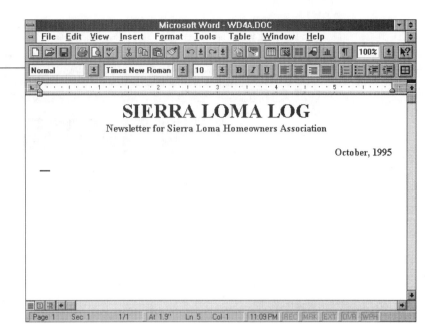

Figure 4-2

INSERTING A HORIZONTAL LINE

You will use the Border command in the Format menu to insert the line. Although a border can be inserted from the Format menu's Borders and Shading command, you will use the tool button here.

■ You may want to show all non-printing characters so that you know exactly where you are positioning the insertion point. Remember, this is done from the Tools menu's Option command.

■ Position the insertion point to the right of the date, and drag upward to select the entire text.

■ Click on the Border tool button, at the mouse pointer in Figure 4-3.

▶ *The Border toolbar is inserted, as shown in Figure 4-3.*

Various buttons on the toolbar let you insert a line above the selection, below the selection, at the left edge, right edge, and so on. Also, the leftmost selection lets you specify the thickness of the line.

■ Click on the down arrow at the right of the line width selector, then select 2¼ point as the width.

■ Specify drawing line at the bottom of the selected text. That is, click on the second button from the left.

▶ *The line has been inserted.*

■ Save the document as **WD4B** on your data disk.

Figure 4-3

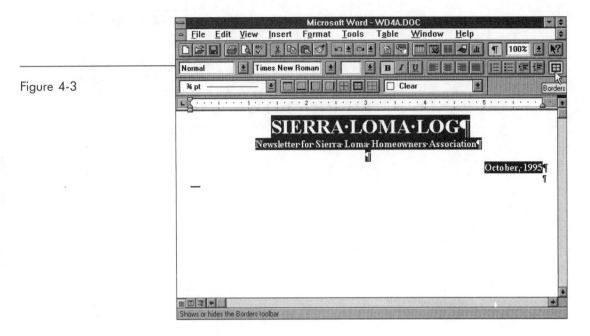

■ Click on the Border tool button again to return to the normal mode.

■ Position the insertion point on the blank line below the border.

You will now insert the text for the newsletter. The text will be long enough to cover two columns.

■ Press ⌈Enter⌉ to insert a blank line.

■ Change the alignment to Left.

■ Enter the following text in 12-point type. The headings are in bold.

HOSE BIBS
Many residents have not disconnected their hoses from the outside hose bib since we have had such warm weather. The hose will act as a vacuum and trap the water inside the faucet extension behind the wall. When the water freezes and expands, the pipe may crack under the pressure of the ice. Then when the hose is used, the water runs under your house or into the wall causing substantial damage. Please disconnect your hoses. Should you have a problem, the <u>Association will not be responsible</u> for either the repair to the hose bib or the resulting damage to your home.

HEAT IN UNOCCUPIED UNITS
If your unit is left vacant, it is important to leave enough heat so as to prevent your water pipes from freezing. Any subsequent damage resulting from frozen pipes will be the homeowner's responsibility, and not subject to insurance claims.

WINDOW WASHING

The Association has had several inquiries as to homeowners wanting their windows washed. The Association does not provide this service. If you check the Yellow Pages, there are several licensed and insured companies available.

MAINTENANCE AND LANDSCAPE

There will be a "skeleton" maintenance crew from November 1, 1995, through March, 1996. Should, if, or when we have snow, they will be shoveling it from the walks. For your safety, please do not use salt of any kind on the sidewalks. The snow melts when the salt is applied, and refreezes to a slick, icy and dangerous condition. If you have an area needing "special attention," contact Fred Leisler, maintenance supervisor, at 747-7600.

ASSOCIATION DUES

The monthly homeowners dues per unit will be raised to $96.00, effective January 1, 1996, in order to keep up with escalating insurance, utility fees, and maintenance costs.

Remember, the dues must be paid on or before the first of each month. There is a $10.00 late fee after the 20th. If you have questions regarding your account or your payment history, feel free to call Cindy Anderson, bookkeeper for Sierra Loma Association.

BOARD MEETING DATES

The Board of Directors' meetings are held on the third Wednesday of each month at the Clubhouse, starting at 7:00 p.m. All owners are welcome to attend.

■   Check spelling, then save as **WD4C**.

CREATING NEWSPAPER-TYPE COLUMNS

Now you are ready to define the columns, but first let's change the view so that the true layout of the document is displayed onscreen.

■   From the View menu, select Page Layout.

▶   *The display shows the true layout of the document.*

■   Place the insertion point before the word "Hose" on the first line of text.

■   Click on the Column button ▦ on the toolbar. You will see a small diagram that represents four columns, as shown in Figure 4-4.

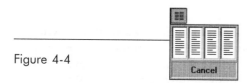

Figure 4-4

■   Click on the second column from the left to indicate two columns.

▶   *The entire document appears in two columns, not just the text from the insertion point down. You can see the result on the Print Preview screen shown in Figure 4-5.*

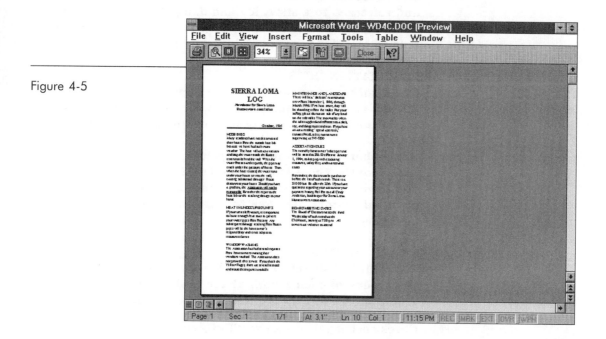

Figure 4-5

If you want some of the text on a page to cross multiple columns, the page must be divided into two **sections**—one formatted to one column, and the other to two columns. Ordinarily, you would create a section by inserting a section break at the appropriate location and defining display format for each section. However, right now, you will use the Column command to do both.

■   Click on the Column tool button, and select the first column in the diagram to put the entire document back in one column.

■   Make sure that the insertion point is located just before the word "Hose" on the first line of text.

■   From the Format menu, select Columns.

▶   *The Columns dialog box is displayed, as shown in Figure 4-6.*

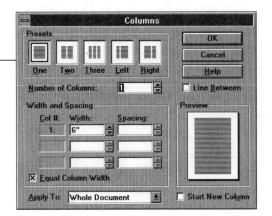

Figure 4-6

- ■ Type **2** in the Number of Columns text box.

- ■ Click on the down arrow key on the Apply To box.

- ■ Select This Point Forward, then complete the command.

  - ▶ *The document is in two columns from the insertion point down.*

- ■ Save the file as **WD4D** on your data disk.

ADDING GRAPHIC PICTURES

You now decide that it might be nice to add a picture. You will insert the picture in the file houses.wmf at the beginning of the section "Heat in Unoccupied Units."

N O T E : If the standard installation procedure for Microsoft Word was followed, this picture is available in the Clipart directory within the directory containing Microsoft Word. You may want to check with your instructor to be sure.

- ■ Place the insertion point at the beginning of the article on "Heat in Unoccupied Units." Be sure the insertion point is at the body of the article, not the heading.

- ■ From the Insert menu, select Picture.

  - ▶ *The Insert Picture dialog box, as shown in Figure 4-7, is displayed.*

- ■ Specify the appropriate drive and directory where Microsoft Word clipart is found.

- ■ Select the file houses.wmf in the Find Name list box.

  - ▶ *The image appears in the Preview display.*

Figure 4-7

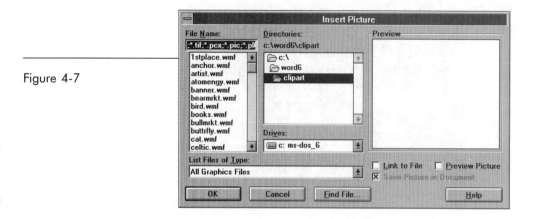

■   Complete the command.

▶   *The picture is inserted at the insertion point position, as shown in Figure 4-8.*

Figure 4-8

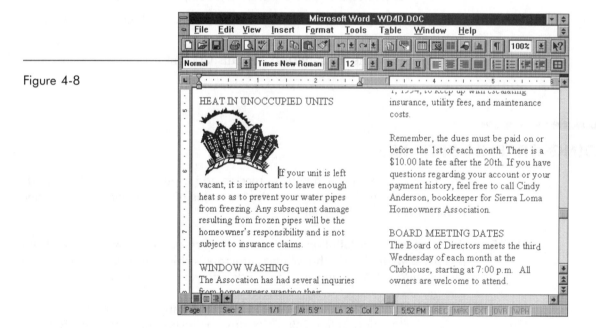

The picture is too big. You can change the size, however.

■   Click on the picture.

▶   *A box appears around the picture, as shown in Figure 4-9.*

The little black squares on the box are called **handles**. These are used to change the size of the picture.

■   Position the mouse on the lower-right handle and drag the handle slightly up and to the left until the picture is about half the original size.

Figure 4-9

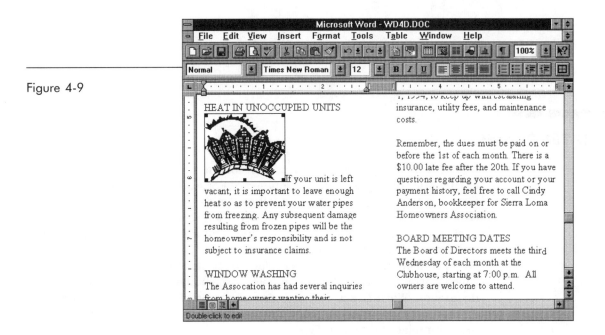

You might notice that the area to the right of the picture is left blank. That is, text is not wrapping around the picture. You can change this, too.

- Make sure that the picture is still selected.

- From the Insert menu, select Frame.

  ▶ *The text now wraps around the picture, as shown in Figure 4-10.*

Figure 4-10

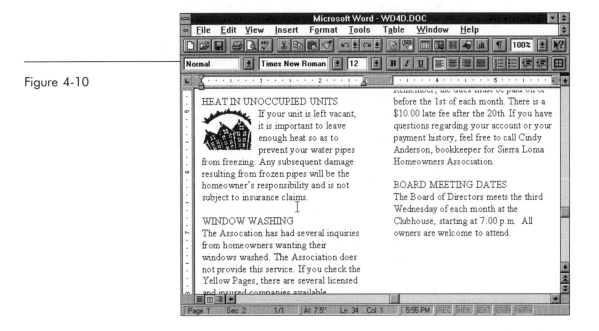

   ■   Save your file as **WD4E**.

   ■   Print the document.

USING TEMPLATES

A document ***template*** is a special document you can use as a pattern to create other documents of the same type. For example, you can use a letter template to produce letters that follow the same format. When you use a template, you needn't start from scratch each time you create a document. Tasks such as setting the margins, choosing a font, and creating headers and footers have already been done.

As explained earlier, every Word document is based on a template called Normal. That is, if you don't select a template when you create a new document, Word bases the new document on the Normal template. Any existing document can be made into a template by specifying it as a Document Template in the File Type.

You may wonder why you need a template. You can always open a document and edit it to suit your needs. However, when you do this, you have to make sure that you do not save the file using the same filename, thus destroying the original. When you open a template file, the new document will have the standard default name, such as Document 1.

Right now, you will create a memo using the memo2.dot template.

   ■   From the File menu, select New.

      ▶   *The New dialog box is displayed.*

   ■   Scroll the Template list box to select Memo2, then complete the command.

      ▶   *A new document opens, displaying the template, as shown in Figure 4-11.*

You can see that the memo has already been laid out nicely and the current date has already been entered. All you need to do is to substitute your entries to those enclosed in brackets.

   ■   Drag to select [*Names*] that follows "TO:."

   ■   Type **John Callahan**.

   ■   Drag to select [*Names*] that follows "FROM:."

   ■   Type ***your name***.

   ■   Similarly, enter **Cost Estimate** as the entry to follow "RE:" and type **Michael Myers** as the name to follow "CC:."

Figure 4-11

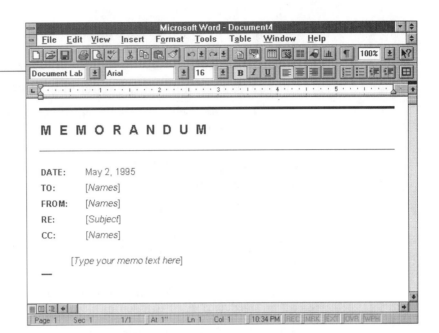

- For the text, drag to select [*Type your memo text here*], then type the following:

  As per our conversation, the following is a cost estimate for a new computer for your office.

- Press (Enter) twice to insert a blank line.

- Save the document as **MEMO1** on your data disk.

Next, you want to insert a table showing various costs.

INSERTING TABLES

Microsoft Word's **table** feature lets you add a grid to a document and fill it with text. This feature can be used to create a variety of documents, including forms, calendars, and documents similar to spreadsheets. Tables can perform simple arithmetic calculations, similar to the calculations a spreadsheet program can perform.

Before you begin working with tables, you must learn the basic vocabulary associated with them. Tables are made up of **rows**, which run horizontally across the page, and **columns**, which run vertically down the page. Rows are assigned numbers (starting with number 1 and going down the page), and columns are assigned letters of the alphabet (starting with A). The location where a row and column intersect is called a **cell**. Cells are assigned names based on their relative position within the table. The cell at column C, row 4 is referred to as cell C4.

Using tables is a two-step process. First, you create the table by defining the number of columns and rows that make up the table. The second step is adding the text and numbers to the table.

■   From the T<u>a</u>bles menu, select <u>I</u>nsert Table.

▶   *The Create Tables dialog box is displayed as shown in Figure 4-12.*

Figure 4-12

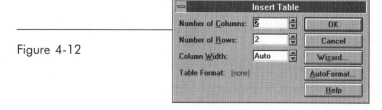

You need to enter the number of columns and rows to be created for the table. Here, you want two columns and five rows.

■   Enter **2** for the number of columns and **5** for the number of rows.

■   Complete the command.

Alternative: You can also specify the number of rows and columns through the Column button 🔲 by dragging the mouse to the appropriate row and column on the grid that is displayed.

▶   *A table with the appropriate number of rows and columns is inserted, as shown in Figure 4-13. The insertion point is located in cell A1.*

Figure 4-13

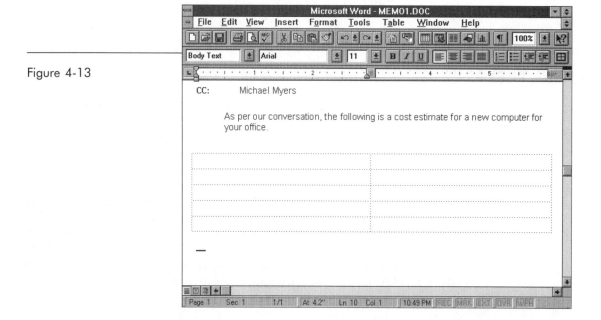

WORD PROCESSING

- Type the following information in cell A1. The text will wrap within the cell, so there is no need for you to press Enter at the edge of the cell.

  486DX with 8 MB RAM, dual floppy, 120 MB Hard Disk, extended keyboard

- Position the insertion point in cell B1 by pressing Tab or clicking in the cell.

- Type **1299**.

- Enter the following in the cells indicated:

cell A2	**Super VGA monitor**
cell B2	**350**
cell A3	**Mouse, DOS, Windows**
cell B3	**85**
cell A4	**Ethernet Card**
cell B4	**69**
cell A5	**TOTAL**

You look at the screen and decide that the first column should be wider.

- Position the mouse pointer on the line between two columns.

  ▶ *The pointer changes, as shown in Figure 4-14.*

Figure 4-14

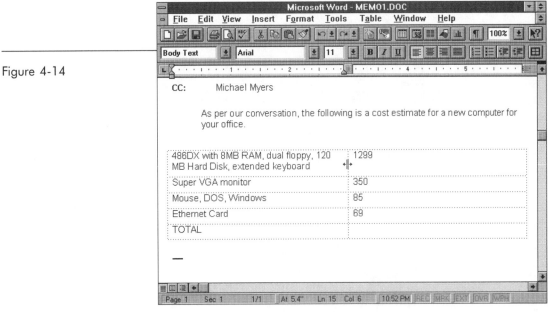

■ Drag the line to the right, to the 4″ position on the ruler. That is, hold down the left mouse button and move the mouse pointer to the right. When you are at the 4″ position, release the mouse button.

▶ *The column width, as well as the text in cells, adjust.*

P R A C T I C E   T I M E   4 - 2

Drag the left edge of the table to the right so that it is aligned to the paragraph above.

Figure 4-15 shows the correct alignment.

Figure 4-15

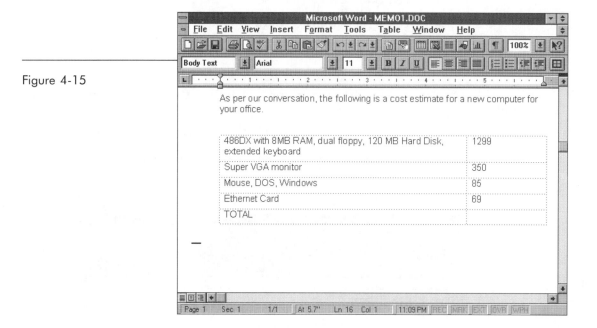

Since the second column contains monetary figures, you'd like to change the way it is displayed. First you need to select the column.

■ Position the insertion point in cell B1.

■ From the Table menu, select Select Column.

▶ *The column is selected.*

The following are two alternatives for selecting a column.

To select a column using the *keyboard*, position the insertion point in cell B1, then hold down the Shift key and press the ↓ key repeatedly.

To select a column using the *mouse*, move the mouse pointer just above the top border of cell B1 so that the mouse pointer turns into an arrow, as shown in Figure 4-16, then click the left button on the mouse.

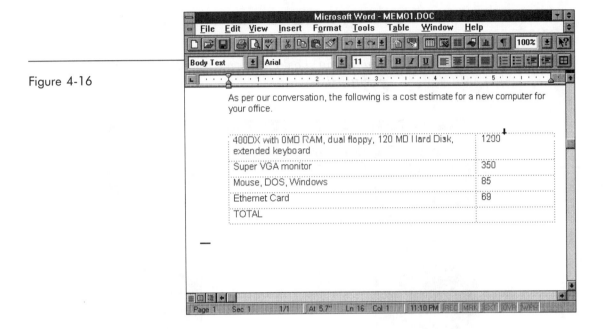

Figure 4-16

Now you can change the display format of column B.

■   Change the alignment to Right using either the Format, Paragraph command or the tool button.

In cell B5, you want to display the total cost.

■   Position the insertion point in cell B5.

■   From the Table menu, select Formula.

▶   *The Formula dialog box appears as shown in Figure 4-17.*

Notice that the default formula is the one to sum the entries above.

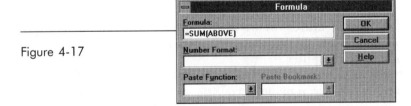

Figure 4-17

■   Complete the command.

▶   *The sum of values in cells B1 through B4 appears in cell B5.*

■ Position the insertion point below the table.

■ Insert a blank line.

■ Finish the memo by entering the text below:

If I can provide further information, please feel free to call me.

▶ *Your memo should look similar to the one displayed in Figure 4-18.*

Figure 4-18

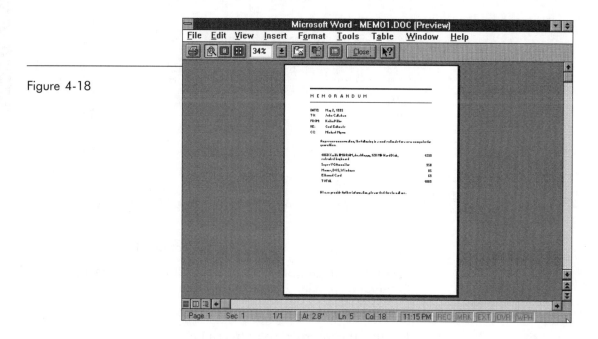

■ Save the document as file **MEMO2** on your data disk.

ENDING LESSON 4

There are many more features to Microsoft Word; these should be explored on your own. Just remember, the only way to learn to use a word processor is by working on the computer.

Exit Microsoft Word and Windows as explained in Lesson 1. There is no need to save changes you made to your file.

WORD PROCESSING

S U M M A R Y

☐ **The four basic steps in creating newspaper-type documents are: (1) Creating the title; (2) Entering text; (3) Defining the format; and (4) adding graphics.**

☐ **A line can be inserted in a document using the Border command in the Format menu.**

☐ **A graphic picture can be inserted in a document as text is being entered or after all text has been entered.**

☐ **A graphic picture can be sized using the handles.**

☐ **A document template is a special file you can use as a pattern to create other documents of the same type.**

☐ **The table feature lets you add a grid to a document and fill it with text. It can even perform some simple calculations similar to the ones used in spreadsheet programs.**

K E Y T E R M S

cell	rows	table
column	section	template
handles		

C O M M A N D S U M M A R Y

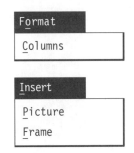

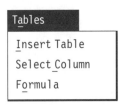

R E V I E W Q U E S T I O N S

1. Explain the steps involved in inserting a horizontal line using the Border command.

2. When using the Column tool button to specify the number of columns, how do you indicate two columns?

3. What do you have to do to display both single-column text and double-column text on a single page?

4. When you insert a graphic picture, where is it inserted within a document?

5. How do you change the size of a graphic picture?

6. What command do you give to make text wrap around a graphic picture?

7. What is a template?

8. Define the following terms: row, columns, and cell.

9. How do you change the column width of a table?

10. How do you display total of all values that appear above a given cell?

EXERCISES

1. Create a résumé using a template.
   a. Save it as **WD4EX1** on your data disk.
   b. Print the résumé.

2. Create the document shown in Figure 4-19. The graphics picture is disk.wmf in the Clipart directory of the MS Word directory.
   a. Save the document as **WD4EX2**.
   b. Print the document.

Figure 4-19

Care and Handling of Floppy Disks

 You must use proper care in handling floppy disks. They are very fragile. Here are some suggestions for their care and handling:

Insert the disk in disk drive, access window (for 5 1/4") or disk drive metal (for 3 1/2") end first, label side up.

- For 5 1/4" disk, always keep the disk in its envelope when not in use.
- For 3 1/2" disk, never open the mechanical shutter while a disk is out of the drive. Doing this exposes the surface to dirt, dust, fingerprints, etc.
- Do not touch the surface of the disk through the access window or wipe the surface with rags or tissue paper.
- Do not let disks collect dust.
- Keep disks out of the sun and away from other sources of heat, which can cause them to warp or lose data.
- Keep disks at least 2 feet away from magnetic fields, such as those generated by electrical motors, radios, televisions, tape recorders, library theft detectors, and other devices. A strong magnetic field will erase information on a disk.
- When writing on a disk label already attached to the disk, use only a felt-tipped pen. Never use any sort of instrument with a sharp point. Also, never use an eraser. Eraser dust is abrasive and may get on the mylar surface.
- Keep disks at room temperature before use (a disk just brought in from a cold blizzard has shrunk enough in size that its tracks are not where the system expects to find them).
- Never open the drive door or remove a disk while the drive is running--that is, while the red in-use light on the front of the disk drive is on. If you do, you can damage the data on your disk.
- Check to make sure that the gummed tab and external labels are on securely.

3. Create the document shown in Figure 4-20. The graphics picture is computer.wmf in the Clipart directory of the MS Word directory.

    a. Save the document as **WD4EX3**.

    b. Print the newsletter.

Figure 4-20

CAMPUS COMPUTER CLUB
WEEKLY NEWSLETTER

Volume 5, No. 2   October 7, 1993

SEMESTER DUES DUE
Fall semester dues of $5.00, to help cover the cost of computer paper and online file storage, are due by October 10. A fee of $10.00 will be assessed to those who are late with dues.

FALL WORKSHOP SCHEDULE
Due to a mix-up in scheduling with the Computer Science Department's seminars, the Campus Computer Club seminars schedule published last week is void. Please stay tuned for a revised schedule.

IMPORTANT ANNOUNCEMENT
Anyone attempting to infect the campus computer with a worm or virus will be prosecuted. See next item for related info.

SEMINAR SPEAKER
FBI agent Mort Merriweather will speak next Friday at 3 p.m. on Computer Bugs, Worms, and Viruses. Mort has been involved in several Federal investigations of computer chaos. He says he will give some hints on keeping personal computers "well," and will show us some examples of destructive viruses (including the penalties that their perpetrators incurred).

THIS WEEK'S TIP
Keep your files in order. Use the TIDY_FILE utility written by Kitty Hawkins to delete obsolete versions that clutter disk space. See Chet Williams in the Lab for details.

TWENTY YEARS AGO
Randy Kondo's father has provided us with a newsletter that the computer club published in 1969. An enlarged photocopy is available in our office for those of you interested in stone age computing. To wit:

The IBM 1620 in use has a memory size of 20,000 characters.

Users can submit one job per day on punched cards.

The new card reader reads 10 cards per second.

The newsletter doesn't say it, but there is no on-line storage for student programs or data, and no magnetic tape drives.

The programming languages most used are FORTRAN IV and Assembler.

The newsletter is typed, get this, using a manual typewriter!

Word 6.0 Projects

PROJECT 1

1. Create the memo shown below, save it as **WDP1**, and print it.

   MEMORANDUM

   DATE: *current date*

   TO: **Dallas Irving, President**

   FROM: *your name*

   SUBJECT: **Water Saddle Market Evaluation**

   Our recent survey of market prospects for the water saddle yielded the following conclusions.

   1. **The projected sales for five years should be about 1,600 saddles.**

   2. **The dude ranch market is but one of three viable markets: private owners and horseback riding stables are other strong markets.**

   3. **It is important to get in first with a quality product. Potential buyers are very conservative. If our initial product has serious flaws, all our subsequent products will not sell.**

   4. **Cowpokes, Inc. is currently well-positioned to enter this market.**

   Some details of our findings include the following items.

   <u>Breakdown by Market and Year</u>

Year	Dude Ranches	Privates	Horse Rides	Total
1	50	100	50	200
2	100	100	50	250
3	150	100	50	300
4	200	100	100	400
5	250	100	100	450
Total	750	500	350	1600

<u>**Consumer Concerns about a New Product**</u>

- **Is it produced by a company that can be relied upon?**

- **Does it represent an improvement, not just a trendy twist?**

- **Is it reasonably priced?**

- **Is it durable?**

PROJECT 2

1. Enter the following in the data source file to be used in a merge. Save it as file **WDP2DAT** on your data disk.

Field Definition

Field 1   **Borrower**

Field 2   **Lender**

Field 3   **Principal**

Field 4   **Payment**

Field 5   **Date**

Field 6   **Rate**

Field 7   **City**

Field 8   **State**

Field 9   **Day**

Field 10   **Month**

Field 11   **Year**

Data to Be Entered

Field 1	**Marty Python**	Field 1	**Roni Andrews**
Field 2	**Bank of Arizona**	Field 2	**Bank of Nevada**
Field 3	**$100,000**	Field 3	**$67,000**
Field 4	**$1,300**	Field 4	**$612.88**
Field 5	**May 11, 1995**	Field 5	**October 14, 1995**
Field 6	**10%**	Field 6	**10.5%**
Field 7	**Phoenix**	Field 7	**Reno**
Field 8	**Arizona**	Field 8	**Nevada**
Field 9	**11**	Field 9	**14**

Field 10 **November**   Field 10 **September**

Field 11 **1994**   Field 11 **1994**

2. Enter the following document as the main document to be used in a merge. Save it as **WDPMAIN** on your data disk.

Promissory Note

The <BORROWER> agrees to pay <LENDER> the principal sum of <PRINCIPAL>. By this note, <BORROWER> agrees to make monthly installments in the sum of <PAYMENT> or more, until said obligation is paid in full. The first payment is due on or before <DATE>, and all successive payments are due on the first day of each succeeding month thereafter until paid in full.

This obligation shall bear interest on the declining principal balance at a rate of <RATE> per annum. In the event the undersigned fails to make a required payment within thirty days when due, then the remaining balance of the obligation shall become due and payable in full. Furthermore, if <BORROWER> is more than 30 days late on a required payment, <LENDER> can elect to recover the collateral securing this obligation, as described below, and dispose of same in any commercially reasonable manner, applying the proceeds of such sale toward the balance remaining hereon.

Additional payments or prepayment in full may be paid by <BORROWER> without penalty.

No delay on the part of <LENDER> in the exercise of any right or remedy shall operate as a waiver thereof, and no single partial exercise by the same of any right or remedy shall preclude further exercise of any right or remedy.

The obligation evidenced hereby has been made in <CITY,> <STATE>, and shall be governed by the laws of the State of <STATE>.

Dated this <DAY> day of <MONTH>, <YEAR>.

_____

<BORROWER>, borrower

_____

<LENDER>, lender

3. Merge the files and get a printout.

Microsoft Word 6.0 for Windows Command Summary

This section is a quick reference for Microsoft Word commands covered in this manual. This is *not* a complete list of all Microsoft Word commands.

Command	from Menu	Shortcut
Alignment	Format, Paragraph	
Center text		Ctrl+E or ▤
Justified		Ctrl+J or ▤
Left alignment		Ctrl+L or ▤
Right alignment		Ctrl+R or ▤
Appearance	Format, Font	
Bold		Ctrl+B or **B**
Italic		Ctrl+I or *I*
Underline		Ctrl+U or U̲
Arranging window	Window, Arrange All	
Bullet		▤
Column	Format, Columns	▥
Copy a text	Edit, Copy	Ctrl+C or ▤
Cut a text	Edit, Cut	Ctrl+X or ✂
Date—inserting current	Insert, Date and Time	
Display actual layout	View, Page Layout	
Display non-printing characters	Tools, Options	¶
Display ruler	View, Ruler	
Exit Word	File, Exit	Alt+F4
Find text	Edit, Find	Ctrl+F
Font	Format, Font	formatting toolbar
Frame—insert	Insert, Frame	
Header or footer	View, Header and Footer	
Help	Help, Contents	F1 ▤

Command	from Menu	Shortcut
Insert a horizontal line	Format, Borders and Shading	⊞
Line indentation	Format, Paragraph	ruler
Line spacing	Format, Paragraph	
Margin Setting	File, Page Setup, Margins	ruler
Merge document	Tools, Mail Merge	
Open an existing document	File, Open	Ctrl+O or 📂
Open a new document	File, New	Ctrl+N or 🗋
Page break	Insert, Break	Ctrl+Enter
Page numbering	Insert, Page Numbers	
Paper orientation	File, Page Setup, Paper Size	
Paragraph indentation	Format, Paragraph	▤ or ruler
Paste text	Edit, Paste	Ctrl+V or 📋
Pictures—insert	Insert, Picture	
Preview a file	File, Preview	🔍
Print a file	File, Print	Ctrl+P or 🖨
Replace text	Edit, Replace	Ctrl+H
Save file with new name	File, Save As	
Save file with same name	File, Save	Ctrl+S or 💾
Size of characters	Format, Font	formatting toolbar
Spelling check	Tools, Spelling …	✓
Tables		
Insert a table	Tables, Insert Table	▦
Select a column	Tables, Select Column	
Insert a formula	Tables, Formula	
Tabs	Format, Tabs	ruler
Thesaurus	Tools, Thesaurus	Shift+F7
Undo typing	Edit, Undo Typing	Ctrl+Z or ↺
Windows—switching	Window, filename	

Glossary

active window   The window to which the next command will apply. If a window is active, its title bar changes color to differentiate it from other windows.

align   To line up.

application window   A window that contains a running application. The name of the application appears at the top of this window.

border   The outer edge of a window.

bullets   A text format in which each item in a list of items is preceded by a small circle.

byte   A single character.

cell   Intersection of a row and a column in a table.

centered   Text that is centered, line by line, on the page.

check box   A small square box that appears in a dialog box and that can be selected or cleared. When the check box is selected, an X appears in the window.

click   To press and release a mouse button quickly.

clipboard   The temporary storage location used to transfer data between documents and between applications.

close   To remove a document window or application window from the desktop.

collapse a directory   To hide additional directory levels below a selected directory.

configuration   The arrangement of hardware and software in a computer system.

control menu box   The icon that opens the control menu for the window. It is always at the left of the title bar.

column   Vertical entries in a table.

cpi (characters per inch)   A measurement of type size.

current directory   The directory that is currently highlighted in the directory tree or whose directory window is the active window.

cursor   A symbol or flashing underscore that shows the position onscreen where an entry is made.

cut   To remove selected text from a document and place it temporarily on the clipboard; the text can then be pasted to a new location.

data source   In a merge operation, the file that contains the data to be merged into the main document.

default   A value, action, or setting that is automatically used when no alternate instructions are given. For example, the default drive is where the program looks for data files unless explicitly instructed otherwise.

desktop   The screen background for Windows on which windows, icons, and dialog boxes appear.

dialog box   A rectangular box that either requests or provides information. Many dialog boxes present options to choose among before Windows can carry out a command. Some dialog boxes present warnings or explain why a command cannot be completed.

dictionary   A list of correctly spelled words used by the Speller.

directory   A file or a part of a disk that contains the names and locations of other files on the disk.

directory tree   A graphic display in File Manager of the directory structure of a disk.

document window   A window within an application window that contains a document you create or modify by using an application. There can be more than one document window in an application window.

double-click   To rapidly press and release a mouse button twice without moving the mouse. Double-clicking usually carries out an action, such as opening an icon.

drag   To hold down the mouse button while moving the mouse.

drag and drop   To move an item onscreen by pointing to it, then dragging it to the desired position.

drop-down list box   A single-line dialog box that opens to display a list of choices.

drop-down menu   The sub-option menu that appears when an option in the menu bar is highlighted.

endmark   An underscore that shows the end of the document.

expand directory   To show currently hidden levels in the directory tree.

field   A distinct data element used in the merge feature. Each record in a secondary file is composed of fields.

file   A collection of data records with related content; data stored as a named unit on a peripheral storage medium such as a disk.

filename   The name assigned a file; must be no more than eight characters long, and may include an optional extension of a period plus up to three characters.

find   A utility that allows you to look for all occurrences of specific words or characters in a document.

first-line indent marker   A symbol on the ruler that indicates how far the first line of paragraph is to be indented.

font   The appearance of characters on your screen and printout, which is determined by the typeface, size, and special treatment such as bold, underline, italics, and so on.

footer   Lines of text that appear at the bottom of every page.

frame   A container into which you can put an object (such as a graphic). Once an object is in a frame, it can be dragged to anywhere in the page.

format a disk   To prepare a blank disk to receive data.

function keys   Keys ([F1] to [F10] or [F12]) that allow special functions to be entered with a single keystroke.

group   A collection of programs in Program Manager. Grouping your programs makes them easier to find when you want to start them.

group icon   The graphic that represents a minimized Program Manager group. Double-clicking on the group icon opens the group window.

group window   A window that displays the items in a group within Program Manager.

handles   Black squares that appear on the box around a graphic that can be used to change the size of the picture.

hanging indent   Text layout in which the first line of a paragraph is flush left, while runover lines are indented.

hard page break   A page break code that is specially inserted into the text.

header   Lines of text that appear at the top of every page.

header record   In a merge, the first row of the data source where field names appear. The header records act as column headings for the information on the data source.

I-beam   The shape taken by the mouse pointer when it is in the workspace.

icon   A graphic representation of various elements in Windows, such as disk drives, files, applications, and documents.

inactive window   Any open window in which you are not currently working.

insert mode   An editing mode in which the characters you type are inserted at the insertion point, pushing previous characters tothe right.

insertion point   The place where text will be inserted when you next type a character.

justified   Text that is aligned on both the left and right margins.

landscape   Paper orientation in which the document is wider than it is long.

launching   Starting an application program. This is usually done by double-clicking on the application icon.

left-aligned   Text that is aligned on the left margin.

left indent marker   A symbol on the ruler that shows how far the text is to be indented from the left margin.

list box   Within a dialog box, a box listing available choices, for example, the list of all available files in a directory. If all the choices won't fit, the list box has a vertical scroll bar.

main document   The file containing the document in a merge operation. Using the merge feature, you can print multiple copies, each incorporating data in the data file.

maximize button   The small box containing an up arrow at the right of the title bar. It can be clicked to enlarge a window to its maximum size.

menu   A list of items, most of which are commands. Menu names appear in the menu bar near the top of the window.

menu bar   The horizontal bar containing the menu choices.

merge   A feature that allows you to insert the data from a data source into specified positions in the main document.

minimize button   The small box containing a down arrow at the right of the title bar. It can be clicked to shrink a window to an icon.

monospaced characters   A font in which all letters have the same width.

mouse   A cursor-control device that resembles a small box on wheels. As the box is rolled on a flat surface, the movement of the wheel signals the computer to move the cursor on the display screen in direct proportion to the movement of the mouse.

multitasking   The ability to run more than one application at a time without interrupting the execution of any of the active applications.

newspaper-style columns   Text format in which there are multiple columns on a single page. Text flows from column to column.

non-printing characters   Special characters entered into a document to indicate where certain keys, such as Enter and Tab, were pressed. These characters are not displayed when the document is printed.

open   To display the contents of a file in a window or to enlarge an icon to a window.

page layout view   Document display which reflects the way document will be printed.

paste   To insert text from the clipboard to a new location in a document; see cut.

pathname   The direction to a directory or file within your system. For example, C:\DIR1\FILEA is the pathname for the FILEA file in the DIR1 subdirectory on drive C.

point   To move the pointer onscreen until it rests on the item you want to select.

point size   The unit of measure commonly used to indicate font size. There are 72 points to an inch.

pointer   The arrow-shaped cursor on the screen that indicates the position of the mouse.

portrait   Paper orientation in which a sheet is longer than it is wide.

print preview   The feature that allows you to view the text onscreen as it will be printed.

program group   See group.

proportionally spaced characters   Font that uses varying widths for different letters; for example, an *m* is wider than an *i*, as it is here.

record   A single block of data used in the merge feature. Each block of data pertaining to a separate person or item is a record.

replace   A utility that searches for all occurrences of specific words or characters and replaces them with words or characters you specify.

restore button   The small box at the right of the title bar that contains a down arrow and an up arrow. The restore button appears after you have enlarged a window to its full size. It can be clicked to return the window to its previous size.

right-aligned   Text that is aligned on the right margin.

right indent marker   A symbol on the ruler that shows how far the text is to be indented from the right margin.

row   Horizontal entries in a table.

ruler   The bar at the top of the workspace that displays current settings for margins, tabs, justification, and spacing.

scroll   To move through a document by moving lines off the top or bottom of the screen. Word does this automatically as you enter text, or you can scroll through a document using the scroll bar.

section   A portion of the text. A section can be as short as a single paragraph or as long as an entire document. Each section can be formatted differently.

selection bar   An unmarked area along the left side of the text area. It is used to select text with the mouse. When the mouse pointer is in the selection bar, it turns into a right-pointing arrow.

soft font   A font that is downloaded to your printer's memory from a disk provided by the font's manufacturer.

soft page break   A page break that is inserted automatically by the program, based on specified margin and page length settings.

soft return   A line break that is inserted automatically by the program, based on specified margin settings.

status bar   A horizontal bar at the bottom of the document window that displays such information as the font style and type size being used and the insertion point position.

subdirectory   A directory contained within another directory. All directories are subdirectories of the root directory.

table   A grid that can be filled with text and numbers.

tabs   Settings that determine indents, or the new position of the insertion point each time you press Tab; by default, tabs are set at every half-inch.

task   An open application.

template   A special document you can use as a pattern to create other documents of the same type.

text area   The area of a window between the menu bar and the status bar which displays the document you are working with or information about the application you are working on.

text box   A box within a dialog box where you type information needed to carry out the chosen command.

title bar   The horizontal bar located at the top of a window containing the title of the window.

toggle   A command that alternatively turns a feature on and off.

tool bar   A section of the window containing buttons with icons, called tools, which you can click to perform certain operations.

typeface   The graphic style applied to characters; common typefaces are Couricr, Helvetica, and Times Roman. The typeface is often referred to as the font.

typeover (OVR) mode   An editing mode that replaces the character the insertion point is on with the character you type.

window   A rectangular area onscreen in which you view an application or document.

wordwrap   A feature that automatically moves a word at the end of a line to the next line.

work area   The area of a window that displays the information contained in the application window of the document with which you are working.

zoom   A feature that allows you to look at the text preview screen close up or from a distance.

Index

Introducing
Microsoft Excel 5.0
FOR
WINDOWS

Introducing

Microsoft Excel 5.0

FOR

WINDOWS

KEIKO PITTER

Mitchell **McGRAW-HILL**

New York St. Louis San Francisco Auckland Bogotá Caracas
Lisbon London Madrid Mexico Milan Montreal New Delhi
Paris San Juan Singapore Sydney Tokyo Toronto

Mitchell **McGRAW-HILL**
San Francisco, CA 94133

Introducing Microsoft Excel 5.0 for Windows

4 5 6 7 8 9 0   SEM SEM   9 0 9 8 7 6

ISBN 0-07-051596-4

Sponsoring editor: Roger Howell

Editorial assistant: Rhonda Sands

Technical reviewer: Bill Barth

Production supervisor: Leslie Austin

Project manager: Gary Palmatier, Ideas to Images

Interior designer and illustrator: Gary Palmatier

Cover designer: Christy Butterfield

Composition: Ideas to Images

Printer and binder: Semline, Inc.

Library of Congress Card Catalog No. 93-78721

Contents

1 Creating a Simple Spreadsheet

1

SPREADSHEET

2 Changing the Worksheet Format   26

3 Modifying the Worksheet   48

4 Using Charting Features

73

SPREADSHEET

5 Functions, Macros, and a Customized Toolbar   98

Introduction

INTRODUCING EXCEL 5.0 FOR WINDOWS

Electronic spreadsheets are used to analyze, summarize, and present numeric data. They simplify the mechanics of calculating and allow you to apply "what-if" scenarios to your formulas.

Spreadsheets can be used for finanical forecasting, budgeting, stock portfolio analysis, cost analysis—even for maintaining a household budget, tracking cash flow, or determining whether you can afford a new car.

Introducing Microsoft Excel 5.0 for Windows gives you the knowledge and expertise to develop simple to advanced spreadsheets. This tutorial helps you become comfortable with the essentials of Excel for Windows and feel confident exploring the program's capabilities.

Using This Module

To use this book, you need an 80286 computer (or higher) with at least 4MG of memory (RAM). The computer should also have a diskette drive, a mouse, MS DOS version 3.1 or higher, Windows 3.1 software or higher, and Excel 5.0 for Windows. A blank, formatted diskette is also required. If your configuration deviates from this, consult your instructor. This book assumes that you are familiar with both the basic operation of a computer system and of Microsoft Windows.

Each lesson in this book begins with goals that are listed under the heading "Objectives". Key terms are introduced in ***bold italic*** type; text to be typed by the user is shown in **bold**. Also, keep in mind the following:

■   This symbol is used to indicate the user's action.

▶   *This symbol is used to indicate the screen's response.*

Alternative: Presents mouse or keystroke alternatives to the command given above.

N O T E :   This format is for important user notes and tips.

P R A C T I C E   T I M E

These brief drills allow you to practice features previously discussed.

Finally, a series of projects, a command summary, and a glossary of key terms are found at the end of the book.

To study this book, you should first go through Lessons 1, 2, and 3. These lessons acquaint you with the basics of electronic spreadsheets. Lesson 4 introduces the charting features of Excel, and Lesson 5 covers functions, macros, and customized toolbars. The last two lessons can be studied in any order once you are familiar with the basics.

Creating a Simple Spreadsheet

O B J E C T I V E S

Upon completing the material presented in this lesson, you should understand the following aspects of Excel 5.0 for Windows:

- ☐ **Starting Excel**
- ☐ **Using spreadsheet terminology**
- ☐ **Identifying parts of the Excel window**
- ☐ **Creating a workbook**
- ☐ **Selecting cells**
- ☐ **Using the Name box**
- ☐ **Entering data into a workbook**
- ☐ **Clearing the contents of a cell**
- ☐ **Making text and numeric entries**
- ☐ **Using the AutoSum feature**
- ☐ **Entering simple formulas**
- ☐ **Saving a file on a disk**
- ☐ **Naming a sheet in a workbook**
- ☐ **Closing a worksheet**
- ☐ **Printing a workbook**
- ☐ **Exiting Excel**

STARTING EXCEL

Before starting Excel, start the Microsoft Windows program.

■   Start the Windows program. Make sure that the Program Manager is the only window displayed onscreen.

▶   *The installation procedure for Excel created a program group icon for Microsoft Excel 5.0 in the Program Manager window. See Figure 1-1.*

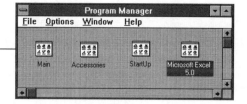

Figure 1-1

N O T E :   It is possible that on your computer, the Excel program was installed in the Microsoft Office group or as a part of the Windows Application group. If so, the procedure you use to load Excel may vary slightly. Check with your instructor for your particular setup.

■   Maximize the Program Manager window.

■   Double-click on the Microsoft Excel 5.0 group icon to open the Excel window.

▶   *The Microsoft Excel 5.0 group window, similar to the one in Figure 1-2, is displayed.*

Figure 1-2

The group window contains icons representing the Excel program and associated utility programs.

■   Launch the Excel program by double-clicking on the Microsoft Excel icon.

▶   *A copyright screen briefly appears, then the initial Excel screen appears, as shown in Figure 1-3.*

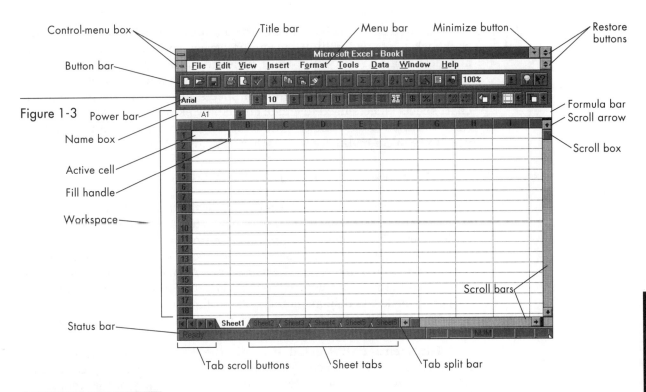

Figure 1-3

Labels (clockwise): Control-menu box, Title bar, Menu bar, Minimize button, Restore buttons, Formula bar, Scroll arrow, Scroll box, Scroll bars, Tab split bar, Sheet tabs, Tab scroll buttons, Status bar, Workspace, Fill handle, Active cell, Name box, Power bar, Button bar

THE EXCEL SCREEN

Figure 1-3 labels parts of the Excel window described in this lesson. The Microsoft Excel application window has all the basic components of a Windows screen—a title bar; a menu bar; a control-menu box; minimize, maximize, and restore buttons; and scroll bars. Also, at the bottom of the screen is the status bar, whose function is explained later.

You might notice that there are two restore buttons and two control-menu boxes. This is because, on the screen right now, two windows are displayed: the Excel application window and a new workbook window. The new workbook is contained within the **workspace**, or the area between the menu bar and the status bar, of the Excel application window, and the new workbook is already maximized.

■ Restore the workbook window by clicking on the lower restore button.

▶ *The workbook window is no longer maximized within the workspace of the Excel application window.*

Now you can see the workbook window more distinctly within the workspace. The workspace can hold several workbooks, depending on the available memory of your computer. The title bar of the Excel window displays "Microsoft Excel", and that of the workbook contains the workbook name: "Book1".

A **workbook** is a collection of sheets, arranged as though they are one on top of the next; they are identified by the **sheet tabs**, labeled "Sheet1",

"Sheet2", and so on, as indicated at the bottom of the window. By default, a workbook is opened with 16 sheets. However, you can insert new sheets and delete ones you do not want included. This feature enables you to maintain logically related data as sheets in a common workbook file.

There are six different kinds of sheets in a workbook: worksheets, chart sheets (sheets used to create charts), two kinds of sheets for use with the Microsoft Visual Basic programming language, and two kinds of sheets used to keep compatibility with earlier versions of Excel.

NOTE: Microsoft Visual Basic is a language used to program instructions for Excel.

To switch to a sheet, click on the sheet tab for the desired sheet. You can see sheet tabs only for sheets #1 to 6 right now. The tab scroll buttons are used to view more. The leftmost and rightmost buttons allow you to jump directly to the first sheet and the last sheet, respectively. The middle two tab scroll buttons are used to move one sheet at a time. Also, the **tab split bar** can be dragged to the right to display more sheet tabs (and less horizontal scroll bar) or to the left to display more scroll bar (and less sheet tabs). As will be described later, sheet names that appear on sheet tabs can be changed to a more descriptive name.

The **menu bar**, located beneath the Excel application title bar, contains nine menus. Excel's commands are accessed either by clicking on the desired menu option or by pressing [Alt] and the key of the underlined letter in the menu option you want. When you select a menu option, a drop-down menu containing the commands appears below that option. To make a selection in the drop-down menu, click on the desired menu option or press the key of the underlined letter.

Beneath the menu bar, there are two or three **toolbars** which contain buttons with icons, called tools, which you can click on to perform certain operations. Tools are shortcuts—they perform the most commonly used commands, including bold, italic, text justification, AutoSum, and ChartWizard. Many of the tools are explained in this book.

■   Move the mouse pointer on top of the first tool button.

▶   *A pop-up description of the tool appears, as shown in Figure 1-4. Also, a description of the tool is displayed in the status bar.*

Figure 1-4

P R A C T I C E   T I M E   1 - 1

Move the mouse pointer over other tool buttons. Notice all the various shapes the mouse pointer adopts, depending on where it is located on the worksheet.

Under the toolbar is the *formula bar*. This is where you enter or edit data in a workbook. The first area of the formula bar is called the Name box. Its function is explained later in this lesson.

At the bottom of the Excel window is the *status bar*. On its right side it indicates whether the Caps Lock, Num Lock, and other toggle keys are on. At its left edge it displays the program mode, which indicates what the program expects from you. Right now the mode is "Ready," which indicates that Excel is ready for your next command or entry. There are three other modes: Enter, Edit, and Point.

■   Maximize the workbook window.

▶   *Notice that the title bar now indicates "Microsoft Excel — Book1".*

THE WORKSHEET AREA

The worksheet, currently Sheet1, displays a grid of nine vertical columns (labeled A through I) and 18 horizontal rows, with row and column headings at the left and top edges of the grid. Notice that the mouse pointer is a hollow cross in the worksheet area and changes into an I-beam in the formula bar.

N O T E :   The number of columns and rows displayed depends on the column widths and heights, respectively, as well as the size of your monitor.

The intersection of a row and a column is called a *cell*. Each cell is identified by a unique *address* consisting of its column letter and row number, such as A1 or G8. Because a workbook has 16 sheets, the formal cell address also includes the sheet reference. Using this format, cell A1 on Sheet1 is referred to as Sheet1!A1. This is explained in more detail later.

You might have noticed that cell A1 has a thicker border around it. This is because cell A1 is currently the *active cell*. The address of the active cell appears in the Name box. The third area of the formula bar displays the contents of the active cell. Because the cell is empty, nothing appears there.

N O T E :   Notice the square at the bottom right corner of the active cell border. This is called the fill handle. Its function is explained later.

You can enter data only in the active cell. Other cells can be made active by using either the mouse or keyboard arrow keys. With the mouse, all you have to do is click on the cell you want to make active. With the keyboard, you select the active cell by pressing the arrow keys. Each arrow key moves the active cell border one cell at a time in the indicated direction.

■   Click on cell A2 to make it the active cell.

PRACTICE TIME 1-2

Make cell B6 the active cell.

The **scroll bars** along the right and bottom edges of the workspace window indicate that the worksheet extends beyond column I to the right, and beyond row 18 at the bottom. The worksheet contains 256 columns (A to Z, AA to AZ, and so on to IV) and 16,384 rows. Because of the space limitation imposed by your window size, you can see only as many rows and columns as your window can display at any time.

Using a mouse, you can scroll the window by dragging the **scroll box** on the scroll bar in the direction you wish to move or by clicking on the **scroll arrows** at either end of the scroll bar. When you use the scroll bars to view a different area of the worksheet, the currently active cell does not change as the view scrolls. Therefore, you must point and click on a cell in the current view if you wish to change the active cell. On the other hand, scrolling the view with the keyboard arrow keys is directly related to moving the active cell.

■   Scroll to the right using the mouse or by pressing → several times.

■   Scroll down using the mouse or by pressing ↓ several times.

N O T E :   The End key followed by an arrow key moves the active cell in the direction of the arrow either to the end of a row or column of data, or, if no data is present in the initial active cell, to the end of a row or column of blank cells.

USING THE NAME BOX

Another way to select a particular cell to make it active whether or not that cell is currently displayed in the window is by using the **Name box**. Suppose you want to make H21 the active cell.

■   Click on the Name box.

▶   *The cell address in the Name box is highlighted, as shown in Figure 1-5.*

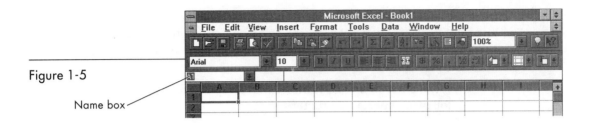

Figure 1-5

Name box

Enter the cell address of the cell to be made active.

■ Type **H21** and press ⏎Enter.

▶ *Cell H21 becomes the active cell.*

N O T E : You can also change the active cell by using the Edit menu Goto command or by pressing F5. You will be prompted to enter the address of the desired cell.

PRACTICE TIME 1-3

Use either the mouse or keyboard to do the following:

1. Make G15 the active cell.

2. Make K125 the active cell.

3. Use Page Up and the arrow keys to make K37 the active cell.

4. Go to cell AT5000.

5. When you are satisfied that you can make any cell active, make A1 the active cell.

ENTERING DATA

The data you enter into a cell can take one of three forms: text, a number, or a formula. A **text entry** is a combination of characters or words and is not used in calculations. An example of a text entry would be a heading, or label, that describes the entries in a column or row. **Numeric entries** are values or dates which can be used in calculations. Text entries are displayed left justified, meaning they are aligned with the left edge of the cell, and numbers are displayed right justified in the cell. **Formulas** are mathematical expressions that, when evaluated, yield values which are displayed in their cells. They are discussed in more detail later.

Text and numbers are known as **constant values**. To enter a constant value, you select a cell, type the entry, then complete the entry. Excel determines whether an entry is text or a number on the basis of what you enter.

- If the entry is a valid number, made up of the digits 0–9 and the following special characters

  + – / $ % , . E e ( )

then Excel interprets the entry as a number. Examples of numbers include $1,000.25 (currency), 15% (percent), 3⅐ (fraction), –2.3E–1 (scientific or exponential notation), and 12/14/94 (date).

- If the entry does not begin with = or \, and it does not begin with one of the above numerical special characters, Excel interprets it as text.

If you are entering a number as a text entry (such as a Social Security number like 123–45–6789 or phone number like 555–1212), type an apostrophe (') first, then enter the text. The apostrophe is a signal that you're typing text. The apostrophe appears in the formula bar, but not in the cell.

Uppercase

To type a letter in uppercase, hold down ⇧Shift while you type that letter, just as you would on a typewriter. If you want to type the whole entry in uppercase, press Caps Lock once, so that the word "CAPS" appears in the status bar. To exit uppercase, simply press Caps Lock again. When entering nonalphabetic shifted characters, such as $ or %, you must hold down ⇧Shift regardless of the status of Caps Lock.

■   Make sure A1 is the active cell.

■   Type your name, but *do not* press ←Enter when finished.

▶   *If your name is too long to be displayed in the cell, the entry may partially spill off the active cell. The formula bar, immediately above the workspace, displays your entry. See Figure 1-6.*

The formula bar also displays three boxes to the left of the entry: a **cancel box** containing a X, an **enter box** containing a checkmark, and a Function Wizard box that displays "fx". The Function Wizard box is explained later.

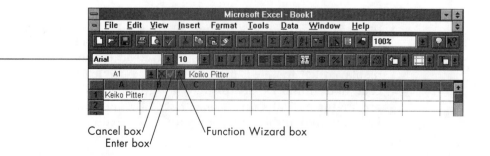

Figure 1-6

Completing an Entry

When you have entered the information, complete the entry either by clicking on the enter box or by pressing [←Enter]. When you use the enter box, the active cell remains the same, whereas using [←Enter] moves the active cell down one row.

- ■ Complete the entry by clicking on the enter box.

    ▶ *Your name appears in the active cell (and may spill over to adjacent cells); the formula bar displays the entry, but no boxes; and the status bar indicates Ready mode.*

Correcting or Canceling an Entry

As you type the entry, it appears in the formula bar. If you notice an error while typing, press [←Backspace] to back up and make corrections. You can also cancel the entry in progress and start over again.

- ■ Make A2 the active cell.

- ■ Type the name **Keiko Pitter**, but *do not* complete the entry.

- ■ Now, cancel the entry by clicking on the cancel box or by pressing [Esc].

    ▶ *The entry is canceled.*

N O T E :   When you cancel an entry, the previous contents of the cell are restored.

CLEARING THE CONTENTS OF A CELL

If you want to erase an entry that was previously made, make that cell active then delete the contents.

- ■ Make sure cell A1 is active.

- ■ Click on Edit to display the menu, then on the Clear command.

    ▶ *The Clear menu appears, as shown in Figure 1-7.*

The menu has four options. The default selection is All, which clears not only the contents of the cell, but also any display format you might have set or Notes that might have been added to the cell (these are explained later). Since you have not set any display format, you can select either All or Contents.

- ■ Select Contents and press [←Enter].

    Alternative: Select the cell and press [Del].

    ▶ *Your name is cleared from the cell.*

SPREADSHEET

Figure 1-7

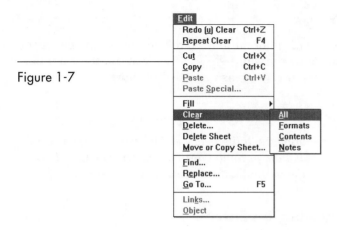

N O T E :   If you use the Edit menu Delete command instead, the command not only removes the contents of a cell, but the cell itself.

CLOSING A WORKBOOK

Before continuing the lesson, you will close the workbook that is currently displayed onscreen. Closing the workbook means removing it from the workspace. This is done here because during the time you were experimenting with changing the active cell and so on, you may have accidentally entered data in a cell. Rather than clearing all the cells in this workbook, you will start a new one.

■   From the File menu, select the Close command.

▶   *A dialog box with a question mark appears. Excel asks if you want to save the changes in workbook Book1.*

■   Click on the No button to indicate that you do not want to save the file.

▶   *The workspace is blank.*

CREATING A NEW WORKBOOK

You will learn the various features of Excel through an example. Bill is the manager of a small company. He needs a weekly record of inflows and outflows of cash, called a cash flow worksheet. It explains the net increase or decrease in cash at specific time intervals, often weekly or monthly. You will open a new workbook and create a worksheet that covers two one-week periods.

First, you need to create a new workbook in the workspace.

■ From the <u>F</u>ile menu, select the <u>N</u>ew command.

Alternative: Press (Ctrl)+(N) or click the New Workbook tool, ▣.

▶ *A new workbook with a title Book2 appears in the workspace.*

■ Maximize the worksheet, if necessary.

ENTERING LABELS

First, you will label the rows. That is, you will make text entries that explain what data are entered in the rows. To enter a label, you select a cell, type the entry, then complete the entry. If the text is too long to fit in one cell, Excel automatically runs the text into *blank* adjacent cells.

■ Select cell A1.

■ Enter the label **Beginning Date**.

■ Leave cell A2 blank and select cell A3.

■ Enter the label **Beginning Balance**.

PRACTICE TIME 1-4

Enter the following labels in the specified cells.

A4   [leave blank]

A5   **Cash Payments**

        B6   **Rent**
        B7   **Utilities**
        B8   **Salaries**
        B9   **Loan Payment**
        B10   **Insurance**
        B11   **Materials**
        B12   **Office Supplies**
        B13   **Owner's Draw**
        B14   **Total Payments**

A15   [leave blank]

A16   **Net Cash Generated**

A17   [leave blank]

A18   **Ending Balance**

When you are finished, the sheet will look like Figure 1-8.

SPREADSHEET

Figure 1-8

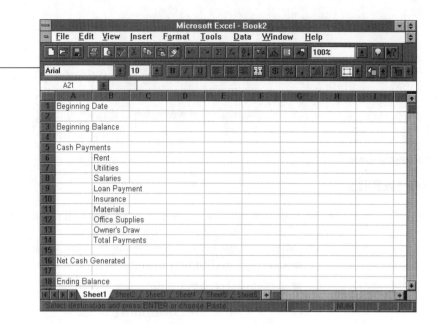

N O T E :   If a label is too long to fit in a cell, the excess characters will be displayed in the consecutive blank cell(s) to the right; if a number is too large to be displayed in a cell, the cell will fill with hash marks (#). In either case, only the display is affected; the correct data remains in the cell.

In the next lesson, you will adjust the column width of column B so that the labels will not spill into adjacent cells. For now, however, you will leave column C blank, which will preserve the labels. The cash data are entered in columns D and E.

ENTERING NUMBERS

The first row is to display the beginning date for each period (week). In Excel, a date entry is considered a number. If you enter a date in one of the predefined formats, Excel automatically displays it in the appropriate format. For example,

Your entry	Format Displayed
3-1-95 or 3/1/95	m/d/yy
1-Mar-95 or 1/Mar/95	d-mmm-yy
1-Mar, 1/Mar, 3-1, or 3/1	d-mmm
Mar-95 or Mar/95	mmm-yy

- In cell D1, enter **3–5**.

   ▶ *Cell D1 reads 5-Mar, and "3/5/1995" (or the current year) is displayed in the formula bar.*

NOTE: The year displayed in the formula bar is the current year, according to the computer's internal clock.

- In cell E1, enter **3–12**.

NOTE: Later, you will specify other display formats for dates.

The remaining numbers you enter for the first two weeks are monetary figures. Monetary figures can be entered with or without commas to separate thousands, and with or without the dollar sign ($). You will initially enter numbers with commas in every three places.

- In cell D3, enter **7,320** as the beginning balance.

   ▶ *The value 7,320 is entered right justified.*

- In cell D6, enter **800**.

- In cell D7, enter **0**.

PRACTICE TIME 1-5

Enter the following numbers in the specified cells.

		E6	**0**
		E7	**500**
D8	**3,250**	E8	**3,250**
D9	**1,000**	E9	**0**
D10	**400**	E10	**0**
D11	**2,000**	E11	**2,510**
D12	**225**	E12	**320**
D13	**700**	E13	**700**
D16	**5,775**	E16	**6,420**

Your worksheet should look similar to the one in Figure 1-9.

Figure 1-9

		Microsoft Excel - Book2					

File Edit View Insert Format Tools Data Window Help

Arial   10   B I U

A24

	A	B	C	D	E	F	G	H	I
1	Beginning Date			5-Mar	12-Mar				
2									
3	Beginning Balance			7,320					
4									
5	Cash Payments								
6		Rent		800	0				
7		Utilities		0	500				
8		Salaries		3,250	3,250				
9		Loan Payment		1,000	0				
10		Insurance		400	0				
11		Materials		2,000	2,510				
12		Office Supplies		225	320				
13		Owner's Draw		700	700				
14		Total Payments							
15									
16	Net Cash Generated			5,775	6,420				
17									
18	Ending Balance								

Sheet1 Sheet2 Sheet3 Sheet4 Sheet5 Sheet6

Ready   NUM

NAMING THE SHEET

As you recall, this is the first sheet of a 16-page workbook, with the default sheet name of Sheet1. You will give it a more meaningful name. Since this is the first version of the cash flow worksheet, you will call this CASH1.

■   From the Format menu, select Sheet then Rename.

    Alternative: Double-click on the sheet tab for Sheet1.

▶   *The Rename Sheet dialog box is displayed, as shown in Figure 1-10.*

Figure 1-10

■   Enter **CASH1** in the Name text box.

■   Complete the entry by clicking on OK or pressing ⏎Enter.

▶   *The sheet tab now reads "CASH1", as shown in Figure 1-11.*

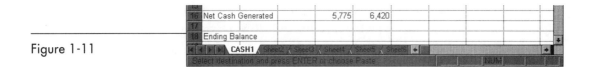

Figure 1-11

SAVING YOUR WORK

Before entering more information on the worksheet, you will save the workbook to the disk. The workbook you see is contained in the workspace, which is the RAM of the computer. If there is a power outage or hardware failure, all the information will be lost. Since you've already entered a considerable amount of information, you want to save it to more permanent storage (on a data disk) right now. Also, by saving the worksheet at this point, should you make a lot of mistakes in the next section, you can retrieve the version that is stored on the data disk and start over from this point.

Save the current worksheet on your data disk.

■ Insert your data disk in a drive.

■ From the File menu, select the Save As command.

▶ *The Save As dialog box appears, as shown in Figure 1-12.*

Figure 1-12

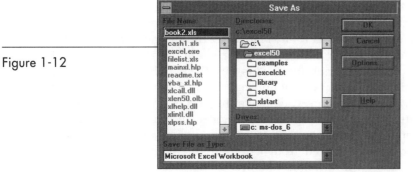

You need to specify the filename and then the drive. When you specify a filename, Excel will automatically give a workbook file the extension .XLS. The filename follows the same convention as any DOS files. That is, it is one to eight characters in length, consisting of letters, numbers, and other symbols *except* for a space and the following characters:

. , " / \ [ ] : ; | < > + = * ?

You can enter the name in upper- or lowercase. Excel will convert all entries to lowercase in the display.

SPREADSHEET

■ Because the entry in the File <u>N</u>ame list box is already highlighted, just type the filename **ASSIGN**. *Do not* press ⎡←Enter⎤ yet.

You need to select the drive containing your data disk.

■ Click on the arrow button located at the right edge of the Dri<u>v</u>es box.

▶ *A drop-down list displaying all available drives appears.*

■ Click on the drive that contains your data disk.

■ Complete the command by clicking on the OK button or by pressing ⎡←Enter⎤.

▶ *A Summary Info dialog box appears, giving you the opportunity to enter information about the workbook.*

For now, you will not enter information in this dialog box.

■ Click on OK or press ⎡←Enter⎤.

▶ *The worksheet is saved to your disk.*

▶ *The filename "ASSIGN.XLS" is displayed in the worksheet title bar.*

ENTERING FORMULAS

Cell D14 is to display the sum of numbers entered in rows 6 through 13. Rather than adding numbers manually and entering the result in cell D14, you will enter a formula that will instruct the computer to calculate the total. When you enter a formula in a cell, the result of the calculation is displayed.

A formula entry always begins with the equals sign (=). When you enter a formula, the formula itself appears in the formula bar as the contents of the cell. The cell, however, displays the numeric result after the formula is calculated. In a formula, the operator + indicates addition, – indicates subtraction, * indicates multiplication, and / indicates division. These operators are evaluated from left to right. As in ordinary mathematics, multiplication and division take precedence over addition and subtraction unless the latter operations are enclosed in parentheses. For example, =6+4/2 yields 8, whereas =(6+4)/2 equals 5.

The formula, then, is =D6+D7+D8+D9+D10+D11+D12+D13, but rather than entering this lengthy formula, you can use the **AutoSum** feature.

■ Make cell D14 the active cell.

■ Click on the Sum button on the toolbar, ⎡Σ⎤.

▶ *The formula bar and the cell display the entry, =SUM(D6:D13), with D6:D13 highlighted at the cell, as shown in Figure 1-13.*

▶ *The range of cells, D6 through D13, is enclosed in a blinking dotted-line border called the marquee border.*

Figure 1-13

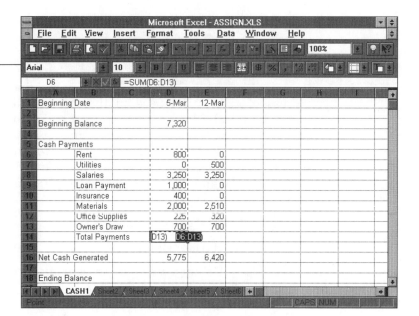

NOTE: The keyboard shortcut for the AutoSum feature is [Alt]+[=] (hold down [Alt] while you press [=]).

The AutoSum feature makes a guess of the values you want totaled. A ***marquee border*** of moving dashes, somewhat resembling the moving lights on a theater marquee, indicates the range of cells selected for summation. In this case, it guessed that you want to total the numbers in the cells immediately above the active cell. D6:D13 refers to the range of cells from D6 through D13. If this was not the range of cells you wanted to sum, you would specify the correct range by entering the addresses of the first and last cells in the range, separated by a colon (:). What you type would replace the highlighted range in the formula. This time, the range displayed is exactly what you want. Range specification is explained in more detail in the next lesson.

▪ Complete the entry by clicking on the enter box.

▶ *The total 8375 appears in cell D14.*

Suppose one of those values should change. For example, upon closer inspection, you determine that the cost for materials was 1,725.

▪ In cell D11, enter **1,725**.

▶ *The total in cell D14 changes to 8100.*

Are you beginning to see the value of electronic spreadsheets? When you change a number in the workbook, all the values that are dependent on that number are automatically updated.

The formula for cell D18, ending balance, is a bit more involved. The number you want displayed is the beginning balance (in cell D3) minus the total payments (which is in cell D14) plus the cash received (in cell D16), or =D3–D14+D16.

■   At cell D18, enter **=D3–D14+D16**.

▶   *The formula bar displays your entry, and cell D18 displays 4,995.*

As you determined this formula, you might have had to check for the address of cells to be used in the formula. If this had been a large spreadsheet and if the cells you wanted had scrolled offscreen, you would have had to scroll to find them. After finding them, you would have had to note their cell addresses, select the cell in which you wanted to enter the formula, and then type the formula. Excel can help you do this a little more easily. You will enter the same formula by using the point method. First, clear the entry at D18.

■   Clear the entry at cell D18.

■   Press ꞏ=ꞏ (*do not* press ꞏ←Enterꞏ).

▶   *"=" appears in the formula bar.*

■   Click on cell D3, the first cell in the formula.

▶   *The formula bar shows "=D3", and the status bar indicates Point mode.*

Here, the marquee border defines the single cell that has been selected for pasting into your formula. In general, the marquee border represents cells or ranges of cells that are selected for copying elsewhere.

■   Press ꞏ–ꞏ (*do not* press ꞏ←Enterꞏ).

■   Click on cell D14, the next cell in the formula.

▶   *The formula bar now reads "=D3–D14".*

■   Press ꞏ+ꞏ (*do not* press ꞏ←Enterꞏ).

■   Point to the last cell in the formula (cell D16).

■   Complete the entry by clicking on the enter box.

▶   *The formula bar contains the formula "=D3–D14+D16" and cell D18 displays the value 4,995.*

As you become familiar with the Excel program, you will find many cases where you can accomplish a task in several different ways. Not all methods are explained in this book. You can explore them on your own.

P R A C T I C E   T I M E   1 - 6

Make the entry for cell E3. Cell E3 is to display the ending cash balance from the previous week, or the contents of cell D18. Hence, the formula at cell E3 is =D18.

FILL RIGHT COMMAND

Cells E14 and E18 are to contain formulas similar to the ones at D14 and D18. That is, E14 is to display the sum of cells E6 through E13, and E18 is to contain the formula =E3–E14+E16. You can enter these manually as you did for cells D14 and D18. However, you will use another method, the Fill Right command.

■ Select cells D14 and E14 by pointing to cell D14 and dragging to cell E14. That is, point to cell D14, hold down the left mouse button, move the mouse to cell E14, and then release the button.

▶ *Cells D14 and E14 are enclosed in a border.*

■ From the Edit menu, select Fill then Right.

Alternative: Press Ctrl+R (hold down Ctrl and press R).

▶ *The number 7280 appears at cell E14.*

■ Make cell E14 the active cell.

▶ *The formula bar indicates that the cell contains the desired formula.*

The Fill Right command copies the contents of the leftmost cell in the selected range to the rest of the cells in the same range. As you've noticed, Excel inserted a **relative formula** in cell E14; that is, rather than copying the formula =SUM(D6:D13) to cell E14, it copied a formula that specified "sum the contents of cells in rows 6 through 13 of the same column." So, at cell E14, it copied =SUM(E6:E13).

N O T E : If you had wanted the **absolute formula**, =SUM(D6:D16), copied to cells in the selected range, you would have entered the original formula in cell D14 with dollar signs ($) preceding the cell's column label and row number; that is, the formula would be =SUM($D$6:$D$13). This is discussed in more detail later.

PRACTICE TIME 1-7

Use the Fill Right command to copy the contents of cell D18 to E18. You should get the result 4,135 displayed in cell E18.

There is an even easier way to copy using the mouse. If you recall, the square at the bottom right corner of the active window is called the **fill handle**. When the mouse pointer is positioned above the fill handle, it turns into a plus sign (+), or cross hair.

SPREADSHEET

■ Clear the contents of cell E18.

■ Make cell D18 the active cell.

■ Drag the fill handle of cell D18 to cell E18. That is, position the mouse pointer on the fill handle of cell D18 (so that the mouse pointer turns into a plus sign), press the mouse button, drag the mouse to cell E18, then release the button.

▶ *The relative formula is copied and cell E18 displays 4,135.*

SAVING THE WORKBOOK A SECOND TIME

Now that you have made changes to the worksheet, you will save the workbook a second time, using the same filename. When you save a file using the same filename, the current version replaces the one on the disk.

■ From the <u>F</u>ile menu, select the <u>S</u>ave command.

Alternative: Press [Ctrl]+[S] or click on the Save tool, ▤.

▶ *The current workbook replaces the one on the disk.*

PRINTING A WORKSHEET

You can quickly print this worksheet. It is assumed that your printer was correctly installed through the Windows program. Before printing, however, you will make sure that your printer is selected for use by Windows.

■ From the <u>F</u>ile menu, select the Page Set<u>u</u>p command.

▶ *The Page Setup dialog box is displayed, as shown in Figure 1-14.*

Figure 1-14

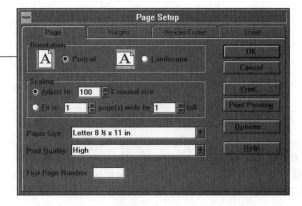

■ Select the Options button.

▶ *The name of the printer you are using should appear on the title bar of the Setup dialog box that is displayed.*

N O T E : If the printer displayed is not correct, consult your instructor.

■ Select OK to return to the Page Setup dialog box.

■ Make sure that the printer is on and ready to print.

■ From the Page Setup dialog box, click on the Print button.

▶ *The Print dialog box appears, as shown in Figure 1-15.*

Figure 1-15

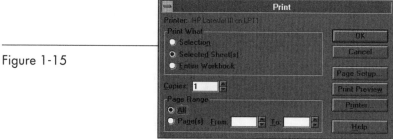

■ Complete the command by pressing ⏎Enter or clicking on OK.

▶ *Your worksheet is printed.*

N O T E : To print without going through Page Setup, select the File menu Print option, or press Ctrl+P, or click on the Print tool, 🖶.

Although the worksheet has 256 columns and 16,384 cells, unless you indicate otherwise, Excel prints only the rectangular area of the worksheet containing entries.

EXITING EXCEL

You should never quit Excel by just turning off your computer. Always exit to Windows and then properly quit Windows before shutting down your system. When you properly exit Excel and Windows, the programs will caution you if any workbooks or other documents have been changed since they were last saved.

■   From the File menu, select the Exit command.

Alternative: Press [Alt]+[F4].

▶   *If any open worksheets were changed since they were last saved, a cautionary dialog box appears, giving you a chance to save the worksheets again. Select yes or no accordingly.*

▶   *You return to Windows.*

ENDING LESSON 1

This is the end of this lesson.

■   Quit the Windows session by clicking on File then on Exit Windows.

Alternative: Press [Alt]+[F4].

■   Remove your data disk from the disk drive.

■   Turn off your computer and monitor.

S U M M A R Y

In this lesson, many of the terms and concepts necessary to use electronic spreadsheets and Excel 5.0 for Windows were introduced.

☐   **The Excel application window consists of a title bar, a menu bar, a tool bar, a formula bar above a workspace, and a status bar beneath the workspace. The window can be moved, sized, maximized, minimized, restored, and closed like other Windows applications.**

☐   **The worksheet is a window contained in the Excel workspace. When the worksheet window is maximized, it incorporates the application window functional parts.**

☐   **A cell can be selected by clicking on it, by using the arrow keys to move the active cell border, or by entering the desired cell address in the Name box.**

☐   **An entry into a cell is completed by clicking on the check box or by pressing [←Enter].**

- ☐ **The AutoSum feature sums a series of adjacent cells. It is invoked by pressing Alt+= or by clicking on the Sum tool.**

- ☐ **Formulas begin with an = and reference the contents of a cell by the cell address.**

KEY TERMS

absolute formula	formula bar	scroll arrows
active cell	formula	sheet tabs
address	marquee border	status bar
AutoSum	menu bar	tab split bar
cancel box	Name box	text entry
cell	numeric entry	toolbar
constant value	relative formula	workbook
enter box	scroll bar	workspace
fill handle	scroll box	

COMMAND SUMMARY

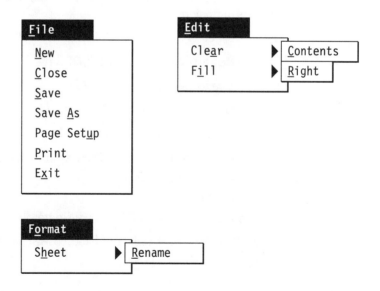

File
New
Close
Save
Save As
Page Setup
Print
Exit

Edit
Clear ▶ Contents
Fill ▶ Right

Format
Sheet ▶ Rename

SPREADSHEET

REVIEW QUESTIONS

1. How do you move the mouse pointer to a cell that is not displayed in the window? Quickly select a cell that is not displayed in the window?

2. How do you invoke commands by using the mouse? The keyboard?

3. What information is displayed in the formula bar?

4. Describe two ways to complete an entry into a cell.

5. How does Excel determine that an entry is text? A formula?

6. How can you make a text entry that consists of numbers only?

7. How can you erase the contents of a cell?

8. How can you copy a formula in one cell to the cell to its right?

9. How can you cancel an entry?

10. How do you print the worksheet?

EXERCISES

1. Create the following budget workbook, with labels in column A and numbers and formulas in column C. You should determine how to enter the formulas indicated in braces.

Row	Label	Value
1	**Revenues**	**$50,322**
2	**Variable Costs**	**$9,255**
3	**Gross Margin**	[Revenues minus Variable Costs]
4	**Fixed Costs**	**$18,240**
5	**Net Profit**	[Gross Margin minus Fixed Costs]

   a. Rename the sheet BUDGET1.
   b. Print the sheet.
   c. Save the workbook as EX1 on your data disk.

2. Create the following schedule of fixed costs. Enter the labels in column A and the values in column C.

Row	Label	Value
1	**Rent**	**650**
2	**Utilities**	**225**
3	**Salaries**	**15,220**
4	**Loan Payment**	**1,000**
5	**Insurance**	**134**
6	**Office Supplies**	**100**
7	**FIXED COSTS**	[sum of all above columns]

a. Rename the sheet FIXCOST1
b. Print the sheet.
c. Save the workbook as EX2 on your data disk.

3. Create the following workbook of checks written. The labels are entered in row 1 in the columns indicated (leave columns D and F blank). The information is entered in the rows that follow.

A	B	C	E	G
Check No.	**Date**	**Paid to**	**Account**	**Amount**
725	**3/1**	**B. Sutton**	**Owner's Draw**	**700**
726	**3/1**	**Colonial Bank**	**Loan Payment**	**1,000**
727	**3/1**	**R. Sutton**	**Salaries**	**800**
728	**3/1**	**G. Winters**	**Salaries**	**700**
729	**3/1**	**M. Allen**	**Salaries**	**700**
730	**3/1**	**B. McCoy**	**Salaries**	**600**
731	**3/1**	**J. Saunders**	**Salaries**	**450**
732	**3/1**	**B.B. Properties**	**Rent**	**800**
733	**3/1**	**Fidelity Insurance**	**Insurance**	**400**
734	**3/1**	**Morgan Co.**	**Materials**	**450**
735	**3/3**	**Concord Stationers**	**Office Supplies**	**225**
736	**3/4**	**Sanford Supplies**	**Materials**	**945**
737	**3/4**	**James & Son**	**Materials**	**330**

a. Rename the sheet CHECKS1.
b. Print the sheet.
c. Save the workbook as EX3 on your data disk.

2 Changing the Worksheet Format

OBJECTIVES

Upon completing the material presented in this lesson, you should understand the following aspects of Excel 5.0 for Windows:

- ☐ **Using the onscreen Help feature**
- ☐ **Retrieving a file from disk**
- ☐ **Copying the contents of a sheet to another sheet**
- ☐ **Selecting a column or row**
- ☐ **Adjusting column widths**
- ☐ **Deleting columns**
- ☐ **Formatting numbers**
- ☐ **Selecting a range**
- ☐ **Setting the font for the workbook**
- ☐ **Setting the font and style for a range or cell**
- ☐ **Selecting multiple rows**
- ☐ **Outlining the worksheet border**
- ☐ **Removing gridlines from the printed worksheet**
- ☐ **Printing the worksheet**

STARTING OFF

Turn on your computer and start the Windows program, then launch the Excel program as you did in Lesson 1. Insert your data disk in a disk drive. If necessary, maximize the Excel application window. You will start by retrieving the file ASSIGN.XLS which you saved during the last lesson. Retrieving a file is also called opening a file.

USING EXCEL ONSCREEN HELP

If you have difficulty understanding or remembering a command, you can use Excel's extensive onscreen help. The onscreen Help feature of Excel is similar to the onscreen Help feature of Windows.

■ From the Help menu, select the Contents command.

Alternative: Press F1.

▶ *The Microsoft Excel Help Contents window appears, as shown in Figure 2-1.*

Figure 2-1

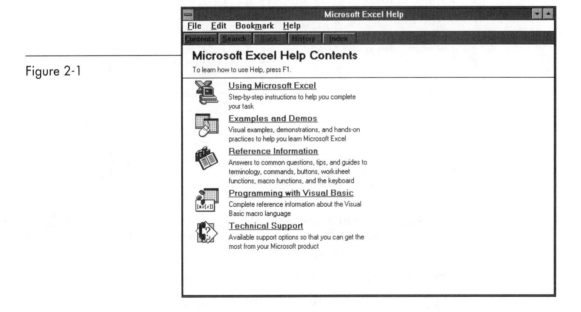

The Help Contents window contains a title bar, a menu bar, and a row of help buttons. Any one of the graphics or their associated underlined topics, called **jump terms**, can be selected either by clicking on it with a mouse, or by pressing Tab or ⇧Shift+Tab to highlight the topic and then pressing ←Enter.

■ Select Using Microsoft Excel.

▶ *The Using Microsoft Excel window appears.*

Again, the underlined jump terms can be selected to reveal further information.

■ Select Essential Skills.

▶ *The Essential Skills window opens.*

■ Select Managing Workbook Files.

▶ *The Managing Workbook Files window opens.*

■ Select Opening a workbook.

▶ *The How To/Opening a workbook window is displayed, as shown in Figure 2.2.*

Figure 2-2

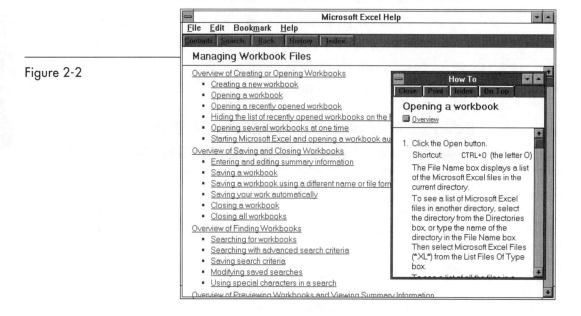

Help explains that you can open a file by clicking on the Open tool, ⬛. If you scroll this window, several more jump terms are listed, so you can obtain further information.

■ Select the Close button to close the How To window.

■ Exit the help screen by double-clicking on the control-menu box in the upper left corner of the window.

The tool with a question mark icon (⬛) is the Help tool. If you want information about a menu command or tool, click on the Help tool first, then click on the tool or command you want help on.

■ Click on the Help tool.

▶ *The cursor turns into the Help pointer,* ⬛*.*

■ Click on the Open tool.

▶ *The help screen on the Open command is displayed, as shown in Figure 2-3.*

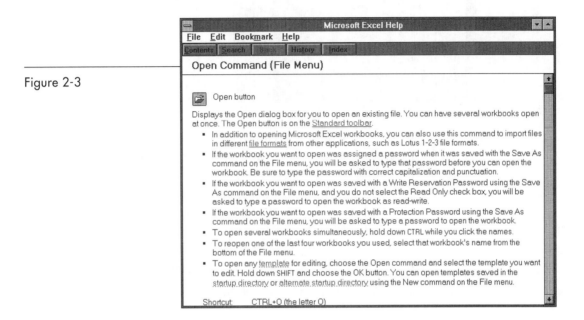

Figure 2-3

■ Close the help screen by double-clicking on the control-menu box.

The onscreen help contains much more information than is covered in this book. You can use, for instance, the Examples and Demo commands to explore other available features.

OPENING A FILE

You will now open a file from the data disk.

■ From the File menu, select the Open command.

Alternative: Press Ctrl+O or click on the Open tool.

▶ *The Open dialog box appears, as shown in Figure 2-4.*

This dialog box is similar to the Save As dialog box you saw in the previous lesson. It lets you specify the drive, directory, and filename of the workbook you want retrieved from disk. When you specify the drive and directory, the name of the file you want should appear in the File Name list box on the left. The drive is specified in the Drives drop-down list box at the bottom center of the dialog box.

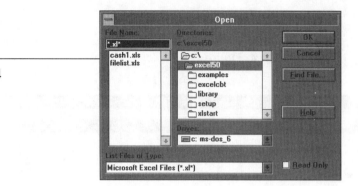

Figure 2-4

■ If the drive containing your data disk does not appear in the Dri̲ves list box, click on the down arrow at the right. A drop-down list box appears. Click on the disk drive you want.

▶ *The D̲irectories list box above the Dri̲ves list box displays all directories on the disk. The name of the current directory appears above the box. In the D̲irectories list box, the icon for the current directory is an open folder.*

■ If necessary, double-click on the directory you want.

▶ *The filenames in the selected directory appear in the File N̲ame list box.*

■ Select ASSIGN.XLS in the File N̲ame list box by double-clicking on it or by highlighting it and then pressing ⏎Enter.

▶ *The worksheet you prepared in the previous lesson is displayed, as shown in Figure 2-5.*

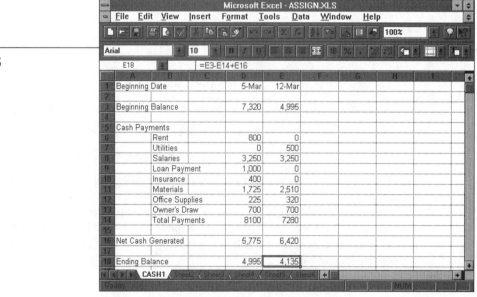

Figure 2-5

COPYING A WORKSHEET
TO ANOTHER WORKBOOK SHEET

To provide you with the ability to review the work done in each successive lesson, you will copy the data from CASH1 onto the second sheet of the workbook, rename it CASH2, and use it in this lesson.

■ Press Ctrl and drag the CASH1 sheet tab over the Sheet2 tab (*do not* release the mouse button).

▶ *As you move the pointer, a document icon with a plus sign appears beneath it, as shown in Figure 2-6.*

Figure 2-6

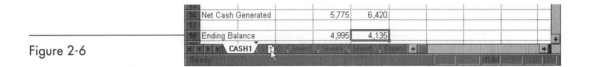

■ With the mouse pointer over the Sheet2 tab, release the mouse button.

▶ *A copy of CASH1, named CASH1 (2), is inserted, shifting the rest of the sheets to the right, as shown in Figure 2-7.*

Figure 2-7

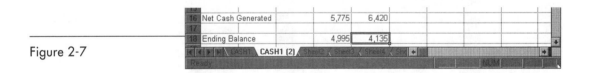

N O T E :   If you drag the sheet tab without holding down Ctrl, the sheet is moved rather than copied.

■ Rename CASH1 (2) as CASH2.

HANDLING MULTIPLE SHEETS

CASH1 and CASH2 are two sheets in a workbook. You can switch from one to another simply by clicking on the sheet tab for the desired sheet.

■ Click on the CASH1 sheet tab.

▶ *The CASH1 sheet is displayed.*

■ Click on the CASH2 sheet tab.

▶ *The CASH2 sheet is displayed.*

You can also display both sheets at the same time.

■ From the <u>W</u>indow menu, select <u>N</u>ew Window.

▶ *A second window displaying the ASSIGN workbook is displayed, as indicated by the title ASSIGN.XLS:2.*

■ Click on the CASH1 sheet tab so that this window displays CASH1.

■ From the <u>W</u>indow menu, select <u>A</u>rrange.

■ Make sure that the <u>T</u>iled radio button is selected and complete the command.

▶ *The screen displays ASSIGN.XLS:1 and ASSIGN.XLS:2, as shown in Figure 2-8.*

Figure 2-8

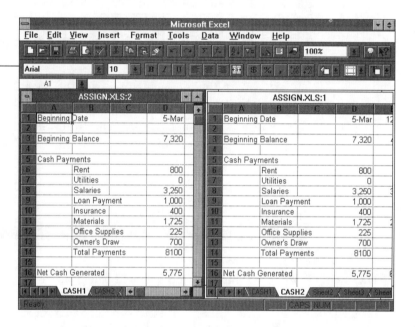

■ In the ASSIGN.XLS:2 window, click on the Sheet2 sheet tab.

▶ *Blank Sheet2 is displayed.*

Note that cell A1 in CASH1 contains the label Beginning Date. When you refer to a cell address, such as A1, you are referring to a cell in the sheet that is displayed. A complete name for a cell is actually sheetname!cell-address. For example, cell A1 in the CASH1 sheet is CASH1!A1.

■ In the ASSIGN.XLS:2 window, in cell A1 of Sheet2, enter the formula **=CASH1!A1**.

▶ *Cell A1 of Sheet2 now displays the contents of cell A1 in CASH1.*

If you were to change the contents of CASH1!A1, Sheet2!A1 will reflect the change.

■ Clear the contents of Sheet2!A1.

■ Close one of the workbook windows by double-clicking on the control-menu box in the upper left corner of that window.

▶ *The title bar now reads "ASSIGN.XLS", meaning that there is only one window for the workbook.*

■ Maximize the worksheet window, and click on the CASH2 sheet tab, if necessary.

Right now, you will continue to work with just one sheet, CASH2. All cell addresses will refer to those in this sheet.

SELECTING A COLUMN

To achieve a desired look in a worksheet, it is often necessary to adjust the width of one or more columns. In the current worksheet, you want to change the width of column B so that the longest entry will fit in the column. To do this, first select the entire column and then specify the width.

■ Select column B by clicking on the column heading at the top of the column.

▶ *The entire column B is selected. That is, all the cells in column B are surrounded by a thick border and all the cells except the selected cell are highlighted.*

N O T E : To select a row, you can click on the row label at the left of the worksheet. You can also select rows and columns from the keyboard by positioning the active cell in the row or column and pressing [⇧Shift]+[Spacebar] to select the row or [Ctrl]+[Spacebar] to select the column.

USING AUTOFIT COLUMN WIDTH

Now you are ready to widen the column. Rather than you specifying the column width, Excel can determine the longest entry in the column and set the column width to accommodate it.

■ From the Format menu, select Column then AutoFit Selection.

Alternative: Double-click on the right border of the column heading.

▶ *Column B widens enough to display the longest entry in the column.*

DELETING COLUMNS

Now that you've adjusted the width of column B, column C is no longer needed.

■   Select column C by clicking on the column heading.

■   From the Edit menu, select Delete.

▶   *The numbers in columns D and E now appear in columns C and D.*

FORMATTING NUMBERS

Numbers in columns C and D were entered with commas. However, you might have noticed that numbers in cells C14 and D14 appear without commas. You can change the format of the numbers in those cells to be consistent with the rest.

■   Select cells C14 and D14 by clicking on cell C14 and dragging to the right so that D14 is also highlighted.

■   From the Format menu, select the Cells command.

Alternative: Press Ctrl + 1.

▶   *The Format Cells dialog box appears, as shown in Figure 2-9. If your display is different, select Number on index tabs at the top.*

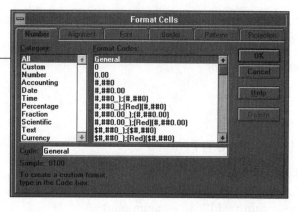

Figure 2-9

The Category list box on the left divides formats into categories. As you select a different category, all possible formats for that category are listed in the Format Codes list box on the right. The All category, however, lists all available formats for numbers.

Below the list boxes, the Code text box displays the highlighted format (from the Format Codes list box). A sample displays how the selected cell would look with the highlighted format. Right now, General is highlighted. When a cell is set to the General format (the default), Excel determines the display format based on the entry in the cell.

■ Select #,##0 so that it is highlighted.

▶ *The Code text box displays #,##0 and the Sample display is 8,100.*

This format displays commas in every three positions, but no digits to the right of decimal point.

■ Complete the command by clicking on the OK button or by pressing ⌐←Enter⌐.

▶ *The values at cells C14 and D14 have the same format as the rest.*

You can also format numbers using one of the number-formatting tools: Currency Style (■), Percent Style (■), Comma Style (■), Increase Decimal (■), or Decrease Decimal (■). All you need to do is select a range of cells to be formatted and click on the appropriate formatting tool. A **range** is a rectangular array of cells, specified by the address of its top left and bottom right cells, separated by a colon (:).

NOTE: Currency and comma tools are in the accounting format. Hence, if the amount is zero, a hyphen appears instead.

Here, you want to select the range from C3 to D18.

■ Select the range C3:D18 by pointing to cell C3 and then dragging until the range C3 to D18 is highlighted, then release the mouse button. (If you don't quite get it right the first time, try again.)

▶ *All the specified cells except the selected cell—the one where the entry is made—are highlighted.*

The first three number-formatting tool buttons are for currency ($), percent (%), and comma (,) formats. The two buttons on the right are used to set the number of places to the right of the decimal.

■ Click on the Currency Style tool.

▶ *The numbers are displayed with a dollar sign and two places to the right of decimal. Several cells fill with hash marks (#), indicating that the column width is not wide enough.*

You will eliminate the display of decimal.

SPREADSHEET

■   Click on the Decrease Decimal tool twice.

▶   *Each time you click, the number of decimal places decreases by one.*

PRACTICE TIME 2-1

1. Change the display format for cells C3 to D18 back to #,##0 (the comma style) either using the Format Cells menu option or the tool button.

2. Save the workbook on your data disk, using the same name.

SELECTING FONTS

The appearance of characters onscreen and in printed output is determined by three factors collectively called the **font**: the typeface, the size, and the type style.

*   **Typeface** is the graphic design applied to the characters, and given a name such as Courier or Times Roman.

*   **Point Size** is the height of a capital letter, measured in points. One point equals $1/72$ inch. Typical fonts are 10 or 12 point.

*   **Type style** includes regular, **bold**, *italic*, and underline. Bold, italic, and underline can be used in any combination.

You can select an appropriate font for display and printing of the worksheet. The style can be varied to emphasize certain information. Also, the font and size determine how much text can fit on one page of a document.

Right now, you will select the entire worksheet and change the font.

■   Select the entire worksheet by clicking on the Select All button at the top left corner of the sheet where row and column headings meet, as indicated in Figure 2-10.

■   From the Format menu, select Cells.

Alternative: Press Ctrl + 1 .

▶   *The Format Cells dialog box appears.*

■   Click on the Font index tab at the top.

▶   *The dialog box appears, as shown in Figure 2-10.*

The dialog box has list boxes for Font, Font Style, Size, Underline, and Color. The Effects group box has check boxes for Strikethrough, Superscript, and Subscript. There is also a check box for Normal Font. The Color and Underline boxes are drop-down list boxes. Each option has an

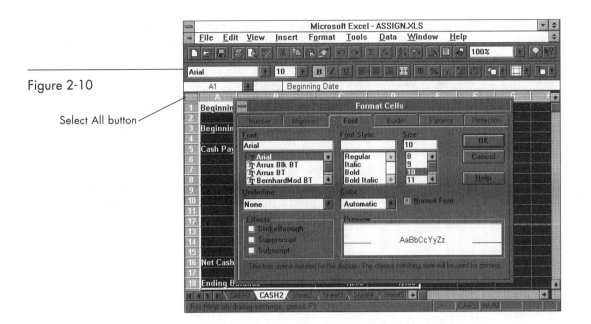

Figure 2-10

Select All button

underlined letter to make it accessible from the keyboard by pressing [Alt] and then the key of the underlined letter. The Preview box displays how the selected font looks onscreen. All fonts (typefaces) in Excel belong to one of three categories:

printer font   Font used for printing. The closest screen font is used for display.

screen font   Font for display. The closest printer font is used for printing.

TrueType   Matching fonts exist for printing and display.

As you highlight different fonts in the list box, a message appears at the bottom of the dialog box, indicating what kind of font it is.

You should experiment with several fonts to determine which are compatible with your printer and suitable for your worksheet display. In the following examples, if you are not sure which font to select, highlight various options to see the effect in the Preview box and then reset the option to the initial setting.

■ Use the arrow keys or mouse to select a font.

▶   *The selected font is highlighted in the list box and also appears in the text box just above.*

Styles appear in the Font Style list box. A style can be selected to emphasize selected cells in the worksheet. For now you will leave the style as Regular.

Font sizes are indicated in points (not characters per inch). Typical sizes used are 10 and 12 point, but the best font size for any worksheet depends on how well the worksheet fits onto a page. If the worksheet is small, a 12- or 14-point font may be used. Larger font sizes mean larger characters are printed or displayed. Sometimes a worksheet may fit onto one page only if a 10- or 8-point font is selected. You will have to experiment to determine what fits and looks best.

- ■   Set the font size to 12 point.

- ■   Complete the command by clicking on OK or pressing ←Enter.

   ▶   *The screen display reflects the font size selected.*

Notice the Font and Size drop-down list boxes on the toolbar. When you click on the down arrow on the right, the list of available typeface or size options is displayed, as shown in Figure 2-11. All you need to do is select the cell(s) and then select the desired typeface and size from these list boxes.

Figure 2-11

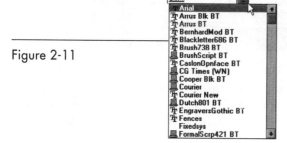

Type styles can be changed in a similar manner using the tools: Bold (■), Italic (■), and Underline (■).

CHANGING THE FORMAT OF SELECTED CELLS

It is possible to change typeface, style, or size of selected cells, rows, or columns. Generally, you should limit your variations within any worksheet to styles and sizes. To change the appearance of certain cells in the worksheet, select the cells (a range, row, or column) then specify the font for those cells. Right now, you will change the font so that rows 1, 3, 5, 14, 16, and 18 are displayed in bold characters for emphasis.

- ■   Select row 1.

- ■   Click on the Bold tool or press Ctrl+B.

P R A C T I C E   T I M E   2 - 2

Change row 3 to bold.

SELECTING MULTIPLE ROWS

Rather than changing rows 5, 14, 16, and 18 to bold individually, you will select them all and then click on the Bold tool.

■ Select row 5.

When using a mouse, you can select a second range without removing the first selection by holding down Ctrl while you select the second range.

■ Hold down Ctrl while you click on the row heading for row 14.

■ Hold down Ctrl while you click on the row headings for row 16 and then 18.

P R A C T I C E   T I M E   2 - 3

Make the four rows bold.

Since bold characters are displayed wider than normal characters, you will need to adjust the column width. However, you will do this after changing some labels to italic.

ITALIC STYLE

Suppose you want to display labels in column A, rows 5 through 12, in italic. You can do this by setting the Italic style in the Cells-Font dialog box accessible from the F̲ormat menu. However, it is much more convenient to do this using a shortcut.

■ Select the range B6:B13.

■ Click on the Italic tool or press Ctrl+I.

▶ *The Italic tool button has a depressed appearance and the selected range is displayed in italic.*

ADJUSTING COLUMN WIDTH

Before you print this worksheet, you should adjust the widths of columns B through C. This time, rather than letting Excel set the column widths, you will specify the width.

■ Place the mouse pointer on the line between the headings for columns B and C.

▶ *The pointer changes to an arrow pointing left and right. This lets you drag the end of column B to a new position in the heading.*

■ Drag to the end of column C in the heading.

▶ *Column B becomes wider. You should be able to see all the labels.*

Columns C and D contain similar information. You would like columns C and D to be the same width. To set several columns the same width, select those columns before setting the width.

■ Select columns C and D by clicking on the column heading for column C and dragging to the right until columns C and D are selected.

At this point, you could drag the right edge of one of the headings as mentioned above. However, you will specify it through the Column Width dialog box. There are two ways to display the Column Width dialog box; one is through the F̲ormat, C̲olumn, W̲idth command sequence, and the other is to use the Shortcut menu.

■ With the mouse pointer over the selected area, press the *right* mouse button.

▶ *The Shortcut menu is displayed, as shown in Figure 2-12, listing commands that can be applied to the selected range.*

Figure 2-12

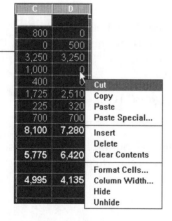

■ Select Column Width.

▶ *The Column Width dialog box is displayed, as shown in Figure 2-13.*

Figure 2-13

■ Enter **12** in the Column Width text box and complete the
   command.

▶ *The widths of both columns reflect the change.*

OUTLINING THE WORKSHEET BORDER

For printing, the worksheet range A1:D18 could use a border. This is
easily done.

■ Select the range A1:D18.

■ From the F<u>o</u>rmat menu, select the C<u>e</u>lls command.

■ Select the Border index tab.

▶ *The Format Cells dialog box appears, as shown in
   Figure 2-14.*

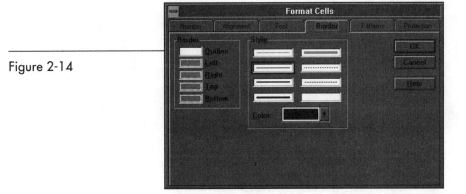

Figure 2-14

The Border box has five options, and the Sty<u>l</u>e box has eight line options
and a color option. You will activate the outline and select the thickest line
in the Sty<u>l</u>e option.

■ Click on the first option, <u>O</u>utline.

■ Select the thickest line option in the Sty<u>l</u>e box.

▶ *The Outline box displays a thick line.*

■   Complete the command.

▶   *The selected range has a thick border around it.*

PREVIEWING THE WORKSHEET

Let's look at the worksheet onscreen before actually printing it.

■   From the File menu, select Print Preview.

Alternative: Click on the Preview tool, 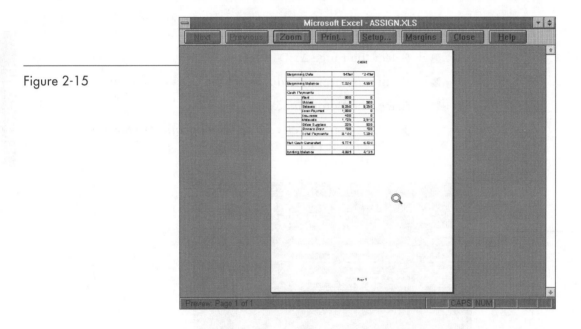.

▶   *A preview of the output is displayed, as shown in Figure 2-15.*

Figure 2-15

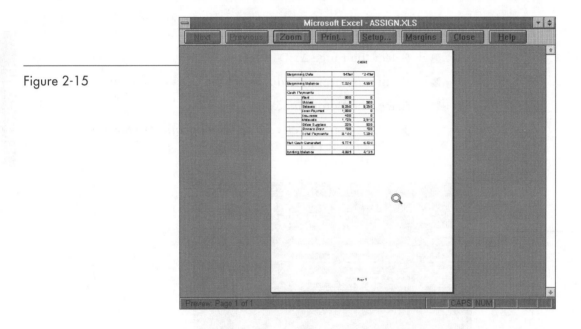

■   Enlarge the display by selecting the Zoom button.

▶   *The display enlarges.*

N O T E : If you selected either a screen font or a printer font, the display and printing are controlled by similar, but not identical fonts. It is possible for the column widths to be fine for screen display but too narrow for printing.

You decide that you'd like the spreadsheet printed centered on the page and that the gridlines should not be printed.

■ Select <u>S</u>etup, or select the Margins index tab.

▶ *The Page Setup dialog box appears, as shown in Figure 2-16. If the display is different, select the Page index tab.*

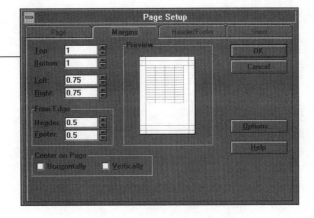

Figure 2-16

The dialog box contains a Center on Page box.

■ Click on the Hori<u>z</u>ontally check box.

Now turn off the gridlines.

■ Select the Sheet index tab.

▶ *The Page Setup dialog box is displayed, as shown in Figure 2-17.*

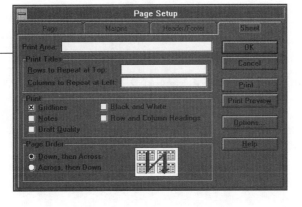

Figure 2-17

■ Click on the <u>G</u>ridlines check box so that the X disappears.

■ Complete the command by selecting OK.

▶ *The preview screen should look similar to Figure 2-18.*

Figure 2-18

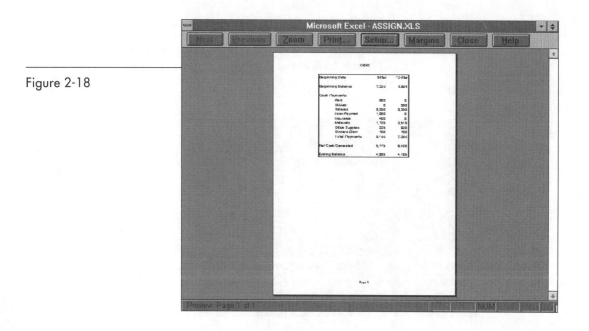

P R A C T I C E   T I M E   2 - 4

1. Select the Setup button in the preview screen and center the spreadsheet vertically as well.

2. When you are satisfied, use the Print tool to print the worksheet.

ENDING LESSON 2

This is the end of Lesson 2. Exit Excel and Windows as explained in Lesson 1. Do not save the changes to the ASSIGN worksheet.

SUMMARY

In this lesson, ways to change and enhance the printing and screen display are presented. The following topics are covered:

☐ **The onscreen Help feature provides information on the use of Excel.**

☐ **Files are retrieved from disk by using the File menu Open command.**

☐ **A sheet can be copied to another sheet by dragging the sheet tab.**

☐ **Two sheets on a workbook can be displayed by using the Window, New Window command to create a second window for the same workbook.**

☐ **A column is selected by clicking on the column heading or by selecting a cell in the column and pressing Ctrl + Spacebar.**

☐ **A row is selected by clicking on the row label or by selecting a cell in the row and pressing Alt + Spacebar.**

☐ **A range is selected by dragging the mouse or by holding down ⇧Shift while using the arrow keys to expand the range from a single cell.**

☐ **Multiple rows can be simultaneously selected by holding down Ctrl while the mouse is used to select another row.**

☐ **The gridlines in the spreadsheet can be removed by specifying the option through the Page Setup dialog box.**

☐ **The File menu Print Preview feature lets you examine a document's layout before printing.**

KEY TERMS

font	range	typeface
jump term	point size	type style

SPREADSHEET

COMMAND SUMMARY

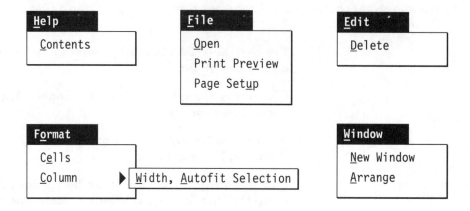

REVIEW QUESTIONS

1. What is meant by opening a file?

2. How do you select an entire column or row?

3. How do you delete a column?

4. How do you set two or more columns to the same width?

5. What is a range?

6. How do you select a range?

7. What three attributes describe a font?

8. What are gridlines, and how can you turn them off for printing?

9. What does the Outline option in the Border command do?

10. Why should you preview a document before printing it?

E X E R C I S E S

1. Open the workbook EX1 on your data disk.
   a. Copy the BUDGET1 sheet to the second sheet and rename it BUDGET2. You will work with BUDGET2.
   b. Delete column B.
   c. Make cells A1, A2, and A4 italic.
   d. Make cells A3 and A5 bold.
   e. Set the column B format to comma, with 0 decimal places.
   f. Adjust the widths of columns A and B so they print correctly.
   g. Print sheet BUDGET2.
   h. Save the workbook on your data disk, using the same filename.

2. Open the workbook EX2 on your data disk.
   a. Copy the FIXCOST1 sheet to the second sheet and rename it FIXCOST2. You will work with FIXCOST2.
   b. Delete column B.
   c. Make cell A7 bold.
   d. Format cell B7 as currency, with 0 decimal places.
   e. Adjust the widths of columns A and B so they print correctly.
   f. Print sheet FIXCOST2.
   g. Save the workbook on your data disk, using the same filename.

3. Open the workbook EX3 on your data disk.
   a. Copy the CHECKS1 sheet to the second sheet and rename it CHECKS2. You will work with CHECKS2.
   b. Delete columns D and F (delete column F first).
   c. Make row 1 bold.
   d. Adjust the widths of the columns to fit the data.
   e. In cell F1, enter the beginning balance of **10,575**.
   f. Adjust the width of column F.
   g. Write formulas in column F to give the balance: at F2 enter **=F1–E2** and copy to the rest.
   h. Print sheet CHECKS2.
   i. Save the workbook on your data disk, using the same filename.

LESSON 3 Modifying the Worksheet

OBJECTIVES

Upon completing the material presented in this lesson, you should understand the following aspects of Excel 5.0 for Windows:

- [ ] **Copying, cutting, and pasting information**
- [ ] **Extending a series of dates**
- [ ] **Setting date formats**
- [ ] **Inserting rows**
- [ ] **Using functions**
- [ ] **Using the Fill, Down command**
- [ ] **Right-justifying text entries**
- [ ] **Freezing panes**
- [ ] **Hiding and unhiding columns**
- [ ] **Splitting windows**
- [ ] **Using print titles**
- [ ] **Printing sideways**
- [ ] **Adjusting page margins**
- [ ] **Sorting a range**
- [ ] **Scaling a printed page**
- [ ] **Using the AutoFormat feature**

STARTING OFF

Turn on your computer and start Windows. Launch the Excel program and place your data disk in a disk drive.

■ Open the ASSIGN workbook from your data disk.

■ Copy worksheet CASH2 to the third sheet and rename it CASH3.

▶ *The worksheet should look like Figure 3-1.*

Figure 3-1

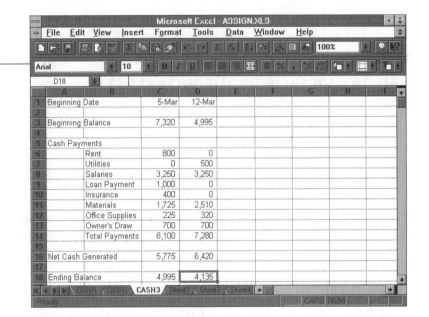

COPYING INFORMATION TO THE CLIPBOARD

The cash flow worksheet contains two weeks of information. Suppose you want to add another week to the sheet. The formulas in cells D3, D14, and D18 can be copied into the same rows in column E. You've used the F̲ill R̲ight command and the fill handle. In this lesson, you will copy data using the Clipboard. The **Clipboard** is a temporary storage place in your computer's memory. You can cut or copy data to the Clipboard, then paste it elsewhere in the workbook, even on a different sheet. When you cut, you move the original to the Clipboard; when you copy, the original stays intact and a copy is placed on the Clipboard.

■   Make cell D3 active.

■   From the Edit menu, select the Copy command to copy the cell to the Clipboard.

Alternative: Press Ctrl+C or click on the Copy tool, 🖫.

▶   *A marquee border appears around the selected cell.*

The marquee border around cell D3 indicates that the cell has been copied to the Clipboard.

N O T E :   If you were to cut, use the Edit menu Cut command, Ctrl+X, or the Cut tool, ✂.

PASTING INFORMATION INTO THE WORKSHEET

The information on the Clipboard can now be pasted elsewhere in the worksheet.

■   Select cell E3.

■   From the Edit menu, select the Paste command to paste the contents of the Clipboard into the cell.

Alternative: Press Ctrl+V or click on the Paste tool, 🖫.

▶   *The formula bar displays "=D18". The value displayed in the cell is 4,135, the ending cash balance for the previous week.*

N O T E :   You will notice that cell D3 still has a marquee border. This is because its contents are still on the Clipboard and hence can be copied to another cell if desired.

The formula in cell D3, =C18, was copied to E3 as a relative formula. That is, the formula was copied in terms of the offsets of the referenced cell from the selected cell.

P R A C T I C E   T I M E   3 - 1

Use the Clipboard to copy the formulas in cells D14 and D18 to E14 and E18, respectively.

EXTENDING A SERIES OF DATES

You are almost ready to enter the values for the week. First, you should put the beginning date in cell E1. You could simply enter 3/19, but Excel can automatically extend your series of dates. Since there are seven days between March 5 and March 12, you can specify that the same interval be used for the next cell in the row.

■ Select the range C1:D1.

■ Extend the series of dates by dragging the fill handle to E1. That is, position the mouse pointer on the square at the bottom right corner of cell D1 so that it turns into a cross hair, and drag it to cell E1.

▶ *The date 19-Mar appears in cell E1.*

DATE FORMATTING

The dates are displayed in the format d-mmm, which is European standard. You may prefer to display them as mmm-d. Excel lets you change the format code; it even lets you create display codes that are not on its list. The formatting is done through the Format Cells dialog box. Here, you will display the dialog box through the Shortcut menu.

■ Select the range C1:E1, but leave the mouse pointer over the selected area.

■ With the mouse pointer over the selected range, click the *right* mouse button.

▶ *A Shortcut menu appears, as shown in Figure 3-2, listing commands that can affect the selected range.*

■ Select Format Cells.

▶ *The Format Cells dialog box is displayed, as shown in Figure 3-3.*

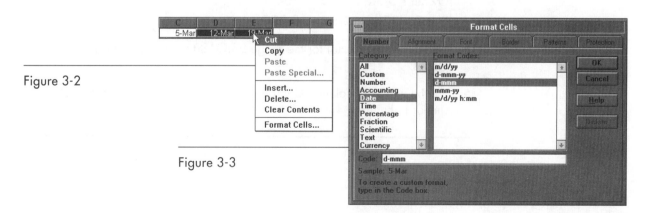

Figure 3-2

Figure 3-3

Excel noted the fact that the selected cells contained dates, so it displayed date-formatting information. Notice that the mmm-d format is not displayed as an option.

■ Enter mmm-d in the C*o*de text box. Make sure any previous codes are deleted.

■ Complete the command by clicking on OK or pressing [←Enter].

▶ *The date format is now changed.*

EXPANDING THE WORKSHEET

Bill would like the cash flow worksheet to cover 13 weeks, beginning with the week of March 5. Before you enter the data in column E, you can copy the formulas in rows 3, 14, and 18 to the next 10 columns and similarly extend the date series. First, copy the formulas in column E to columns F through O, then extend the dates to those columns.

P R A C T I C E   T I M E   3 - 2

1. Copy the formulas in column E, rows 3, 14, and 18, to columns F through O.

2. Extend the date series to columns F through O.

3. In column E, enter the third week's values, as follows:

Rent	**0**
Utilities	**0**
Salaries	**2,800**
Loan Payment	**0**
Insurance	**0**
Materials	**1,950**
Office Supplies	**145**
Owner's Draw	**700**
Net Cash Generated	**6,850**

4. Set the display format for the range E3:O18 to comma with 0 decimal places.

5. Set the widths of columns C through O to 12. Your screen should look similar to Figure 3-4.

Figure 3-4

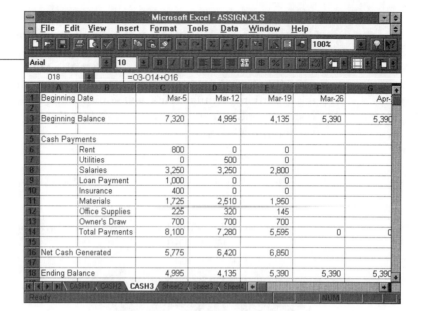

INSERTING ROWS

The cash flow worksheet is ready for the next 10 weeks of data. You decide it would look better if there were two rows—a title and a blank row—above the dates. This will require the insertion of two rows.

- Select rows 1 and 2.

- From the Insert menu, select Rows.

    ▶ *The entire worksheet moves down two rows.*

PRACTICE TIME 3-3

1. In cell A1, enter the title **CASH FLOW**.

2. Change the display of A1 to bold.

USING FUNCTIONS

You want to display the totals spent in different categories. In column P, rows 8 through 15, you will enter the sums for each row, columns C through O. You could use the Sum tool, but here you will use a function.

A **function** is a formula that is built into Excel and given a name. Each function uses one or more values, called **arguments**, as input; it then performs its operation, then returns, or produces, a value. Some common functions include SUM, AVERAGE, COUNT, MAX, and MIN. Excel contains a variety of mathematical, financial, trigonometric, logical, and character-manipulation formulas. To assist you in using these functions, Excel has an Insert, Function command. You will use this command to enter the SUM function at cell P8.

■   Select cell P8.

■   From the Insert menu, select Function.

    Alternative: Click on the Function tool, ![fx].

    ▶   *The Function Wizard dialog box appears, as shown in Figure 3-5.*

Figure 3-5

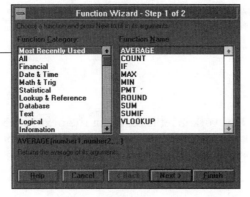

■   If necessary and possible, move the dialog box so that cell P8 and the formula bar are visible. The dialog box can be moved by dragging the title bar.

The dialog box contains two list boxes: the Function Category and the Function Name. When you choose an option in the Function Category list box, only those functions belonging to the category are displayed in the Function Name list box.

Below the Function Category list box, the highlighted function (from the Function Name list) is displayed along with its arguments, enclosed in parentheses. If there are several arguments, they are separated by commas. Arguments are the values the function uses, and may be values (1, 2, 3), references to cells (A1), ranges (D1:H24), mathematical formulas (6*26), or other functions.

■   Select Math & Trig in the Function Category list box.

■ Scroll the Function <u>N</u>ame list box and select the SUM function.

▶ *SUM(number1,number2,...) appears below the list box, as well as in cell P8 and the formula bar. The ellipses (...) in the arguments of the SUM display indicate that additional arguments are optional.*

■ Select the Next> button.

▶ *Another dialog box appears, as shown in Figure 3-6.*

Figure 3-6

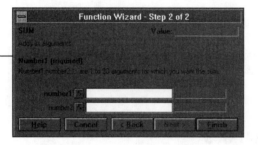

■ If necessary, drag the dialog box so that row 8 is visible.

Here, you are to enter arguments to be used in the function. The values you want added together are in the range C8:O8. You can either type the range (C8:O8) or select the range with the mouse.

■ Drag the mouse to select range C8 to O8. When you drag to select a range, you can start from any corner of the range.

▶ *Range C8:O8 appears in the number1 text box.*

■ Complete the command by selecting <u>F</u>inish or pressing ⏎Enter.

▶ *The value 800 appears in cell P8.*

P R A C T I C E   T I M E   3 - 4

1. Copy the formula at cell P8 to cells P9 through P15. You can do this using the F<u>i</u>ll, <u>D</u>own command, the <u>C</u>opy and <u>P</u>aste commands, or dragging the fill handle. The F<u>i</u>ll, <u>D</u>own command is very similar to the F<u>i</u>ll, <u>R</u>ight command.

2. In cell P3 enter the label **Totals**.

3. Make cell P3 bold.

4. Adjust the width of column P to be the same as columns C through O. Your screen should look similar to Figure 3-7.

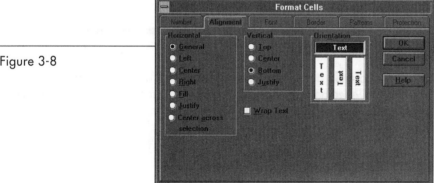

Figure 3-7

RIGHT-JUSTIFYING TEXT ENTRIES

Does anything about the Totals column heading bother you? It doesn't line up above the values in the column. Values are displayed right justified in a cell, whereas text is displayed left justified. You can change the text alignment to right justified through the Format Cells dialog box or by using a justification tool: Left-justify (▒), Center-justify (▒), or Right-justify (▒).

■   Select cell P3.

■   From the Format menu, select Cells then Alignment.

▶   *The Alignment dialog box is displayed, as shown in Figure 3-8.*

Figure 3-8

The dialog box contains three selection boxes. The Horizontal and Vertical selection boxes contain radio buttons for selecting the type of alignment in a cell, and the Orientation box contains four examples of text orientation.

- Select the <u>R</u>ight radio button in the Horizontal selection box, then complete the command.

  Alternative: Select the cells and click on the Right-justify tool.

  ▶ *The text in cell P3 is right justified.*

P R A C T I C E   T I M E   3 - 5

In column Q, you will enter the average amount for expenditures.

1. In cell Q3, enter the label **Averages** displayed in bold, right justified.

2. Change the width of column Q to 12.

3. In cell Q8, use the AVERAGE function (in the Statistical category) using the range C8:O8 as the argument.

4. Change the display format of cell Q8 to comma with 2 decimal places.

5. Copy the entry in cell Q8 to Q9 through Q15.

6. Save the workbook using the same filename.

FREEZING PANES

While you view columns P and Q, you cannot see columns A and B, which contain the row labels. Since this worksheet does not contain many rows, you may not have any trouble remembering what each row represents, but it would be better if the row labels were displayed. You can *freeze panes*, that is, keep selected rows and/or columns displayed even as you scroll through the worksheet. When you give the <u>W</u>indow menu <u>F</u>reeze Panes command, the rows and columns above and to the left of the selected cell are frozen. You should make sure the rows and columns containing titles are displayed and the appropriate cell is selected before issuing the <u>F</u>reeze Panes command.

P R A C T I C E   T I M E   3 - 6

Select cell A1, then select cell C4 so that cell A1 is visible in the workspace.

■   From the <u>W</u>indow menu, select the <u>F</u>reeze Panes command.

▶   *The workspace is divided into four panes, as shown in Figure 3-9. The horizontal and vertical lines dividing the panes are darker than the gridlines.*

Figure 3-9

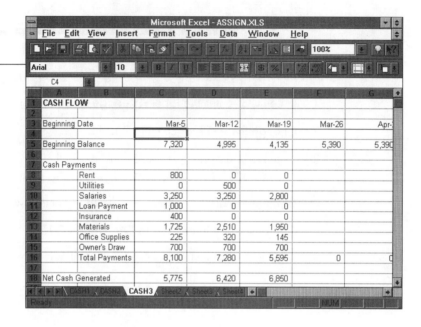

■   Now select cell P8.

▶   *The row labels in columns A and B remain displayed in the workspace.*

■   Press ⬇ until cell P20 is selected.

▶   *The upper right and lower left panes scroll synchronously with the lower right pane, so the appropriate titles are always displayed.*

The <u>F</u>reeze Panes command is useful when you have row and column titles that you want to keep displayed as you scroll to other areas of the worksheet.

■   From the <u>W</u>indow menu, select Un<u>f</u>reeze Panes.

SPLITTING WINDOWS

There are times when it is convenient to see two different sections of a sheet at the same time. The <u>F</u>reeze Panes command is limited to freezing rows or columns to the left or above the selected cell. The <u>S</u>plit command, on the other hand, divides the screen into either two or four panes, and you can display whichever portion of the worksheet in each pane. There are two ways to do this. The first method is to use the Window menu Split command, which splits the screen to the left and above the selected cell. The second method is to use the Split boxes. You will try both.

■ Scroll the screen so that columns A through G are in view.

■ Select cell E1.

Since the Split command divides the window above and to the left of the selected cell, by selecting a cell in row 1, the screen will be divided only horizontally, or into two panes.

■ From the Window menu, select Split.

▶ *The window is divided into two panes, as shown in Figure 3-10.*

Figure 3-10

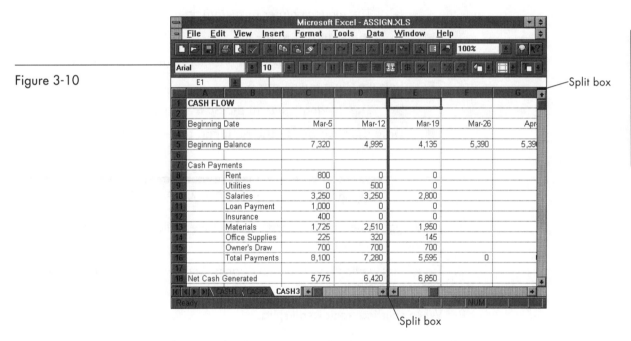

Split box

Split box

■ Scroll the pane on the right so that it displays columns P and Q.

■ Select cell C11 in the left pane and enter **1,200**.

▶ *The values in cells P11 and Q11 change in the right pane.*

■ Change the value in cell C11 back to **1,000**.

▶ *Again the values in cells P11 and Q11 change.*

■ Press ↓.

▶ *Notice that both panes scroll together.*

■ From the Window menu, select Remove Split.

▶ *The window is no longer split.*

P R A C T I C E   T I M E   3 - 7

1. Select a cell in the middle of the window and issue the Split command.

2. Try scrolling each pane.

3. When satisfied, remove the split.

The second method is to use the **Split boxes**, which are indicated in Figure 3-10.

■   Position the mouse pointer on the Split box to the right of the horizontal scroll bar.

▶   *The mouse pointer turns into* ◄||▶.

■   Drag the Split box to the left.

▶   *As you drag, a vertical bar moves along the window.*

■   Release the mouse button.

▶   *The window splits at the Split box position.*

■   Drag the Split box to the right end to remove the split.

P R A C T I C E   T I M E   3 - 8

1. Try dragging the Split box located above the vertical scroll bar to split the window horizontally.

2. Try splitting vertically to make four panes. Scroll vertically and horizontally and see the effect.

3. When satisfied, remove all splits.

HIDING COLUMNS

In order to view columns P and Q while entering data in column F, you can also hide columns G through O. When you **hide columns**, the contents are preserved but the columns are not displayed onscreen or in printouts. Hiding a column is the equivalent of setting the column width to zero.

■   Freeze panes so the rows above and columns to the left of cell C4 will remain in view.

■   Select columns G through O.

■   From the Format menu, select the Column then Hide.

■   Scroll the worksheet so that columns E, F, P, and Q are displayed, as shown in Figure 3-11.

Figure 3-11

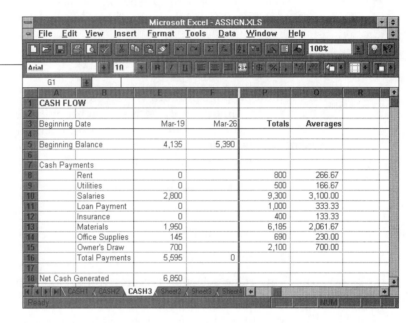

P R A C T I C E   T I M E   3 - 9

1. Unhide columns G through O.

    Hint: First select columns F through P.

2. Unfreeze panes.

PRINTING A MULTIPLE PAGE DOCUMENT

The cash flow worksheet is 17 columns wide. A large worksheet is printed on multiple sheets. The Excel Print Preview screen would be used to fine-tune your printouts without wasting a lot of paper. When you are satisfied with the way the printout looks, you can print the worksheet.

■   From the File menu, select the Print Preview command.

Alternative: Click on the Preview tool.

▶   *The Print Preview screen appears.*

The status bar indicates that this worksheet will require three pages to print.

NOTE: The number of columns displayed on the first page and the number of pages needed to print the worksheet vary depending on fonts and column widths.

■   Select the Next button.

▶   *Page 2 is displayed.*

If the multiple page printout is stapled together in a report, the reader might have a hard time identifying what each row represents on pages 2 and 3. Columns A and B should be printed on each page. This is called setting **print titles**. You need to exit (close) Print Preview and return to the worksheet document to do that.

■   Click on the Close button.

▶   *You return to the worksheet document.*

■   From the File menu, select the Page Setup command.

■   Select the Sheet index tab.

The Print Titles selection box lets you set the titles you want repeated for each page. You want columns A and B.

■   In the Columns to Repeat at Left box, enter **A:B**.

■   Complete the command.

P R A C T I C E   T I M E   3 - 1 0

Preview the printout. Note that columns A and B appear on each page. Do not close the Print Preview screen.

PRINTING SIDEWAYS (LANDSCAPE)

There are two page orientations. The usual orientation is **portrait**, named because most portraits of people are taller than they are wide. A sheet printed sideways on the page is printed in **landscape** orientation, named because many landscapes are painted on canvases that are wider than they are high. Sometimes, a short, wide worksheet may look better printed in landscape orientation. You can set the page orientation.

■ From the preview screen, click on the <u>S</u>etup button.

■ Select the Page index tab.

▶ *The Page Setup dialog box appears, with an Orientation selection box.*

■ Select <u>L</u>andscape and complete the command.

▶ *The preview screen displays the page in landscape orientation. The worksheet still prints on three pages.*

REDUCING THE NUMBER OF PAGES

If you want to reduce the number of pages for the report, you have several options to try: you can use narrower columns, you can reduce the page margins, you can scale the output, and you can use a smaller font. You will practice the first three options here.

Since columns B through N are almost twice as wide as they need to be, narrowing the column width is feasible in this case.

P R A C T I C E   T I M E   3 - 1 1

1. Close the Print Preview feature.

2. Change the width of columns C through O to 7, and columns P and Q to 9.

3. Preview, but do not close the preview screen.

N O T E :   If any values are displayed as ### in the cell, the column width is too narrow to print. This is because of differences between screen display and printed characters. If this happens, you should return to the worksheet and widen the columns slightly so that they will print properly.

The page margins can be set via the Page Setup dialog box, but the Print Preview feature also lets you drag margins to dynamically display the effects of your change.

■ Display page 1 on the preview screen.

■ Select the <u>M</u>argins button.

▶ *The page borders display margin and column-width handles, as shown in Figure 3-12.*

Figure 3-12

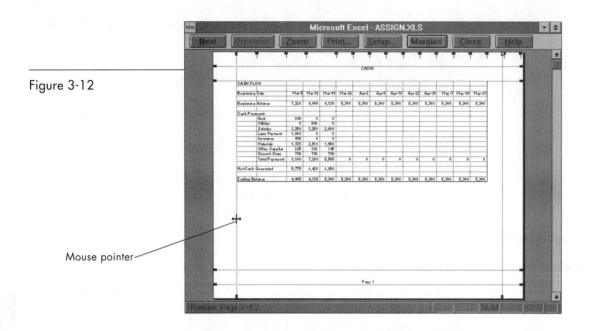

Mouse pointer

When the mouse pointer is located on one of the margin handles, as shown in the figure, the pointer becomes a cross hair with two arrows indicating the directions you can drag the margin or column width.

■ Drag the left margin to about half its initial width.

▶ *The page setup dynamically adjusts when you release the mouse button.*

■ Drag the right margin to about half its initial width.

▶ *Again, the preview screen reflects the change. In the example here, the sheet still takes two pages to print.*

Scaling the output means you can tell Excel to print the output at a percentage of the normal size. The percentage can be less or more than 100%. You can even ask it to automatically figure out the percentage so that a worksheet will fit on one page.

■ Select the Setup button.

■ If necessary, select the Page index tab.

In the Scaling selection box, you have option of specifying the percentage or specifying over how many pages you'd like the sheet to print (Excel figures out the percentage). You want this sheet to print on one page.

■ Select the Fit to radio button and complete the command.

▶ *The entire worksheet now fits on one page.*

Now center the worksheet horizontally on the page.

■ Select the Setup button, then the Margins index tab.

■ In the Center on Page list box select Horizontally so that an X appears in front of it.

■ Complete the command.

▶ *The report is now centered horizontally.*

CHANGING HEADERS AND FOOTERS

You now decide that you do not want the filename appearing at the top of the page nor the page number at the bottom.

■ Select the Setup button, then the Header/Footer index tab.

▶ *The dialog box similar to the one in Figure 3-13 is displayed.*

Figure 3-13

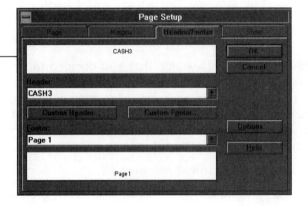

The upper half of the dialog box describes the current header information, and the bottom half describes the footer. The current header is the sheet number, and the footer is the page number. Notice that you have several predefined headers and footers to choose from. Right now, however, you do not want any headers or footers.

NOTE: If none of the displayed header/footer options meet your needs, you can create custom headers and footers.

■ Click on the down arrow at the right of the Header list box.

▶ *Various options for the header are displayed.*

■ Scroll to the top of the option and select [none].

PRACTICE TIME 3-12

1. Change the footer to [none].

2. Complete the command.

■ Print the worksheet by clicking on the Print button.

▶ *The Print dialog box appears. All the options should be correct for printing.*

■ Complete the command by clicking on OK.

▶ *The worksheet is printed.*

■ Save the workbook using the same filename.

SORTING

Just for practice, assume that you decided to alphabetize various uses of cash. This means you want the entries in rows 8 through 15 rearranged. Excel lets you reorder a range of rows in whatever sequence you want. You can arrange data in regular or reverse alphabetical order (A to Z or Z to A) or in ascending or descending numerical order, based on any column in the range. Such rearranging of rows is called *sorting*.

■ Select rows 8 through 15.

■ From the Data menu, select the Sort command.

▶ *The Sort dialog box appears, as shown in Figure 3-14.*

Figure 3-14

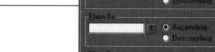

You can sort based on the entries in up to three columns. Currently, column A, in ascending (alphabetical) order, is displayed as the column to sort by, or the key. The second and third columns are not specified. The second column needs to be specified when there may be duplicate entries in the first column and you want to sort those duplicates based on a second-column entry, such as when the first column contains last names and the second column contains first names. The third column is used if the entries in the first two columns are identical, and might be used, for example, for middle names. Because you are sorting on the type of cash payment, you need to specify only one column, column B, in ascending order.

■   Select Column B in the Sort By text box.

■   Complete the command.

▶   *The range is sorted in alphabetical order.*

P R A C T I C E   T I M E   3 - 1 3

1. Try sorting in descending order of amounts displayed in column C.

2. Sort again in alphabetical order by type of use.

USING THE AUTOFORMAT FEATURE

Bill believes that you are a great computer expert, and you don't want to let him down. Although the table needs several more weeks of data to be complete, you would like to give it a professional look. Excel's AutoFormat feature can help. The **AutoFormat** feature is principally used for screen displays, not for printouts. Since AutoFormat affects the font, number format, row and column sizes, and borders, you should always save the worksheet before using AutoFormat. Here, you've already saved the file before practicing the sort feature.

■   Hide columns F through O.

■   Select the range A1:Q20.

■   From the Format menu, select the AutoFormat command.

▶   *The AutoFormat dialog box appears, as shown in Figure 3-15.*

Figure 3-15

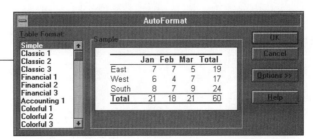

The AutoFormat feature has 16 professionally designed table formats. As you highlight different selections in the Table Format list box, the sample displays the effects.

■   Scroll through the various table formats and look at the sample.

■   Select the Classic 1 format style.

■   Complete the command by clicking on OK.

▶   *The selected range is formatted.*

■   Select a cell outside the range of the formatted table so that you can see the effect.

The gridlines on the screen distract from the formatting.

■   From the Tools menu, select Options then the View index tab.

▶   *The Options dialog box is displayed, as shown in Figure 3-16.*

Figure 3-16

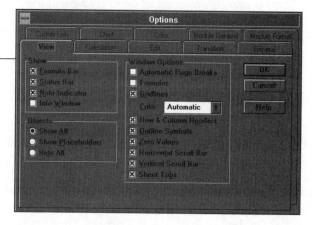

■   From the Window Options selection box choose Gridlines so that the X in front of the option disappears.

■   Complete the command.

▶   *The gridlines disappear from the display.*

■   Now delete any blank rows. Your display will look similar to Figure 3-17.

Figure 3-17

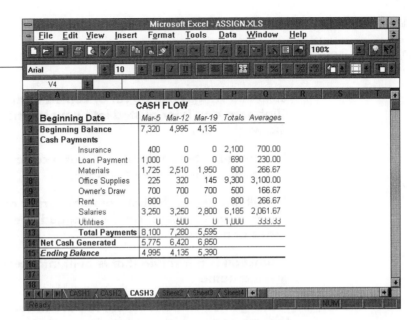

PRACTICE   TIME   3-14

1. Try other AutoFormat options.

2. When satisfied, close the workbook. Do not save the changes.

ENDING LESSON 3

This is the end of this lesson. Exit Excel and Windows before turning off your computer, as described previously. You do not need to save any of the open documents.

S U M M A R Y

In this lesson, ways to modify and expand the worksheet are presented. The following topics are discussed:

- [ ] **Cells and ranges can be cut or copied to the Clipboard and later pasted into new locations in the workbook.**

- [ ] **The marquee border indicates that a cell or range has been copied to the Clipboard.**

- [ ] **The fill handle, at the bottom right corner of the selected cell or range, can be dragged to extend a series of numbers.**

- [ ] **A function is a formula that is built into Excel and given a name.**

- [ ] **The arguments of a function, in parentheses, are the values on which the function operates.**

- [ ] **Although hidden columns are not displayed, their data remains unaffected.**

- [ ] **Freezing panes allows row and column titles to remain in view while the rest of the spreadsheet scrolls.**

- [ ] **Splitting a window allows you to display two or four sections of a worksheet at the same time.**

- [ ] **Worksheets can be printed in portrait or landscape orientation on many types of printers.**

- [ ] **Print titles are labels that are printed on every page of a multiple page printout.**

- [ ] **A range can be sorted in numeric or alphabetical order on up to three keys.**

- [ ] **The Excel AutoFormat feature has predesigned formats for effective presentation of tables of data.**

- [ ] **Scaling the output allows you to specify the percentage of normal size you'd like your output printed in.**

- [ ] **Gridlines on the display can be eliminated.**

KEY TERMS

argument	function	print titles
AutoFormat	hide columns	scaling
Clipboard	landscape	sorting
freeze panes	portrait	Split boxes

COMMAND SUMMARY

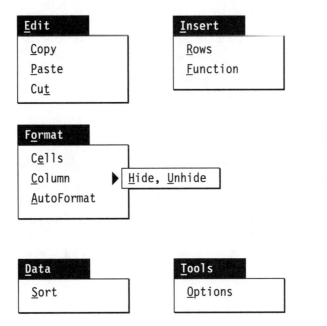

Edit
Copy
Paste
Cut

Insert
Rows
Function

Format
Cells
Column ▶ Hide, Unhide
AutoFormat

Window
Freeze Panes
Unfreeze Panes
Split
Remove Split

Data
Sort

Tools
Options

SPREADSHEET

REVIEW QUESTIONS

1. What is the difference between the Cut and Copy commands?

2. The information on the Clipboard is represented in the worksheet by the range with the _____ border.

3. How do you hide columns D through H in a worksheet?

4. How do you unhide columns?

5. How do you split a window?

6. How do you instruct Excel to print sideways on a page?

7. Why do you need to set the print titles when you have multiple page output?

8. Describe what the AutoFormat feature does.

9. What purpose does freezing panes serve?

10. When do you have to specify the second column to sort by?

E X E R C I S E S

1. Open the workbook EX1 on your data disk.
   a. Copy the BUDGET2 sheet to the third sheet and rename it BUDGET3. You will work with BUDGET3.
   b. Insert two rows above the table.
   c. Add the title **JANUARY BUDGET** above the table.
   d. Use AutoFormat to configure the table to a style you like.
   e. Eliminate gridlines from the display.
   f. Print the worksheet.
   g. Save the workbook on your data disk, using the same filename.

2. Open the workbook EX2 on your data disk.
   a. Copy the FIXCOST2 sheet to the third sheet and rename it FIXCOST3. You will work with FIXCOST3.
   b. Add two rows and two columns above and to the left of the table.
   c. Add the titles **FIXED COSTS** and **Greyback Division** in cells C1 and C2.
   d. Use AutoFormat to configure the table to a style you like.
   e. Eliminate gridlines from the display.
   f. Print the worksheet.
   g. Save the workbook on your data disk, using the same filename.

3. Open the workbook EX3 on your data disk.
   a. Copy the CHECKS2 sheet to the third sheet and rename it CHECKS3. You will work with CHECKS3.
   b. Add a row at row 2.
   c. Move the contents of cell F1 to cell F2 and remove bold from the entry.
   d. At F1, enter the label **Balance** and make it bold.
   e. Change the display format of columns E and F to accounting, no dollar sign, with 0 decimal places (the second option). This option displays negative numbers enclosed in brackets.
   f. At row 13, insert a row.
   g. You made a deposit of $2,250 on March 2. Enter **3/2** in cell B13, **DEPOSIT** in cell C13, and **–2250** in cell E13.
   h. Copy the formula at cell F12 to cells F13 and F14. This will calculate the correct balance.
   i. Print the worksheet.
   j. Save the workbook on your data disk, using the same filename.

4 Using Charting Features

OBJECTIVES

Upon completing the material presented in this lesson, you should understand the following aspects of Excel 5.0 for Windows:

- [ ] **Recognizing chart types**
- [ ] **Creating charts**
- [ ] **Selecting a chart type**
- [ ] **Entering a title in a chart**
- [ ] **Adding axis labels to a chart**
- [ ] **Inserting text and arrows in a chart**
- [ ] **Adding borders around text in a chart**
- [ ] **Saving a chart document**
- [ ] **Embedding a chart in a worksheet**
- [ ] **Saving a notebook with an embedded chart**
- [ ] **Using multiple data series in a chart**
- [ ] **Adding a legend to a chart**
- [ ] **Removing axis labels and data labels from a chart**
- [ ] **Using the ChartWizard feature**
- [ ] **Making an exploded pie chart**

STARTING OFF

Turn on your computer and start Windows. Maximize the Program Manager window, if needed, then launch the Excel program. Place your data disk in a disk drive.

CHARTING CONCEPTS IN EXCEL

A chart you create can be displayed on the monitor or printed. Furthermore, a chart can be in its own separate chart document or it can be inserted in the worksheet that contains the data used in the chart. Either way, a chart contains **dynamic references** to the worksheet. This means there is a dynamic link between the worksheet and the chart, so if the contents of relevant cells change in the worksheet, the chart is automatically updated to reflect those changes.

Different types of charts are used for different purposes.

A **pie chart** shows how a certain quantity is divided up. For example, it may depict the categories of expenses, as shown in Figure 4-1.

Figure 4-1

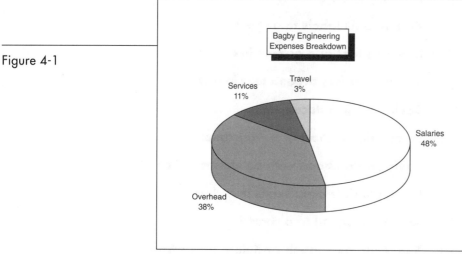

A **column chart**, or bar chart, shows how some quantity varies between different categories. For example, it may compare budgeted and actual costs for various categories of expenses, as shown in Figure 4-2.

A three-dimensional or **3-D chart** enhances the visual effect over that of a two-dimensional chart. For example, Figure 4-3 displays a 3-D column chart of the same data that was depicted in Figure 4-2.

A **line chart** often shows how something varies over time. For example, it may display how cash on-hand fluctuates from week to week, as shown in Figure 4-4.

Figure 4-2

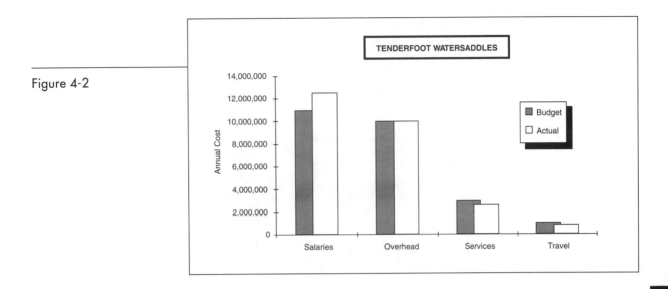

Figure 4-3

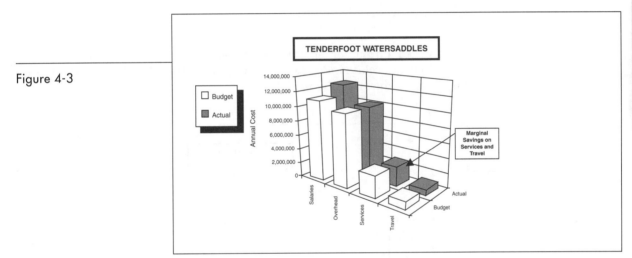

Figure 4-4

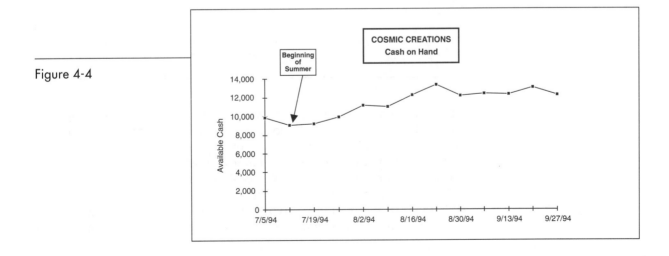

An ***area chart*** is similar to a line chart. It is often used to compare two or more trends. For example, it may illustrate a company's income and profits over time, as shown in Figure 4-5.

Figure 4-5

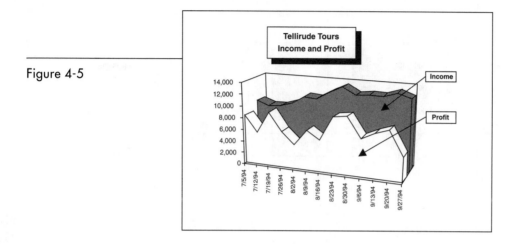

An ***xy chart***, or scatter chart, often displays how two numerical quantities are related. For example, it may portray the effect of advertising on sales, as shown in Figure 4-6.

Figure 4-6

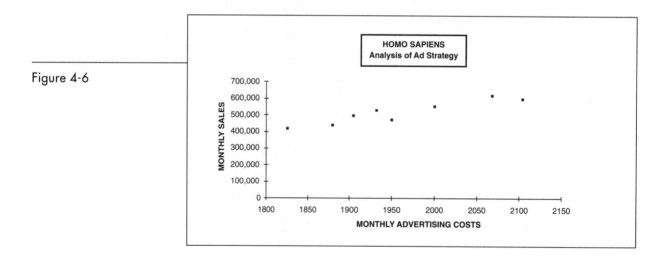

Sometimes a mixture of chart types presents different types of data effectively. In Excel, you can build a ***combination chart***, also called an overlay chart, which has a second chart of a different type plotted on top of the main chart in the same chart window, such as the combination of weekly sales and closing stock prices, as shown in Figure 4-7.

You will explore most of these options in this lesson. Although it is possible to make many different types of charts with the same data, some types of charts may be more appropriate than others. This lesson

Figure 4-7

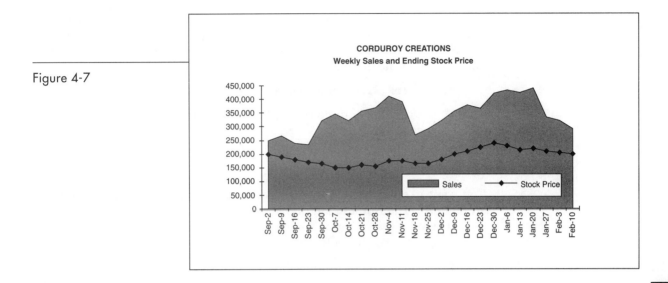

concentrates on the commands and options available in charting, not on the reasons for using the different types of graphs in business. In Excel, a chart consists of a series of ***chart items***, such as the title, the axis labels, and legends. Figure 4-8 labels items that are used in charts. This lesson describes how to use these items.

Figure 4-8

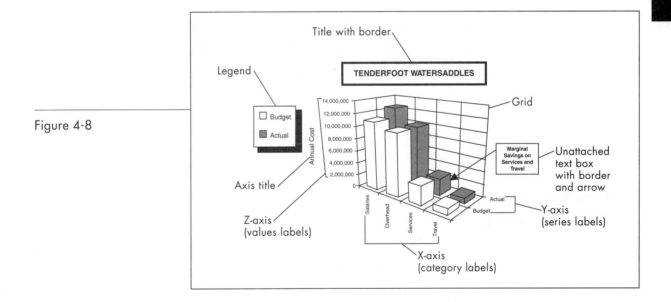

You will create a workbook containing daily sales figures and use this worksheet for several exercises on charts.

- Start a new workbook if needed.

- In cell A1, enter the title **DAILY SALES** and make it bold.

You want to enter titles for Monday through Saturday in cells B2 through G2. The AutoFill feature in Excel recognizes days of the week and months of the year, so you can extend either type of label across columns or down rows by using the fill handle.

■   In cell B2, enter **Monday**.

■   Drag the fill handle to cell G2 to extend the title across the columns.

▶   *The days of the week, from Tuesday to Saturday, are automatically filled in.*

You want to enter the week dates, March 5 through March 19, in cells A3 through A5. The AutoFill feature can use a range of two cells to establish a sequence of dates or numbers which can be extended across columns or down rows by using the fill handle.

■   In cells A3, A4, and A5, enter dates **3/5**, **3/12**, and **3/19**, respectively.

P R A C T I C E   T I M E   4 - 1

1. Enter the following data for three weeks of sales.

	Mon	Tues	Weds	Thurs	Fri	Sat
5-Mar	885	975	1045	1105	1035	730
12-Mar	840	1080	1140	1350	1400	610
19-Mar	900	1040	1210	1365	1480	855

2. Adjust the widths of all columns to display the contents of all the cells.

3. Save the workbook on your data disk as DAILY.

CREATING A CHART

Many situations arise where information is better presented graphically than in the worksheet table format. Before you create a chart, however, you should decide how you want to use it. If a chart is intended to supplement worksheet data and be displayed with it, it would be better to embed the chart in the worksheet. You can also display a chart on a separate sheet in your workbook. A chart sheet is inserted into the workbook just to the left of the worksheet it is based on. Either way, the chart is dynamically linked to the worksheet data on which it is based, and both are updated when you update the worksheet.

Charts are created using commands or buttons that display the ChartWizard. The **ChartWizard** is a series of dialog boxes that guides you through the steps required to create a new chart or modify settings for an existing chart. When creating a chart with the ChartWizard, you can specify the worksheet range, select a chart type and format, and specify how you want your data to be displayed. You can also add a legend, a chart title, and title to each axis. A **legend** is descriptive text that identifies each series of data on a chart.

In our current example, you decide that a column chart will provide a good comparative view of daily sales figures for the week of March 5. The sales figures for a week are in the range B3:G3. You also want to include the day labels in row 2. Thus the chart consists of labels and data in the range B2:G3. You will create this in its own chart sheet.

■ Select the range B2:G3.

■ From the Insert menu, select Chart.

▶ *You are asked if you want the chart inserted in the current worksheet or created on a new sheet.*

If you were to select the first option, On This Sheet, the chart would be embedded in the same sheet as the data. To select this option, you can also click on the ChartWizard tool, ■. You will do this later in the lesson.

■ Select As New Sheet.

▶ *The first ChartWizard dialog box appears, as shown in Figure 4-9, and a sheet tab for Chart1 is inserted to the left of the Sheet1 sheet tab.*

Figure 4-9

The selected range, B2:G3, should appear in the Range text box (as an absolute range, with dollar signs). Also a sheet, Chart1, was inserted to the left of the current sheet.

■ Select the Next> button.

▶ *The second ChartWizard dialog box appears, as shown in Figure 4-10.*

The column chart is the default chart type.

■ Make sure that Column is selected, then click on Next>.

▶ *The third ChartWizard dialog box is displayed, as shown in Figure 4-11.*

Figure 4-10

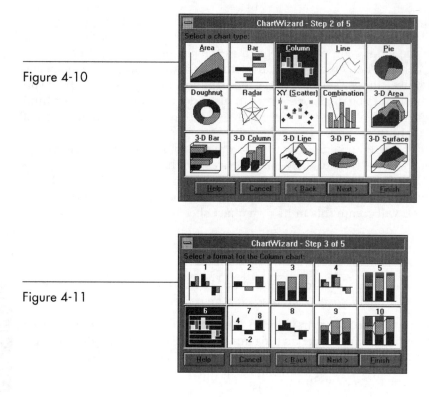

Figure 4-11

Figure 4-12

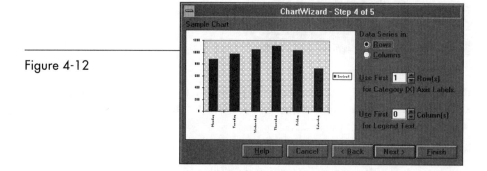

You have ten options for column chart.

■   Select 1 then Next>.

▶   *The fourth ChartWizard dialog box is displayed, as shown
     in Figure 4-12.*

In addition to letting you preview the chart, this dialog box lets you specify
the row that contains labels for the horizontal axis (x-axis) of the chart. The
horizontal axis is also called the **category axis**. The default is the first row
of the specified range. You can also specify the column that contains the
information for the legend. Since this chart contains just one data series,
you will not insert a legend.

■   Select Next>.

▶   *The last ChartWizard dialog box is displayed, as shown in Figure 4-13.*

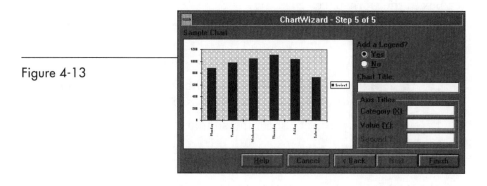

Figure 4-13

This dialog box lets you indicate whether you want to add a legend and also lets you specify the chart title and axis labels. Enter a chart title and the title for the ***series axis*** (vertical or y-axis).

■   Click on the No radio button for legend.

■   In the Chart Title text box, enter **DAILY SALES**.

■   In the Value (Y) text box, enter **Sales ($)**.

■   Click on the Finish button.

▶   *The chart sheet is displayed, as shown in Figure 4-14.*

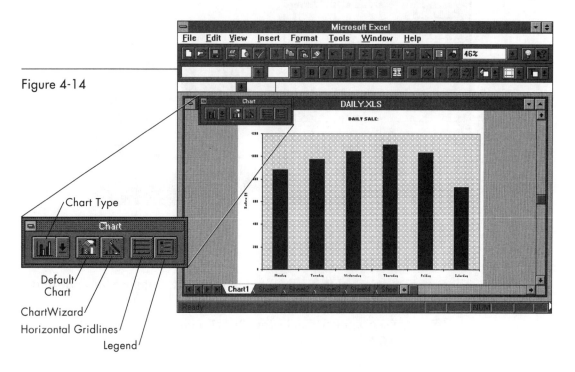

Figure 4-14

Chart Type

Default Chart

ChartWizard

Horizontal Gridlines

Legend

Note the box containing the Chart tools that appeared onscreen (see Figure 4-14). This is actually the Chart toolbar. This toolbar can be moved anywhere onscreen by dragging its title bar. Also, if you were to move it above the workspace, it would turn into a regular toolbar. Keep the toolbar as a box in the workspace.

To view the dynamic nature of the link, you will display both Chart1 and Sheet1 onscreen.

■ From the <u>W</u>indow menu, select <u>N</u>ew Window.

▶ *A second window displaying the DAILY workbook appears, as indicated by the title DAILY.XLS:2.*

■ Click on the Sheet1 sheet tab so that this window displays the data.

■ From the <u>W</u>indow menu, select <u>A</u>rrange.

■ Make sure that the <u>T</u>iled radio button is selected, and complete the command.

▶ *The screen displays both Sheet1 and Chart1, as shown in Figure 4-15.*

Figure 4-15

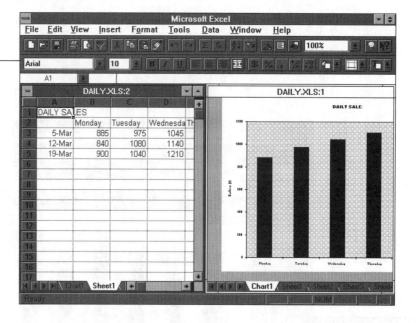

■ Scroll both windows so that the data and the column for Saturday is displayed.

The Saturday sales value is the lowest in the chart. Suppose its value in the worksheet is changed to 1000.

■ On the window displaying Sheet1, change the sales value at G3 to **1000**.

> ▶ *The chart on the right reflects the change.*

- ■ Change the value of G3 back to **730**.

> ▶ *Again, the chart immediately reflects the change.*

CHANGING CHART TYPE

You can easily change the chart type.

- ■ First, make the window containing Chart1 the active window.

- ■ From the F<u>o</u>rmat menu, select Chart <u>T</u>ype.

> ▶ *The Chart Type dialog box appears, as shown in Figure 4-16.*

Figure 4-16

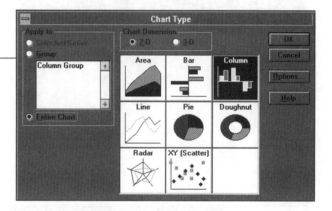

You have a choice of two-dimensional or three-dimensional charts.

- ■ Select the <u>3</u>-D radio button to see the options for three-dimensional charts.

> ▶ *Options for 3-D charts appear.*

- ■ Select 3-D Column and complete the command.

> ▶ *The chart is changed.*

- ■ Maximize the window containing the Chart1 sheet.

> ▶ *The display should look similar to Figure 4-17.*

You can also select the chart type from the Chart Type tool. When you click on the right arrow next to the Chart Type tool in the Chart toolbar, a drop-down menu displaying various chart types appears, as shown in Figure 4-18.

Figure 4-17

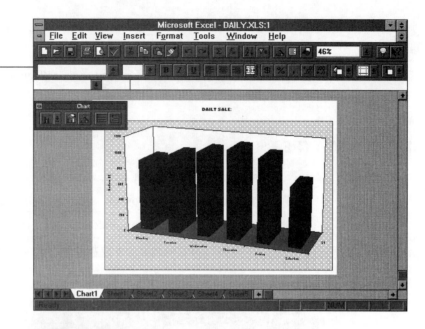

Figure 4-18

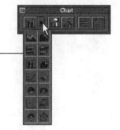

P R A C T I C E   T I M E   4 - 2

1. Select other chart types. If the option you select is inappropriate for the data, a warning box is displayed.

2. When you are satisfied, select the 3-D Column chart, as shown in Figure 4-17.

ADDING HORIZONTAL GRIDLINES

You will add horizontal gridlines to the graph so that it will be easier to visually compare values. Although you can do this through the Insert menu Gridlines command, here you will use the Horizontal Gridlines tool in the Chart toolbar.

■ Click on the Horizontal Gridlines tool.

▶ *Gridlines are added.*

SELECTING CHART ITEMS

Each part of a chart is a specific item. If you want to format, move, size, or edit an item, you must first select it. To select an item, simply point and click on the item with the mouse. When you do, either a box with little squares, called **handles**, appears around the item, or simply a couple of handles appear to indicate that you've selected the item. The reference area at the far left of the formula bar tells you which item is selected. If the title is selected, for example, the formula bar displays the word "Title".

EDITING THE CHART TITLE

You decide that you would like to edit the chart title to make it more descriptive and also add a second line. The first line is to say "COSMIC CREATIONS", and the second line is "Daily Sales for Week of Mar 5".

■ Click on the chart title.

▶ *A box appears around the title.*

■ Click on the formula bar so that the insertion point appears.

■ Type **COSMIC CREATIONS** then press Ctrl + ←Enter.

▶ *The formula bar expands and the insertion point moves one line down.*

■ Type **Daily Sales for Week of Mar 5** and press ←Enter.

▶ *The title is now expanded.*

In a two-dimensional chart, the horizontal direction is called the category axis or x-axis, and the vertical direction is the series axis or y-axis. In a three-dimensional chart, the two-dimensional portion lies on the surface. That is, the x-axis is still the horizontal direction, but the y-axis is now the depth. The z-axis becomes the vertical direction. You may notice that there is an "S1" that appears along the y-axis. This is a label for a y-axis that is not needed.

■ From the Insert menu, select Axes.

■ Click on the Series (Y) Axis so that the X in front of it disappears.

■ Complete the command.

▶ *The S1 disappears.*

SPREADSHEET

PRACTICE TIME 4-3

Preview the chart. It should look similar to Figure 4-19.

Figure 4-19

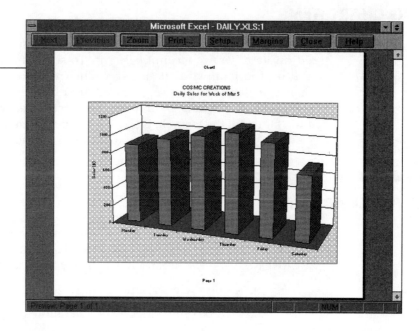

ADDING A TEXT ITEM

Suppose that a fire occurred down the street on Saturday, and you think it may have affected your sales that day. You want to note this somewhere on the chart. To add a text item, you must first make sure that another text item is not selected within the chart. Otherwise, the selected text item gets edited.

■ Make sure that a chart item is not selected. You can do this by clicking somewhere outside the chart display.

■ Type the text **Fire at Albrights affected sales** and press ⎴Enter⎵.

▶ *The text you typed appears on the chart, surrounded by handles, as shown in Figure 4-20.*

You would like the text in the box to appear three or four lines high and narrower. You can use the mouse to change the size of the box.

■ Drag one of the corners of the box to change the size until the box is about half as wide as its original size and two times the original height. That is, position the mouse pointer on one of the corner handles so that it turns into a double arrow. Then drag it.

Figure 4-20

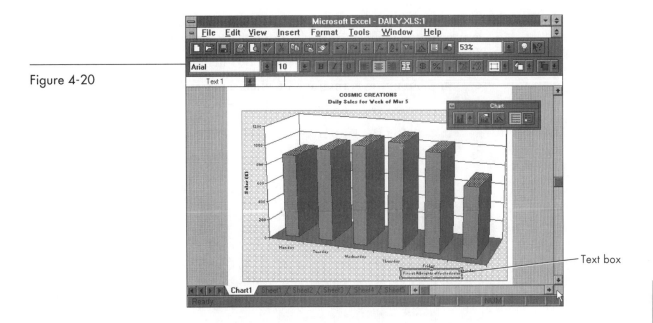

Text box

NOTE: It may take several tries until it looks just right.

You will now move this text box above the Saturday column in the upper right corner of the chart.

■   Move the mouse pointer to just below this text box so that the tip of the pointer touches the box. The mouse pointer must remain an arrow.

■   Drag the box to the upper right corner of the chart, above the Saturday column, as shown in Figure 4-21.

Figure 4-21

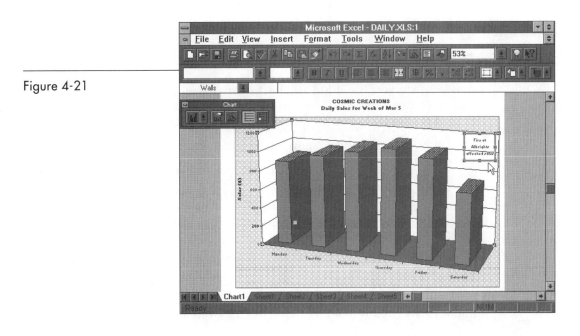

Although better, this text box still does not stand out. You will put a box around it and change the background to a solid color.

■ Make sure that the desired text item is selected.

■ From the Format menu, choose Selected Object.

Alternative: Press Ctrl+1.

■ Select the Patterns index tab.

▶ *The Format Object dialog box is displayed, as shown in Figure 4-22.*

Figure 4-22

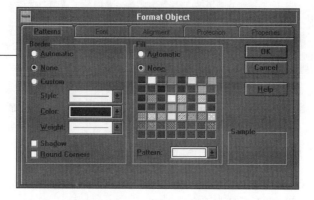

■ In the Border selection box, click on the Automatic radio button.

■ In the Fill selection box, click on the Automatic radio button.

■ Complete the command.

■ Click elsewhere on the sheet to deselect the text item.

▶ *The text item now has border and a solid background.*

ADDING A TOOLBAR

Another item you can add to a chart is an arrow that visually connects two items. You will use an arrow to connect the text you just entered to the Saturday sales column. An arrow is added using the Drawing toolbar.

■ From the View menu, select Toolbars.

▶ *The Toolbars dialog box appears, as shown in Figure 4-23.*

■ Select Drawing by clicking on the box in front of it so that an X appears.

■ Complete the command.

▶ *The Drawing toolbar appears, as shown in Figure 4-24.*

This toolbar is similar to the Chart toolbar in that if you drag it above the workspace, it turns into a regular toolbar. Drag it back over the workspace and it turns back into a box that can be moved anywhere.

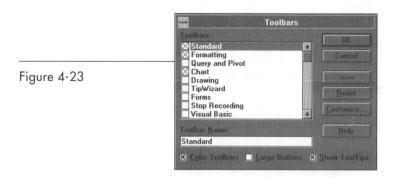

Figure 4-23

Figure 4-24

Arrow tool

■ Click on the Arrow tool.

▶ *The pointer turns into a cross hair.*

■ Drag the cross from the bottom border of the text box to the Saturday column.

▶ *An arrow appears.*

NOTE: If you need to, you can adjust the position of the arrow by dragging the handle on each end.

■ Click elsewhere in the workspace.

▶ *The screen should look similar to Figure 4-25.*

■ Close the Drawing toolbar by double-clicking on its control-menu box.

Figure 4-25

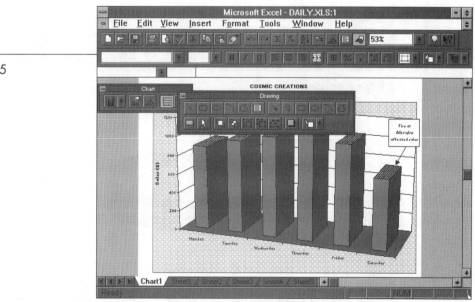

CLOSING A WORKBOOK WINDOW

As you recall, we still have two windows for the same workbook. You will now close one of them.

■ With either window in view, double-click on the control-menu box in the upper left corner of the window.

▶ *One of the workbook windows is now closed, as indicated by the filename that appears in the title bar.*

■ Save the workbook using the same filename.

PIE CHARTS

Pie charts use a single data series and show how something is divided up. You will examine the weekly cash outflow using a simple pie chart.

■ Select the Sheet1 sheet tab.

■ Select range B2:G3.

P R A C T I C E   T I M E   4 - 4

Create a new chart on a separate sheet. It is to be a 3-D Pie chart (option 7), using the first row as Pie Slice labels, with the chart title COSMIC CREATIONS, and no legend. The screen should look similar to Figure 4-26.

Figure 4-26

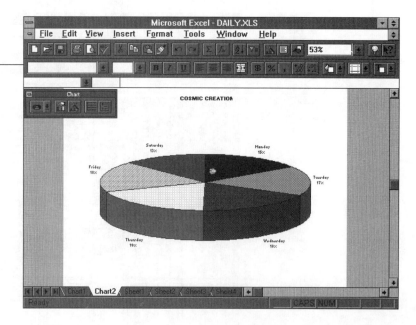

MAKING AN EXPLODED PIE CHART

You may have noticed that you had options to create an ***exploded pie chart*** while creating the chart using the ChartWizard. Pieces of a pie chart can be exploded, or removed from the circle, for emphasis.

■ Click anywhere on the pie.

▶ *Handles appear around the whole pie.*

■ Click on the slice for Tuesday.

▶ *Handles appear around the slice for Tuesday.*

■ Drag the slice away from the center of the pie.

▶ *The slice is now exploded, as shown in Figure 4-27.*

Figure 4-27

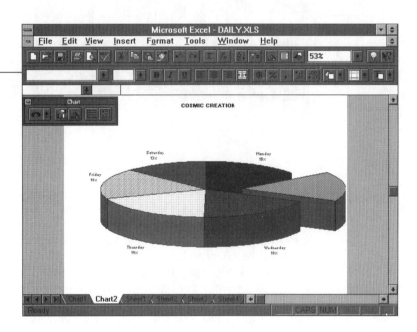

EMBEDDING A CHART IN A WORKSHEET

You may want the chart and the worksheet data to be displayed or printed together. This can be done by simply specifying that the chart be inserted in the worksheet. You will first copy the data from Sheet1 to another sheet, and will work with the new sheet.

■ Copy the contents of Sheet1 to the next sheet. This is accomplished by holding down Ctrl while dragging the Sheet1 tab over Sheet2.

■ Click on the Sheet1 (2) tab.

You have three weeks of data in the worksheet. You can display all three data series in one chart. Each data series is plotted as a different line, in different color, as a row of bars, or as a column. This time, you need to include row labels in column A in the selected range.

■   Select the range A2:G5.

■   From the Insert menu, select Chart then On This Sheet.

Alternative: Click on the ChartWizard tool.

▶   *A marquee border appears around the A2:G5 range, and the mouse pointer indicates the ChartWizard, as shown in Figure 4-28.*

Figure 4-28

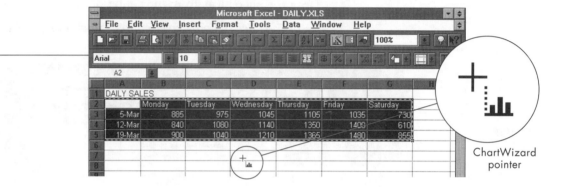

ChartWizard pointer

To have the ChartWizard automatically place the chart on the worksheet, click on the worksheet where you want the top left corner of the chart to be positioned. If you want to specify the chart's location and size, however, you need to position the mouse pointer on the worksheet where you want one corner of the chart to be, and then drag until the rectangle is the shape you want. Right now, you will use the default size.

■   Click on cell B7.

▶   *The first ChartWizard dialog box is displayed, showing A2:G5 as the range.*

■   Select Next>.

▶   *The second ChartWizard dialog box is displayed, with Column as the default selection.*

■   Select Next>.

▶   *The third dialog box is displayed.*

■   Select 1, then Next>.

▶   *The fourth dialog box is displayed.*

The ChartWizard has selected the first row of the range as the x-axis label, and the first column for the legend text. The information is correct.

■   Select Next>.

▶   *The fifth dialog box is displayed.*

This time you do want to display the legend. You need to insert the chart title and the y-axis title.

■   Enter **COSMIC CREATIONS** for the chart title, and **Sales ($)** for the y-axis title.

■   Select <u>F</u>inish.

▶   *A chart is embedded, similar to Figure 4-29.*

Figure 4-29

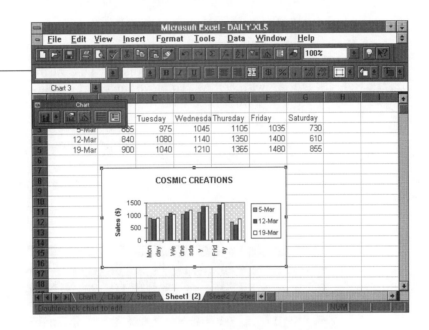

This chart does not look quite right, especially the labels along the x-axis. This can be corrected by changing the following in any combination: the size of the chart, the font size of the label text, and the alignment of the label text. To edit the chart (in this case, changing the font or alignment), you need to make the chart active.

■   Double-click anywhere on the chart to make it active.

▶   *A thicker border appears around the chart.*

■   Click on the x-axis (the line itself) so that handles appear on each end.

■   From the F<u>o</u>rmat menu, choose S<u>e</u>lected Axis.

Alternative: Press Ctrl+1.

▶   *The Format Axis dialog box appears.*

First you will change the alignment.

■ Select the Alignment index tab.

■ Change the orientation to vertical.

You will now change the font size.

■ Select the Font index tab.

■ Change the Font size to 8.

■ Complete the command.

■ Click elsewhere on the worksheet.

You will now change the size of the chart.

■ Click on the chart to select it.

▶ *A box with handles appears around the chart.*

■ Now move the chart display so that the top left corner aligns with cell A7. To move the chart display, position the mouse pointer on the bottom edge of the box surrounding the chart, and then drag.

■ Change the size of the chart by dragging the bottom right handle to cell F25.

▶ *The chart should look similar to Figure 4-30.*

■ Save the workbook again, using the same filename.

Figure 4-30

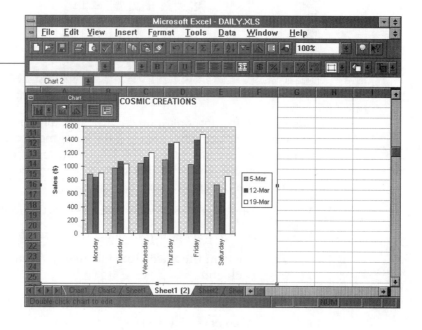

ENDING LESSON 4

This ends the lesson. Exit Excel. You do not need to save any open files.

S U M M A R Y

In this lesson, the graphic features of Excel are presented. The following topics are covered:

- ☐ **To create a chart, a range of the data and labels is selected in the worksheet and a new chart is created as a part of the sheet containing the data or as a new sheet within the workbook.**

- ☐ **The ChartWizard guides you through the creation of a chart, with a series of easy-to-follow dialog boxes.**

- ☐ **The chart is dynamically linked to the data in the worksheet on which it is based.**

- ☐ **A text item may be positioned anywhere in the chart. It can be formatted to add a border and background color.**

- ☐ **Arrows may be added and positioned in the chart using a Drawing tool.**

- ☐ **Charts may contain several data series.**

- ☐ **A legend is added to identify the data series.**

- ☐ **Pie charts may contain exploded segments.**

K E Y   T E R M S

area chart	combination chart	line chart
category axis	dynamic references	pie chart
chart item	exploded pie chart	series axis
ChartWizard	handles	3-D chart
column chart	legend	xy chart

COMMAND SUMMARY

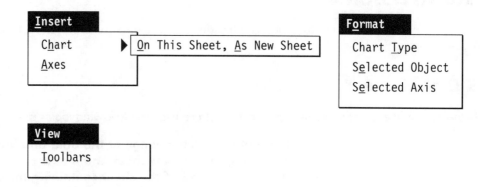

REVIEW QUESTIONS

1. How do you create a chart in Excel?
2. Name at least five types of charts that can be created in Excel.
3. What are axes? Describe the x, y, and z axes.
4. What is a data series, and what does it mean when a chart has two data series?
5. What is a text item in a chart?
6. How do you display both a chart and a worksheet from the same workbook?
7. How do you add an arrow? What is the purpose of adding an arrow?
8. How do you add a border to a text item?
9. How do you embed a chart in a worksheet?
10. What is an exploded pie chart?

EXERCISES

1. Start a new workbook.
   a. Enter the data shown in Figure 4-31 and create a 3-D exploding pie chart (embedded in the same worksheet).
   b. Print the worksheet.
   c. Save the workbook on your data disk as CHART1.
2. Start a new workbook.
   a. Enter the data shown in Figure 4-32 and create a combination chart (embedded in the same worksheet).

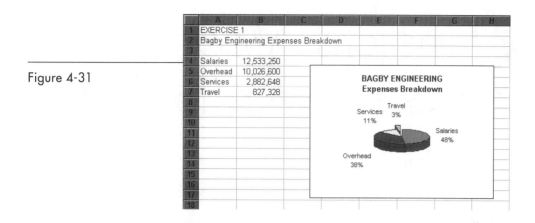

Figure 4-31

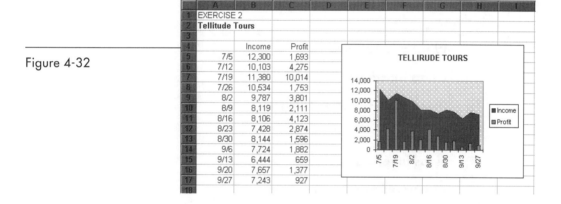

Figure 4-32

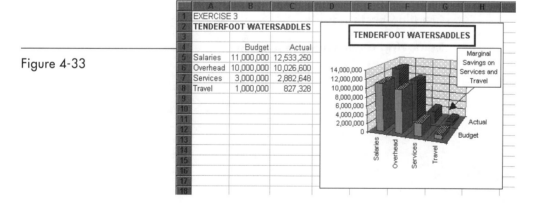

Figure 4-33

b. Print the worksheet.

c. Save the workbook on your data disk as CHART2.

3. Start a new workbook.

   a. Enter the data shown in Figure 4-33 and create a 3-D column chart (embedded in the same worksheet).

   b. Print the worksheet.

   c. Save the workbook on your data disk as CHART3.

OBJECTIVES

Upon completing the material presented in this lesson, you should understand the following aspects of Excel 5.0 for Windows:

- ☐ **What a function is**
- ☐ **Using functions**
- ☐ **Using the Goal Seek feature**
- ☐ **What a macro is**
- ☐ **Steps involved in recording a macro**
- ☐ **Two ways to run a macro**
- ☐ **Customizing the toolbar**
- ☐ **Creating custom tools**
- ☐ **Removing tools from the toolbar**

STARTING OFF

Turn on your computer and start Windows. Maximize the Program Manager window, if needed, then launch the Excel program. Place your data disk in a disk drive.

FUNCTIONS

A ***function*** is a prewritten formula that is named and incorporated into Excel. You can use a function by specifying its name and ***arguments***. Arguments contained within parentheses following the function are the values on which the function operates to produce a result. Arguments may consist of text, numbers, cell addresses or ranges, or other functions. The function is said to *return* a result, meaning the result (or value) replaces the function in the display. A function that is contained in a formula or another function is evaluated and its value is used in the formula or function. Often, functions have more than one argument. Those arguments are separated by commas within the parentheses.

The Insert menu Function command or the Function tool can be used to place Excel functions in a cell entry.

■ From the Insert menu, select the Function command.

Alternative: Click the Function tool, ⨍×.

▶ *The Function Wizard dialog box is displayed, as shown in Figure 5-1.*

Figure 5-1

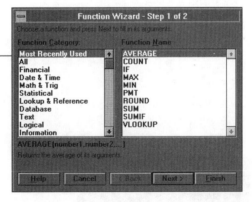

The dialog box contains two list boxes: The Function Category and the Function Name. When you choose an option in the Function Category list box, only those functions belonging to the category are displayed in the Function Name list box.

Below the Function Category list box, the highlighted function (from the Function Name list) is displayed along with its arguments, enclosed in parentheses. If there are several arguments, they are separated by commas.

The functions are in 10 different categories, including Financial, Date & Time, Math & Trig, and Statistical. Some of these categories, such as Financial or Statistical, require knowledge about those subjects to use their functions. The examples in this lesson are restricted to subjects with which most users are familiar.

■   Select Cancel to close the Function Wizard dialog box.

DATE AND TIME FUNCTIONS

Excel treats dates as serial numbers, with January 1, 1900, being 1. The display format chosen allows you to see it as a date.

■   Rename the current sheet Date & Time.

■   Select cell A1.

■   From the Insert menu, select the Function command.

Alternative: Click the Function tool.

■   Select the Date & Time category in the Function Category list box.

▶   *The function names displayed in the Function Name list box are those that deal with dates and times.*

■   Select to highlight the DATE function, but do not press anything.

▶   *Below the Function Category list box, the text "DATE(year,month,day)" appears, and the formula "=DATE()" is displayed in the formula bar.*

■   Select Next>.

▶   *The Function Wizard Step 2 dialog box is displayed, as shown in Figure 5-2.*

Figure 5-2

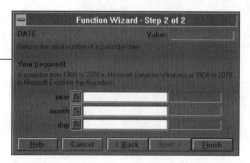

You can make the entries for arguments from this dialog box. Because the insertion point appears in the year text box, the explanation for the year argument appears in the dialog box.

■ Click on the month text box to position the insertion point.

▶ *The explanation for the month argument is displayed.*

Because an argument can be a function, the Function tool appears in front of each argument text box to make it easy to insert a function.

■ In the year text box, enter **98**.

▶ *The formula bar reads "=DATE(98)".*

■ In the month text box, enter **2**.

▶ *The formula bar reads "=DATE(98,2)".*

■ In the day text box, enter **28**.

▶ *The formula bar reads "=DATE(98,2,28)", and in the Value text box in the upper right corner of the dialog box, the number 35854 is displayed.*

The serial number 35854 represents February 28, 1998.

■ Select Finish.

▶ *Cell A1 displays 2/28/98.*

By changing the display format of cell A1, you can see the serial number instead.

■ With the insertion point over cell A1, press the right mouse button.

▶ *The Shortcut menu is displayed.*

■ Select Format Cells.

▶ *The Number index tab of the Format Cells dialog box is displayed.*

■ Change the display format to Number, 0.

▶ *The contents of cell A1 change to 35854.*

■ Change the display back to Date, m/d/y.

Because dates are actually serial numbers, it is possible to add or subtract them. For example, if you need to enter in a cell the date that occurs 180 days after February 28, 1998, you can use the DATE function which translates February 28, 1998, to a serial number, then adds 180 to it.

NOTE: Excel assumes that the Century is the present century. You also could have entered the year as 1998. Also, if you were to enter 2/28/98+180, Excel interprets the entry as a text entry, not a date.

- ■ In cell A2, enter **150**.

- ■ Select cell A3 and click on the Sum tool.

  - ▶ *A marquee border appears around cell A2.*

- ■ Select cells A1 and A2 so that A1:A2 appears as the argument for the SUM function.

- ■ Complete the entry.

  - ▶ *The cell A3 displays 7/28/98, a date 150 days after February 28, 1998.*

Excel also has a function that displays the present day, according to the computer's internal calendar. This is useful when you want a record of the date a worksheet is printed.

PRACTICE   TIME   5 - 1

In cell A4, insert the TODAY function. Follow the Function Wizard and complete the entry. (This function does not require any argument.) The current date (according to the computer's internal clock) should appear.

Because dates are kept as serial numbers, you can find the number of days between two dates by subtracting one from the other.

- ■ In cell A5, enter the formula **=A3–A4**.

  - ▶ *An integer (whole number) displays the number of days between those dates.*

The time of day is stored in Excel as a fraction of a day.

PRACTICE   TIME   5 - 2

1. In cell C1, paste the NOW function, follow the Function Wizard, and complete the entry.

2. Adjust the width of column C so that the entire entry is displayed. The present date and time, according to the computer's internal clock, are displayed.

3. Change the display format of cell C1 to Number, 0.00. You can see the fraction part.

4. When satisfied, change back to the original format.

N O T E :   The TIME function returns the current time, but not the date.

The YEAR, MONTH, DAY, HOUR, MINUTE, and SECOND functions all use a serial number (representing a date) for their argument. Each of these functions returns a whole number representing the appropriate quantity. MONTH returns 1 for January, 2 for February, and so on. Day returns 1 for the first day of a month, et cetera. A similar function is WEEKDAY, which returns a number representing the day of the week: 1 for Sunday, 2 for Monday, and so forth. Suppose you want a cell to display today's day of the week.

■ In cell A7, enter the formula WEEKDAY, and for the argument, serial_number, enter the function TODAY. The entry on the formula bar should read "=WEEKDAY(TODAY())".

Hint. Click on the Function tool that appears in the second dialog box. You must finish the Function Wizard for TODAY before finishing the Function Wizard for WEEKDAY.

▶ *Cell A5 displays a number between 1 and 7.*

N O T E : If you know the name of the function along with the required argument, you can simply type the entry in a cell rather than go through the Function Wizard.

LOOKUP AND REFERENCE FUNCTIONS

Although the MONTH and WEEKDAY functions return the number of the month and day of the week, you might want the name of the month or day displayed. You can create a table of month or day names and have Excel replace the number with the appropriate name. In this example, you want to replace the value generated by the formula =WEEKDAY(TODAY()) with the name of the day. This needs to be done automatically so that, if you open the worksheet tomorrow, the correct day is displayed. The table consists of two columns. The first column contains the number you want to replace, and the second column contains the name of the day that number represents.

■ In the range G1:H7, enter the following information:

G	H
1	SUNDAY
2	MONDAY
3	TUESDAY
4	WEDNESDAY
5	THURSDAY
6	FRIDAY
7	SATURDAY

The range G1:H7 is a vertical lookup table consisting of two columns. Given a number (representing the day of the week) that appears on the first column of the table, you can retrieve the appropriate day name in the second column using the VLOOKUP function. Now you will edit cell A5 to display today's day of the week.

■ Select cell E1.

■ From the Insert menu, select the Function command.

Alternative: Press the Function tool.

■ Highlight the Lookup & Reference category.

■ Highlight the VLOOKUP function and select Next>.

The first argument, lookup_value, is the number that is returned from the WEEKDAY function, with the TODAY function as the argument.

■ Click on the Function tool that appears on the lookup_value entry line.

■ Enter the same function that was entered in cell A7. That is, the entry for this argument should read WEEKDAY(TODAY()). Be very cautious as you respond to the Function Wizard. Right now, you are just entering the first argument for the VLOOKUP function—you should not "Finish" the Function Wizard.

The second argument, Table_array, is range G1:H7.

■ Enter **G1:H7** as the second argument.

The final argument is the column in the table to be used in the lookup. The names of the days of the week are in the second column of the table.

■ Enter **2**.

The fourth argument is not required.

■ Now select Finish.

▶ *Cell E1 contains the appropriate day of the week and the formula bar reads "=VLOOKUP(WEEKDAY(TODAY()),G1:H7,2)".*

NOTE: The HLOOKUP function is similar to VLOOKUP, except that the table is arranged by rows rather than columns.

Rather than having the lookup table on the same sheet, you will place it in a different sheet named Reference. By doing this, the entries in the lookup table will not interfere with the rest of the entries on the current sheet.

■ Move cell range G1:H7 on the Date & Time sheet to Sheet5, cell range A1:B7.

■ Rename Sheet5 as **Reference**.

■ Display the Date & Time sheet.

▶ *Cell E1 displays #REF!. It can no longer reference the lookup table.*

■ Edit the entry in cell E1 by replacing #REF! with **Reference!A1:B7**.

▶ *The entry should now read "=VLOOKUP(WEEKDAY(TODAY())),Reference!A1:B7,2)" and the correct result should appear in cell E1.*

In the sheet named Reference, you can enter other lookup tables as well, such as ones to show the month of the year, names of products, and so on. These tables can be used by all sheets in the same workbook.

LOGICAL FUNCTIONS

An IF function is used to insert different numbers or labels in a cell based on a specific condition. The three arguments of the IF function are condition, true condition, and false condition. The **condition** is actually a comparison of two values that is evaluated to be true or false. If the condition is true, you are to make the entry in the second argument; if the condition is false, you make the entry in the third argument. For example, you may want to look at the quantity of an item in stock. If it falls below a certain number, say 50, you want to enter REORDER as the status. On the other hand, if the quantity is 50 or more, you want to enter OK as the status.

■ Click on the Sheet2 sheet tab.

■ Rename the sheet as **Logical**.

■ Enter the following in columns A, B, and C.

	A	B	C
1	**Item Number**	**Quantity**	**Status**
2	**L1327**	**57**	
3	**L2111**	**3**	
4	**L2733**	**50**	

■ Adjust the column widths as needed.

Conditions are evaluated with logical operators. A **logical operator** is a symbol that instructs Excel to evaluate the relationship between two values. Six of the most common logical operators and the type of relationship they check for are shown as follows, using cell B2 as the cell to evaluate.

Operator	Relationship	Example
<	less than	B2<50
>	greater than	B2>50
<=	less than or equal to	B2<=50
>=	greater than or equal to	B2>=50
<>	not equal to	B2<>50
=	equal to	B2=50

As you can see, the quantity at cell B2 can be compared to 50 in several ways. Depending on the condition used, actions to take for "true" or "false" changes. One way is to check to see if the quantity is less than 50. If so, enter REORDER. If not, enter OK. If the condition you check is "compare and see if quantity is equal to or greater than 50," then under the true condition you would enter OK, and under the false condition you would enter REORDER.

■ In cell C2, insert the logical function IF. Enter **B2<50** in the logical_test text box, **REORDER** in value_if_true, and **OK** in value_if_false.

▶ *Cell C2 displays OK because the value in B2 is greater than 50.*

■ Copy the formula in cell C2 to cells C3 and C4.

▶ *The screen should look similar to Figure 5-3.*

Figure 5-3

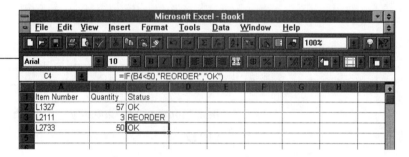

P R A C T I C E   T I M E   5 - 3

1. Change the condition on the IF statement so that you are checking to see if the quantity is greater than or equal to 50. What do you have to do to the second and third arguments?

2. Save the workbook as PRACTICE on your data disk.

MATHEMATICAL FUNCTIONS

Worksheets often involve mathematical calculations. There are a number of mathematical and trigonometric functions available.

Suppose you need to calculate a 7.75% tax on a sale of $1,758.41.

- Click on the Sheet3 sheet tab.
- Rename the sheet as **Math & Trig**.
- In cells A1, A2, and A3, enter **SALES**, **TAX**, and **TOTAL**, respectively.
- In cell B1, enter **1758.41**.
- First, enter the formula **=7.75%*B1** in cell B2.

  ▶ *Cell B2 displays 136.27678.*

Since you are dealing with monetary figures, you want the number rounded to the nearest penny.

- Clear cell B2.
- In cell B2, enter the Math & Trig function **ROUND**. The first argument, number, is to be **7.75%*B1**, and the second argument, num_digits, is to be **2**.

  ▶ *The value displayed in cell B2 is 136.28.*

PRACTICE TIME 5-4

1. In cell B3, sum the values in cells B1 and B2.

2. Save the workbook again, using the same filename.

FINANCIAL FUNCTIONS

Excel has several useful financial functions. One very useful and popular function is the PMT (payment) function. It calculates the payments on a loan given the principal, the rate of interest for each period, and the number of periods. Let's say that you are planning to borrow $18,000 to buy a new car. The current interest rate is 12% annually, and you are looking at a five-year loan.

- Click on the Sheet4 sheet tab and rename it **Financial**.
- On cells A1, A2, A3, and A5, enter **Loan Amount**, **Interest Rate**, **Term (in years)**, and **Payment**, respectively.

■ Adjust column widths accordingly.

■ In cell B1, enter **$18,000**.

■ In cell B2, enter **12%.**

■ In cell B3, enter **5**.

■ Select cell B5.

■ Enter the Financial formula **PMT** and proceed to step 2 of the Function Wizard.

▶ *Your screen should look similar to Figure 5-4.*

Figure 5-4

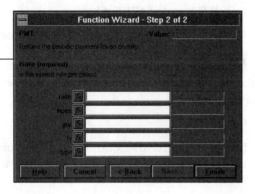

The first argument, rate, is the rate per period. Since your payment is monthly, you need to divide the rate by the number of months in a year, or 12.

■ Enter **B2/12** as the first argument.

The second argument, nper, is the total number of payment periods. This is the number of months in five years.

■ Enter **B3*12** as the second argument.

The third argument, pv, stands for present value, or the amount of your loan.

■ Enter **B1** as the third argument.

Fourth and fifth arguments are not required.

■ Select **F**inish.

▶ *Cell B5 displays ($400.40).*

Your payment is $400.40 a month. The amount is shown as a negative number because by *subtracting* $400.40 each month for the duration of the loan, with the interest amount specified, you can pay up the loan.

GOAL SEEK

Now that you see the payment amount, you gasp. You cannot afford to pay more than $400 a month on a car. You wonder how much you can borrow if you want to keep the payment at $300. You could keep entering various amounts for the loan until you get the result you want, but this can be unnecessarily time-consuming. Instead, the task can be accomplished using the ***Goal Seek*** feature. When you use Goal Seek, Excel varies the value in a cell you specify until a formula depending on that cell returns the result you want.

■ Select cell B5, the cell containing the formula.

■ From the Tools menu, select the Goal Seek command.

▶ *The Goal Seek dialog box is displayed, as shown in Figure 5-5.*

Figure 5-5

In the Set Cell box, enter the cell containing the formula for which you want to find a specific solution. Cell B5 is already displayed.

In the To value box, enter the value that you want.

■ Enter **–300**, which is the payment you want (specified as the negative number).

In the By changing cell box, enter the cell containing the value to be changed in solving for the result you want.

■ Enter **B1**, the cell containing the loan amount.

■ Complete the command.

▶ *A dialog box that shows the status of the goal seek is displayed, as shown in Figure 5-6.*

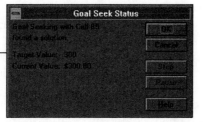

Figure 5-6

When the goal seek is complete, Excel displays the result on the worksheet. If the specific solution that you want cannot be reached, Excel displays a message. According to the dialog box, the goal seek has found a solution. If you want to keep the solution value on the worksheet, click on OK. If you want to retain the original values on the worksheet, select the Cancel button.

■   Click on OK.

▶   *Cell B1 indicates that in order to keep the payment at $300, you can borrow only $13,487.*

If you change your mind about keeping the new values, you can still restore the old values.

■   From the Edit menu, select Undo Goal Seek to clear its result.

Alternative: Press Ctrl+Z.

▶   *The original values are restored.*

PRACTICE TIME 5 - 5

1. You are studying alternatives. Hence, this time you want to do the same goal seek (To value is to remain the same) but vary the number of years. That is, the cell to change is B3. The result should be 7.673856. Do not accept the result.

2. Do another goal seek. This time your goal is to set the payment to $350 by varying the loan amount. The result should be $15,734. Do not accept the result.

3. Save the workbook, using the same filename.

MACROS

Sometimes you may have a task to do over and over that requires several keystrokes and commands. Of course, the more keystrokes you make, the greater the chance of making mistakes.

A **macro** is a recorded sequence of frequently used keystrokes and mouse actions that can be played back at a later time. When you play back a macro, Excel runs, or automatically performs, all the actions you recorded. You can use macros to reduce a series of actions to a single keystroke or push of a button. When you record a command macro, Excel creates an instruction for each action you complete. These instructions are stored in a sheet, named Module by default, in the current workbook or in a separate file you specify.

RECORDING AND USING MACROS

To demonstrate the mechanics of recording and using a macro, you will create a macro that enters your name in the selected cell.

■ Click on Sheet6 sheet tab and rename it **Macro**.

■ From the Tools menu, select the Record Macro command then Record New Macro.

▶ The Record New Macro dialog box appears, as shown in Figure 5-7.

Figure 5-7

■ Select Options>>.

▶ *The dialog box, shown in Figure 5-8, is displayed.*

Figure 5-8

The dialog box contains a text box for the macro name. The macro name must begin with a letter or an underline character. The rest of the name can be letters, numbers, periods, or underlines. The name cannot look like a cell reference, and you must use an underline or a period, not a space, to separate words. The name must be less than 256 characters long.

■ Type **My_Name** as the macro name.

The description can be edited to whatever you want. You may want to include information on what this macro does. Right now, you will leave it as is.

In the Assign To box, you are given two options. The second option, Shortcut Key, allows you to enter a letter to be used with Ctrl as a shortcut key to run the macro. The default, as shown in Figure 5-8, is Ctrl+e. That is, you can run this macro by holding down Ctrl and pressing e. In the macro key, the case of the letter is important. For example, one macro can be run by using Ctrl+E and another by using Ctrl+e.

■   Select Shortcut Key with e as the character.

The Store in selection box lets you choose whether to store the macro in this workbook, in your personal macro workbook, or in a new workbook. Macros that you may want to use with all workbooks should be stored in a personal macro workbook. Macros stored in a workbook are available for use within that workbook only. You will leave it at the default setting, This Workbook.

The Language selection box lets you specify the language in which the macro instructions are stored. The default is Visual Basic, which is the programming language used by many Windows applications. As you will see later, you need to learn Visual Basic if you want to edit the macro (as displayed on the macro sheet). If you were to set it to MS Excel 4.0 Macro, the format is very similar to keystrokes. However, you would still need to study the way macros are written in Microsoft Excel 4.0 in order to edit it. You will leave this at its default value as well.

■   Complete the command.

▶   *The Stop Recording Macro button appears onscreen, as shown in Figure 5-9.*

Figure 5-9

Stop Recording Macro button

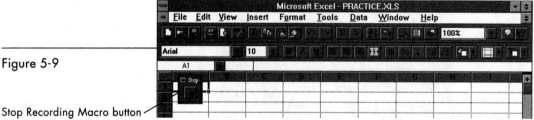

■   Type your name and click on the enter box.

■   Click on the Stop Recording Macro button.

You have recorded a macro named My_Name in a macro sheet. When you run the macro, it should enter your name at the selected cell. You will run the macro to enter your name into cell B3.

■   Select cell B3.

■   Press Ctrl+e to run the macro.

▶   *Your name appears in cell B3.*

When you have several macros, you might forget which keystroke combination is associated with a macro. That's when the macro name is useful. You will now run a macro using the macro name.

■ Select cell D1.

■ From the <u>T</u>ools menu, select the <u>M</u>acro command.

▶ *The Macro dialog box appears, as shown in Figure 5-10.*

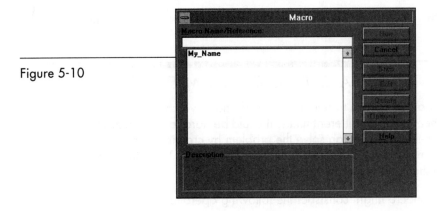

Figure 5-10

■ Select the My_Name macro and click on Run.

▶ *Your name is entered in cell D1.*

As mentioned earlier, this macro was recorded using a language called Visual Basic. Just to satisfy curiosity, let's see what it looks like.

■ From the <u>T</u>ools menu, select <u>M</u>acro.

■ Select My_Name and click on Edit.

▶ *A screen similar to Figure 5-11 is displayed.*

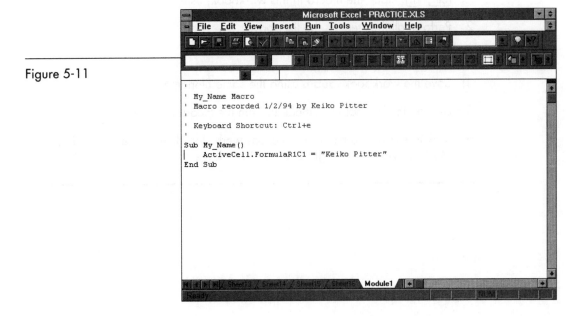

Figure 5-11

Notice that the macro is recorded on a sheet called Module1, toward the back of this workbook. Learning how to write or edit a macro (rather than record) written in Visual Basic is a course on its own, and will not be discussed here.

■   Save the workbook, using the same filename.

■   Click on the first sheet of the workbook, Date & Time.

P R A C T I C E   T I M E   5 - 6

Some worksheets are frequently updated and, if you have printouts of the worksheet made at different times, it could be hard to tell which worksheet is more up-to-date. You can solve the problem by creating a macro that adds your name and the date at the top of the worksheet. Then, just before printing a worksheet, you can run the macro.

The macro might consist of the following operations:

Step 1   Select rows 1 and 2.

Step 2   Insert new rows for the titles.

Step 3   Select cell A1.

Step 4   Enter your name in the cell. You can use the previously written macro.

Step 5   Select cell D1.

Step 6   Enter today's date in the cell using the TODAY function.

1. Begin recording a macro. Give it the name **Heading** and the shortcut Ctrl+h. Place the macro in this workbook, using Visual Basic.

2. Perform all the steps in the list above.

3. Stop recording the macro.

4. Save the workbook, again using the same filename.

5. Display the Logical worksheet and run the Heading macro.

6. Look to see where macro instructions were stored. They were stored in the Module1 worksheet, right after the My_Name macro.

CUSTOMIZING THE TOOLBAR

Right now, a tool to run a macro does not appear on the toolbar. You can customize the toolbar by adding, deleting, or rearranging the tools. If a tool you need does not exist, you can create a new tool to perform exactly the task you want.

■ From the View menu, select Toolbars.

▶ *The Toolbars dialog box is displayed, as shown in Figure 5-12.*

Figure 5-12

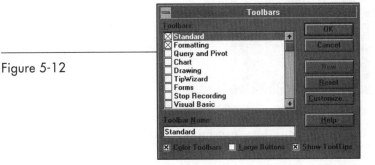

Toolbars you can add are displayed in the list box. If you need to display the toolbar for Visual Basic, for example, select it (so that an X appears in front). Right now, however, you want to customize the existing toolbar by adding new tools.

■ Select Customize.

▶ *The Customize dialog box is displayed, as shown in Figure 5-13.*

Figure 5-13

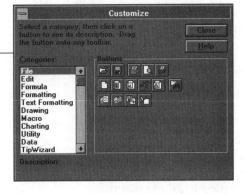

As you select an option in the Categories list box on the left, the Buttons list box on the right shows all the available tool buttons. When a tool button is dragged onto the toolbar, it becomes a tool that can be utilized.

■   Select Macro in the Categories list box.

▶   *The display changes to the one shown in Figure 5-14.*

Figure 5-14

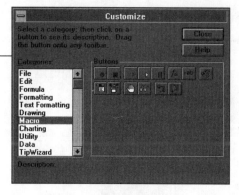

As you click on a button, the description (function) of the button is displayed at the bottom.

■   Click on the third button from left ( ), which is the Macro Run button.

▶   *The description "Runs macro at insertion point" is displayed.*

You want to include this tool on the toolbar.

■   Drag the Macro Run button to the toolbar, just to the left of the Cut tool, .

▶   *The new tool has been added to the toolbar.*

Now try the Macro Run tool.

■   Click on the Macro Run tool on the toolbar.

▶   *The Macro dialog box is displayed, ready for you to select and run a macro.*

■   Select Cancel.

CUSTOMIZING A TOOL BUTTON

Let's go one more step toward making a custom tool. You will create a tool that will run the My_Name macro.

■   From the View menu, select Toolbars.

■   Select Customize.

■   In the Categories list box, select Custom.

▶   *The Customize dialog box is displayed, as shown in Figure 5-15.*

Figure 5-15

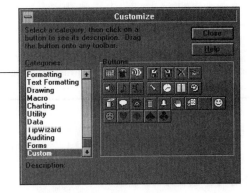

All the buttons displayed in the Buttons list box are blank buttons that can be assigned to a macro. You can use a button that is representative of the function of the macro to which the button is assigned. In this example, however, you will use the happy-face tool button.

■   Drag the happy-face tool button to the toolbar, just to the left of the Sum tool.

▶   *The button now appears on the toolbar, and the Assign Macro dialog box is displayed, as shown in Figure 5-16.*

Figure 5-16

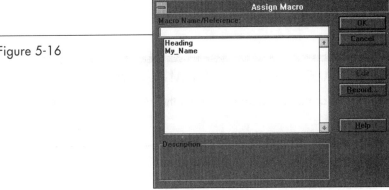

For a button to become a tool, some function must be assigned to it.

■   Select the My_Name macro and complete the command.

▶   *The Customize dialog box is displayed.*

■   Close the Customize dialog box.

Now you are ready to try out your new tool.

- Select cell E6.
- Click on the happy-face tool, 😊.

  ▶ *Your name is inserted in cell E6.*

P R A C T I C E   T I M E   5 - 7

Create a custom tool that runs the Heading macro. Use any appropriate button.

REMOVING A TOOL FROM THE TOOLBAR

Built-in buttons, such as Macro Run, are not deleted from Microsoft Excel when you remove them from the toolbar. However, a button that you customized is permanently deleted once you remove it from the toolbar. Right now, you will remove the built-in Macro Run button.

- From the View menu, select Toolbars, then Customize.

  Alternative: With the mouse pointer over the toolbar, press the right mouse button to display the Shortcut menu, then select Customize.

  ▶ *The Customize dialog box is displayed.*

- Drag the Macro Run button off the toolbar and release the mouse button.

P R A C T I C E   T I M E   5 - 8

Remove from the toolbar the tool buttons that run the My_Name and Heading macros.

NOTE: If you want to delete a custom button from a toolbar but save it for later use, create a toolbar for storing unused buttons, and then move the button that you want to save to this storage toolbar.

ENDING LESSON 5

This is the end of the lesson. Exit Excel without saving any changes to open documents. Quit Windows. Remove your data disk from the disk drive.

SUMMARY

In this lesson, functions and macros are described.

- ☐ **A function is a prewritten formula in Excel.**

- ☐ **A function uses arguments as input and returns a result.**

- ☐ **Functions can be pasted into an entry. The arguments may optionally be pasted in with the function.**

- ☐ **A macro is a series of commands or entries that is stored in a macro sheet.**

- ☐ **You can run a macro with a** Ctrl **keystroke combination or by using the Run command.**

SPREADSHEET

KEY TERMS

argument	function	logical operator
condition	Goal Seek	macro

COMMAND SUMMARY

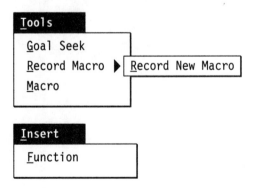

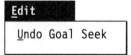

REVIEW QUESTIONS

1. What is a function?
2. How does a function use its arguments?
3. What can you use for arguments in a function?
4. Can you add and subtract dates? Explain.
5. What do you use the WEEKDAY function for?
6. What is a macro?
7. How can you create a macro in Excel?
8. What are two ways to run a macro?
9. Where are macros stored?
10. How do you edit a macro?

EXERCISES

1. Start a new workbook.
   a. Enter the following:

	A	B	C
1	**Name**	**Score**	**P/F**
2	**Ann Brown**	**74**	
3	**Carolyn Jones**	**63**	
4	**John Smith**	**80**	

   b. In column C, enter the IF function so that if the score is greater than or equal to 75, the word PASS is entered, otherwise FAIL.
   c. Print the worksheet and also specify the formula entry for column C.
   d. Save the workbook as FNMAC1 on your data disk.

2. Start a new workbook.

   a. Create and test a lookup table and function that converts the result of the MONTH function (with the TODAY function as the argument) to the name of the month.

   b. Print the worksheet(s) containing the formula entry and the lookup table. Specify the formula entry used.

   c. Save the workbook as FNMAC2 on your data disk.

3. Start a new workbook.

   a. Create and test a macro that makes the entry at the current cell centered and bold. Name the macro as appropriate with a shortcut key.

   b. Print the macro sheet.

   c. Save the workbook as FNMAC3 on your data disk.

Excel Projects

You are interested in keeping track of your car's gasoline mileage (miles per gallon, or mpg). Each time you get gas for the car, you note the mileage and the amount of gasoline you add. You want to calculate miles per gallon in two ways: the fill-up mpg (mpg since the last fill-up) and the cumulative mpg (mpg since you started to keep track).

1. Start a new workbook. Rename Sheet1 as **MILEAGE** and enter the following:

Date	Miles	Gallons	Fill-up mpg	Cumulative mpg
Nov. 6	8943	19.0		
Nov. 18	9296	20.0		
Nov. 30	9643	19.4		
Dec. 7	9951	18.3		
Dec. 20	10296	17.7		
Jan. 1	10592	20.1		
Jan. 12	10966	20.7		
Jan. 21	11354	20.7		
Feb. 2	11732	19.6		
Feb. 14	12097	20.2		
Feb. 24	12475	19.2		
Mar. 6	12821	20.4		

Hints: On November 18, both the fill-up mpg and the cumulative mpg are the miles (9296–8943) divided by the gallons (20.0).

On November 30, the fill-up mpg is (9543–9296)/19.4, and the cumulative mpg is (9643–8943)/(20.0+19.4).

2. Create a line graph on a new sheet that shows how the fill-up mpg changes over time. Incorporate titles and other graphic options to improve the graph.

   Hint: To select cells in columns A and D, first select cells in column A, then hold down Ctrl as you select cells in column D.

3. Print the graph and the sheet MILEAGE. Indicate formulas used in cells D3:E4.

4. Save the workbook as MILEAGE on your data disk.

PROJECT 2

You are starting a lawn/garden-care service, and you want to establish prices for the services you offer. You want to be sure to make a profit, even if your costs change. The three standard services you offer are lawn seeding, monthly lawn care (mowing and fertilizing), and yard cleanup (pruning and raking). The yards you service are all about the same size.

- Seeding takes 4 hours of labor, 7 pounds of seeds, 6 pounds of fertilizer, and 1 round trip in the truck.

- Monthly lawn care takes 2 hours of labor, 2 pounds of fertilizer, 1 gallon of weeder, 1 cubic yard of disposal, and 5 round trips in the truck.

- Yard cleanup takes 3 hours of labor, 4 cubic yards of disposal, and 2 round trips in the truck.

When you have found the total cost of a service, you add 15% profit to arrive at your charge for the service. Initially, your costs are as follows:

Labor	$10.00 per hour
Seed	$2.25 per pound
Fertilizer	$0.75 per pound
Weeder	$9.00 per gallon
Disposal	$3.00 per cubic yard
Truck	$7.00 per round trip

You can use the spreadsheet to find the prices you will charge customers and to update the prices as your costs change.

1. Start a new workbook. Rename Sheet1 as **LAWNCARE** and make appropriate entries, using the following as a guide.

	A	B	C	D	E	F	G	H	I
1				**SEEDING**		**LAWN CARE**		**CLEANUP**	
2				**NO. OF**		**NO. OF**		**NO. OF**	
3	**ITEM**	**UNIT**	**COST**	**UNITS**	**COST**	**UNITS**	**COST**	**UNITS**	**COST**
4	Labor	10.00	/ hr	4		2		3	
5	Seed	2.25	/ lb	7		0		0	
6	Fertilizer	0.75	/ lb	6		2		0	
7	Weeder	9.00	/ gal	0		1		0	
8	Disposal	3.00	/ cu yd	0		4		2	
9	Truck	7.00	/ trip	1		5		2	
10				___		___		___	
11		**Total Cost**							
12		**15% Profit**		___		___		___	
13									
14		**Charge for Service**							

a. Enter the labels and values as shown in the table. Note that there are two columns for UNIT COST; column B contains values under the heading of UNIT, and column C contains the other information under the heading of COST.

b. Individual costs are calculated by multiplying the number of units by the unit cost.

c. For total costs, use the SUM function at cells E12, G12, and I12 to add the values in the respective columns.

d. Profit is the total cost multiplied by the percentage that is specified in cell B12.

2. Save the workbook as LAWNCARE.

3. Print the worksheet.

4. After a month of service, you realize that it takes 2.5 hours of labor per month for lawn care, and the cost of disposal has been raised to $3.25 per cubic yard.

   a. Copy the content of the LAWNCARE sheet to Sheet2. Rename Sheet2 as LAWNCARE2 and make the specified changes.

   b. Print LAWNCARE2.

5. Save the workbook again, using the same filename.

Microsoft Excel 5.0 for Windows Command Summary

This section is a quick reference for Excel commands covered in this manual. This is *not* a complete list of all Excel commands.

Task	Menu Command	Shortcut Keys	Tool Buttons
Auto-format a worksheet	Format, AutoFormat		
Arrange windows	Window, Arrange		
Check setup for printing	File, Page Setup		
Clear the selected cell	Edit, Clear, Contents	Del	
Close the file	File, Close		
Copy across row	Edit, Fill, Right	Ctrl+R	
Copy an entry down a column	Edit, Fill, Down	Ctrl+D	
Copy range to Clipboard	Edit, Copy	Ctrl+C	🗐
Copy Clipboard to worksheet	Edit, Paste	Ctrl+V	🗐
Create a new workbook	File, New	Ctrl+N	🗋
Customize toolbar	View, Toolbars, Customize		
Delete selected row or column, or row or column of selected cell(s)	Edit, Delete		
Display toolbars	View, Toolbars		
Exit Excel	File, Exit		
Format cell contents	Format, Cells	Ctrl+1	💲 % , 🔢 🔢
Freeze row or column titles	Window, Freeze Panes		
Goal Seek	Tools, Goal Seek		
Help contents	Help, Contents	F1	▶?
Hide column	Format, Column, Hide		
Insert rows	Insert, Rows		
Insert functions	Insert, Function		f_x
Move range to Clipboard	Edit, Cut	Ctrl+X	✂
Name a sheet	Format, Sheet, Rename		

Task	Menu Command	Shortcut Keys	Tool Buttons
Open a file	File, Open	Ctrl+O	◩
Open a new window	Window, New Window		
Paste from Clipboard	Edit, Paste	Ctrl+V	▣
Preview a sheet	File, Print Preview		▣
Print a worksheet	File, Print	Ctrl+P	▣
Remove gridlines from display	Tools, Options, View		
Remove split	Window, Remove Split		
Save file with new name	File, Save As		
Save file	File, Save	Ctrl+S	▣
Search on Help	Help, Search	F1 , Search	
Set alignment	Format, Cells, Alignment	Ctrl+1	▣ ▣ ▣
Set/change header/footer	File, Page Setup, Header/Footer		
Set print titles	File, Page Setup, Sheet		
Sort a range	Data, Sort		
Splitting windows	Window, Split		
Undo commands	Edit, Undo	Ctrl+Z	
Undo Goal Seek	Edit, Undo Goal Seek	Ctrl+Z	
Unfreeze row or column titles	Window, Unfreeze Panes		
Unhide columns	Format, Column, Unhide		

C h a r t i n g

Task	Menu Command	Shortcut Keys	Tool Buttons
Add borders around title and text	Format, Selected Object	Ctrl+1	
Change chart type	Format, Chart Type		▣
Create a chart sheet	Insert, Chart, As New Sheet		
Embed a chart	Insert, Chart, On This Sheet		▣
Format selected axis	Format, Selected Axis	Ctrl+1	
Format selected object	Format, Selected Object	Ctrl+1	
Insert/delete axes label	Insert, Axes		

M a c r o

Task	Menu Command	Shortcut Keys	Tool Buttons
Edit Macro	Tools, Macro, Edit		
Record macro	Tools, Record Macro, Record New Macro		
Run macro	Tools, Macro, Run		▣

Glossary

absolute address Cell address that does not change in the course of copying a formula to other cells. In a cell marked for absolute address, the formula contains dollar signs.

absolute formula Formula containing absolute addresses.

active cell Cell that is selected.

active window The window to which the next command will apply. If a window is active, its title bar changes color to differentiate it from other windows.

address A way to refer to the cell location using column and row designations. For example, the cell at column C row 4 is referred to as C4.

application window A window that contains a running application. The name of the application appears at the top of this window.

area chart A chart in which the size of the area indicates the magnitude of the various items represented.

argument Items contained between parentheses to pass data to a function.

AutoFormat Built-in combinations of formats that you can quickly select and apply to a range of data.

AutoSum A feature that enables Excel to guess which cells you are adding together (to display the sum) when you press the Sum button.

axis labels Descriptive text that can be displayed next to an axis on a chart.

cancel box Box that you select to cancel the current entry.

category axis X-axis; axis that displays category names.

cell Intersection point of a row and a column, where an individual piece of information is stored.

chart item A component of a chart.

click To press and release a mouse button quickly.

Clipboard A temporary storage location used to transfer data within a document and between documents and applications.

close To remove a document window or application window from the desktop.

column chart A chart in which heights of columns (bars) indicate the magnitude of the various items represented.

combination chart Chart that combines more than one type of display. For example, one data series is displayed as a lein chart and a second data series is displayed as column chart within a single chart document.

constant value Text and numbers that you enter.

control-menu box The icon that opens the control menu for a window. It is always at the left of the title bar.

default A value, action, or setting that is automatically used when no alternate instructions are given. For example, a default drive is where the program looks for data files unless explicitly instructed otherwise.

dialog box A box that either requests or provides information. Many dialog boxes present options to choose among before Windows can carry out a command. Some dialog boxes present warnings or explain why a command can't be completed.

directory A file or a part of a disk that contains the names and locations of other files on the disk.

document window A window within an application window. A document window contains a document you create or modify by using an application. There can be more than one document window in an application window.

double-click To rapidly press and release a mouse button twice without moving the mouse. Double-clicking usually carries out an action, such as opening an icon.

SS**127**

drag   To move an item onscreen by holding down the mouse button while moving the mouse.

drop-down list box   A single-line dialog box that opens to display a list of choices.

drop-down menu   The suboption menu that appears when an option in the menu bar is highlighted.

dynamic reference   A link between a chart and a worksheet. If the contents of a relevant cell change, the chart is automatically updated to reflect that change.

enter box   Box that you click on to complete an entry.

exploding pie chart   A pie chart in which one or more slices (category) is detached.

file   A collection of data records with related contents; information stored as a named unit on a peripheral storage medium such as a disk.

fill handle   A little black square on the bottom right corner of the selected cell. When it is dragged, you can copy the cell entry or enter series of constant values to adjoining cells in the same row or column.

font   The graphic design applied to all numerals, symbols, and characters in the alphabet. A font comprises the point size, typeface, and appearance of the text, such as bold, italic, and underlining.

formatting a disk   Prepare a blank disk to receive information.

formula   Series of characters containing cell references and arithmetic operators for numeric data manipulation.

formula bar   A section of the window where you enter or edit data in a worksheet.

freeze panes   Keep selected rows and/or columns displayed even if you scroll the window.

function   A series of commands that are already resident in Excel. A user simply references the function and passes parameters to the function in order to get the desired result.

Goal Seek   A feature in which Excel varies the value in a specified cell until a formula that's dependent on that cell returns the result you want.

gridlines   Lines dividing the columns and rows.

handles   Little black boxes that surround selected text items; you can change the size of the item by dragging a handle.

hide columns   Specify column to not display (set column width to 0). For all calculation purposes, however, these columns exist.

icon   A graphical representation of various elements in Windows, such as disk drives, applications, and documents.

inactive window   Any open window in which you are not currently working.

insertion point   The place where text will be inserted when you type.

jump terms   Underlined terms in the Help function that can be selected to display further information.

landscape   Paper orientation in which a sheet is wider than it is long (e.g., $11 \times 8\frac{1}{2}$).

launching   Starting the execution of an application program. This is usually done by double-clicking on the application icon.

legend   Descriptive text that identifies the information on a graph.

line chart   A chart made of lines that connect points in the horizontal range.

list box   Within a dialog box, a box listing available choices—for example, the list of all available files in a directory. If all the choices won't fit, the list box has a vertical scroll bar.

logical operation   operators used to compare two values and produce the logical value true or false.

lookup table   A table used by the LOOKUP function. The value is compared with the entry in the first column/row to retrieve information in the second column/row.

macro   A series of worksheet commands or data entries stored in one or more cells and activated, or invoked, with a keystroke command.

marquee border   A border that blinks. For example, when you select cells to copy, those cells are surrounded by a marquee border.

maximize button   Small box containing an up arrow at the right of the title bar. It can be clicked to enlarge a window to its maximum size.

menu   A list of items, most of which are Windows commands. Menu names appear in the menu bar near the top of the window.

menu bar   The horizontal bar containing the menu choices.

minimize button The box containing a down arrow at the right of the title bar. It can be clicked to shrink a window to an icon.

mouse A cursor-control device that resembles a small box on wheels. As the box is rolled on a flat surface, the wheel positions signal the computer to move the cursor onscreen in direct proportion to the movement of the mouse.

name box Area at the left end of the formula bar, used to move to and select a specific location on a worksheet.

numeric entries Numbers or formulas that can be used in a calculation.

open To display the contents of a file in a window or to enlarge an icon to a window.

pathname The direction to a directory or file within your system. For example, C:\DIR1\FILEA is the pathname for the FILEA file in the DIR1 subdirectory on drive C.

pie chart A chart consisting of a circle divided into slices representing data series.

point To move the pointer onscreen to rest on the item you want to select.

point size The unit of measure used to indicate font size. There are 72 points in an inch.

pointer The arrow-shaped cursor onscreen that indicates the position of the mouse.

portrait A paper orientation in which a sheet is longer than it is wide (e.g., 8½ × 11).

print titles Rows or columns that will appear as titles on every printed page.

radio button Buttons found within a selection box of which, like the station selectors in many automobiles, only one may be selected at a time.

range Rectangular block of cells within a worksheet.

relative address Automatic changing of a cell address in a Copy or Move operation to reflect a new location.

relative formula Formula containing relative addresses.

restore button The box containing a down arrow and an up arrow at the right of the title bar. The restore button appears after you have enlarged a window to its full size. It can be clicked on with a mouse to return the window to its previous size.

scaling Sizing the output to fit more or fewer pages than it would at normal size.

scroll arrows Arrow at either end of the scroll bar. By clicking on the arrow, you are able to scroll through the window in the corresponding direction.

scroll bars Bars along the right and bottom edges of the workspace that allow you to scroll the window.

scroll box A box on a scroll bar. You can drag it up or down to scroll the window.

series axis Y-axis in a 3-D chart; displays the data series in the chart.

sheet tabs Tabs along the bottom of a spreadsheet that display sheet names. By clicking on the tabs you can move from sheet to sheet within a workbook.

size Height of a capital letter, measured in points; there are 72 points in an inch.

soft font A font that is downloaded to your printer's memory from a disk provided by the font manufacturer.

sorting Reordering; arranging items in a desired sequence.

sort keys The column or row to sort by.

Split boxes Boxes that appear at the end of scroll bars; you can drag the Split box to divide a window.

status bar Bar at the bottom of the Excel window that displays such information as the program mode and the status of various toggle keys.

style Appearance of characters, such as regular, bold, italic, and underline.

subdirectory A directory contained within another directory. All directories are subdirectories of the root directory.

tab split bar A little bar that appears between the sheet tabs and the scroll bar at the bottom of the document window; a Split box can be dragged to display more or less of the scroll bar.

task An open application.

text entries A combination of character(s) or word(s) that are not used in calculations.

text box A box within a dialog box where you type information needed to carry out the chosen command.

SPREADSHEET

title bar The horizontal bar located at the top of a window that contains the title of the window.

toggle A command that alternately turns a feature on and off.

toolbar A section of the window that contains buttons with icons, called tools, which you can click on to perform certain operations.

type style The way characters appear, such as bold, italic, or underline.

typeface Graphic design applied to the characters, and given a name such as Courier or Times Roman.

3-D Three-dimensional.

value axis Axis that has labels based on the range of values plotted in the chart. In a 2-D chart, it is the y-axis. In a 3-D chart, it is the z-axis.

window A rectangular area onscreen in which you view an application or document.

workbook The file in which you work and store your data.

workspace The area of a window that displays the information contained in the application of the document you are working with.

xy chart Also called a scatter chart—a chart that displays how two numerical quantities are related.

Index

SPREADSHEET

Introducing
Microsoft Access 2.0
FOR
WINDOWS

TIMOTHY TRAINOR & JEFFREY STIPES

Introducing

Microsoft Access 2.0

FOR

WINDOWS

McGRAW-HILL

New York St. Louis San Francisco Auckland Bogotá Caracas
Lisbon London Madrid Mexico Milan Montreal New Delhi
Paris San Juan Singapore Sydney Tokyo Toronto

McGRAW-HILL
San Francisco, California

Introducing Microsoft Access 2.0 for Windows

2 3 4 5 6 7 8 9 0 SEM SEM 9 0 9 8 7 6

ISBN 0-07-065257-0

Sponsoring Editor: Roger L. Howell
Editorial Assistant: Rhonda Sands
Production Supervisor: Richard DeVitto
Project Manager: Books International
Interior Design: Gary Palmatier
Cover Designer: Christy Butterfield
Printer: Semline, Inc.

Library of Congress Catalog Card Number 93-78714

Contents

1 Creating Database Tables and Forms — 1

2 Database Queries and Modifications — 26

DATABASE

3 Creating Reports and Two Table Queries   51

4 Enhancing Database Applications   75

DATABASE

Introduction

INTRODUCING ACCESS 2.0 FOR WINDOWS

Database programs are used to organize, store, manipulate, and retrieve important facts and figures. They simplify the mechanics of producing professional-looking data entry screens and reports. Databases can be used to organize inventory, customer lists, transactions, and other business or personal data.

Introducing Access 2.0 for Windows gives you the knowledge and expertise to develop simple to complex queries, data entry forms, and reports using integrated databases. This tutorial helps the user become comfortable with the essentials of Microsoft's Access 2.0 for Windows and feel confident exploring the program's capabilities.

Using This Module

This section is designed to assist you in completing each lesson. Lessons begin with goals listed under the heading Objectives. Key terms are introduced in **bold italics** type; text to be typed by the user is shown in **bold**. Also keep in mind the following:

■   This symbol is used to indicate the user's action.

▶   *This symbol is used to indicate the screen's response.*

Alternative: Presents an alternative keystroke or icon "shortcut."

NOTE: This format is for important user notes or tips.

P R A C T I C E   T I M E

These brief drills allow the user to practice features previously discussed. Each lesson assumes all previous Practice Times have been completed.

Finally, a series of projects, a command summary, and a glossary of key terms are found at the end of the book.

BEFORE YOU START

Access 2.0 operates within Microsoft's graphical user interface called Windows. Many operating procedures are common to all Windows-compatible software packages and Intel-based microcomputers. We are assuming you are familiar with the following procedures:

- Turning on your computer, printer, and screen
- Using a mouse and keyboard
- Formatting a disk
- Displaying a disk's directory
- Copying files to another disk
- Loading a formatted disk (referred to as the data disk) into a disk drive
- Activating Microsoft's Windows graphical user interface
- Working within Window's desktop

If any of these assumptions are incorrect, ask your instructor for help.

To use this book, you need Access 2.0 for Windows installed in the Microsoft Windows 3.1 operating environment. In addition, you must have a formatted floppy disk containing data supplied by your instructor. A standard hardware configuration with floppy disk (drive A), mouse, and printer installed through Windows is also assumed.

The data disk contains several tables used in Lessons 3 and 4. These files are supplied by your instructor to reduce the amount of data entry necessary to complete these lessons.

In some situations, you will be working with a personal computer that is connected to other computers in a Local Area Network or LAN. You will need additional information concerning commands for linking your computer into the network. Use the space below to write out each step.

Printer type: _____

Access disk drive: _____

LAN procedures: _____

_____

_____

_____

_____

_____

_____

_____

DATABASE

ACKNOWLEDGMENTS

We would like to acknowledge the contribution of the following people who reviewed the manuscript:

Louis Adelson, Clarion University

Carolyn Alexander, Phillips County Community College

Barbara Felty, Harrisburg Area Community College

Lanny Felty, Harrisburg Area Community College

Krystal Scott, Oklahoma Baptist University

Paula Thompson, Delta State University

F. Stuart Wells, Ph.D., Tennessee Technological University

We would also like to thank the entire Microcomputer Applications Using Windows 3.1 class at the 1994 National Computer Educator's Institute who class-tested this text in a preliminary form.

Tim Trainor
Jeff Stipes

Creating Database Tables and Forms

OBJECTIVES

Upon completion of the material presented in this lesson, you should understand the following aspects of Access:

- ❑ **Launching Access**
- ❑ **Using database terminology**
- ❑ **Setting up new database**
- ❑ **Creating data tables**
- ❑ **Locating data values within a table**
- ❑ **Setting up a data entry form**
- ❑ **Saving data tables and forms on disk**
- ❑ **Printing data**
- ❑ **Exiting Access**

DATABASE

OVERVIEW

In our modern society, there is a growing need to manage data. A *database management system (DBMS)* is a software tool that permits people to use a computer's ability to store, retrieve, modify, organize, and display key facts. Stored data is an extremely valuable asset for any person or organization using a computer system. People rely on organized data in the form of telephone books, airline schedules, meeting agendas, etc., to conduct their daily activities.

DBMS helps organize data based on the user's need; for instance, a video store might organize data concerning video tape rentals.

- Letters, numbers, and special symbols are the simplest forms of data people use. These characters make up a customer's name or the title of a movie. A DBMS needs to know what type of character combinations to expect. You might want it to limit acceptable characters to numbers or valid dates.

- When characters are combined together, they form data *fields.* Fields are the facts that can be transformed into information through processing. For each video tape the computer would store a field for the movie's title, release date, replacement cost, etc. Data fields are given generic *field names* as a means of reference, like Video Title field or Last Name field. Data management software will also require that each field be identified by type. Common field types would include text, number, date/time, or yes/no.

- Collections of related fields form records. A *record* describes a person, place, object, or event. In the video store rental system, the data about each customer would make up a customer record. There also would be a record for each video tape and each time a tape is rented.

- *Tables* contain groups of records related by a common theme. For example, video tape records would be in a different table from the customer records. The table that contains all video tape records would be called the inventory table. All the customer records become the customer table.

The power and sophistication of data management software varies greatly. The software dictates whether data in tables are independent or can be integrated. The more sophisticated DBMS, for example, Microsoft's Access 2.0 for Windows, can integrate data from several tables into a *relational database.* As shown in Figure 1-1, a relational DBMS can retrieve and integrate data from several tables at the same time.

The video store could integrate data from the inventory and customer tables. When customers rent a video, a store employee scans the customer number from their ID card. The DBMS then uses this number as a *key* field to uniquely identify the customer's record. The record is retrieved from disk to extract a name and other data from the customer table. The same procedure is used to retrieve the video's tape number from the inventory table. As a result, only the customer number and tape number are entered

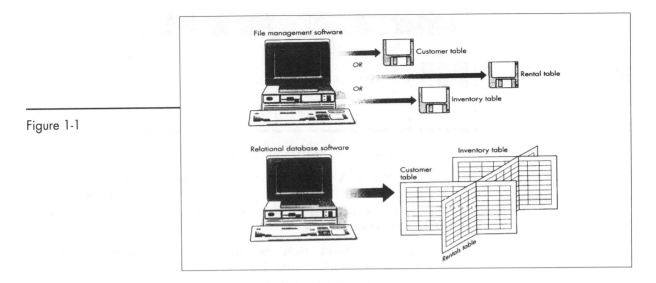

Figure 1-1

to rent a video. A less sophisticated file management system would also require entering the movie's title along with the customer's name, address, and telephone number each time tapes are rented.

Each DBMS package has special features and specific approaches to database development and management. However, the basic operating procedures for any database management system take one of two approaches. The first approach is to initiate action through a series of key words or commands. Users enter commands from the keyboard like "Create CUSTOMER.DBF" or "Display Last-Name, Telephone When State = "MI"." These command-driven packages often have special menu-driven help screens for beginners. Other database management systems rely on menus and icons (pictures) that depict the action in which users wish to engage. Access falls into this category with its graphical user interface that is compatible with Microsoft's Windows operating environment. Tables are created and accessed by selecting the appropriate icon or menu option.

STARTING ACCESS

Before starting Access, turn on your computer system and start Microsoft's Windows program.

- Turn on your computer, screen, and printer.

- If necessary, link to a local area network.

- Place your formatted data disk into a disk drive.

- Start the Windows program.

- Make sure the Program Manager is the only window displayed on the screen.

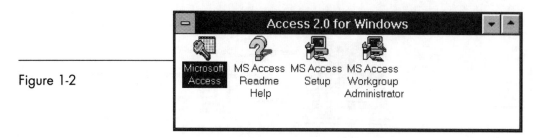

Figure 1-2

- Maximize the Program Manager window.

- Double-click on the Access for Windows or Microsoft Office group icon, ⬛ or ⬛ . Your computer system might use another label for this group icon. Check with your instructor for your particular setup.

  ▶ *The installation procedure for Access creates a program group which includes icons for Microsoft Access and associated utility programs, as shown in Figure 1-2.*

NOTE: If you do not double-click fast enough, Windows displays the control menu. When this happens, just click on the <u>R</u>estore option or press R to launch Access.

- Launch Access by double-clicking on the Microsoft Access icon, ⬛ .

  ▶ *After the logo screen the Access application window opens. This window may display the Access Cue Cards dialog box, as shown at the bottom of Figure 1-3.*

The Cue Cards option offers step-by-step instructions for tasks you are performing. It is one of several types of help provided by Access. Other types of online help will be discussed at a later time. If the Cue Cards dialog box is displayed, you can close it. You will not be using Cue Cards in this book.

- If the Cue Cards dialog box is open, select the Don't display this startup card again check box and double-click on the control box.

  Alternative: Press ALT+F4.

  ▶ *The Access application window is displayed, as shown at the top of Figure 1-3.*

- Maximize the Access window.

THE ACCESS APPLICATION WINDOW

The Access window contains the same basic elements of any application window. As shown in Figure 1-4, a *title bar* along the top identifies the

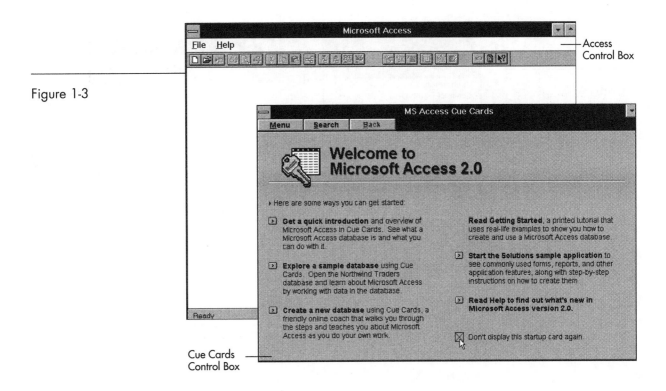

Figure 1-3

Cue Cards
Control Box

application (Microsoft Access) and the *menu bar* underneath it offers *drop-down menus*, in this case File and Help. Access commands are activated by clicking on the desired menu name or by holding down the Alt key and pressing the key of the underlined letter in the menu name. For example, holding down the Alt key and pressing F, ALT+F, opens the File menu. When a menu is selected, the available commands appear in the drop down menu. Dimmed menu options cannot be activated.

Don't be fooled by this simple layout. The Access desktop comes alive with options once you open a database.

Tool Bar

Beneath the menu bar is the **tool bar** which contains a row of **tool buttons** that you can click to quickly perform Access's most commonly used commands. Tool buttons exist for copying, printing, saving files, etc. Access provides a brief explanation of each button in the tool bar when you move the pointer over the button and pause for a moment.

■   Move the pointer over each button and pause.

▶   *A description of each button's function appears under the pointer and in the status bar.*

NOTE: If the descriptions *do not* appear, press ESC and try again.

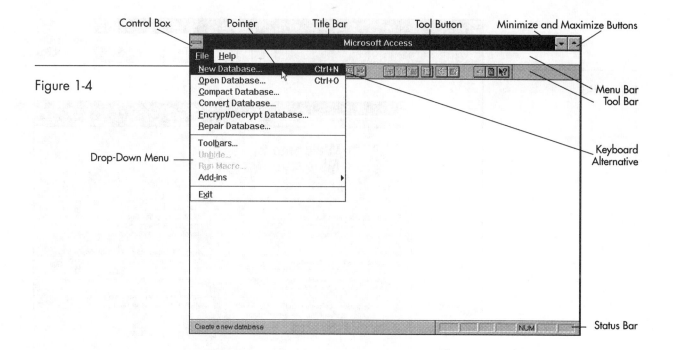

Figure 1-4

Status Bar

The **status bar**, found at the bottom of every Access window (see Figure 1-4), also displays information about the highlighted menu option. In addition, this area is used to display input prompts. When questions occur, glance down to this screen location to see if a helpful description or example is provided.

■   Click on the File menu name and hold down the mouse button.

▶   *File menu opens, as shown in Figure 1-4.*

■   Drag the mouse pointer along the menu bar and down the menus as they open.

▶   *The status bar displays descriptions of each option as the pointer passes over it.*

■   Move pointer into an open area of the screen and release the mouse button.

CREATING A NEW DATABASE

Tables, data entry forms, reports, and other objects you use Access to create are placed in a database. The design and development of a usable database are somewhat like building a new house. The architect must understand the needs of the home owner before a compatible design can be achieved. To

Figure 1-5

CUSTOMER TABLE

Customer Number	First Name	Last Name	Address	City	State/Prov	Zip/Postal Code
881464	Alice	Harris	734 Mercury Drive	Hackley	MI	49442
882882	John	Wilson	12456 East Stone R	Grand Lake	MI	49457
884317	George	Miller	789 Robins Road	Wilson Park	MI	49480
886951	Sandy	Davis	4533 Ritter Drive	Hackley	MI	49442
891254	Todd	Evans	1351 Willow Lane	Hackley	MI	49441
894239	Mary	Richardson	1728 Apple Avenue	Grand Lake	MI	49457
896444	Frank	Stevens	96381 Pinewood	Hackley	MI	49442
897062	Charles	Billings	1879 Strong	Wilson Park	MI	49480
898837	Carol	Taylor	8845 Garfield Road	Grand Lake	MI	49457
899111	Roxanne	Little	3657 Wilson	Hackley	MI	49442
913271	Bill	Alberts	682 Williams	Wilson Park	MI	49480
915988	Martha	Young	226 E. 120th	Hackley	MI	49443
916389	Judy	Harris	3226 Wolf Lake Roa	Hackley	MI	49441
917222	Alan	McCarthy	17984 Cove Harbor	Hackley	MI	49441
919977	Dan	Kamp	456 State	Hackley	MI	49443

Customer Number	Tape Number	Date Out	Date In			
881464	16828	8/8/92	8/9/92	d Lake	MI	49457
881464	44332	8/19/92	8/20/92	kley	MI	49442
881464	47739	8/30/92		on Park	MI	49480
881464	48419	8/9/92	8/10/92	d Lake	MI	49457
881464	48800	8/12/92	8/13/92	kley	MI	49441
881464	50613	8/5/92	6/6/92			
882882	40013	8/22/92	8/23/92			
882882	46599	8/16/92	8/17/92			
882882	48422	8/18/92	8/19/92			
882882	48799	8/3/92	8/4/92			
882882	48801	8/21/92				
882882	63456	8/11/92	8/12/92			
884239	47315	8/24/92	8/25/92			
884317	16828	8/15/92	8/17/92			
884317	37612	8/8/92	8/9/92			
884317						
884317						
884317						
886951						
886951						

RENTALS TABLE

Tape Number	Movie ID	Available	Purchase Date	Purchase Price
16827	101	Y	1/5/93	$39.75
16828	101	Y	1/5/93	$39.75
23184	113	Y	3/5/93	$42.85
23185	113	Y	3/5/93	$42.85
23186	113	Y	3/5/93	$42.85
23187	113	Y	10/5/93	$42.85
37611	114	N	3/17/93	$35.60
37612	114	Y	3/17/93	$35.60
39955	111	Y	4/2/93	$29.95
39956	111	Y	4/2/93	$29.95
40012	102	Y	3/27/88	$39.75
40013	102	Y	3/27/88	$39.75
40014	102	Y	3/27/88	$39.75
42137	109	Y	7/9/93	$35.60
42138	109	Y	7/9/93	$35.60
42139				

INVENTORY TABLE

Tape Number list (MOVIES TABLE area):
43765, 43766, 44331, 44332, 46130, 46131, 46599, 47314, 47315

Movie ID	Movie Title	Production Company	Category	Release Date	Rating
101	Casablanca	Warner Bros.	O	9/11/42	None
102	African Queen	20th Century-Fox	O	10/12/51	None
103	Dirty Harry	Warner Bros.	A	3/18/71	R
104	Star Wars	20th Century-Fox	S	5/25/77	PG
105	Friday the 13th	Paramount	H	1/9/80	R
106	Star Trek	Paramount	S	12/20/79	G
107	Raiders of the Lost Ark	Paramount	A	7/23/81	G
108	Ghostbusters	Columbia	C	7/16/84	PG
109	Jaws	Universal	H	4/20/75	R
111	The Godfather	Paramount	D	10/11/72	R
112	Die Hard	20th Century-Fox	A	6/30/88	R
113	Ghost	Paramount	D	2/24/90	PG13
114	Pretty Woman	Touchstone	C	5/20/90	R
115	Dances with Wolves	Orion	A	11/9/90	PG13
116	Jurassic Park	Amblin	A	5/1/93	PG13
117	Adventures of Your Name	Your Course Name	A	11/27/95	PG
118	Your selection #1	Touchstone	D	2/4/89	G
119	Your selection #2	Orion	A	7/9/83	PG

MOVIES TABLE

DATABASE

make this point in regards to database applications, we will take a closer look at the needs of our local video store—Boomtown Video Rentals.

The video store's relational database, called VIDSTORE, would use several integrated tables (see Figure 1-5). The CUSTOMER table maintains the names, addresses, telephone, and rental status of the people with whom we do business. A unique customer number is assigned to everyone and serves as a key field. A separate RENTALS table tracks each customer transaction (rental). The INVENTORY table lists each tape carried by the store.

To reduce the data redundancy caused by stocking several copies of the same movie, the title and other information common to several tapes is kept in a separate MOVIES table. The MOVIES and INVENTORY tables are linked by the movie's ID number. As a result, we can carry three copies of the movie *ET,* but we only need to include the title, release date, category (adventure, comedy, horror, etc.), and other related information once in the MOVIES table. Three different tape numbers are assigned to the tapes and become independent records in the INVENTORY table.

Working Disk Drive

In this lesson you will create the VIDSTORE database and MOVIES table. The MOVIES table is then loaded with some of your favorite movie titles. You need to designate a **working disk drive** for Access to store the VIDSTORE database. When using this tutorial, you should always select the drive into which you placed your data disk as the working drive. The STUDENT database with CUSTOMER, RENTALS, and INVENTORY tables should have been provided on your data disk. In later lessons you will integrate these tables into the VIDSTORE database.

■   Open the File menu.

■   Select the New Database command, as shown in Figure 1-4.

   Alternative: Press ALT+F, then N, or use the new database tool button, ▣ .

▶   *The New Database dialog box is displayed.*

At this time a formatted data disk with the STUDENT database should already be inserted into the computer's disk drive. If you do not have a data disk with this database, ask your instructor for a copy before continuing. In this tutorial, examples will always use drive A.

■   Click on the Drives down-arrow button.

▶   *The Drives list box opens.*

■   Select the drive letter for the disk drive holding your data disk.

▶   *The Directories list box displays all the directories currently on your data disk. If you need to specify a directory, do so by clicking on the directory name.*

■   Click in the File Name text box.

▶   *An I-beam pointer appears in text box.*

Figure 1-6

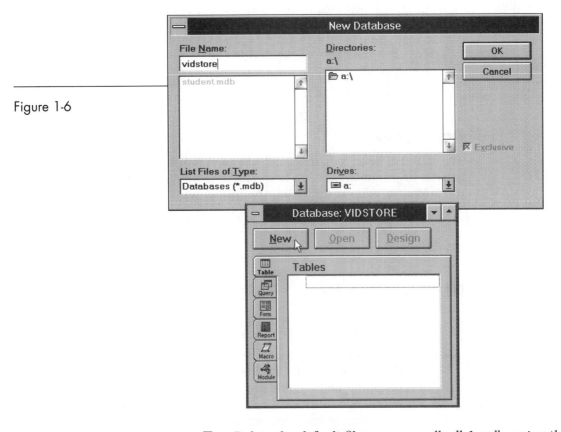

■ Delete the default filename, usually db1.mdb, using the BACKSPACE and DELETE keys.

■ Type **vidstore,** as shown at the top of Figure 1-6, and complete the command by clicking on OK or pressing ENTER.

▶ *The VIDSTORE database window opens, as shown at the bottom of Figure 1-6.*

Access automatically adds the filename extension .MDB to all database files.

CREATING A DATA TABLE

Next, the MOVIES table needs to be added to the VIDSTORE database. The Table button should currently be active and Tables displayed on top of the list box as shown at the bottom of Figure 1-6. Other objects, like forms and reports, are created or opened by selecting the appropriate button found on the left side of the database dialog box. The buttons on the top—New, Open, and Design—initiate the desired actions.

■ Select the New button.

> ▶ *The New Table dialog box is displayed, containing the Table Wizards, New Table, and Cancel buttons.*

- ■ Select the New Table button.

> ▶ *The Table 1 window opens. Figure 1-7 shows how this window will be filled out.*

Data Types

The MOVIES table contains five fields for every record. We need to establish generic field names for each field. At the same time Access needs to know the field type, size, and whether the field is used as a key.

- ■ Type **Movie ID** in the first row under Field Name and press ENTER.

> ▶ *Text in the Data Type column is highlighted.*

NOTE: Data type options are displayed by clicking on the down arrow button, as shown in Figure 1-7.

Access uses 8 different field types:

- *Text* fields contain letters, numbers, special symbols (!,@,#,$,%), or any of the standard ASCII characters used by personal computers. These alphanumeric fields are limited to a maximum length of 255 characters. When in doubt it is best to designate a field as text. Telephone numbers, social security numbers, and similar fields that appear to be numeric often include hyphens and spaces which make them text.

- *Memo* fields are reserved for text fields that exceed the limit of 255 characters. These fields can be up to 32,000 characters long. Like text fields, memo fields can contain any combination of characters.

- *Number* fields only contain numbers and an optional decimal point or minus sign. You should use number field types when the field will be used in numeric calculations. For example, Hours Worked and Pay Rate would be number fields because they are used to compute a person's wages.

- *Date/Time* fields contain any valid date or time. Several date formats are available from the long date (July 9, 1994), to the medium date format (9-Jul-94) and short date (7/9/94). The time format appears as 2:24 P.M. Access checks each entry for validity. If you enter an invalid date or time, an error dialog box displays the message "The value you entered isn't appropriate for this field."

- *Currency* fields are special number fields that are preset to show two decimal places and a leading $ sign.

- *Counter* fields contain integer (whole) numbers that Access auto-matically increments as you add records. These fields could be used

Figure 1-7

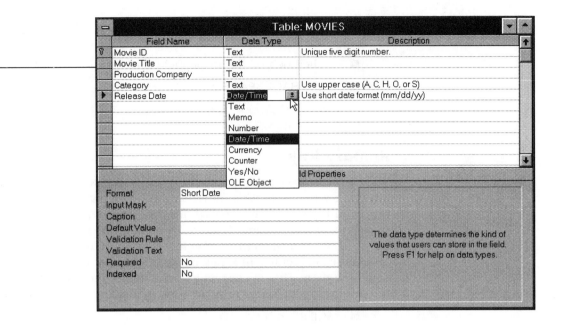

to increment the customer number as new customers are added to a table.

- *Yes/No* fields are set to one of two values. You could create a Yes/No field in each inventory record to indicate whether a tape is available for a customer to rent. In this case, "Yes" means the tape is in the store and available to rent while "No" means the tape is out or unusable for some reason.

- *OLE* (Object Linking and Embedding) fields take advantage of features associated with the Windows operating environment. An OLE field can contain an object, for instance, 50 pages of text or a complete spreadsheet, that is created and maintain by other software. Any changes to the object after it is installed in the Access table are automatically updated. This field type is limited to advanced applications.

Enter each field name, type, and size as described. Press the Enter key after each entry. The Movie ID is the key field and must be the first field.

NOTE: Fields can be inserted or deleted if necessary. Highlighting any part of a field definition and pressing the Ins key will insert a new field. Likewise, pressing the two key combination of Ctrl + Del will delete a field entry.

■   Press ENTER to select Text as the data type.

▶   *A flashing cursor moves to the Description column.*

■   Type **Unique five digit number.**

This description will appear in the status bar of any data entry form using this field. Next, to save storage space, you need to change the maximum field size from 50 characters to 5. This still leaves the store room for 99,999 separate movie titles.

- ▪ Click behind 50 in the Field Size box.
- ▪ Use BACKSPACE to delete the 0.
  - ▶ *Field Size is 5.*

Primary Key

While Access does not require a table to have a key field, there are several advantages to designating Movie ID as the **primary key.** Since a primary key is unique to each record in the table, Access does not permit duplicates. If two records had the same key, the key field could no longer be used to identify either record. Another advantage is that Access automatically creates an index using the key field. Indexes help speed up access to data. This is especially important when using large tables with hundreds of records. Records are always displayed in the key field order.

- ▪ Click on Movie ID.
  - ▶ *A flashing cursor appears in the field name.*
- ▪ Click on the key button (🔑) in the Tool bar.
  - ▶ *A key is inserted in front of the black pointer (current field indicator) to the left of the field name.*

PRACTICE TIME 1-1

Using Figure 1-7 as a model, enter the remaining field names, types, description, and sizes.

Field 2: Movie Title, Text, (none), 25

Field 3: Production Company, Text, (none), 20

Field 4: Category, Text, Use upper case (A, C, H, O, or S), 1

Date/Time Fields

The Release Date uses the Date/Time data type which is selected from the Data Type list box. When this option is selected, the size option disappears from the Field Properties area because the field size is determined by the date option you select. You will use the Format list box to select the short date format for this field.

- ▪ Type **Release Date** as the fifth field name and press ENTER.
  - ▶ *The text in the Data Type area is highlighted, and the arrow button is activated, as shown in Figure 1-7.*

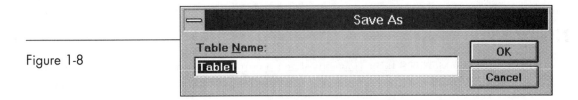

Figure 1-8

■ Click on the arrow button.

▶ *The Data Type list box opens.*

■ Select Date/Time format.

▶ *Access closes the list box and removes the Size option from Field Properties.*

■ Move the pointer into the Field Properties Format area and click.

▶ *A flashing cursor and an arrow button appear in the text area.*

■ Click on the arrow button and select Short Date.

▶ *Short Date is added to the Format text box.*

We have just scratched the surface of possibilities when it comes to defining database records. The text boxes marked Validation Rule and Validation Text help database designers prompt the correct data entry and check for errors. Unfortunately, these topics and other validity checks must be left for another time.

SAVING THE TABLE DESIGN

Before continuing, you need to save the **table design** you just entered. The table design includes the field names, data types, data entry descriptions, and field formats.

■ From the File menu, select Save As.

▶ *The Save As dialog box appears with Table 1 highlighted in the Table Name text box (see Figure 1-8).*

■ Type **MOVIES** and complete the command by clicking on OK or pressing ENTER.

▶ *The table is added to the VIDSTORE database, and the table name is changed to Movies in the title bar.*

■ From the File menu, select Close.

▶ *The display returns to the Access application window with the VIDSTORE database dialog box active.*

NOTE: If a table by the same name already exists, Access gives you the option of copying over the old table with the new or using a different name.

ENTERING DATA

The MOVIES table now exists as an empty shell on your disk. Your next step is to fill it with the names of the video tapes rented by Boomtown Video.

■ Make sure that MOVIES is highlighted in the VIDSTORE database dialog box.

■ Select Open.

▶ *A window with the empty MOVIES table is displayed.*

■ Maximize the MOVIES table window.

▶ *The MOVIES table fills the application window.*

Entering data into the table is basically the same as entering field names. After entering each field value, you press either the Tab or Enter keys to continue to the next entry. Access saves each record after all the fields are entered and checked for incompatibilities. As the insertion point moves from field to field the description (if any) you entered when setting up the MOVIES table appears in the status line. Furthermore, if incompatibilities are found, an error message appears in a special dialog box.

Should you discover that you neglected to enter one of the fields or made a mistake in a field definition or spelling of a field name, correcting the error is easy. From the View menu select Table Design and correct the error. You can then continue entering data by using the View menu's Datasheet option.

■ Type **101** for the record 1 Movie ID and press ENTER.

▶ *The insertion point is moved to the record 1 Movie Title field.*

NOTE: When you make a mistake, use the Backspace key to back up and erase the problem. If the data has been entered, click the pointer when it is over the problem to move the insertion point. Then either use the Backspace or Delete keys to delete the entry. Remember Ctrl + Del and Ins will delete and insert records.

■ Type **Casablanca** for the record 1 Video Title and press ENTER.

▶ *The Production Company field is highlighted.*

■ Type **Warner Bros.** for the record 1 Production Company field and press ENTER.

▶ *The Category field is highlighted.*

■ Type **O** for Oldie in Category field and press ENTER.

▶ *The Release Date field is highlighted.*

■ Type **9/11/42** in the Release Date field and press ENTER.

▶ *After a pause to save the record, the record 2 Movie ID field is highlighted.*

PRACTICE TIME 1-2

Enter the following data into the MOVIES table. Do not be concerned if some titles are not fully displayed in the area provided. Arc in Raiders of the Lost Arc is purposely misspelled.

Record 2:	**102**	**African Queen**	**20th Century-Fox**	**O**	**10/12/51**
Record 3:	**103**	**Dirty Harry**	**Warner Bros.**	**A**	**3/18/71**
Record 4:	**104**	**Star Wars**	**20th Century-Fox**	**S**	**5/25/77**
Record 5:	**105**	**Friday the 13th**	**Paramount**	**H**	**1/9/80**
Record 6:	**106**	**Star Trek**	**Paramount**	**S**	**12/20/79**
Record 7:	**107**	**Raiders of the Lost Arc**	**Paramount**	**A**	**7/23/81**
Record 8:	**108**	**Ghostbusters**	**Columbia**	**C**	**7/16/84**
Record 9:	**109**	**Jaws**	**Universal**	**H**	**8/14/86**
Record 10:	**110**	**Platoon**	**Hemdale**	**A**	**12/5/86**
Record 11:	**111**	**The Godfather**	**Paramount**	**D**	**10/11/72**
Record 12:	**112**	**Die Hard**	**20th Century-Fox**	**A**	**6/30/88**

LOCATING RECORDS

The row/column format currently used to display the MOVIES table is called a **datasheet.** This format displays multiple records on the same screen and is one of several options you have for displaying data. A black triangle, the **record selector**, in the far left column identifies the active record. In Figure 1-9, record 4 is the active record. The record number box above the status bar also identifies the active record as well as the current record count.

The contents of our MOVIES table are relatively small. However, you can imagine that a popular video rental store would have hundreds, if not thousands, of video tapes. As the table expands, you need ways of quickly finding records and moving around the table. The **navigation buttons** in Figure 1-9 let you move anywhere from the first to the last record in a table. These buttons also help you to move the record selector to the next or previous record. The navigation buttons are modeled after the forward and reverse buttons found on most tape players. The Record menu's Goto option provides the same alternatives (First, Last, Next, and Previous) along with a New record option.

■   Click on the First record navigation button, ⏮ .

Alternative: ALT+R, G then F.

Figure 1-9

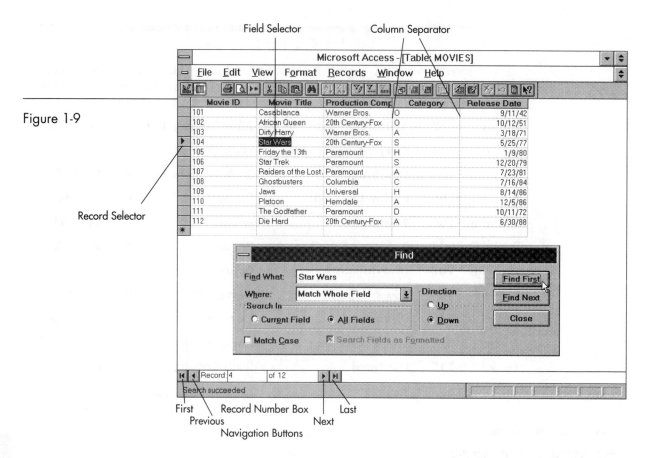

Field Selector

Column Separator

Record Selector

First

Previous

Record Number Box

Next

Last

Navigation Buttons

> ▶ *The record selector moves to the first record (Casablanca).*

■ Click on the Next record navigation button, ▶.

Alternative: ALT+R, G then N.

> ▶ *The record selector moves to record 2 (African Queen).*

■ Click on the Last record navigation button, ▶|.

Alternative: ALT+R, G then L.

> ▶ *The record selector moves to record 12 (Die Hard).*

Access also lets you locate specific data, like a movie title or release date, by using the Edit menu's Find option. For instance, you could find information about the *Star Wars* movie using this method.

■ From the Edit menu, choose Find.

Alternative: Press CTRL+F or use the Find tool button, 🔍.

> ▶ *The Find dialog box opens.*

■ Select the All Fields button.

■ Type **Star Wars** (don't forget space between words) into the Find What text box.

■   Select the Find Fir<u>s</u>t button.

▶   *Access highlights the Star Wars movie title; however, it may be hidden behind the dialog box.*

■   If necessary, drag the Find dialog box away from Movie ID 104 and the other Star Wars data as shown in Figure 1-9.

■   Select Close.

▶   *The Find dialog box closes, and the MOVIES table returns.*

PRACTICE TIME 1-3

Make record 12 the active record.

CHANGING COLUMN WIDTHS

On close examination of the datasheet, you will notice that the designated column widths are not wide enough to handle some data and field names. For example, the field name Production Company does not fit in the space provided. Neither does the movie title for record 7. While this will bother some people more than others, it is very simple to adjust the column widths. The line that falls between field names in the column headings is referred to as the ***column separator.*** When the pointer is moved over the column separator, it changes to a double arrow. At this time you can drag the column separator left or right to change the associated column width.

■   Move the pointer over the column separator between Production Company and Category.

▶   *The pointer changes to a double arrow.*

■   Drag the column separator to the right until the field name Production Company is completely visible.

PRACTICE TIME 1-4

1. Widen the Movie Title column until all of the title can be read.

2. Reduce the column width of the Movie ID and Category columns leaving enough space for the field names.

DATABASE

Figure 1-10

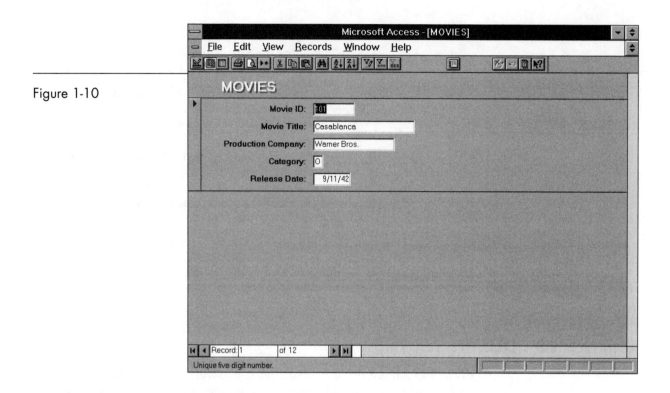

CREATING A FORM

While there are advantages in seeing several records at the same time when entering data using a datasheet, it can be cumbersome when long records are involved. In addition, business applications, like video rentals, often require special data entry screens that handle one record (rental) at a time. To meet these needs, Access offers users the option of displaying fields from a single record as a *form.* Figure 1-10 displays record 1 from the MOVIES table using the View menu's Forms option.

Wizards

The layout of a record when displayed as a form is completely flexible. You can customize the look, add your own labels, and change the field order used by the insertion point during data entry. However, an Access *Wizard* provides a fast and easy alternative. Wizards help users design database objects by automating common procedures. The AutoForm wizard will automatically create a professional-looking form for you at the click of a button. The form design in Figure 1-10 was created using the AutoForm wizard.

■   Click on the AutoForm tool button, ⬛ .

> ▶ *After a pause, Access creates a data entry form for displaying MOVIES records.*

■ Maximize the form window.

> ▶ *Record 1 is displayed, as shown in Figure 1-10.*

■ Press PAGE DOWN.

Alternative: Use Next button, ▶ .

> ▶ *The next record is displayed.*

The Page Down and Page Up keys are practical alternatives to the Previous and Next navigation button. In addition, pressing the Home key highlights the first field in the record while pressing the End key highlights the last field. These keyboard alternatives work in both a form view and a datasheet view.

PRACTICE TIME 1-5

Display record 8 in the MOVIES table.

Using a Data Entry Form

Data entry procedures using the form view are the same as those you used with the datasheet. After each entry press the Tab or Enter key to move to the next field. Any descriptive information about the field is displayed in the status line. To get to any empty screen for entering a new movie, you can either page down or use the Records menu's New option.

■ From the Records menu, choose Goto and select New.

> ▶ *An empty form is displayed, and the record number box indicates record 13 of 13.*

■ Enter the following data, pressing ENTER after each entry.

Movie ID: **113**

Movie Title: **Ghost**

Production Company: **Paramount**

Category: **D**

Release Date: **2/24/90**

> ▶ *A blank data entry form is displayed.*

DATABASE

PRACTICE TIME 1-6

Using the form view, enter the following records into the MOVIES table:

Record 14:	114	Pretty Woman	Touchstone	C	5/20/90
Record 15:	115	Dances with Wolves	Orion	A	11/9/90
Record 16:	116	Jurassic Park	Amblin	A	5/1/93
Record 17:	117	Adventures of *your name*	*your course name*	A	*Today's Date*

Records 18 & 19: Now enter your two favorite movies. Use Movie ID numbers 118 and 119. The category choices are as follows: A - Adventure, D - Drama, C - Comedy, H - Horror, O - Oldie (classics), and S - Science Fiction. Enter your best guess for release date and production company.

Saving the Form

Each database record is saved before the next record is entered. However, Access does not automatically save a new form. Before you continue, it would be best to store this form for future use. We will use Movies as the form name which also matches the table name.

■   From the File menu, select Close.

   Alternative: Press CTRL+F4.

   ▶   *The Save As dialog box opens, asking if you wish to save changes to Form 'Form1'.*

■   Select Yes.

   ▶   *The Save As dialog box opens displaying default name Form1.*

■   Type **Movies** and complete the command.

   ▶   *The datasheet with the MOVIES table returns.*

NOTE: If the MOVIES table is not currently on the screen, open the Window menu and select the Table:MOVIES option.

   On close examination of the datasheet you will notice that it does not contain records beyond number 12. Access does not automatically update a datasheet window when the table is updated using another window. The next time the datasheet opened, it will contain an updated view of the MOVIES table.

■   From the File menu, select Close.

   ▶   *Dialog box opens asking if you want to save changes to Table 'Movies'.*

■   Select Yes.

   ▶   *The display returns to the Access application window with the VIDSTORE database window active.*

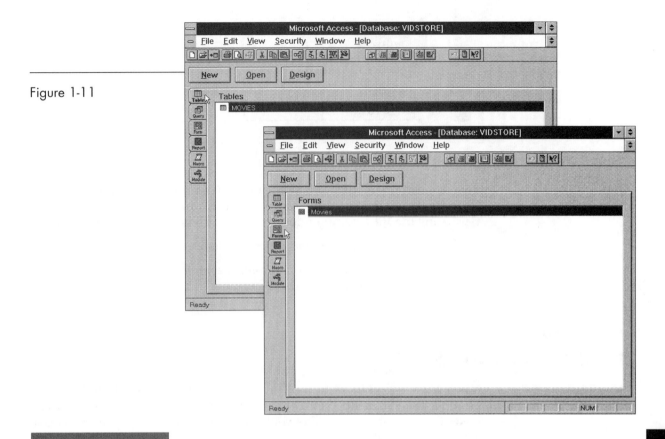

Figure 1-11

DATABASE

DATABASE OBJECTS AND VIEWS

The basic building block within an Access database is an ***object.*** You have already worked with two important objects: table and form. Other database objects, like query and report, are listed in the VIDSTORE database window currently on your screen. The sole purpose of these database objects is to organize data in a way that is easily accessible to you and others.

Currently, the VIDSTORE database contains two objects: the MOVIES table and the Movies form.

■   If necessary, select the Table button.

▶   *The window displays the MOVIES table, as shown at the top of Figure 1-11.*

■   Select the Form button.

▶   *The window lists the Movies form, as shown at the bottom of Figure 1-11.*

■   Click on the Open button.

▶   *The Movies form opens.*

The datasheet, form, and design views available to you are one way Access makes database data accessible. You will find that you can bounce

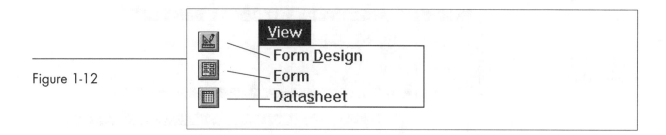

Figure 1-12

from one view to another depending on what you need to do with the data. From the form view currently on your screen, you can quickly change the view using the View menu options or tool buttons shown in Figure 1-12.

■   From the View menu, select Datasheet.

▶   *View changes to a row/column format showing all the MOVIES records you entered.*

PRINTING YOUR WORK

It is always a good habit to confirm the correct printer is selected prior to printing. The File menu Print Setup option enables you to make this check. If you have any question as to what the printer selection should be, check with your instructor.

■   From the File menu, select Print.

Alternative: Press CTRL+P or use the Print button, 🖨 .

▶   *The Print dialog box is displayed, as shown in Figure 1-13.*

Figure 1-13

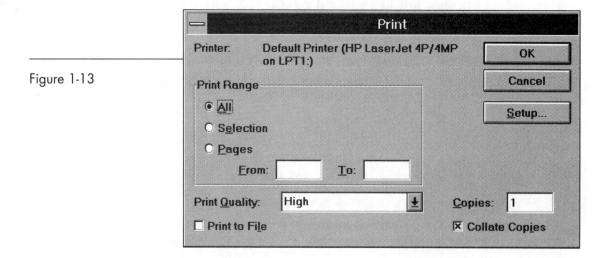

Take a close look at the dialog box on the screen. You will want to make sure you are printing one copy of all pages. These options should be the default settings.

■ Complete the command.

▶ *The printer displays a message box giving you a chance to cancel printing, then prints the table.*

CLOSING ACCESS WINDOWS

After the MOVIES table has been printed, you are done with this lesson and can close the table.

■ From the File menu, select Close.

▶ *The display returns to the VIDSTORE database window.*

EXITING ACCESS

It is a good habit to close all open windows before exiting Access. If you have made any recent changes to the database, Access will give you the option of saving these changes.

■ From the File menu, choose Close Database.

▶ *If recent changes have been made, Access gives you a chance to save changes, then returns to an empty Access application window.*

The procedure for exiting Access is similar to exiting any Windows-compatible software package. Selecting the Exit option from the File menu returns control back to Windows.

■ From the File menu, select Exit.

▶ *The program manager window is displayed.*

ENDING LESSON 1

Always end your Windows session from the Program Manager. This will guarantee you an opportunity to save any work you forgot to store on disk earlier. Before turning off your computer and the other associated hardware, ask your instructor about system shutdown procedures used at your school.

DATABASE

SUMMARY

❑   **Sophisticated database management systems (DBMS) integrate tables into relational databases.**

❑   **The Access DBMS works within the Windows operating environment and uses associated concepts and procedures.**

❑   **The Access application window offers a tool bar under the menu bar. The tool bar contains tool buttons representing common menu options.**

❑   **Access stores the user's database in the working directory. Each database is made up of objects which include tables and forms.**

❑   **Data records within a table are subdivided into fields. Each field is given a field name and designated as either text, memo, number, date/time, currency, counter, yes/no, or object-linking and embedding.**

❑   **When a field is designated as a primary key, it is required. Access will not add a new record to a table unless unique data is entered in the key field.**

❑   **Data is displayed in a row/column format as a datasheet or one record at a time in a form.**

❑   **Navigation buttons or the Edit menu's Find option are used to locate data within a table.**

❑   **Users can automatically create a data entry form using a wizard.**

❑   **Access uses Window's print manager to print data.**

❑   **As with all Windows compatible software, users quit Access by pulling down the File menu and selecting the Exit option.**

KEY TERMS

column separator	key	status bar
database management system (DBMS)	navigation buttons	table
	object	table design
datasheet	primary key	tool bar
field	record	tool button
field name	record selector	wizard
form	relational database	

COMMAND SUMMARY

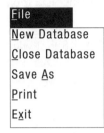

File
New Database
Close Database
Save As
Print
Exit

Edit
Find

View
Table Design
Datasheet

Record
Goto

DATABASE

REVIEW QUESTIONS

1. How do fields, records, and tables form a relational database?
2. What steps do you follow to launch Access for Windows?
3. What is the function of the tool bar and the status bar?
4. Give an example of invalid data for each of the following field types: number, currency, date/time, and yes/no.
5. Why would having two records with the same primary key field value cause problems?
6. What information is included as part of the table design?
7. How do you save the table design?
8. How are navigation buttons used?
9. How do you change the column width in a datasheet?
10. What Access feature automatically creates a data entry form for users?
11. Identify three different Access views and explain how you change the view.
12. How do you print the contents of a datasheet?
13. How do you exit from Access?

EXERCISES

1. Create a database called PERSONAL.
   a. Set up a new table called FRIENDS that will store information about people you know. Include in the table names, addresses, telephone number, birthday, and other information you would like to maintain about friends and relatives.
   b. Create a data entry form.
   c. Use data entry form to create five fictitious records. Use your name for record 1.

    d. Save the form as FRIENDS.

    e. Print the datasheet view of the FRIENDS table.

2. Create a new database called BUSINESS.

    a. Set up a new table called STOCKS that will serve as a personal stock portfolio manager. Include in the STOCKS table the following fields:

    Field 1 - Transaction Number (text, 6 characters, designate as primary key)

    Field 2 - Stock Name (text, 15 characters)

    Field 3 - Number of Shares (number)

    Field 4 - Purchase Price per Share (number)

    Field 5 - Date Purchased (date)

    Field 6 - Current Price per Share (number)

    b. Create a data entry form.

    c. Use the data entry form and financial page of your favorite newspaper to pick six stocks and enter related information into table. Transaction numbers should start at 1001 and increment by one, i.e., 1002, 1003, etc.

    d. Save the form as STOCKS.

    e. Print the datasheet view of the STOCKS table.

3. Create a table called SUPPLIER in the VIDSTORE database.

    a. Include the following fields in the table:

    Field 1 - Supplier Number (text, 6 characters, designate as primary key)

    Field 2 - Name (text, 25 characters)

    Field 3 - Street Address (text, 30 characters)

    Field 4 - City (text, 15 characters)

    Field 5 - State/Province (text, 2 characters)

    Field 6 - Zip/Postal Code (text, 10 characters)

    Field 7 - Telephone Number (text, 15 characters)

    Field 8 - Balance (number)

    b. Create a data entry form.

    c. Enter five records using a data entry form. Use your name for the first supplier and your imagination to fill in the remaining names, addresses, and other data.

    d. Save the form as SUPPLIER.

    e. Print the datasheet view of the SUPPLIER table.

2 Database Queries and Modifications

OBJECTIVES

Upon completing the material presented in this lesson, you should understand the following aspects of Access:

- ❏ **Using context-sensitive help**
- ❏ **Opening a database**
- ❏ **Updating (adding, deleting, or changing) data in a table**
- ❏ **Modifying a table's design**
- ❏ **Filtering data using query by example**
- ❏ **Sorting a dynaset**
- ❏ **Saving a query**
- ❏ **Printing a query dynaset**
- ❏ **Modifying a query**
- ❏ **Using comparison and logical operators in complex queries**

STARTING OFF

Database management systems, like Access 2.0 for Windows, allow you to access and organize vast amounts of data. If you know how to use this tool, significant increases in personal productivity can be achieved. All of this hinges on your ability to locate and access the databases holding information of use to you.

Turn on your computer and start the Windows program. Insert your data disk and then launch the Access program as you did in Lesson 1.

■   Turn on your computer.

■   Insert your data disk into the disk drive.

■   Launch Windows.

■   Open Access 2.0 group icon and Launch Access.

▶   *The Access application window is displayed.*

■   If necessary, maximize the application window.

When you start this lesson, you need access to the VIDSTORE database created in Lesson 1. The MOVIES table, shown in Figure 2-1, contains information customers like you could use when planning this weekend's video viewing.

When opening VIDSTORE you could encounter the **error message** shown in Figure 2-2. Error messages result when the computer system is unable to function properly or when you are about to do something you might regret. Well-written error messages provide explanations related to the problem or offer alternative courses of action.

Figure 2-1

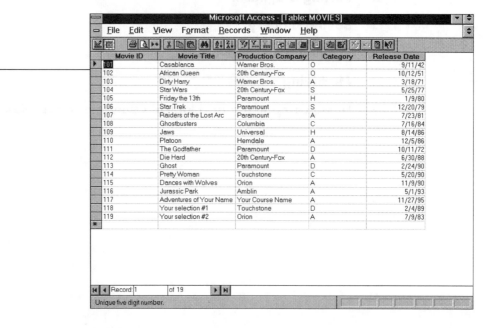

GETTING HELP

You encounter two different types of "problem" situations when working with software systems like Access. You initiate some situations by asking questions: "How do I do _____?" Other situations are forced upon you by the computer, as illustrated by the error message in Figure 2-2. This particular error message occurs when you attempt to access the database from a floppy disk drive that does not contain a formatted diskette or has its disk drive latch open.

Selecting the Retry button or pressing R clears the error message and the computer tries to read the diskette again. Selecting the Cancel button returns the display back to the Access application window. The most commonly used course of action is usually highlighted as the default button in the error message box. In Figure 2-2, the Retry button is the default option that you initiate by pressing the Enter key. You will also find the Access *User's Guide* a good reference source for additional information about error messages and other software features.

Situations where you ask "How do I do _____?" are handled by several Help features. These features include the Help menu and cue cards that walk you through different operations step-by-step. Both of these features provide **context-sensitive help**. This means the information supplied by the help screens changes based on the Access feature currently being used.

Figure 2-2

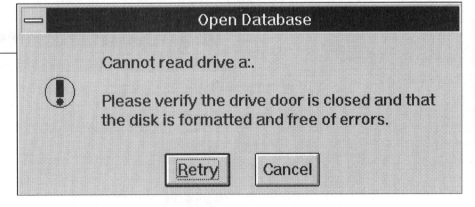

NOTE: If any table is currently open, close it using the File menu's Close Database option.

■   Click on the Help menu.

   Alternative: Press F1.

   ▶   *The help options are displayed.*

■   Select Contents.

   ▶   *A Help window with general information about Access appears, as shown at the top of Figure 2-3.*

DATABASE

The Help window contains a title bar and a row of help buttons above the workspace. The workspace contains information on a topic, here a short description of different Access features. The workspace can be scrolled. More information is available for any of the underlined topics called *jump terms*. The top screen in Figure 2-3 contains the jump term <u>Using Microsoft Access</u>. A jump term or related icon is selected either by clicking on it using the mouse or by pressing Tab or Shift+Tab keys to highlight the topic and then pressing Enter. The Contents help button displays common concepts and jump terms. The Search help button is used to locate a new jump term and related description.

■ Position the pointer over the <u>Using Microsoft Access</u> jump term.

▶ *The pointer changes to a pointing finger,* 🖑 *.*

■ Select the jump term.

▶ *The Using Microsoft Access window opens, as shown at the bottom of Figure 2-3.*

Figure 2-3

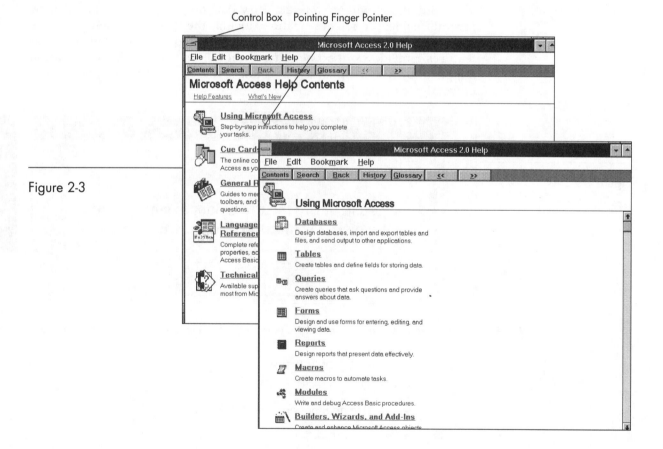

Since you need to open the VIDSTORE database, let's see what Help has to say about opening an existing database.

■ Click on the Databases jump term.

▶ *The Databases help window opens with a list of database-related jump terms.*

■ Select <u>Opening, Printing, Copying, Renaming, and Deleting</u> found at the bottom of the jump term list.

▶ *Opens a box with another list of jump terms.*

■ Choose Opening an Existing Database.

▶ *The Opening an Existing Database help window is displayed.*

■ After reading the help screen description, exit the Help window using the <u>F</u>ile menu.

Alternative: Double-click on the Help window control box.

▶ *The Help window is cleared from the Access application window.*

Another useful help feature is the Context-sensitive Help button. This feature helps you answer questions about icons and menu options found in the Access application window. Selecting this button and clicking on a menu option or toolbar button, automatically opens the related Help window.

■ Click on the Context-sensitive button, 🔲 .

▶ *Pointer changes to Context-sensitive pointer,* 🔲 *.*

■ Open the <u>F</u>ile menu and use the Context-sensitive pointer to select <u>O</u>pen Database.

▶ *The Open Database Command (File Menu) window is displayed.*

■ After reading the help screen description, close the Help window.

▶ *The Help window is cleared from the Access application window.*

OPENING AN EXISTING DATABASE

The help screens you reviewed detailed the basic procedures for opening an existing database. Currently, at least two databases should be on your data disk: VIDSTORE and STUDENT as shown in Figure 2-4. Each database uses Access's default filename extension .MDB. The VIDSTORE database was created as part of the Lesson 1 tutorial and STUDENT is supplied to you by your instructor.

■   From the File menu, select Open Database.

Alternative: Use the Open Database button, 📂 .

▶   *The Open Database dialog box is displayed.*

In figure 2-4, the Exclusive check box is checked. When this option is active like this, only one user at a time can access the database. That person would have to close the database before someone else could open it. The VIDSTORE database can be designated ***exclusive*** when working with it as a part of this lesson because there is no reason for more than one person to be using the data at the same time. In a real video store application, there could be reasons for turning this option off and having several clerks accessing movie titles and other data at the same time.

■   Verify that the disk drive and directory with your databases are shown in the Drives and Directories list boxes.

■   Click on VIDSTORE.MDB and finish the command by clicking on OK or pressing Enter.

Alternative: Double-click on VIDSTORE.MDB.

▶   *The database: VIDSTORE dialog box opens.*

■   With the Tables button active, select MOVIES, and click on Open.

▶   *The MOVIES table is displayed.*

Figure 2-4

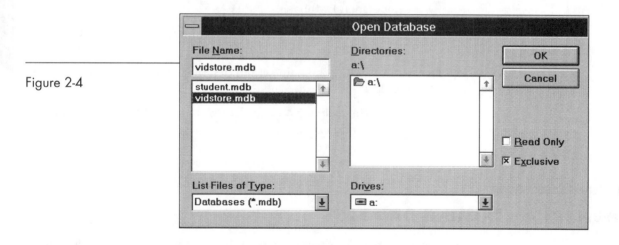

PRACTICE TIME 2-1

When necessary, complete the following actions. When you are done, your screen should look like Figure 2-1.

1. Display the MOVIES table as a datasheet.

2. Maximize the MOVIES window.

3. Widen the Movie Title column to fit the longest name.

4. Widen the Production Company column to fit the field name.

UPDATING A TABLE

Updating a table involves either adding, changing, or deleting records. In creating the MOVIES table in Lesson 1, you added 19 records to the empty table. Changing and deleting records is just as easy.

Changing a Field Entry

Making changes to field entry works just like the text editing feature of most word processing packages. Both the Delete (Del) and Backspace keys remove text. Delete removes text to the right of the flashing cursor (*insertion point*), while the Backspace key removes text to the left of the cursor. If a mistake is immediately caught the Edit menu's Undo Saved Record option or the Ctrl + Z keyboard alternative returns the changes back to the original format.

■ Position the pointer to the right "c" in Raiders of the Lost Arc and click.

▶ *A flashing cursor appears behind the "c" in "Arc."*

■ Use the keyboard to backspace over "c" and then type **k**.

▶ *Record 7's movie title now reads "Raiders of the Lost Ark."*

■ Press the down arrow key.

▶ *The cursor moves down to record 8's movie title after saving changes to record 7.*

Deleting a Record

The Delete key or Edit-Delete menu option removes highlighted records from a database table. The easiest way to highlight a record is to click on the record selector as shown in Figure 2-5. Because Access cannot undo

Figure 2-5

Record
Selector

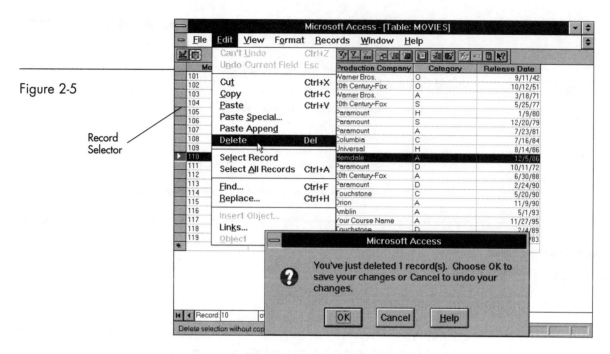

actions associated with removing a record, a warning box appears for you
to verify that the record is to be deleted.

■   Click on the record selector to the left of Movie ID 110.

▶   *Platoon record is highlighted, as shown in Figure 2-5.*

■   From the Edit menu, select Delete.

Alternative: Press Delete.

▶   *A Warning message asks you to OK the deletion of this
record.*

■   Complete the command by clicking on OK or pressing the
Enter key.

▶   *The record Platoon is removed from the table.*

PRACTICE TIME 2-2

Change the release date for *Jaws* to **4/20/75**.

MODIFYING A TABLE'S DESIGN

To allow for an expanded movie inventory, you need to increase the Movie
ID field to six characters and add a field called Ratings to the MOVIES

table. Ratings is a text field that stores the film industry rating of the movie (G, PG, PG13, and R for our purposes). Changes to a table's basic structure are made using the design view.

- ■ From the View menu, select Table Design.

   Alternative: Use the Design button, 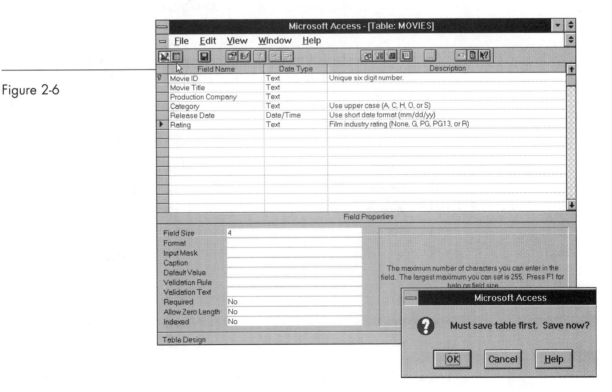 .

   ▶   *Display changes to design view similar to Figure 2-6.*

Expanding the Field Size

Making modifications to the Movie ID's field size is as simple as changing the 5 to a 6. However, great care is required when it comes to changing the design of a table because of the great potential for losing data. For example, changing the Movie ID field type from text to number would require the re-entry of related data. Expanding the ID field from three to four characters would not cause any problems. Making the ID field smaller would generate a warning message and potentially cause the loss of data that exceeded the new field size.

- ■ Select the Movie ID field name and change the 5 in the Field Size text box to a **6**.

- ■ Change the Movie ID Description to read "Unique **six** digit number".

Related error messages do not appear until you try to save the changes.

Figure 2-6

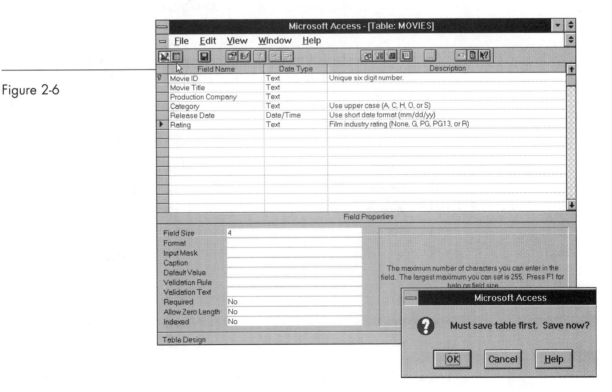

Adding a New Field

New fields are added to the table by inserting a new field name along with the related type, size, and description when appropriate.

■ Move the insertion point to the empty Field Name area under Release Date.

■ Type **Rating**.

▶ *The new field name is added to the table design.*

■ Complete the field design with the following information:

Data Type: **Text**

Description: **Film industry rating (None, G, PG, PG13, or R)**

Field Size: **4**

▶ *The table design should look like Figure 2-6.*

■ From the <u>V</u>iew menu, choose Datasheet.

Alternative: Use the Datasheet View button, ▦ .

▶ *A dialog box asking you to save table first is displayed as seen in Figure 2-6.*

■ Select OK.

▶ *The new table design is stored, and you return to the datasheet view of the MOVIES table. Notice the empty Rating field next to Release Date.*

P R A C T I C E   T I M E   2 - 3

Update the MOVIES table with the following ratings. There are 18 ratings to add because *Platoon* was deleted.

ID	RATING	ID	RATING
101	**None**	111	**R**
102	**None**	112	**R**
103	**R**	113	**PG13**
104	**PG**	114	**R**
105	**R**	115	**PG13**
106	**G**	116	**PG13**
107	**G**	117	**PG**
108	**PG**	118	*your choice*
109	**R**	119	*your choice*

CREATING A QUERY

What is the point of having information if you can't use it? Every DBMS has some means of answering user queries about data. A **query** is a question you ask concerning database data which is in a format that prompts Access to display selected data. The selected data is called a **dynaset**, which looks like a table, but is really a special view of data from one or more tables. A video store customer might ask for a list of all the movies classified as adventure. The dynaset set would be the movie titles of all the adventure movies. Someone else could ask for the list of adventure movies in order from oldest to newest or for a printed copy of the list.

■   From the File menu, choose New, and then select Query.

    Alternative: Use the New Query button, ⊡.

▶   *Opens New Query dialog box.*

■   Select New Query.

▶   *The Select Query window is displayed.*

The top screen in Figure 2-7 illustrates a **select query**. The field names Movie Title, Category, and Rating are in the QBE (Query-By-Example) grid that makes up the bottom half of the query window. When an X appears in the check box under each field name, Access adds related data to the dynaset, also shown in Figure 2-7. If a check mark does not appear in the Show area, the related field can be used as a basis for selecting data, but is not included in the dynaset.

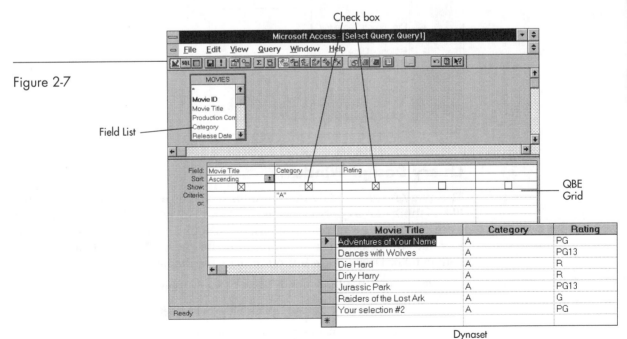

Figure 2-7

Dynaset

As you can see, the select query gets its name because it allows the user to selectively display database data. A select query is one of the most common types of queries. Other types will be discussed later. Building queries is fun and represents the true power of a DBMS.

To select all movie titles:

■ Move the pointer into the first Field area of the QBE grid and click.

▶ *An insertion point and a down arrow appear in the Field area.*

■ Click on the down arrow.

▶ *The list box that displays field names from the MOVIES table opens, as shown in Figure 2-8.*

■ Select Movie Title.

▶ *The field name is added to the first Field area ,and an X is placed in the Show check box.*

■ From the Query menu, select Run.

Alternative: Press the Run button, ▮ .

▶ *A dynaset is displayed with all 18 movie titles.*

Figure 2-8

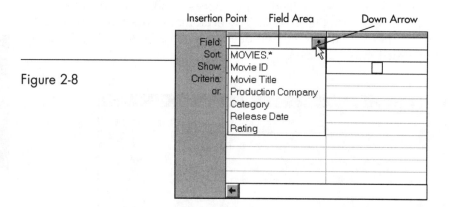

Query Design Window

The query results, the dynaset, are displayed as a datasheet. Some people like to think that a query works like a filter, displaying only the data selected from one or more tables. The QBE grid found in the query design view identifies the selection criterion used by the query. The View-Query Design command or Design View button returns the display to the design view.

■ From the View menu, select Query Design.

Alternative: Use the Design View button, ▮ .

▶ *The Select Query window is displayed.*

Selection Criteria

Field names can also be added to the QBE grid by dragging the name from the field list down into the Field area of the grid. To demonstrate this *drag-and-drop* alternative, you will drag the Category field name into the QBE grid and use it to identify all the adventure movies in the MOVIES table. On closer inspection of Figure 2-7, you will see the ***expression*** *"A"* below the Category check mark in the Criteria area. It specifies that only movies where the *category* = *"A"* are listed. An expression identifies the criteria Access uses to add data to the dynaset. Where an exact match, like uppercase A, is needed, enclose the character(s) in double quotes.

To select all the adventure movies:

■   Click on the field name Category in the MOVIES list box and drag it into the field area to the right of Movie Title.

▶   *Category is added to the QBE grid (similar to Figure 2-7).*

■   Click the pointer under the Category check box in the Criteria area.

▶   *The insertion point is activated.*

■   Type **"A"**.

▶   *Adds expression to Criteria area.*

■   Run the query by clicking on the Run button, 🔲.

▶   *A new Dynaset window appears with at least six adventure movie titles. The number of adventure movies could exceed six if you added movies in this category.*

Sorting the Dynaset

In addition, movie titles can be displayed in alphabetical order from A to Z by designating the Sort area under movie title as ascending. Your other options are descending order (Z-A) or not sorted. When sorting number fields, ascending order is from smallest number to the largest, while descending order is from the largest number to the smallest.

To sort adventure movies by Movie Title:

■   Return to the query design view by clicking on the Design button, 🔲.

■   Click the pointer under Movie Title in the Sort area.

▶   *The insertion point is activated, and a down arrow is displayed.*

■   Click on the down arrow.

▶   *The list box that displays sorting options opens.*

■   Select Ascending.

■   Run the query.

▶   *The dynaset includes adventure movies in alphabetical order.*

PRACTICE TIME 2-4

Use Figure 2-7 as a model for the final results.

1. Add the Rating field to the QBE grid and then run the query.

2. Use the column separator to widen the Movie Title column to fit the longest name in the dynaset.

Saving a Query

Saving regularly used queries will improve your productivity because you can quickly answer commonly asked What-if questions by opening the query and running it again. If the table has been recently updated, the new dynaset reflects these changes.

You save a new query by using the File-Save As command. Otherwise, Access will ask you if you want to save the query when you close it. In either case, you will be given a chance to change the default query name, Query1, to a more descriptive name. The query name can be up to 64 characters, and spaces are acceptable. If you use the File-Save command or Save button at this time, Access still asks if you want to change the default query name.

■   From the File menu, select Save Query As.

Alternative: Use the Save button, 🖫 .

▶   *The Save As dialog box opens.*

■   Type **Adventure Movies** and complete the command.

▶   *The Select Query window returns with the new query name in the title bar.*

Before printing, you will turn off the gridlines.

Turning Off Gridlines

While gridlines help the eye track field entries across the screen, some people like to use Format-Gridlines to turn them off when printing. A check mark appears in front of the Gridlines menu option when the lines are on as shown in Figure 2-9. Selecting the same menu option again turns it off.

■   From the Format menu, select Gridlines.

▶   *The check mark is removed from the menu, and the lines are removed from the display.*

Figure 2-9

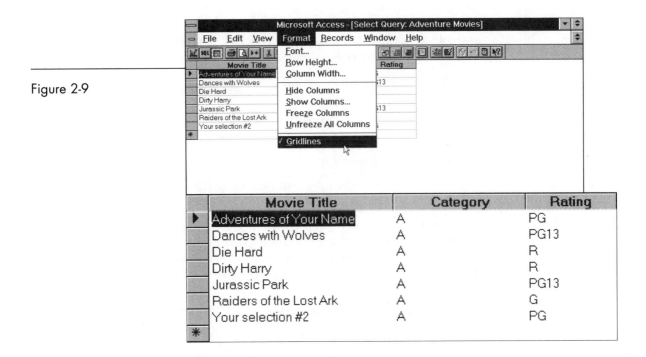

Printing a Dynaset

Access's <u>F</u>ile-<u>P</u>rint command creates a printed report from data in any active window.

■   Check to make sure the printer is on and ready to print.

■   Click on the Print button, 🖨️ .

▶   *The Print dialog box is displayed.*

■   Make sure you are printing one copy and complete the command.

▶   *One copy of the dynaset is printed, with the query name Adventure Movies at the top.*

PRACTICE TIME 2-5

1. Turn on the gridlines.

2. Return to the query design view.

Removing Fields from a Query

Fields are not transferred to the query dynaset when the X is removed from the Show area in the QBE grid. However, queries can still be based on field values even when the field itself is not included in the dynaset. For example, if the X in the Category check box is removed, but the expression "A" remains, the query is still limited to adventure movies.

■   From the query design view, click on the X in the Category Show area.

▶   *The X is removed from the box, but the expression "A" remains in the Criteria area.*

■   Run the query.

▶   *The dynaset contains adventure movie titles and the movies' ratings.*

Fields are removed from the QBE grid by highlighting the field name and pressing the Delete key or, one character at a time, by using the Delete or Backspace keys. Related search criteria, sorting order, and other information in the QBE grid are not removed until the insertion point is moved to another field by pressing one of the arrows keys or Enter.

■   Return to the query design view.

■   Click to the left of the Category field name in the QBE grid.

▶   *An insertion point appears in front of the field name.*

■   Use the BACKSPACE or the DELETE key to remove the field name, then press LEFT ARROW.

▶   *The expression "A" is removed from the QBE grid, and the insertion point moves to the next field.*

P R A C T I C E   T I M E   2 - 6

Create a query that identifies all the movie titles and related ratings for movies produced by Paramount. The dynaset should include the Movie Title and Rating fields, but not Production Company. Use **Paramount Movies** as the query name and print the dynaset.

COMPLEX QUERIES

Quite often, the selection criteria used within a query will involve data from several fields or different field values from the same field. These *complex queries* use multiple criteria along with two *logical operators*: *AND* and *OR*. For example, a complex query could search for information from two separate fields, such as adventure movies with a PG13 rating. In this case the Category field must equal A *and* the Rating field value must equal

PG13. Other times, complex queries search for different values within the same field, such as a customer who wants a list of either adventure or drama movies. In this situation the category field equals A *or* D.

Using the OR Operator

When using the OR operator, only one of the criteria needs to exist for the data to be included in the dynaset. In Figure 2-10, either adventure movies or dramas meet the selection criteria. In this situation no movie would fall into both categories so the OR operator has to be used.

To get a list of all the adventure movies or dramas:

- ■ Display the query design view.

  - ▶ *The Movie Title and the Rating fields in the QBE grid should already be marked for inclusion in the dynaset.*

- ■ Remove any other field names from the QBE grid.

- ■ Add the Category field name to the QBE grid.

  - ▶ *Three fields should appear in the QBE grid: Movie Title, Rating, and Category.*

- ■ In the Criteria area under the Category field, type **"A" Or "D"**.

  - ▶ *The Select Query window should look like Figure 2-10.*

NOTE: Access changes the *o* in *or* to an uppercase *O*.

- ■ Run the query.

  - ▶ *You get a list with at least eight records including one with your name.*

Figure 2-10

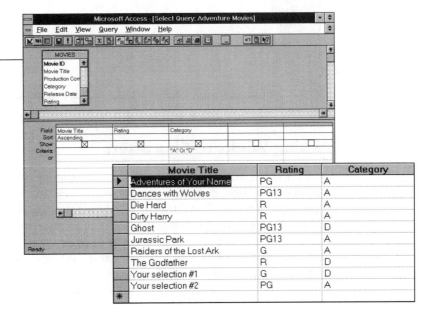

When different fields are used, the second condition is placed in the "or" area found below the Criteria area. Consider a situation where you are looking for movies with a G rating *or* adventure movies. For this query to work, "A" is placed in the Criteria area below Category, while "G" is placed in the or area below Rating.

Access defaults to using the AND operator when more than one Criteria area is filled-in. A query with "A" and "G" in their respective Criteria areas would produce a dynaset listing G rated adventure movies.

Using the AND Operator

When the AND operator is used, every selection criteria must be met before the data is added to the dynaset. In the next query you are to develop, a movie must be rated PG13 as well as have a Category field equal to A.

To select all adventure movies with a rating of PG13:

- ■   Return to the query design view.

- ■   Remove **Or "D"** from the Category Criteria area.

- ■   Type **"PG13"** in the Rating Criteria field.

    ▶   *The QBE grid should look like Figure 2-11.*

- ■   Run the query.

    ▶   *You get a dynaset which includes at least 2 records: Dances with Wolves and Jurassic Park.*

Figure 2-11

Field:	Movie Title	Rating	Category
Sort:	Ascending		
Show:	☒	☒	☒
Criteria:		"PG13"	"A"
or:			

Using Wildcard Characters

In some situations, you need to give Access flexibility in determining which fields are included in the dynaset. For example, some video store customers might find either PG or PG13 movies acceptable. You could use the OR operator to define the selection criteria as *"PG" Or "PG13"*. An interesting alternative is to use the expression *Like "PG*"*. The asterisk (*) is a **wildcard character.** This means that any combination of characters are acceptable where the * is located in the expression. In this case, the rating meets the selection criteria if it starts with PG.

Figure 2-12

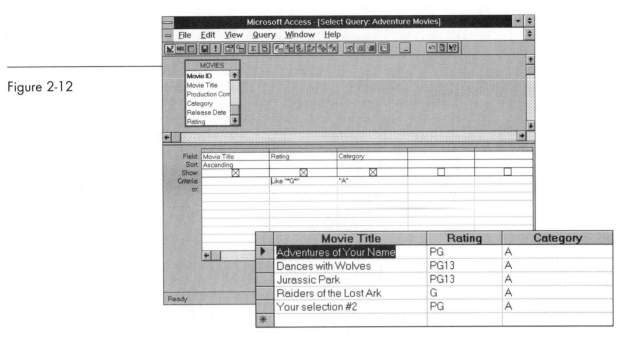

To select all the adventure movies with some type of PG rating:

- Return to the query design view.

- Replace the expression "PG13" with **Like "PG*"**.

- Run the query.

    ▶   *You get a list that includes the movies with your name.*

Wildcard characters can precede or follow selected characters in the selection criteria. Movies with a PG, PG13, or G rating all contain the letter G in the rating. Modifying the Ratings Criteria area to *Like "*G*"* would cover any movie except those with an R rating.

- Return to the query design view.

- Replace the Rating Criteria Like "PG*" with **Like "*G*"**.

    ▶   *The QBE grid should look like the top of Figure 2-12.*

- Run the query.

    ▶   *You get a dynaset that includes all adventure movies with a G, PG, or PG13 rating, as shown in Figure 2-12.*

Using Comparison Operators

Data ranges can be identified as part of the selection criteria by using the following *comparison operators*:

<	less than
<=	less than or equal to

>   greater than
>=   greater than or equal to

These operators work with text, dates, numbers, and other types of data. For instance, movies released before 1980 are identified by the expression *<1/1/80* as shown in Figure 2-13. An expression can contain several comparison and logical operators. If you added a field that identified how many minutes each movie ran, you could use the expression *>60 And <120* to identify movies running over 60 minutes but under 120 minutes.

You should always double-check the logic behind complex queries. It is easy to create a query that does not produce the expected results because the operators are used incorrectly within the selection criteria. Consider again the example above that used movie run times. If the expression used OR instead of AND, then the expression *>60 Or <120* would not eliminate any movies from the dynaset.

Movies released before 1980:

- ■   Return to the query design view.

- ■   Remove **Like "*G*"** and **"A"** from the Criteria areas.

- ■   Add Release Date to the QBE grid.

- ■   Make **<1/1/80** the Release Date criteria.

  ▶   *The QBE grid should look like the top of Figure 2-13.*

- ■   Run the query.

  ▶   *You get a dynaset that includes all movies released before 1980, as shown in Figure 2-13.*

NOTE: Access adds the # symbol to the beginning and end of the date when it recognizes the entry as a date.

Figure 2-13

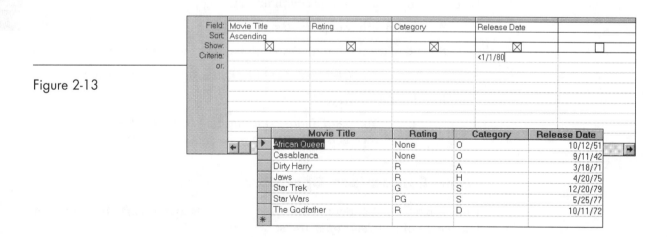

PRACTICE TIME 2-7

1. Print a dynaset with the movie titles and the release dates of all movies released before 1980 in ascending order by release date. Save the query using the query name **Released Before 1980**.

2. Print a list of all the horror movies by title and rating. Do NOT include the Category field in the dynaset and save the query using the name **Horror Movies**.

3. Print a list with the movie title, rating, and category of any movie with the word "Ghost" in the title or in the horror category. Save the query using the name **Ghost Movies**.

4. Close all open query windows.

5. Return to the VIDSTORE database dialog box and maximize the window if necessary.

6. Displays the Query list as shown in Figure 2-14.

DELETING QUERY FROM DATABASE

New queries are developed when they help answer often-asked questions. In these situations the query can be saved and opened again whenever it is needed. Having the query saved on disk is better than using a printed copy of the results because the most up-to-date data is used every time the query is opened and run.

However, every computer user must do a little "housekeeping" once in a while and delete from disk queries, forms, and other database objects that are not being used. Because Access objects are interlinked in many applications, great care must be taken when deleting any object. You could delete a query that is used as a basis for a report, making the report useless.

You are going to delete the Ghost Movies query you created as part of the last Practice Time. The procedure is straightforward. You simply highlight the object name in the database dialog box and press the Delete key. The object is deleted once you confirm that the correct object has been selected.

■ Select Ghost Movies in the Queries list box.

▶ *The query name is highlighted, as shown in Figure 2-14.*

■ Press DELETE.

▶ *The confirmation dialog box opens, also shown in Figure 2-14.*

Figure 2-14

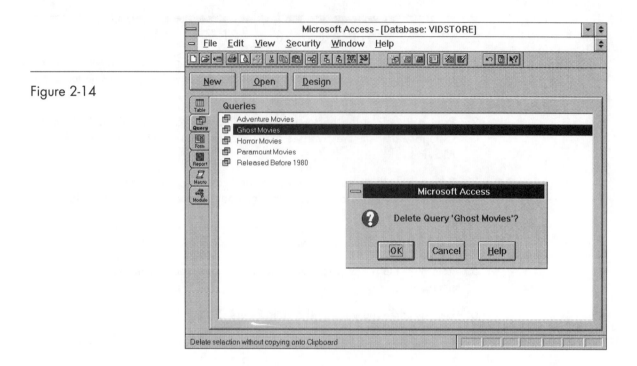

■   Confirm the deletion by clicking on OK or pressing ENTER.

▶   *Ghost Movies is removed from the query list.*

ENDING LESSON 2

This is the end of Lesson 2. Close all open windows and exit Access. If you are done with the computer, follow the recommended procedures for shutting down the computer system.

■   Close all open Access windows.

■   Exit Access.

SUMMARY

❑   **Error messages occur when the computer cannot perform a task or the user is about to get into trouble.**

❑   **Context-sensitive help answers your questions about specific software features. The *User's Guide* also explains software features and error messages.**

❏ **Updating a table involves adding, changing, or removing records.**

❏ **Access organizes records in a table by the key field, also known as the primary key. Tables without a primary key organize records in data entry order.**

❏ **Take special precautions when modifying a table's design. Some changes result in the loss of data.**

❏ **You can extract and sort information from a table using a query. Access uses a query-by-example (QBE) format within the query design view.**

❏ **A query's QBE grid can include expressions that filter the data going into the dynaset.**

❏ **Dynasets can be printed just like data from a table.**

❏ **Data in a dynaset can be sorted into another order.**

❏ **Any object can be removed from the database by highlighting its name in the database dialog box and pressing the Delete key.**

KEY TERMS

comparison operators	exclusive	select query
complex queries	expression	updating
context-sensitive help	jump term	wildcard character
dynaset	logical operators	
error message	query	

DATABASE

COMMAND SUMMARY

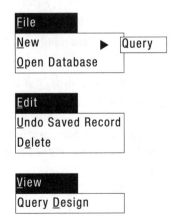

File	
New ▶	Query
Open Database	

Edit
Undo Saved Record
Delete

View
Query Design

Format
Gridlines

Query
Run

Help
Contents

REVIEW QUESTIONS

1. What are two resources, not counting the instructor, you could use to help solve problems that arise when using Access?

2. How do you access data from an existing database?

3. What procedures are used to change existing data in a table or to delete a record?

4. Identify two situations in which data would be lost when modifying a table's structure.

5. How is a dynaset created?

6. What are two ways to add a field to the dynaset?

7. How is data sorted in a dynaset?

8. How do you remove gridlines from a table or dynaset?

9. Explain how you can use a field value as part of a query's selection criteria without including the value within the dynaset.

10. What is the difference between using the OR operator in a complex query and using the AND operator?

11. Explain how a wildcard character is used in an Access QBE grid selection criteria.

12. Identify four different comparison operators.

13. How do you delete a query from the database?

EXERCISES

1. Update the FRIENDS table in the PERSONAL database and set up queries.
   a. Add four new records that reflect the following data:
      - Two male names with birth dates in April and September.
      - Two female names with birth dates in September and December.
   b. Change the addresses and phone numbers of any two of the original five entries.
   c. Delete one of the original five records, but do not delete your record.
   d. Create queries that look for the following information. Print each dynaset as a datasheet and save each query. Include in each dynaset all the fields used by the FRIENDS table. Hint: More than one wildcard character can be used and Access makes a distinction between 09 and 9 when used in a date.
      - All September birth dates.
      - All September or December birth dates.

    e. Print the FRIENDS table.

2. Update the STOCKS table in the BUSINESS database and set up queries.

    a. Modify the table design by changing the Purchase Price per Share and Current Price per Share fields to a currency data type.

    b. Update the Current Price per Share in each record to reflect the most current closing share price.

    c. Add four new stocks to the portfolio. Incorporate the following data into these records:

Transaction #	# of Shares	Purchase Price	Current Price
1007	**100**	**$18.27**	**$21.00**
1008	**400**	**$10.15**	**$11.75**
1009	**700**	**$7.36**	**$6.50**
1010	**200**	**$14.95**	**$12.00**

    d. Increase by 100 shares the number of shares you own for transactions 1002 and 1005.

    e. Delete transaction 1003.

    f. Create queries that look for the following information. Print each dynaset as a datasheet and save each query. Include in each dynaset all six fields found in the STOCKS table.

      - All holdings of more than 300 shares.

      - All holdings of more than 300 shares where the current price is higher than $10.

3. Update the RENTALS and INV table in the STUDENT database and set up queries.

    a. Add four new rentals to the RENTALS table and include the following data:

Customer No.	Tape No.	Date Out	Date In
941111	**42138**	**09/16/94**	**09/17/94**
941111	**47739**	**09/21/94**	**09/22/94**
941111	**50616**	**10/05/94**	**10/07/94**
941111	**48419**	**10/11/94**	**10/12/94**

    b. Movies with tape numbers 48420 and 50617 have been returned damaged. Change their available status in the INV table to an uppercase **N**.

    c. Tape number 48929 is damaged beyond repair and should be deleted from the INV table.

    d. Using the INV table, create queries that look for the following information. Print each dynaset as a datasheet and save each query. Include in each dynaset all five fields found in the INV table.

      - All movies with a purchase price over $35.

      - The movies with a purchase price over $35 that were purchased before 1990.

DATABASE

3 Creating Reports and Two Table Queries

OBJECTIVES

Upon completing the material presented in this lesson, you should understand the following aspects of Access 2.0:

- ❏ **Attaching a database to other tables**
- ❏ **Using the Mailing Label wizard**
- ❏ **Understanding report design terminology**
- ❏ **Using the Groups/Totals wizard**
- ❏ **Creating a two-table query**
- ❏ **Reassigning a report to a new query or table**
- ❏ **Customizing headings**
- ❏ **Printing reports**

STARTING OFF

Turn on your computer, start Windows, and then launch the Access 2.0 for Windows program as you did in previous lessons. Insert your data disk and set the working directory if necessary. Maximize the Access application window.

■   Insert your data disk into the disk drive.

■   Launch Access.

▶   *The Access application window is displayed.*

■   Open the VIDSTORE database.

■   If necessary, maximize the application window.

ATTACHING OTHER DATABASE TABLES

It is time to link the VIDSTORE database to the customer, inventory (inv), and rentals tables found in the STUDENT database supplied by your instructor. Access provides two ways of incorporating files used by other database management software, including other Access files. When you **import** a file, it is converted into an Access format. **Attaching** to another database table leaves the data in its original format, while allowing you to display and update it. However, you cannot change the design of any objects in the attached database.

The three tables, CUSTOMER, INV, and RENTALS, are all in a native Access format and do not need to be imported. You will attach the VIDSTORE database to each of these tables. Together with the MOVIES table (see Figure 3-1), they represent an integrated relational database system.

■   From the File menu, select Attach Table.

▶   *The Attach dialog box opens, as shown at the top of Figure 3-2.*

■   Verify that the data source is Microsoft Access and complete the command by clicking on OK or pressing Enter.

▶   *The Select Microsoft Access Database dialog box opens.*

The dialog box on your screen is essentially the same as the Open dialog box. You identify the drive, directory, and database name of the data you want to attach. The Exclusive check box is also found in the Open dialog box. When this option is active, only one user can access the database. That person would have to close it before someone else could open it. Since you could be sharing these tables with other students on a network, you should make sure the Exclusive option is NOT active.

DATABASE

Figure 3-1

CUSTOMER TABLE

Customer Number	First Name	Last Name	Address	City	State/Prov	Zip/Postal Code
881464	Alice	Harris	734 Mercury Drive	Hackley	MI	49442
882882	John	Wilson	12456 East Stone R	Grand Lake	MI	49457
884317	George	Miller	789 Robins Road	Wilson Park	MI	49480
886951	Sandy	Davis	4533 Ritter Drive	Hackley	MI	49442
891254	Todd	Evans	1351 Willow Lane	Hackley	MI	49441
894239	Mary	Richardson	1728 Apple Avenue	Grand Lake	MI	49457
896444	Frank	Stevens	96381 Pinewood	Hackley	MI	49442
897062	Charles	Billings	1879 Strong	Wilson Park	MI	49480
898837	Carol	Taylor	8845 Garfield Road	Grand Lake	MI	49457
899111	Roxanne	Little	3657 Wilson	Hackley	MI	49442
913271	Bill	Alberts	682 Williams	Wilson Park	MI	49480
915968	Martha	Young	226 E. 120th	Hackley	MI	49443
916389	Judy	Harris	3226 Wolf Lake Ro	Hackley	MI	49441
917222	Alan	McCarthy	17984 Cove Harbor	Hackley	MI	49441
919977	Dan	Kamp	456 State	Hackley	MI	49443

Customer Number	Tape Number	Date Out	Date In			
881464	16828	8/8/92	8/9/92	d Lake	MI	49457
881464	44332	8/19/92	8/20/92	kley	MI	49442
881464	47739	8/30/92		on Park	MI	49480
881464	48419	8/9/92	8/10/92	d Lake	MI	49457
881464	48800	8/12/92	8/13/92	kley	MI	49441
881464	50613	8/5/92	6/6/92			
882882	40013	8/22/92	8/23/92			
882882	46599	8/16/92	8/17/92			
882882	48422	8/18/92	8/19/92			
882882	48799	8/3/92	8/4/92			
882882	48801	8/21/92				
882882	63456	8/11/92	8/12/92			
884239	47315	8/24/92	8/25/92			
884317	16828	8/15/92	8/17/92			
884317	37612	8/8/92	8/9/92			
884317						
884317						
884317						
884317						
886951						
886951						

RENTALS TABLE

Tape Number	Movie ID	Available	Purchase Date	Purchase Price
16827	101	Y	1/5/93	$39.75
16828	101	Y	1/5/93	$39.75
23184	113	Y	3/5/93	$42.85
23185	113	Y	3/5/93	$42.85
23186	113	Y	3/5/93	$42.85
23187	113	Y	10/5/93	$42.85
37611	114	N	3/17/93	$35.60
37612	114	Y	3/17/93	$35.60
39955	111	Y	4/2/93	$29.95
39956	111	Y	4/2/93	$29.95
40012	102	Y	3/27/88	$39.75
40013	102	Y	3/27/88	$39.75
40014	102	Y	3/27/88	$39.75
42137	109	Y	7/9/93	$35.60
42138	109	Y	7/9/93	$35.60
42139				
43765				
43766				
44331				
44332				
46130				
46131				
46599				
47314				
47315				

INVENTORY TABLE

Movie ID	Movie Title	Production Company	Category	Release Date	Rating
101	Casablanca	Warner Bros.	O	9/11/42	None
102	African Queen	20th Century-Fox	O	10/12/51	None
103	Dirty Harry	Warner Bros.	A	3/18/71	R
104	Star Wars	20th Century-Fox	S	5/25/77	PG
105	Friday the 13th	Paramount	H	1/9/80	R
106	Star Trek	Paramount	S	12/20/79	G
107	Raiders of the Lost Ark	Paramount	A	7/23/81	G
108	Ghostbusters	Columbia	C	7/16/84	PG
109	Jaws	Universal	H	4/20/75	R
111	The Godfather	Paramount	D	10/11/72	R
112	Die Hard	20th Century-Fox	A	6/30/88	R
113	Ghost	Paramount	D	2/24/90	PG13
114	Pretty Woman	Touchstone	C	5/20/90	R
115	Dances with Wolves	Orion	A	11/9/90	PG13
116	Jurassic Park	Amblin	A	5/1/93	PG13
117	Adventures of Your Name	Your Course Name	A	11/27/95	PG
118	Your selection #1	Touchstone	D	2/4/89	G
119	Your selection #2	Orion	A	7/9/83	PG

MOVIES TABLE

Figure 3-2

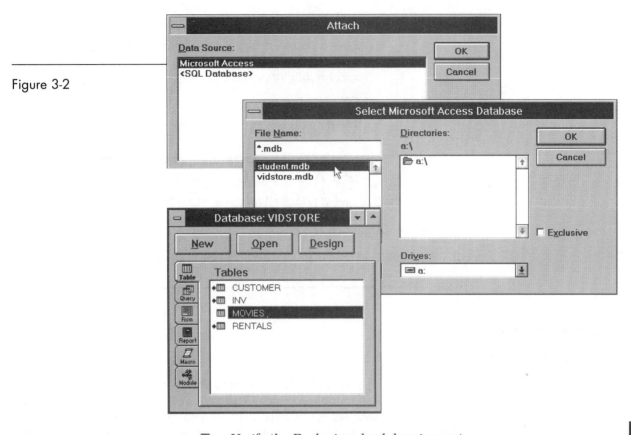

- Verify the E**x**clusive check box is empty.

- Select **student.mdb** and complete the command.

  ▶ *The Attach Tables dialog box opens, as shown at the bottom of Figure 3-2.*

Figure 3-3

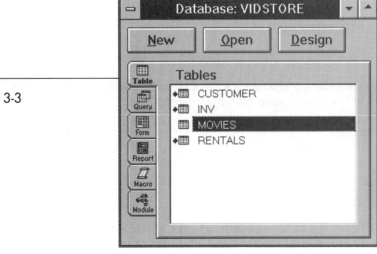

■   Choose the CUSTOMER table and complete the command.

▶   *After a pause, a confirmation box confirms that the table was successfully attached. Do not continue until you have successfully attached the table.*

■   Select OK.

▶   *The display returns to the Attach Tables dialog box.*

PRACTICE TIME 3-1

1.   Attach the INV and RENTALS tables to the VIDSTORE database.

2.   Close the Attach Tables dialog box.

The VIDSTORE Database dialog box should look like Figure 3-3.

CREATING REPORTS

The queries used in earlier lessons were practical demonstrations of how users can access database tables in ways that meet their personal needs. The need for concise, up-to-date, and easy-to-read information is behind the development of many relational databases. Reports represent another Access feature that allows you to customize data presentations. A report is designed to be printed on paper and used away from the database and computer system that created it. This lesson focuses on the design and development of printed reports using tables or queries.

PRACTICE TIME 3-2

1.   Open the CUSTOMER table.

2.   Maximize the CUSTOMER window, if necessary.

3.   Add your name and address to the CUSTOMER table. Your customer number is 941111, and your rental status is U (unrestricted).

MAILING LABELS

The CUSTOMER table contains customer names, addresses, telephone numbers, and rental status. Rental status is either U (unrestricted) or R (restricted). You will use Access's report wizard to create mailing labels for fliers being sent to all customers.

New Report Wizard

Mailing labels are just one of several report formats that can be automatically generated by an Access wizard. The Report Wizard is used to quickly create professional looking documents. Quite often, the wizard report design is then customized. Figure 3-4 illustrates samples of the different report formats that are available through the New Report wizard. The last option shown in Figure 3-4, the AutoReport wizard, has its own button in the tool bar (▨) and produces a Single-Column report without additional questions to the user.

■ From the File menu, choose New, then select Report.

   Alternative: Use the New Report button, ▨ .

   ▶ *The New Report dialog box is displayed with CUSTOMER highlighted in the Select a Table/Query text box.*

■ Select the Report Wizards button.

   ▶ *The Report Wizards list box opens; it is similar to the one in Figure 3-4.*

■ Choose the Mailing Label wizard and complete the command.

   ▶ *After a pause, Access displays the Mailing Label Wizard dialog box.*

You will use this wizard to create mailing labels that use fields from the CUSTOMER table. Spaces, commas, and other common punctuation found on mailing labels are added to the design by selecting the appropriate button. Pressing the associated key on the keyboard *does not* work and can have unexpected results. The mailing label design in Figure 3-5 produced the mailing labels shown in Figure 3-4. You will use the same design.

■ Select **First Name** in the Available fields list box.

   ▶ *The field name is highlighted.*

■ Click on the single right arrow button, ▨ .

   ▶ *The First Name moves to Label appearance area.*

NOTE: Clicking on the left arrow button (▨) would move unwanted fields or punctuation marks out of the appearance area.

■ Click on the Space button to add a space after the first name field.

   ▶ *A small dot is placed after the First Name in the Label appearance area, as shown in Figure 3-5.*

Figure 3-4

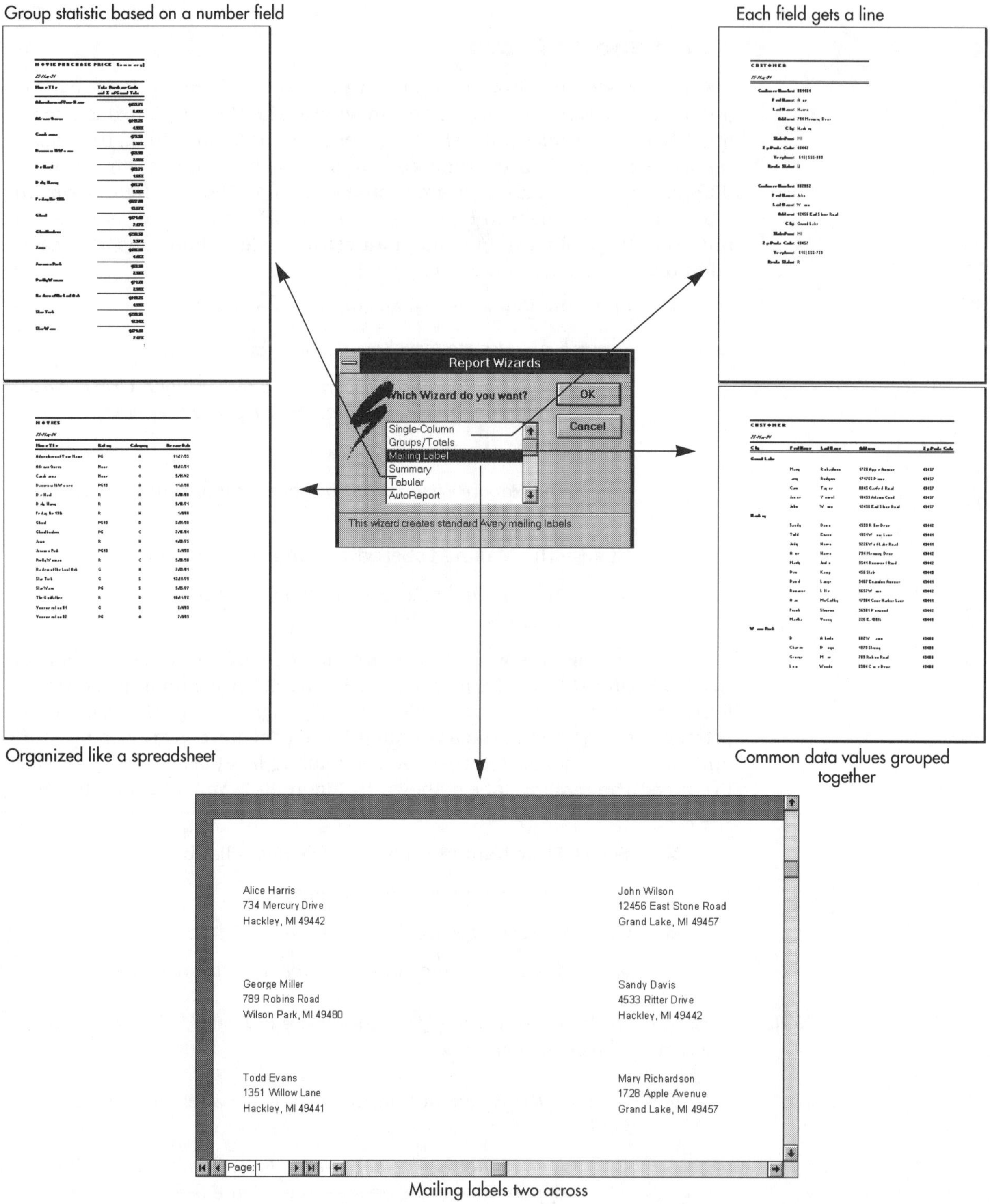

Group statistic based on a number field

Each field gets a line

This wizard creates standard Avery mailing labels.

Report Wizards

Which Wizard do you want?

Single-Column
Groups/Totals
Mailing Label
Summary
Tabular
AutoReport

OK

Cancel

Organized like a spreadsheet

Common data values grouped together

Alice Harris 734 Mercury Drive Hackley, MI 49442	John Wilson 12456 East Stone Road Grand Lake, MI 49457
George Miller 789 Robins Road Wilson Park, MI 49480	Sandy Davis 4533 Ritter Drive Hackley, MI 49442
Todd Evans 1351 Willow Lane Hackley, MI 49441	Mary Richardson 1728 Apple Avenue Grand Lake, MI 49457

Page: 1

Mailing labels two across

■ Select **Last Name** in the Available fields list box.

▶ The field name is highlighted.

■ Click on the single right arrow button, 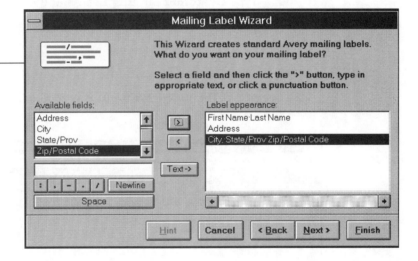.

▶ *The Last Name moves to the Label appearance area.*

■ Click on the New Line button.

▶ *The line under the First and Last Name fields is highlighted.*

PRACTICE TIME 3-3

Finish the mailing label design using Figure 3-5 as a guide.

1. Add the Address field to line 2.

2. Add the City, State/Prov, and Zip/Postal Code fields to the third line with a comma and space after city and at least one space between State/Prov and Zip/Postal Code.

Figure 3-5

The mailing label report format is quite versatile and not limited to mailing labels. For example, given any database with people's names, this report format could be used to make name tags or labels for folders. The Text box under the Available fields list box is used to add permanent labels, like MY NAME IS, to the label. The Text button transfers the permanent label from the text box into the appearance area.

The Mailing Label wizard allows you to sort the labels and gives you the choice of several heights and widths. You also have the choice of printing one, two, or three labels across. Right now you will use the default size and spacing across the page.

■ Select the Finish button.

    ▶   *After a pause, Access displays the report (label) design and then the print preview window with the labels, as shown at the bottom of Figure 3-4.*

NOTE: The default format might vary with 1, 2, or 3 labels displayed across the page preview.

    ■ Maximize the print preview window.

    ■ Click on the Close Window button, 🔲 .

       ▶   *The Report Design window is displayed.*

Saving the Report

The procedure for saving the report is the same procedure you used to save forms and queries. This time you will use the name *Customer Mailing Labels*.

    ■ Click on the Save button, 🔲 .

       ▶   *The Save As dialog box opens.*

    ■ Type **Customer Mailing Labels** and complete the command.

       ▶   *The report design window returns, as shown in Figure 3-6.*

    ■ Close the design window.

    ■ Close the window with the CUSTOMER table.

       ▶   *The VIDSTORE Database dialog box is displayed.*

Figure 3-6

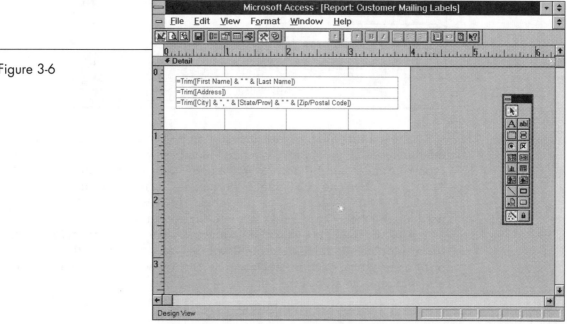

REPORT FORMATTING

Access subdivides a report into the detail section and various bands. The mailing label format you see in Figure 3-6 is the simplest type of report. It contains a **detail section** that identifies which fields from the underlying table or query are included in the report. This detail section is the mailing label design in Figure 3-6. The report design window includes both a horizontal and vertical rulers along with a tool box.

Other report types use page and report bands that contain headers and footers. Headers always precede the related footers as illustrated in Figure 3-9. In long documents, the report band would contain the title page and table of contents in the **report header** and references in the **report footer**. A page band surrounds each page. Therefore, a report will have as many page bands as pages. Column headings that match data presented in the detail section are found in **page headers.** Page numbers, dates, and customized labels can be placed in either the page header or **page footer.**

- Select the Report tab.

  ▶ *The Customer Mailing Labels and other reports, if any, are listed.*

- Choose the New button.

  ▶ *The New Report dialog box is displayed.*

- Click on the Select A Table/Query down arrow.

  ▶ *The list of VIDSTORE tables and queries opens.*

- Highlight **INV** (see Figure 3-7), then select the Report Wizards button.

  ▶ *The Report Wizards dialog box, shown earlier in Figure 3-4, opens.*

- Select **Groups/Totals** from the list and complete the command.

  ▶ *The Group/Totals Report Wizard is displayed.*

Figure 3-7

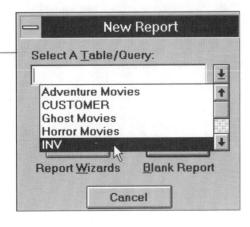

GROUP/TOTAL REPORT WIZARD

Several of the screens used by the Group/Total wizard are similar to the Mailing Label wizard you just used. You are going to use this wizard to create an Inventory Cost report that identifies how much each movie costs and how many tapes of the same movie were purchased. The records will be grouped by Movie ID and sorted by Tape Number. You will have Access compute the total purchase price for all the tapes and for each Movie ID. The final result will look like the bottom of Figure 3-9.

Figure 3-8

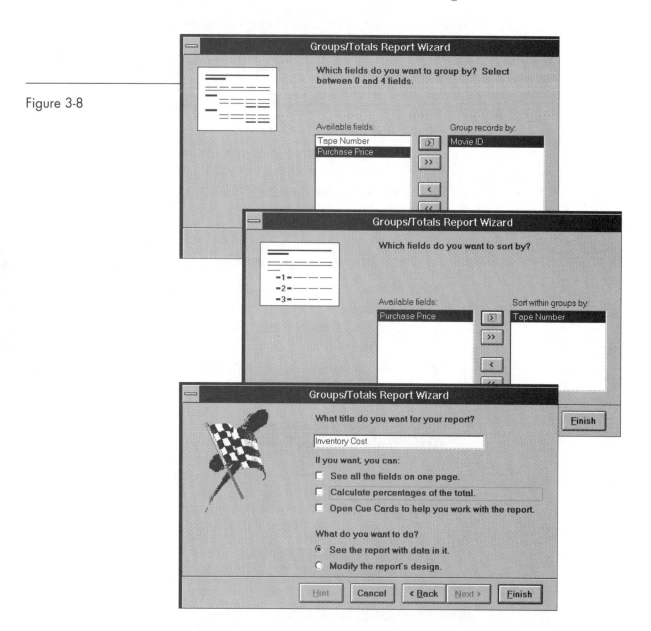

- Use the single arrow key ([›]) to move the **Tape Number**, **Movie ID**, and **Purchase Price** to the Field order on the report list box.

- Select the <u>N</u>ext button.

  ▶ *The wizard displays a dialog box that asks you to group data.*

- Move **Movie ID** to the Group records list box (see Figure 3-8) and select <u>N</u>ext.

  ▶ *The wizard asks how you want to group data.*

- With Normal in the Group text box, select <u>N</u>ext.

  ▶ *The wizard wants to know which field to sort by in the Movie ID group.*

- Move **Tape Number** to the Sort within groups by list box (see Figure 3-8) and select <u>N</u>ext.

  ▶ *The wizard displays different formatting options.*

Page Orientation

The Group/Total wizard lets you choose from three different preset report formats: Executive, Presentation, and Ledger. You will use the default and make sure that a portrait orientation is used. A ***portrait*** orientation means that Access uses an 8.5" by 11" page layout that is taller than it is wide. The other orientation, ***landscape***, uses an 11" by 8.5" page layout that is wider than it is tall.

- Choose the **Portrait** button and select <u>N</u>ext.

  ▶ *The last wizard window where you can change the report title is displayed.*

- Delete INV in the report title area and type **Inventory Costs**.

- Click on X in front of Calculate percentages of total.

  ▶ *The check box is cleared, as shown at the bottom of Figure 3-8.*

- Select the <u>F</u>inish button.

  ▶ *After a long pause, Access displays the report design and then a print preview, as shown in part at the bottom of Figure 3-9.*

- Maximize the print preview design window.

The report is several pages long, with a grand total appearing on the last page.

Figure 3-9

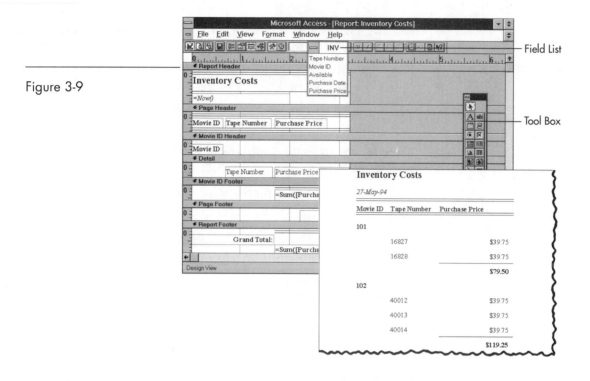

PRACTICE TIME 3 - 4

1. Return the display to the report design window by closing the print preview window.

2. Save the report using the name **Inventory Costs**. Your screen should look like the top of Figure 3-9 except for the appearance of the field list and toolbox.

3. If necessary, use the Field List button (▦) to close the INV field list.

4. If necessary, use the Toolbox button (▨) to close the toolbox.

MODIFYING THE REPORT DESIGN

The report wizard has accomplished a considerable amount of work while you waited. Take another look at the report design in Figure 3-9. In the report header under the title Inventory Costs is the =Now() *function* that returns the current date. This is one of several built-in functions that perform tasks and place the results in an Access object where the function name is located. A few examples from over 150 different Access functions are listed in Table 1. The =Sum function in the report footer displays the results of adding the purchase price from each record together. These results are labeled Grand Total.

TABLE 1 Commonly Used Access Functions

Function	Description
Avg	Calculates the arithmetic mean of a set of values contained in a specified field on a query, table, or form.
Count	Calculates the number of selected records in a query, table, or form.
CurrentUser	Returns the name of the current Access user.
Date	Returns the current date.
Log	Returns the natural logarithm of a number.
Now	Returns the current date and time.
Page	Calculates a report page number.
Pmt	Returns the payment on an annuity based on periodic, constant payments and a constant interest rate.
Rate	Returns the interest rate per period for an annuity.
Rnd	Returns a random number.
Sgn	Returns a value indicating the sign (+, -, 0) of a number.
Sin	Returns the sine of an angle.
Sqr	Returns the square root of a number.
StDev	Returns an estimate of the standard deviation of a population or population sample represented as a set of values contained in a specified field on a query, table, or form.
Sum	Returns the sum of a set of values contained in a specified field on a query, table, or form.
Tan	Returns the tangent of an angle.
Time$	Returns the current time in a 24-hour format.
Timer	Returns the number of seconds that have elapsed since 12:00 A.M. (midnight).
Var	Returns estimates of the variance of a population or population sample represented as a set of values contained in a specified field on a query, table, or form.

Each page starts with a page header that contains column labels for the Movie ID, Tape Number, and Purchase Price. The related page footer uses the =Page function to display the current page number.

Changing Field Properties

One correction that needs to be made to this design involves the Purchase Price label in the page header. Since the purchase price is a right-aligned number field, the related column label should also be right-aligned. Before realigning the column label, let's check the ***property sheet*** box to see the default setting.

■ Click on Purchase Price in the Page Header.

▶   *A border with eight boxes, called sizing handles, surrounds the label.*

■   From the <u>V</u>iew menu, select <u>P</u>roperties.

Alternative: Use the Properties button, 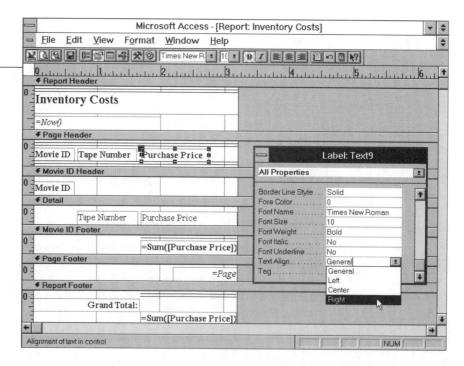 .

▶   *The property sheet that displays the highlighted label's attributes opens.*

NOTE: A property sheet is also activated by clicking once using the right mouse button to open the control menu and then selecting the Properties option.

■   Click on the property sheet's title bar and drag the box to the right, as shown in Figure 9-10.

▶   *The property sheet's location onscreen changes.*

■   Scroll the list box down until you see the Text Align property.

▶   *The default test alignment is General.*

■   Click on the word General.

▶   *The down arrow is displayed at the right side of the list box.*

■   Open the list box by selecting the down arrow.

▶   *The text alignment options are listed, as shown in Figure 3-10.*

■   Select Right.

▶   *The Text Align changes to Right, and the related list box closes.*

Figure 3-10

Adjusting Display Formats

The **label box** assigned to the words Purchase Price needs to be wider so it is even with the purchase price data displayed in the Detail section. It is called a label box because it holds a description, like the report title, that does not change when the report is updated. **Text boxes** are areas of the report which contain data from a table or query. Data in these boxes could change every time the report design is opened. Movie ID in the Page Header is in a text box.

You move or adjust the size of either box type by using the **sizing handles** that surround an active box. In Figure 3-10 the Purchase Price label box is active. Pressing the Delete key at this time removes the field from the report. When the pointer is inside the active box, it is an insertion pointer. Clicking the mouse here allows you to add or delete text or field names.

As you move the pointer over the lines connecting the sizing handles it changes to a hand pointer, ✋. Moving the pointer over the **move handle**, which is in the top left corner of the active box, turns the pointer into a pointing hand, 👆. When either the hand or pointing hand pointer is active, you can move the field to a new location in the report. For example, you could move the page number from the page footer to the page header. Traditional cut and paste procedures also accomplish the same thing.

To widen the Purchase Price label, you will use the sizing pointer (↔) to drag the right side of the box to a new location. When placement precision is called for, the ruler line can be consulted when repositioning an object. You will move the right side of the box until it is on the 3-inch mark of the horizontal ruler.

■ Move the pointer over the middle sizing handle to the right of Purchase Price.

▶ *The pointer changes into a horizontal sizing pointer,* ↔ .

■ Click and drag the sizing handle to the right until it is over the light gray layout line.

▶ *Access highlights the horizontal ruler to the 3-inch mark.*

■ Release the mouse.

▶ *The Purchase Price label is right-aligned 3 inches from the left margin.*

PRACTICE TIME 3-5

1. Adjust the right side of the Purchase Price text box in the Detail section to align with the 3-inch mark on the horizontal ruler.

2. Print the preview report. If necessary, return to the design window to make further adjustments until the Purchase Price and the related column label line up.

3. Close the print preview.

Group Headers and Footers

In addition to page and report bands, the Group/Total wizard adds group bands to the report design. Group bands are divided into headers and footers like the other bands. When displayed, a group band subdivides the detail section into related categories based on values within a designated field. The Inventory Costs report uses a group band based on the Movie ID field. As a result, records with a common Movie ID are grouped together. The =Sum function in the Movie ID Footer adds together all the purchase prices for video tapes of the same movie.

Even the width of a header and footer can be modified. You just drag it up to shorten the width and drag it down to widen it.

PRACTICE TIME 3-6

1. Adjust the right side of the =Sum text box in the Movie ID Footer to align with the 3-inch mark on the horizontal ruler.

2. Print the preview report. If necessary, return to the design window to make further adjustments until the =Sum and Purchase Price text boxes line up.

3. Close the print preview.

4. Close the report design window and save any changes.

TWO-TABLE QUERY

It is easy creating reports using Access wizards. The hard part is making sure the report design is easy to use. The Inventory Costs report is an example of a report that provides the information you need but is difficult to use. The main reason for this is the use of Movie ID as a group identifier. While it is good database design to have a unique identifier for each movie, people using the report would be more comfortable using the movie title. The two report formats are compared in Figure 3-11.

Movie titles were not used because the related field is in the MOVIES table, not in the INV table used for the Inventory Costs report. However, combining data from two tables is not a problem for a relational database as long as both tables have at least one field in common. In this case the Movie ID field occurs in both the MOVIES and the INV tables. Therefore, the Movie ID field would be the ***join field*** (common field) between both tables.

To make the Inventory Costs report easier to read, you will create a query that includes the Movie ID, Tape Number, and Purchase Price from the INV table and the Movie Title from the MOVIES table. You can then use this two-table query instead of the INV table as the underlying source of data for the report.

Figure 3-11

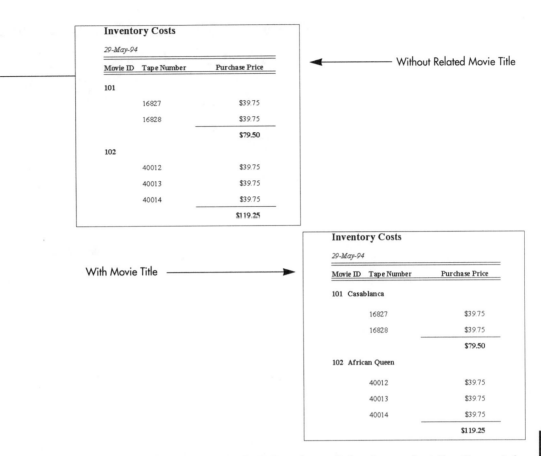

From the VIDSTORE Database dialog box, select the Query tab.

► *Adventure Movies and other queries are displayed.*

Choose the New button.

► *The New Query dialog box is displayed.*

Select the New Query button.

► *The query design window and the Add Table dialog box open.*

Highlight **INV** and choose the Add button.

► *The INV field list is added to the query design.*

Highlight **MOVIES** and select the Add button.

► *The MOVIES field list is added to the query design.*

Close the Add Table dialog box.

When possible, Access identifies a join field in common to both tables that can serve as a link between the two. As discussed earlier, the Movie ID field is the join field in this case. Access draws a line between the field names when identifying the join field. This link can be seen between the Movie ID fields of the INV and MOVIES table in the field list area of Figure 3-12.

DATABASE

Figure 3-12

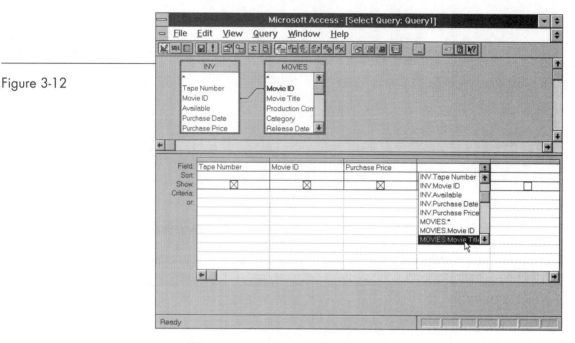

When two or more tables are used, Access precedes the field name with the table name. Therefore, the Tape Number field in the INV table is referenced as INV.Tape Number. In Figure 3-12, the Movie Title field name appears in the list box as MOVIES.Movie title.

PRACTICE TIME 3-7

Use Figure 3-12 as a guide.

1. Add INV.Tape Number to the first Field area in the QBE grid.

2. Add INV.Movie ID to the second Field area.

3. Add INV.Purchase Price to the third field area.

4. Add MOVIES.Movie title to the fourth field area.

5. Save the query using the query name **Inventory Costs**.

6. Close the query design window.

LINKING A REPORT TO A DIFFERENT SOURCE

Report data can be drawn from either a table or query. You can easily reassign a report to a different source using the design window's property sheet. Since the Inventory Costs query contains the Movie Title along with the other data used by the report, it should be used as a data source instead of the INV table.

■ From the VIDSTORE Database dialog box, select the Report tab.

▶ *Inventory Costs and other reports are displayed.*

■ Highlight Inventory Costs and select the <u>D</u>esign button.

▶ *The Inventory Costs design window opens.*

■ Display the active field list by clicking on the Field List button, 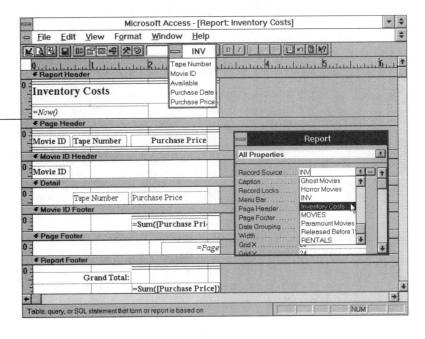 .

▶ *The field names from the INV table are listed.*

■ If necessary, display the property sheet using the Properties button, .

▶ *The property sheet's title bar displays Report.*

NOTE: If the property sheet's title bar references some other label or text box, click on an unused report area to have the property sheet display general report attributes.

■ Click to the right of INV in the Record Source area of the property sheet.

▶ *An insertion point and a down arrow appear.*

■ Select the down arrow and highlight Inventory Costs, as shown in Figure 3-13.

▶ *The Inventory Costs query is reassigned as the Record Source, and the Inventory Costs field list is displayed.*

Figure 3-13

Adding a Field to the Report Design

All you need to do to finish the report modification is to drag the Movie Title field name from the field list box into the Movie ID header. You will also fine tune the design by shortening the width of the Movie ID text box. The Movie Title text box will also need to be widened in order to fit the longest movie name.

PRACTICE TIME 3-8

Adjust the right side of the Movie ID text box in the Movie ID Header to align with the 1/4 inch mark on the horizontal ruler. *Hint:* As shown in Figure 3-14, only *Mo* of Movie ID can be seen in the text box when the size is adjusted properly.

- ■ Drag the Movie Title from the field list into the Movie ID Header to the immediate right of the Movie ID text box.

    - ▶ *The placement of the Movie Title should be similar to Figure 3-14.*

- ■ Drag the middle sizing handle to the right until it is over the light gray layout line, as shown in Figure 3-14.

    - ▶ *Access highlights the horizontal ruler to 2-inch mark.*

- ■ Save the report.

Figure 3-14

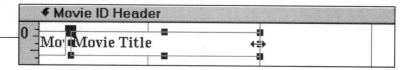

Printing a Report

All that is left to do is to print the report. Since it is several pages long, your instructor might want you to print only a few pages. If this is the case, use the pages option in the Print dialog box.

- ■ Make sure the printer is on and ready to print.

- ■ Click on the Print Preview button.

    - ▶ *A preview of the report is displayed, as shown at the bottom of Figure 9-11.*

- ■ Print the report by clicking on the Print button, ⌨.

    - ▶ *The Print dialog box opens.*

You printed the full report earlier by simply completing the command—either clicking on OK or pressing Enter. To try something different,

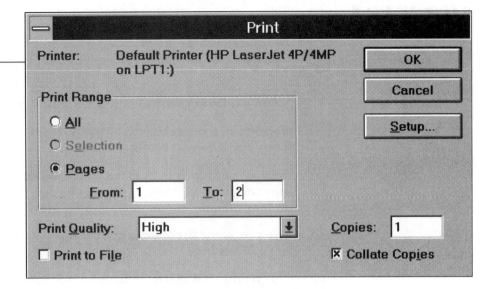

Figure 3-15

let's print pages 1 and 2 only, as shown in Figure 3-15.

- Select the <u>P</u>ages button in the Print Range area.

  ▶ *An insertion point appears in the <u>F</u>rom text box.*

- Type **1** and press TAB.

  ▶ *The insertion point jumps to the <u>T</u>o text box.*

- Type **2**.

  ▶ *The Print dialog box looks like Figure 3-15.*

- Complete the command.

  ▶ *Access prints the first two pages of the report.*

ENDING LESSON 3

There are many more features of an Access report such as adding presentation graphics, internal computations, and an assortment of document design features. These should be explored on your own. Just remember that the only way to learn to use a database management system is by trying it.

This is the end of Lesson 3. Close all open windows and exit Access. If you are done with the computer, follow the recommended procedures for shutting down the computer system.

- Close all open Access windows.

- Exit Access.

SUMMARY

❏   **Database tables created by other relational database systems can be imported or attached to an Access database.**

❏   **Access users create printed documents using different report wizards. Data comes from designated tables or queries.**

❏   **Reports are automatically divided into a detail section, page band, and report band.**

❏   **Special built-in functions perform tasks that insert the current date, averages, sums, or record counts into an Access object.**

❏   **The property sheet box allows users to see and change default settings.**

❏   **The sizing and move handles associated with the active field of a report can be used to fine tune the physical size and placement of the field.**

❏   **A group band organizes records into subgroups based on specific field values. These bands are added or deleted at any time.**

❏   **Queries can use data from several fields and join multiple tables.**

KEY TERMS

attaching	landscape	report footer
detail section	move handle	report header
function	page footer	sizing handles
import	page header	text box
join field	portrait	
label box	property sheet	

COMMAND SUMMARY

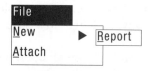

REVIEW QUESTIONS

1. What is the difference between importing and attaching a table to an Access database?

2. In what ways are reports designed to be different from queries?

3. What does the New Report Wizard do?

4. Identify three applications for the mailing label report format.

5. What report formatting features are supported by the detail section, page bands, and report band?

6. What Access functions insert the current date and page number into a report and compute a group total?

7. How are report properties changed?

8. How do you adjust the display size or location of a field in a report?

9. What type of information would be found in a group band?

10. What is needed to link data from two tables into a single query dynaset?

11. How do you reassign a report to a different table or query?

12. How are new fields added to a report?

EXERCISES

1. Use your FRIENDS table in the PERSONAL database to create mailing labels and track birthdays.

   a. Create and print mailing labels for friends and family.

   b. Develop a query called **September Birthdays** that identifies all September birthdays. Include in the dynaset data the Name, Telephone, and Birthday fields. Sort dynaset in ascending order by birthday. Print the dynaset.

   c. Prepare and print a report called **Birthdays**. The report should be based on the September Birthdays query. The report should include the following headings:

   SEPTEMBER BIRTHDAYS   **Today's Date**

   The report itself must use the following data fields in the detail section in this order: Name, Telephone, Birthday (99/99/99 format).

2. Track your earnings and organize your files using your STOCKS table in the BUSINESS database.

   a. Prepare and print a report called HOLDINGS detailing your stock portfolio (STOCKS). The report should have the following data in the detail section: Stock Name, Number of Shares, and Current Share Price.

   b. Create and print mailing labels for all your stock holdings. These labels will be used as folder tags for annual reports and other paper correspondences. Use the mailing label format shown below.

Stock Name - Transaction Number

Date Purchased

c. Develop and print a report called **Holdings** that lists your current stock holdings. The report contains a grand total of the number of shares purchased. The report heading should include your name and today's date in the following format:

***Your Name's* CURRENT STOCK HOLDINGS   Today's Date**

The following data should be included in the detail section in this order: Stock Name, Number of Shares, Purchase Price, Current Price.

3. Use your SUPPLIERS table in the VIDSTORE database to create a report and mailing labels.

a. Prepare and print a report called **Supplier Balances** that shows all the supplier names and balances.

b. Develop a two-table query called **Inventory List** using the MOVIES and INV tables. The Movie ID field is the link between the two tables. The dynaset includes the following fields: Movie Title, Category, Rating, and Tape Number. Sort dynaset by Movie Title and Tape Number.

c. Develop and print a report called **Inventory List** based on the Inventory List query that uses the following fields in the detail section: Movie Title, Tape Number, Category, Rating.

d. Use Mailing Label wizard to prepare and print mailing labels of all suppliers. Mailing labels should be printed two across.

e. Save the mailing labels report as **Supplier Labels**.

4 Enhancing Database Applications

OBJECTIVES

Upon completing the material presented in this lesson, you should understand the following aspects of Access:

- ❏ **Sorting data in a table**
- ❏ **Filtering data**
- ❏ **Adding an index**
- ❏ **Creating Reports with the AutoReport Wizard**
- ❏ **Developing and Running Macros**
- ❏ **Using Parameter Queries**

STARTING OFF

Turn on your computer, start Windows, and then launch the Access 2.0 for Windows program as you did in previous lessons. Insert your data disk and set the working directory if necessary. Maximize the Access application window.

- Insert your data disk into the disk drive.
- Launch Access.
    - ▶ *The Access application window is displayed.*
- Open the VIDSTORE database.
- If necessary, maximize the application window.

SORTING AND FILTERING TABLE RECORDS

You will find that tables are the foundation from which database applications grow. Queries then draw from one or more tables to organize data into usable information. Many of the ways you manipulate data in a query through sorting and selection criteria can be applied directly to data in a table. As a result, a question often arises as to when it is appropriate to create and save a new query dynaset rather than directly manipulating the data in the table.

When to Use a Table

Sorting records into ascending order by movie title or just displaying adventure movies does not require a query. It makes the most sense to manipulate the database table as a datasheet when two situations occur:

1. All the data you need is confined to a single table.

2. The need for data in this arrangement is not likely to occur again.

When to Use a Query

New queries are developed when they help to answer often-asked questions. In these situations, the query can be saved and opened again whenever it is needed. Having the query saved on disk is better than saving a printed copy of the results because the most up-to-date data is used every time the query is opened and run. Printed data can easily become obsolete when the database is constantly being updated. Relying on the disk-based query also provides an additional benefit of reducing the paper clutter that surrounds most desks. Many times a new dynaset may only need to be displayed, not printed.

Queries also work best when the data you need is found in different tables. Queries using data from two or more tables are examined later in the lesson.

Quick Sort

Records are maintained in a table in either key field order or, if a primary key is missing, in the order they were entered. Using the Quick Sort feature to sort records into another order is only maintained until the table is closed or until the records are sorted again. Therefore, any change you make to the order in which records are displayed in a table is temporary. Quick Sort reorganizes the datasheet based on data values in the currently active field. The active field is the one with the flashing insertion point or highlighted field data.

■   Open the MOVIES table.

■   Click on the first movie title.

▶   *An insertion point appears in Casablanca, or the movie title is highlighted.*

■   From the Records menu, select Quick Sort.

   Alternative: Use the Sort Ascending button ( ) or Sort Descending button ( ).

▶   *A secondary menu opens with Ascending and Descending options (see top of Figure 4-1).*

■   Choose Ascending.

▶   *The MOVIES datasheet sorts by movie title, as shown in the bottom of Figure 4-1.*

Figure 4-1

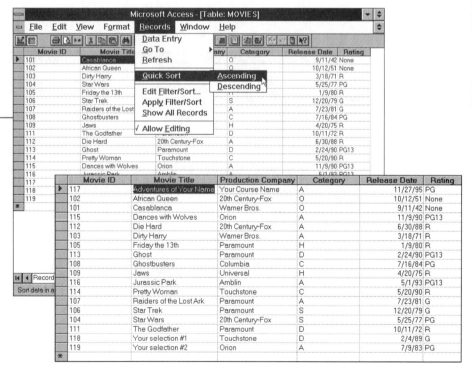

DATABASE

Data Filters

Many of the selection features of a query's QBE grid can be applied to a table's datasheet display as a *filter*. As the name implies, filters are used to selectively display data. To do so requires a selection criterion that works the same as the criterion used in a query. Therefore, it should be of no surprise that the Filter window in Figure 4-2 looks just like a Select Query window.

■ From the Records menu, choose Edit Filter/Sort.

    Alternative: Use the Edit Filter/Sort button, 🔽.

   ▶ *The Filter window opens.*

Notice the grid already contains the Movie Title field name and Ascending in the Sort area. These options were added to the grid when you used the Quick Sort feature. To limit the datasheet display to adventure movies, you will add the Category field name to the grid and the expression "A" to the Criteria area.

■ Add the Category field name to the Field area to the right of Movie Title.

■ Type **"A"** in the Criteria area below Category.

   ▶ *The Filter window should look like the top of Figure 4-2.*

■ From the Records menu, choose Apply Filter/Sort.

    Alternative: Use the Apply Filter/Sort button, 🔽.

   ▶ *The datasheet displays only adventure movies, as shown in the bottom of Figure 4-2.*

Figure 4-2

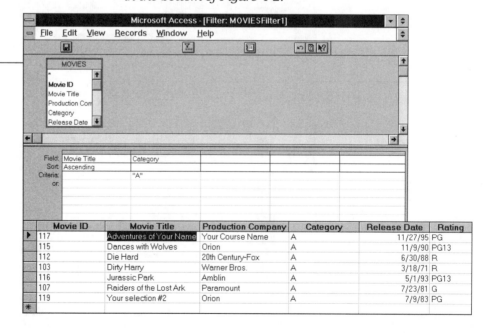

To turn off all filters and sort options, you select Show All Records from the Records menu. This menu option returns the datasheet back to the original settings.

■ From the Records menu, select Show All Records.

Alternative: Use Show All Records button, 🖼️.

▶ *The datasheet displays all the records in Movie ID order.*

PRACTICE TIME 4-1

1. Sort the MOVIES datasheet into ascending order by release date.

2. Display only PG or PG13 rated movies.

3. Print the sorted datasheet with currently active filters.

4. Show all records.

INDEXING A TABLE

As the number of records in a table increases, it takes more time to complete a Quick Sort. To speed up sorting and searching of commonly used fields, you can create an ***index*** for the field in question using the table design window. In the MOVIES table, the Movie Title field would be an ideal index because it is often the basis for a query and the logical order for reports based on the MOVIES table. The Last Name field in the CUSTOMER table would be another good field to index. To start, you will create an index for the Release Date field.

■ Click on the Design button, 🖼️.

▶ *The report design window opens.*

■ Activate the row selector to the left of Release Date

▶ *The Release Date field name, type, and description are highlighted, as shown in Figure 4-3.*

Since it is possible for two movies to have the same release date, duplicate values of this index field are acceptable. If the no duplicates option is selected, Access will not allow the same release date to be entered for different movies.

■ At the bottom of the screen in Field Properties pane, click in the text box to the right of Indexed.

▶ *An insertion point and a down arrow appear.*

Figure 4-3

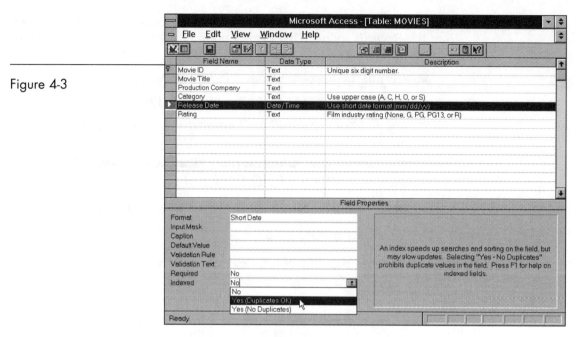

■   Click on the down arrow.

▶   *A list of index options opens, as shown in Figure 4-3.*

■   Select **Yes (Duplicates OK)**.

▶   *The index qualifications are added to the table design.*

Create an index only when searching and sorting speeds need to be improved. Establishing new indexes creates new files that must be updated every time a record is added or deleted from a table. As a result, data entry is often slowed down when a table contains several indexes. Therefore, when adding a new index, the loss of speed during data entry must be weighed against speed gains in sorting and searching.

Removing an Index

When adding an index does not produce expected performance gains or when new indexes bog down data entry, consider removing the index. This is easily accomplished using the Indexes window and Delete key.

■   From the table design window, open the <u>V</u>iew menu, and select Indexes.

▶   *Access opens the Indexes:MOVIES window.*

This window lists all the active indexes for a table and allows users to change the index's sort order.

■   Activate the row selector for Release Date.

▶   *The Release Date index is highlighted, as shown in Figure 4-4.*

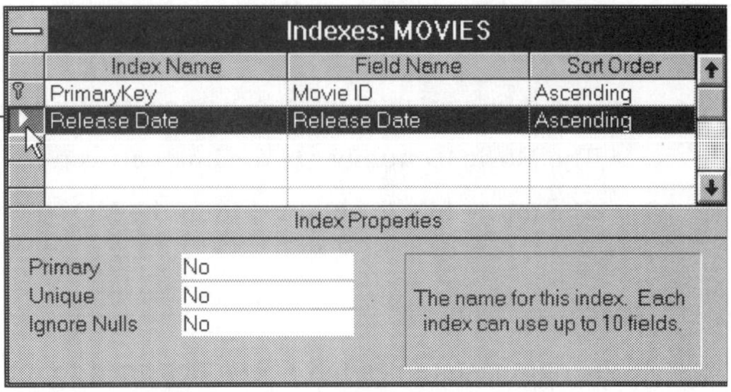

Figure 4-4

■   Press Delete.

Alternative: Use the right mouse button to open the shortcut menu and select Delete Row.

▶   *The Release Date index is removed from the table.*

■   Close the MOVIES indexes window.

▶   *The display returns to the report design window.*

PRACTICE TIME 4-2

Using the MOVIES table, establish Movie Titles as an index field where duplicate titles are acceptable.

QUERY JOINING FOUR TABLES

A two-day limit on video rentals is the current store policy. Boomtown's management periodically needs to identify tape rentals that have been out over two days. You will use Access to create a Late Tape Call List. It will identify the customer's name, telephone number, the movie's title, and the tape's replacement cost. The data necessary for this query must be drawn from all four tables (MOVIES, CUSTOMER, INV, and RENTALS). The resulting dynaset is shown later in this lesson as a part of Figure 4-9. It is based on a query that identifies the following data and links between tables:

- Customer name and telephone number comes from the CUSTOMER table.

- Customer number links the CUSTOMER and RENTALS tables.

- The RENTALS table provides the date the tape was rented—Date Out. An empty Date In field identifies unreturned rentals.

- The tape number from the RENTALS table serves as a link to the INV tables.

- The tape's original purchase price is found in the INV table.

- The Movie ID number is the link between the INV and MOVIES tables.

- The movie title is obtained from the MOVIES table.

Joining Tables

If the database tables have been designed to integrate together, like VID-STORE, creating a query based on data from four tables is straightforward.

■   Close all open windows except for the VIDSTORE database window. This window should be maximized.

■   Select the Query button.

▶   *The Query list with Adventure Movies and other queries you created earlier is displayed.*

■   Choose the New button.

▶   *The New Query dialog box is displayed.*

■   Select the New Query button.

▶   *The Add Table dialog box opens with the select query design window in the background.*

■   Choose CUSTOMER, then select the Add button.

▶   *The CUSTOMER field list is inserted above the QBE grid.*

As you add the other tables to the query Access will attempt to establish join lines between each table. As shown in Figure 4-5, a ***join line*** is automatically drawn between the two tables when a link is found. The line connects the field names of the fields common to both tables. Bold field names identify the table's primary key. You can manually create join lines between tables by dragging the pointer from the field name in one list to a compatible field name in another list.

P R A C T I C E   T I M E   4 - 3

Add the following tables to the query in this order: RENTALS, INV, and MOVIES. Use the scroll bar to bring all the joined tables into view. When you are done, the screen should look like Figure 4-5.

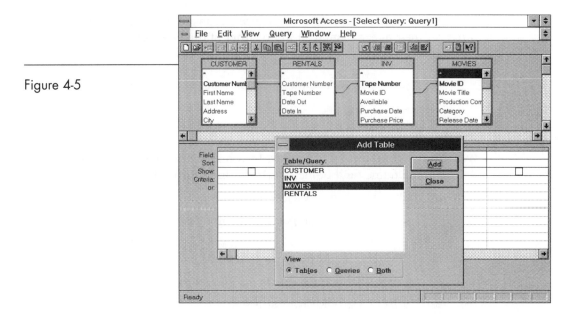

Figure 4-5

Referential Integrity

It is no coincidence that the primary key in each of the tables is used to join records in one table to records in other tables. Good relational database design depends on key fields that uniquely define a record. For example, the Movie ID field is the MOVIES Table's primary key. Movie ID 101 uniquely identifies Casablanca, its release date, rating, and so on. The Movie ID also joins the MOVIES table to the INV table which allows you to match these data with the purchase price and other data about a specific tape.

However, this link between the two tables can be easily corrupted if *referential integrity* is lost. This would be the case if you deleted the Casablanca record from the MOVIES table. Then, the INV table would have tape records that refer to Movie ID 101 when there would no longer be any record in the MOVIES table with a matching Movie ID. Referential integrity would be lost. Therefore, to maintain referential integrity, fields that join tables in a relational database should not be deleted as long as links to other tables still exist.

Two basic rules should be followed for a database to maintain referential integrity:

1. You cannot add a record in a joined table until a record with an acceptable primary key field value is present. In other words, you could not enter a new INV record until an acceptable Movie ID existed in the MOVIES table.

2. You cannot delete a record with a primary key from a table when matching records still exist in other tables. This means you must delete all the Casablanca tapes from the INV table before the Movie ID 101 record can be deleted from the MOVIES table.

Access maintains referential integrity when asked to enforce it. In this case, an error message is displayed when either of the two conditions above exist.

■   Close the Add Table dialog box.

▶   *The select query design window is displayed.*

Multiple Table Query

When more than one table is used by a query, the field list identifies fields by the table name.field name, as shown in Figure 4-6.

■   Click in the first Field area.

▶   *An insertion point and a down arrow appear in the Field area.*

■   Click on the down arrow to open the field list.

▶   *The field list opens, as shown in Figure 4-6.*

■   Select CUSTOMER.First Name.

▶   *First Name is added to the QBE grid.*

Figure 4-6

```
CUSTOMER.*
CUSTOMER.Customer Number
CUSTOMER.First Name
CUSTOMER.Last Name
CUSTOMER.Address
CUSTOMER.City
CUSTOMER.State/Prov
CUSTOMER.Zip/Postal Code
```

Fields are also added to the query dynaset by dragging the field name from a field list down into a QBE grid Field area.

PRACTICE TIME 4-4

1.   Add the following fields to the QBE grid in this order: Last Name, Telephone, Date Out, Date In, Movie Title, and Purchase Price. Use the scroll box to display empty field areas that are currently offscreen.

2.   Turn off the Show option for the Date Out and Date In fields.

3.   Sort the dynaset in ascending order by Last Name.

4.   Save the query using **Late Tape Call List** as the query name.

When you are done, the QBE grid should look like Figure 4-7. Please note that the Field area columns have been adjusted in this Figure to show all fields. Some fields may be scrolled off your screen display.

Field:	First Name	Last Name	Telephone	Date Out	Date In	Movie Title	Purchase Price
Sort		Ascending					
Show:	☒	☒	☒	☐	☐	☒	☒
Criteria:							
or:							

Figure 4-7

Null Fields

Two conditions must exist before we add someone to the late tape dynaset. First, the Date In field must be empty. Access uses a special criteria, **null**, to identify empty fields. In this situation you will add *Is Null* to the Date In Criteria.

■ Type **is null** to the Date In Criteria area.

▶ *Adds search criteria to QBE grid as shown in Figure 4-9.*

Using Dates In Computations

The second condition that must exist is that the Date Out must be over two days—the store's definition of a late tape. Since Access treats dates as sequential numbers, it is possible to subtract 2 from the current date. Any Date Out smaller than today's date minus 2 identifies a tape that was rented over two days ago. The Now() function identifies the current date. Left and right parentheses without any spaces in between are part of the Now() function. Therefore, the search criteria *<Now()-2* will identify late tapes if the Date In is null.

■ Type **<Now( )-2** in the Date Out Criteria area.

▶ *Search criteria are added to the QBE grid, as shown in Figure 4-9.*

The Expression Builder

The last field in the query is purchase price. This is the price Boomtown originally paid for the tape. If the tape needs to be replaced, the customer will actually be charged an additional 10% to compensate the store for time and effort. Access's Expression Builder, see Figure 4-8, is used to place a formula within an object. A new field name, Replacement Cost, is created by multiplying Purchase Price by 1.1. This formula increases the Purchase Price by 10 percent.

■ Click on the Purchase Price field name using the right mouse button.

Alternative: With an insertion point in the desired field, select the Builder button, ▦ .

▶ *The Shortcut menu opens.*

■ Select the Build option.

▶ *The Expression Builder dialog box opens with the Purchase Price in the expression area.*

■ Click in the expression area and move the insertion point to the left of Purchase Price.

■ Type **Replacement Cost:[** (no space after left bracket).

NOTE: Do not confuse the left and right brackets [] with left and right parentheses.

■ Move the insertion point to the right of Purchase Price and type **]*1.1** (no space at end).

▶ *The formula in the expression area should look like Figure 4-8.*

Expression area

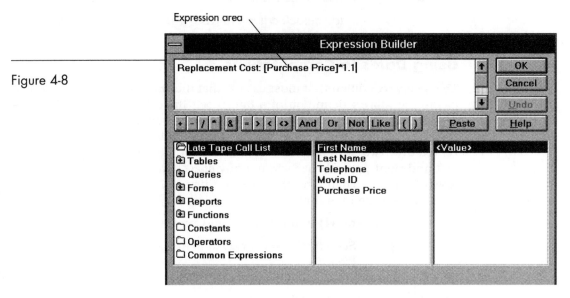

Figure 4-8

■ Complete the command.

▶ *The display returns to the select query design window, as shown at the top of Figure 4-9.*

■ Run the query.

▶ *The dynaset looks like the bottom of Figure 4-9.*

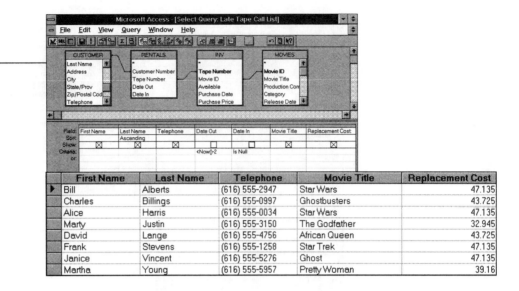

Figure 4-9

PRACTICE TIME 4-5

1. Save the current version of Late Tape Call List query.

2. Close the select query design window.

AUTOREPORT WIZARD

The Late Tape Call List will be a single column report you will create using the Auto Report Wizard. If the Late Tape Call List query is highlighted in the database dialog box, the wizard automatically creates the report using field names from the designated object.

■ Make sure the Late Tape Call List is highlighted in the Query list of the VIDSTORE database dialog box.

■ Click on the Auto Report tool button, 🔲 .

▶ *After a long pause while Access creates the new report, it then displays the report in the print preview window.*

■ Maximize the window.

Notice that the Replacement Cost field should be left aligned and in a currency format. These changes to the way Replacement Cost is displayed can be made by using the report design window, as shown in Figure 4-10.

■ Close the print preview window.

▶ *The report design window is displayed.*

Figure 4-10

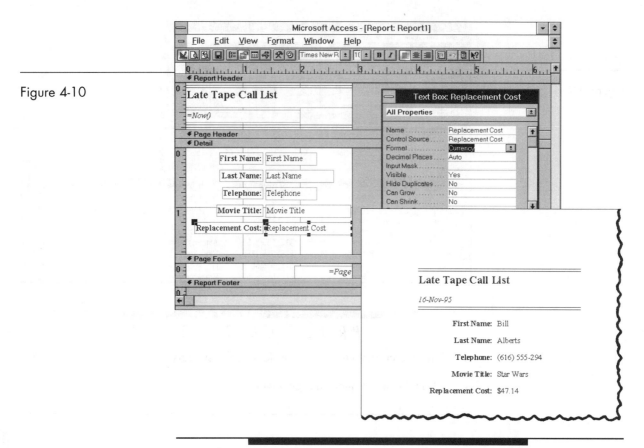

PRACTICE TIME 4-6

1. Use the Replacement Cost properties window to change Format to **Currency** (see Figure 4-10) and Text align to **Left**.

2. Save the report as Late Tape Call List.

3. Close the report design window.

MACROS

The VIDSTORE database is made up of several Access *objects*. Tables, queries, forms, reports, macros, and modules represent different object types. Yet to be discussed are macros and modules. **Macros** are a set of commands users enter to automate routine or repetitive tasks, like the steps to print a report. **Modules** are complete computer programs written in Access's native command language. You would recognize some of these commands, like Open, because they are also menu options. Writing programs using Access commands is beyond the scope of this book.

On the other hand, macros are quick and easy to create. To help streamline procedures for printing the Late Tape Calling List, you will create a macro that automatically opens the report, prints it, and then closes the report.

■   From the VIDSTORE database window, select the Macro tab.

▶   *An empty Macros list opens.*

■   Select the <u>N</u>ew button.

▶   *Access displays the macro window.*

Creating a Macro

You will add action commands to the macro as shown in Figure 4-13. These commands are selected from a list box. Associated comments can be added to the Comment line to the right of the command. While these comments are ignored by Access, they make it easier for users to understand each macro step.

■   Click in the first row of the Action column.

▶   *An insertion point and a down arrow appear in the first action area.*

■   Select the down arrow.

▶   *The list of macro commands opens.*

■   Scroll down the list until OpenReport is found (see Figure 4-11).

■   Select **OpenReport**.

▶   *The OpenReport command is added to the first action area.*

Figure 4-11

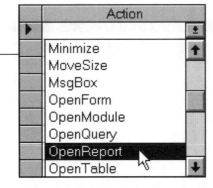

Once an action has been identified, Access prompts the selection of Action Arguments in the lower portion of the screen. These arguments identify specific objects, views, filters, and selection criteria that clarify the command. You will identify two arguments: Report Name and View. The Late Tape Call List is the report. Print preview will be the view.

■ Click in the open area to the right of Report Name.

▶ *An insertion point and a down arrow appear in argument area.*

■ Click on the down area and select **Late Tape Call List**.

▶ *The report name is added to the argument area, as shown in Figure 4-12.*

■ If necessary, click in the View argument area, choose the down arrow, and select **Print Preview**.

▶ *The Print Preview is added to the argument area.*

Figure 4-12

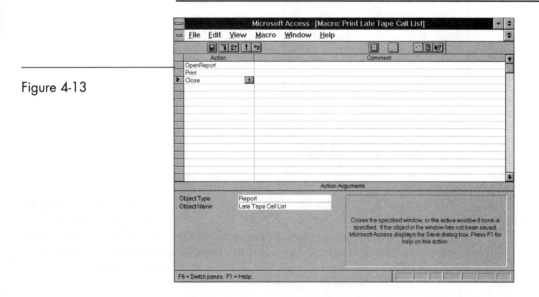

PRACTICE TIME 4-7

1. Insert the **Print** command in the second action row.

2. Insert the **Close** command in the third action row. Use **Report** as the Object Type argument and **Late Tape Call List** as the Object Name argument.

3. Save the macro as **Print Late Tape Call List**. The macro window should look like Figure 4-13.

Figure 4-13

Running a Macro

A macro can be run from either the macro window or the database window. When used on a day-to-day basis, a macro is usually run from the database window. A common scenario would have an employee coming to work and assigned the job of calling customers with late tapes. The employee would then go to the nearest computer and follow a posted set of instructions to turn on the printer, choose on the Macros tab in the VIDSTORE database window, select Print Late Tape Call List, and click on the Run button. The report would automatically be printed and the screen display returned to the VIDSTORE database window. Let's try it!

■ Close the macro window.

▶ *The display returns to the VIDSTORE database window with the Print Late Tape Call List highlighted in the Macros list.*

■ Make sure the printer is on and ready to print.

■ Select the Run button.

▶ *Access displays the print message box with the print preview window in the background, prints the report, and returns the display to the VIDSTORE database window.*

USING PARAMETER QUERIES

Queries can be designed so you can change the search criteria each time a query is run. This type of query, called a **parameter query**, contains a prompt that asks you to enter a parameter Access uses when searching through the table. The prompt replaces the search criteria in the Criteria area of the QBE grid. Prompts are always enclosed in square brackets.

If the prompt [What rating?] is entered in the Rating Criteria area, as shown in Figure 4-14, Access will only include movies with the designated rating in the dynaset. The next time you run the query, you can enter another rating and Access will use it when creating the dynaset.

■ From the VIDSTORE database window, click on the Query tab, then select the New button, and choose the New Query button.

▶ *The Add Table dialog box is displayed.*

■ Add MOVIES, then close the Add Table dialog box.

▶ *The query design window opens.*

■ Place the following field names in the designated order into the Field area of the QBE grid: **Movie Title**, **Category**, **Rating**.

■ In the Rating Criteria area, type **[What rating?]**.

▶ *The QBE grid looks like Figure 4-14.*

■ Run the query.

▶ *The What Rating? prompt is displayed in the message box, as shown in Figure 4-14.*

■ Type **PG13** and press ENTER.

▶ *The dynaset includes at least three movies (see bottom of Figure 4-14).*

■ Return the display to the query design window.

Figure 4-14

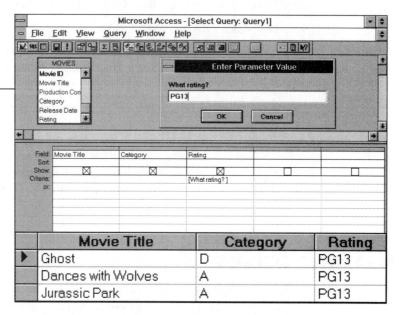

Queries can contain several prompts when desirable. For instance, it may be desirable to select movies by category as well as rating.

PRACTICE TIME 4-8

1. Add the prompt **[What Category (A, C, D, H, O, or S)?]** in the Category Criteria area. Do not be concerned if the prompt scrolls out of the Criteria area. If necessary, the LEFT ARROW and RIGHT ARROW keys can be used to move text back into the Criteria area.

2. Run the query for adventure (A) movies with a PG13 rating.

3. Return the display to the query design window.

Adding Tables to Query

From a practical point of view, this query is of limited use. While it identifies movies carried by the store that match the selection criteria, the user does not know if the movie is currently in the store and available for renting. The VIDSTORE database contains this information, but you need to add the INV table to the query.

■ From the Query menu, select Add Table.

Alternative: Use the Add Table button, 🔲.

▶ *The Add Table dialog box opens.*

■ Add INV and close the Add Table dialog box.

▶ *The INV field list is added to the query design window with Movie ID serving as a link between the MOVIES and INV tables.*

■ Add **Tape Number** and **Available** to the QBE grid.

■ Run the query.

▶ *The prompt asks for a category.*

■ Type A for adventure movies and press ENTER.

▶ *Prompt asks for a rating.*

■ Type PG13 and press ENTER.

▶ *The dynaset displays at least four entries: two for Dances with Wolves and two for Jurassic Park.*

The video store carries several copies of popular movies. Since each tape has a unique tape number in the INV table, multiple copies of the same movie title are included in the dynaset when each tape number is listed.

When the Available field contains a *Y*, the movie is available for customer rentals. Damaged or destroyed tapes contain an *N* and are not available for renting. Notice that two of the four tapes are not available. However, we still do not know if the other tapes are currently in the store or if they have been rented.

To make this final determination, you need to add the RENTALS table to the query. The Date In field from this table will indicate whether the tape is in the store or not.

PRACTICE TIME 4-9

1. Return the display to the query design window.

2. Type **"Y"** into the Available Criteria area.

3. Add the RENTALS table to the query.

4. Place the **Date In** field name into the next available Field area of the QBE grid.

5. Save the query using **Available Movies** as a query name.

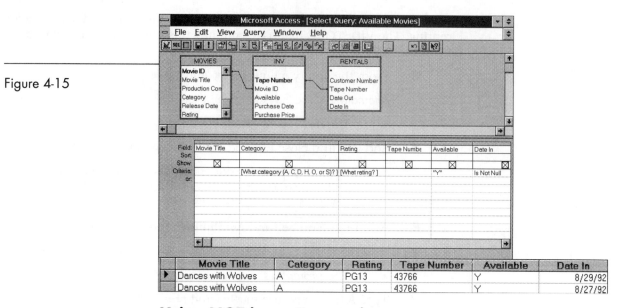

Figure 4-15

Using NOT in an Expression

Previously in the Late Tape Call List, you used the Date In field to determine if a tape was still out. In this situation the Date In field was blank, and the search criteria *Is Null* was used to identify rented tapes. In the Available Movies query, you want to identify the opposite situation, i.e., tapes that have been returned and are available for rental.

The NOT operator is used for this purpose. To identify Date In fields that have a return date and are not blank, you will use the criteria *Is Not Null*.

■   Type **is not null** into the Date In Criteria area.

▶   *The QBE grid should look like the one in Figure 4-15.*

■   Run the query for adventure movies with a PG13 rating.

▶   *Access displays a dynaset similar to the one in Figure 4-15.*

The dynaset in figure 4-15 tells you that Dances with Wolves tape number 43766 is available for renting. This movie is listed twice because the RENTALS table has two different dates; this is because the tape has been rented and returned two times. As a result, you might want to remove the Date In field from the QBE grid to avoid confusion.

■   Save the query.

■   Return the display to the VIDSTORE database window.

ENDING LESSON 4

Access is an extremely powerful software package that is designed to meet the needs of many people in a variety of situations. While this tutorial has only scratched the surface of many Access features, it has given you a valuable foundation from which to explore other features and capabilities. With time, patience, and a handy User's Guide, there is no limit to what you can do with this relational database management system.

This is the end of Lesson 4. Close all open windows and exit Access. If you are done with the computer, follow the recommended procedures for shutting down the computer system.

■   Close all open Access windows.

■   Exit Access.

SUMMARY

❏   **Data can be sorted in a query or within a table's datasheet view.**

❏   **Filters can be placed on a table's datasheet view to limit which records are displayed on the screen. These filters work just like a query's selection criteria.**

❏   **One-of-a-kind data displays from a single table are easily accomplished using filters. Recurring requests for up-to-date data from several tables are best handled and saved as a query.**

❏   **Indexing fields in a table can speed up sorting and searching, but may slow down data entry.**

❏   **An index is removed from a table using the indexes window and the Delete key while within the report design.**

❏   **Two tables are automatically joined together as they are added to a multi-table query when one table has a primary key field that also occurs in the other table.**

❏   **Referential integrity is maintained by not allowing a record with a primary key field to be deleted while joined with records in other tables.**

❏   **Special functions like Now( ) and reserved words like Null are available to enhance query development.**

❏   **The Expression Builder window helps users create a field in a table, query, or form that is based on a formula.**

❏   **The AutoReport Wizard automatically creates a report using the single-column format and the highlighted table or query.**

❏   **The macro window allows users to select a set of Access commands that combine to automate repetitive tasks with Access.**

DATABASE

❑   **A parameter query is designed to allow users to change the search criteria each time the query is run.**

❑   **Tables are easily joined in multiple-table queries using the Add Table button in the tool bar.**

KEY TERMS

filter	macro	parameter query
index	module	referential integrity
join line	null	

COMMAND SUMMARY

REVIEW QUESTIONS

1. When do you create and save a query instead of manipulating data within a table's datasheet?

2. How is a query different from a filter, and how do you turn off a filter?

3. What are the advantages and disadvantages to indexing fields in a table?

4. How do you manually create a join line that connects two tables in a query?

5. Describe a situation using the CUSTOMER and RENTAL tables where referential integrity would be lost.

6. How does Access treat dates?

7. How is the Expression Builder window used?

8. Given that a dynaset or table with the desired data already exists, what is the easiest way to create a single-column report using these data?

9. Identify six different types of Access objects.

10. How are commands added to a macro?

11. How is a parameter query different from a standard select query?

12. How do you add a table to an open query design window?

EXERCISES

1. Reorganize your personal information in the FRIENDS table of the PERSONAL database.

   a. Create and print mailing labels for each friend. The mailing label should include the name, address, city, state/prov, and zip/postal code in a format that is acceptable to the Post Office.

   b. Index the birthday field (Duplicates are OK.).

   c. Create a query called **Birthday List**, that includes the name, complete address, telephone, and birthday of everyone in the FRIENDS table. Sort the dynaset in ascending order by birthday.

   d. Prepare and print a report called **Birthday List** using the Birthday List query. The report should include the following headings:

   BIRTHDAYS BY MONTH   Today's Date

   The report's detail section must use the following data: Name, Address, Telephone, Birthday (mm/dd/yy format). Include a count of how many names are in the list. Hint: Use the =count ([field name]) function to count birthdays or names.

   e. Create a macro called **Print Birthday List** that automatically opens the Birthday List report, prints it, and then closes the report.

2. Update the STOCKS table in the BUSINESS database, create a new Groups/Total report, and a parameter query.

   a. Add at least four new transactions to the STOCKS table. Each purchase should be of a stock you currently own.

   b. Index the Stock Name field (Duplicates are OK.).

   c. Quick Sort the STOCKS table by Stock Name and print the table as a datasheet.

   d. Create and print a Groups/Total report called **Stocks by Company** that groups stocks by Stock Name and provides a total number of shares for each group. A grand total is not necessary. The detail section should include the following: Transaction Number, Number of Shares, Purchase Price, and Date Purchased. The report heading should include your name and today's date in the following format:

   Your Name's STOCK HOLDINGS BY COMPANY Today's Date

   e. Create a macro called **Print Stocks by Company** that automatically opens the Stocks by Company report, prints it, and then closes the report.

   f. Create a parameter query called **Selected Stocks** that allows the user to select a stock name for the search criteria. The dynaset should include all the fields associated with the STOCKS table. Print a dynaset with data about your favorite stock.

3. Restructure the INV table in the STUDENT database, create a new report based on a two-table query.

   a. Index the Supplier Name field in the SUPPLIER table (no duplicates).

b. Quick Sort the SUPPLIER table by Supplier Number and print sorted table as a datasheet.

c. Modify the table design of the INV table by adding a Supplier Number field (text, 6 characters).

d. Add Supplier Numbers to the INV table using Supplier Numbers from the SUPPLIER table.

e. Create a three-table query called **Reorder Movies** using the SUPPLIER, INV, and MOVIES tables. The Supplier Number links the SUPPLIER and INV tables. The Movie Id links the INV and MOVIES tables. The dynaset is limited to records where *Available = N*, sorted in ascending order by Supplier Name, and includes the following fields: Supplier Name, complete mailing address, Telephone, Movie Title, and Purchase Price.

f. Modify the Reorder Movies as a parameter query and save it as **Reorder Movies by Supplier**. This query should include a prompt that allows the user to select which Supplier Number is included in the related dynaset. Print the dynaset with reorder data from the supplier of your choice.

g. Prepare and print a Groups/Total report called **Reorder Movies** which is based on the Reorder Movies query. The report should group records by Supplier Name, lists the Movie Title and Purchase Price in the detail section, and provides the total purchase price for each supplier along with a grand total of all the purchase prices. Add the telephone number field under the supplier's name in the group header. Change properties to align fields and labels.

h. Create a macro called **Print Reorder Movies** that automatically opens the Reorder Movies report, prints it, and then closes the report.

i. Create another macro that automatically runs the Reorder Movies by Supplier query.

Access Projects

PROJECT 1: QUICK PIC FILM DEVELOPMENT

Quick Pic is an overnight film processing service. The company uses a database management system to track the film that customers drop off for processing.

This project uses the CUSTOMER table on your data disk.

1. Create a new database called QUICKPIC.

2. Attach the CUSTOMER table from the STUDENT database to the QUICKPIC database.

3. Create a new table called FILM with the following fields:

   Field 1 - Envelope Number, text, 6 characters, primary key

   Field 2 - Date In, Date

   Field 3 - Customer Number, text, 6 characters

   Field 4 - Film Type, text, 4 characters

   Field 5 - Exposure, number

   Field 6 - Format, text, 1 character

   Field 7 - Date Back, date

   Field 8 - Date Pickup, date

2. Create a data entry form for the FILM table. The form includes the following header: **QUICK PIC Film Development**.

3. Enter the following data into the FILM table using the data entry form:

Env. No.	Date In	Cust. No.	Type	Exp.	Fmt.	Date Back	Date Pickup
101	10/15/94	94111	35	24	C	10/16/94	10/17/94
102	10/15/94	886951	35	36	C	10/16/94	
103	10/15/94	894239	DISC	24	C	10/16/94	10/16/94
104	10/16/94	927494	110	12	C	10/17/94	10/20/94
105	10/16/94	881464	35	36	S	10/17/94	10/17/94
106	10/16/94	881464	35	36	S		
107	10/17/94	915968	35	24	B	10/20/94	
108	10/17/94	884317	110	24	C	10/18/94	10/19/94
109	10/17/94	922232	DISC	24	C	10/18/94	10/20/94

4. Right-align the Film Type field data and center the Format field data in the datasheet.

5. Create a two-table query using the CUSTOMER and FILM tables. The query creates a dynaset that lists customers who have film back and not picked up, which means there is no date in the Date Pickup field.

   Hint: The Date Back field must be greater than 1/1/94 to exclude any film not yet processed.

   Print the dynaset as a datasheet with each customer's name and telephone number along with the envelope number and the date the film came in.

6. Create and print mailing labels for customers with film to pick up. The mailing label must include the customer's full name, street address, city, state/province, zip/postal code.

7. Develop and print a group/total report called **Daily Film Processing** that lists by date the film type, format, and exposure. Use the following guidelines in creating the report.

   a. The report heading should include **Prepared by** *your name* and the date.

   b. The page header identifies the Film Type, Exposure, and Format.

   c. The page footer contains the page number.

   d. The group footer includes a count of the rolls of film processed each day.

   e. The detail section includes the fields Film Type, Exposure, and Format. Align these fields under the related labels in the page header.

8. Create a macro that automatically opens, prints, then closes the Daily Film Processing report.

PROJECT 2: MAGAZINES US

Magazines US is a telemarketing magazine subscription service. The company uses a database management system to track customer subscriptions and telemarketer sales performance.

This project uses the CUSTOMER table from your data disk.

1. Create a new database called SUBSCRIB.

2. Attach the CUSTOMER table from the STUDENT database to the SUBSCRIB database.

3. Create two new tables: MAGAZINE and SALES.

NOTE: The SALES table has a multiple-field primary key, Customer Number + ISS Number. This is accomplished by holding the Ctrl key to highlight both fields before selecting the primary key button.

MAGAZINE

Field 1 - ISS Number, text, 9 characters, primary key

Field 2 - Magazine Name, text, 30 characters

Field 3 - Price, currency

Field 4 - Issues per Year, number

SALES

Field 1 - Customer Number, text, 6 characters, primary key

Field 2 - ISS Number, text, 9 characters, primary key

Field 3 - Date of Sale, Date

Field 4 - Renewal, Yes/No

Field 5 - Sales Rep ID, text, 4 characters

4. Create a data entry form for each table. Each form has the heading MAGAZINES US and an appropriate form identification.

5. Enter the following data into the tables using the data entry forms.

MAGAZINE Table

Issue No.	Magazine Name	Price	Issues per Yr.
0163-6626	Interface	14.00	4
0192-592X	THE Journal	29.00	12
0278-3258	Electronic Learning	23.95	8
0740-1604	PC Week	160.00	52
0888-8507	PC Magazine	44.97	24

DATABASE

Issue No.	Magazine Name	Price	Issues per Yr.
1040-6484	PC Today	24.00	12
1058-7071	Access News	44.95	12
1060-7188	New Media	48.00	12

SALES Table

Cust. No.	ISS No.	Date of Sale	Renew	Sales Rep ID
881464	1060-7188	10/6/94	N	5438
894239	0740-1604	10/7/94	N	5438
894239	0888-8507	10/7/94	N	5438
897062	1040-6484	10/7/94	Y	1432
913271	1058-7071	10/6/94	N	1432
923843	0278-3258	10/5/94	Y	1432
927494	0192-592X	10/6/94	Y	9540
929655	0163-6626	10/5/94	Y	5438
929655	0192-592X	10/5/94	N	5438
929655	0278-3258	10/5/94	Y	5438
941111	1058-7071	10/5/94	N	9540

6. Create a three-table query using the CUSTOMER, MAGAZINE, and SALES tables. The query creates a dynaset that shows customer information on all purchases from sales representative 5438 where the magazine name starts with the letters PC.

   Print the dynaset as a datasheet containing the magazine name, customer name, and sales rep. ID.

7. Develop and print a group/total report called **Sales by Renewal Status** that groups data by renewal status. Use the following guidelines in creating the report.

   a. The report heading should include **MAGAZINES US**, *your name*, and the *date*.

   b. Sort records by renewal status, then ISS Number.

   c. The page header identifies the ISS Number, Date of Sale, Sales Rep Number, and Customer Number.

   d. The page footer contains the page number.

   e. The group footer includes a count of the number of renewals in each group.

   f. The detail section includes the fields ISS Number, Date of Sale, Sales Rep Number, and Customer Number. Align these fields under the related labels in the page header.

8. Create a report based on a two-table query that uses the MAGAZINE and SALES tables. The query should include date of sale, ISS number, and price. Sort the dynaset by date of sale. The group/total report should include the following:

   a. Customized report header:

   MAGAZINES US Daily Sales Report
   prepared by *your name*

   b. Detail section and related page header that display ISS Number and Price fields.

   c. Group band based on Date of Sale field.

   d. Add a calculated field that sums daily sales at the bottom of the group band. Label this field Daily Sales Total.

9. Create macros that automatically open, print, then close the Sales by renewal report and the Daily Sales report.

Access Command Summary

This section is a quick reference for the Microsoft's Access for Windows commands covered in this manual. This is *not* a complete list of all Access commands. -
     ... indicates a dialog box will open

Task	Menu Command	Alternative
DATABASE COMMANDS		
Create a new database	File - New Database...	Ctrl+N
Open an existing database	File - Open Database...	Ctrl+O or
Close database	File - Close Database	
Create new database object	File - New	
Table	Table	
Query	Query	
Form	Form	
Report	Report	
Macro	Macro	
Module	Module	
Rename database	File - Rename...	
Import data from another database	File - Import...	
Export data in another database format	File - Export...	
Attach data from another database	File - Attach...	
Edit import/export specifications	File - Imp/Exp Setup...	
Exit the Access database window	File - Exit	Alt+F4
View list of tables in database	View - Table	
View list of queries in database	View - Query	
View list of forms in database	View - Form	
View list of reports in database	View - Report	
View list of macros in database	View - Macro	
WINDOW COMMANDS		
Display all open windows side by side	Window - Tile	
Overlap all open windows	Window - Cascade	

Task	Menu Command	Alternative

HELP COMMANDS

Task	Menu Command	Alternative
Display Help table of contents	Help - Contents	[icon]
Search for information in Help or Cue Cards	Help - Search...	
Display online couch for designated task	Help - Cue Cards	

EDITING COMMANDS

Task	Menu Command	Alternative
Undo last operation	Edit - Undo	Ctrl+Z
Cut current selection to Clipboard	Edit - Cut	Ctrl+X
Copy current selection to Clipboard	Edit - Copy	Ctrl+C
Paste Clipboard contents	Edit - Paste	Ctrl+V
Delete selection without copying to Clipboard	Edit - Delete	Del
Find specified text	Edit - Find	Ctrl+F
Find and replace specified text	Edit - Replace	Ctrl+H

OBJECT-ORIENTED COMMANDS

Task	Menu Command	Alternative
Create a new database object	File - New	
Close active window	File - Close	
Save active object	File - Save	Ctrl+S or [icon]
Save active object with new name	File - Save As	
Select printer or change printer settings	File - Print Setup...	
Preview printed output	File - Print Preview	[icon]
Print a file	File - Print...	Ctrl+P or [icon]
Select current record	Edit - Select Record	
Select all records	Edit - Select All Records	Ctrl+A
Change font type, size, or style	Format - Font...	
Set height of selected row	Format - Row Height...	
Set width of selected column	Format - Column Width...	

RECORD COMMANDS

Task	Menu Command	Alternative
Move record selector	Records - Goto	
go to first record	First	
go to previous record	Previous	
go to next record	Next	
go to last record Last		
new record New		
Sort records	Records - Quick Sort	
in ascending order	Ascending	[icon]
in descending order	Descending	[icon]
Specify filter or sort criteria	Records - Edit Filter/Sort...	[icon]
Apply filter or sort criteria	Records - Apply Filter/Sort	[icon]
Remove filter and display underlying records	Records - Show All Records	[icon]
Allow changes or prevent changes to data	Records - Allow Editing	

DATABASE

Task	Menu Command	Alternative
TABLE COMMANDS		
Create a new table	File - New	
Save active record	File - Save Record	Shift+Enter
Insert row above selected row	Edit - Insert Row	
Delete selected row	Edit - Delete Row	
Designate selected column(s) as the key	Edit - Set Primary Key	
Display the table in Design view	View - Table Design	
Display the table as a datasheet	View - Datasheet	
View and edit indexes	View - Indexes...	
Turn gridlines on or off	Format - Gridlines	
FORM COMMANDS		
Create a new form	File - New	
Display the form in Design view	View - Form Design	
Display the form	View - Form	
Display as a datasheet	View - Datasheet	
Open or close list of fields	View - Filed List...	
Set form properties	View - Properties...	
Show or hide ruler	View - Ruler	
Show or hide grid	View - Grid	
Open or close toolbox	View - Toolbox	
Open or close palette	View - Palette	
Turn control Wizard on or off	View - Control Wizard	
QUERY COMMANDS		
Create a new query	File - New	
Run query	Query - Run	
Add new table to query	Query - Add Table	
Clear contents of QBE grid	Edit - Clear Grid	
Insert row before selected row in QBE grid	Edit - Insert Row	
Delete row before selected row of QBE grid	Edit - Delete Row	
Insert column to left of selected grid column	Edit - Insert Column	
Delete selected column in grid	Edit - Delete Column	
Display the query in Design view	View - Query Design	
Display the query's dynaset	View - Datasheet	
Set query properties	View - Properties...	
Turn gridlines on or off	Format - Gridlines	
REPORT COMMANDS		
Create a new report	File - New	
Open or close list of fields	View - Field List...	
Set form properties	View - Properties...	

Show or hide ruler	Vew - Ruler
Show or hide grid	View - Grid
Open or close toolbox	View - Toolbox
Open or close palette	View - Palette
Turn control Wizard on or off	View - Control Wizard

MACRO COMMANDS

Create a new macro	File - New	
Execute macro commands	File - Run Macro	
	Macro - Run	

Glossary

alphanumeric   Data that includes both uppercase and lowercase letters, numbers, and symbols.

attaching   Linking a table to a database without changing its native format.

button   Labeled icon that confirms or cancels some program option.

click   To press a mouse button once to select a menu option or icon.

column separator   Vertical line found between column headers. The column separator can be dragged to the left or right in order to adjust the width of the related column.

comparison operators   Operators, like greater than or less than, that are used to describe data ranges as part of a query's or filter's selection criterion.

complex queries   Queries with multiple selection criteria which incorporate the local operators AND/OR.

context-sensitive help   Information supplied by the help window that changes based on the Access feature currently being used.

cursor   Blinking line or box that highlights where the computer will display the next keyboard entry.

data   Facts, figures, and images.

database management system (DBMS)   Software tool that permits people to use a computer's ability to store, retrieve, modify, organize, and display key facts.

datasheet   Row/column format used to display multiple records at the same time.

detail section   Body of a report that contains the fields from the underlying table or query.

dialog box   Window that prompts the user to enter text, select names from a list, or click on an icon to initiate or cancel some program option.

disk directory   Storage area on a disk that contains the filename, size, date, and time of each data file or program saved on the disk.

disk operating system (DOS)   Collection of system software designed to control a computer system using disks for storage.

double-click   To press a mouse button twice in quick succession to run a program or activate a program operation.

drop-down menu (pull-down menu)   Menu options that stay hidden in a menu bar at the top of the screen until the user selects a menu. When the menu is selected, the menu opens to list program options. Once an option is selected, the menu rolls back up into the menu bar.

dynaset   Special view of data from one or more tables that is filtered through a query.

ellipsis   Series of three periods. When found behind a menu option, an ellipsis indicates that additional user input is necessary when using that option.

error message   Screen display that is a result of the computer's failure to function properly or is a warning of a potential problem.

exclusive   Only one user at a time can access designated database.

expression   Identifies the criteria Access uses to add data to a query's dynaset or a table's datasheet display.

field   Combination of characters that represents a single fact.

field name   Generic name given to a data field.

filename   Unique set of letters, numbers, and symbols that identifies a data file or program.

filename extension   A combination of three letters preceded by a period that is added to the end of a filename to identify the file format.

filter   Criteria used to selectively display data.

form   Display format which is limited to fields associated with a single record.

function   Built-in code that performs a specific task, like pagination or statistical computation, and places results where function name is located.

graphical user interface (GUI)   Interface that relies on mouse or keyboard input to select menus or icons that initiate program options.

help screen   Description of software features and explanation of error messages displayed upon demand so the user does not have to refer to a manual.

icon   Picture representing an item, action, or computer operation.

index   An index is used to speed up sorting of records and searching for data in a table. Adding too many indexes to a table could result in slowing down data entry.

import   Linking a table to a database by converting it into the new database's native format.

join field   Field common to two or more tables that Access uses to combine data from both tables into a single dynaset.

join line   Line designating a link between two tables. The line is drawn to connect the field both tables have in common.

jump term   Underlined word or phrase in a help window which references additional help. Double-clicking on the term activates the additional help.

key   Field that uniquely identifies a record.

keyboard   Input hardware containing typewriter-like keys that the user presses.

label box   Displays descriptive data. Label boxes are used for titles and column headings.

landscape   Page orientation that is wider than it is tall.

launch (execute)   To start the execution of a computer program.

list box   Displays a list of names or options. When the list is too long to fit in the box, scroll arrows move the list up and down to display different items within the list box.

logical operators   The AND and OR operators used in complex queries.

macro   Set of Access commands that automate routine or repetitive tasks.

module   Complete computer program written in Access native command language.

move handle   Appears in top left corner of label or text box when it is active. Dragging move handle to a new location in the report repositions the box in the report output.

navigation buttons   Set of four icons found above the status bar that are used to move the selector to the first, previous, next, or last record or page.

null   An empty field.

numeric data   Data containing only numbers (0–9), decimal point, and plus (+) and negative (-) signs.

object   Basic building block of an Access database which includes tables, forms, queries, and reports.

page footer   The bottom of each report page. The page footer could contain custom labels, page number, or date.

page header   The top of each report page. The page header could contain column labels, page numbers, or date.

parameter query   Query designed to let user change search condition every time the query is run.

pointer   Marker that indicates the active record in a table.

portrait   Page orientation that is taller than it is wide.

primary key   Field used by Access to organize and identify a record.

printer   Output hardware that produces information on paper.

property sheet   Lists default report settings.

query   Question user asks concerning database data which is in a format that prompts Access to display selected data.

record   Collection of related fields about a single person, place, object, or event.

record selector   Black triangle that identifies the active record in a table.

referential integrity   Fields that join tables in a relational database are not deleted as long as links to other tables still exist.

relational database   Integrated tables that can be accessed at the same time by a database management system.

report footer   Last part of a report. In long reports the report footer would contain references and possible footnotes.

report header   First part of a report. In long reports the report header would contain a title page and table of contents.

screen pointer Onscreen icon, usually an arrow, that

moves when the mouse or some other pointer device is moved. Program options are activated using a mouse by moving the screen pointer over the desired icon and clicking the mouse button.

scroll To roll onscreen data up, down, or sideways for viewing long or wide documents.

scroll arrows Arrows found at either end of a scroll bar. Users change the view of a window or list box by clicking on one of the scroll arrows.

scroll bar Area that appears on the right or lower edge of a window or list box when only a partial view is available. A scroll bar contains a scroll box and scroll arrows.

scroll box Square within a scroll bar that identifies which portion of the window or list box is currently being viewed. Users can change the view by dragging the scroll box within the scroll bar.

select query Allows users to selectively view data based on the specified criteria.

sizing handles These boxes and connecting lines appear when a label or text is active. Dragging handle to a new report location changes the display size of the box.

status bar Area at the bottom of a window where Access displays field descriptions.

table Group of related records.

table design Information about the contents of a table which includes field names, data types, date entry descriptions, and field formats.

text box Displays data from designated table or query.

tool bar Area beneath the menu bar in an Access application window which contains tool buttons.

tool button Icon found in the tool bar. Clicking on a tool button activates a commonly used program command. Using a tool button is an alternative to using a drop-down menu.

updating Adding, changing, or deleting data.

wildcard character Symbol used to represent any combination of characters.

window Subdivides a screen display to allow the user to look at several menus, dialog boxes, or status reports from more than one program.

wizard Special utility that helps users design database objects by automating common procedures.

working disk drive Disk drive with disk and related directory containing desired Access database.

Index

DATABASE